U.S. Trade Deficit: Causes, Consequences, and Cures

U.S. Trade Deficit: Causes, Consequences, and Cures

Proceedings of the Twelth Annual Economic Policy Conference of the Federal Reserve Bank of St. Louis

edited by
Albert E. Burger
The Federal Reserve Bank of St. Louis

Kluwer Academic Publishers
Boston Dordrecht London

Distributors for North America:
Kluwer Academic Publishers
101 Philip Drive
Assinippi Park
Norwell, Massachusetts 02061 USA

Distributors for the UK and Ireland:
Kluwer Academic Publishers
Falcon House, Queen Square
Lancaster LA1 1RN, UNITED KINGDOM

Distributors for all other countries:
Kluwer Academic Publishers
Distribution Centre
Post Office Box 322
3300 AH Dordrecht, THE NETHERLANDS

Library of Congress Cataloging-in-Publication Data

Economic Policy Conference of the Federal Reserve Bank of St. Louis
(12th: 1987: Federal Reserve Bank of St. Louis)
U.S. trade deficit: causes, consequences, and cures: the proceedings of the 12th Annual Economic Policy Conference of the Federal Reserve Bank of St. Louis/Albert E. Burger, editor.
p. cm.
Includes index.

ISBN-13: 978-94-010-7638-8 e-ISBN-13: 978-94-009-2520-5
DOI: 10.1007/978-94-009-2520-5

1. Balance of trade—United States—Econometric models—Congresses. 2. United States—Commerce—Econometric models—Congresses. I. Burger, Albert E. II. Title.
HF3008.E27 1987
382.1'7'0973—dc19 88-28213 CIP

Softcover reprint of the hardcover 1st edition 1989

Contents

Contributing Authors vii

Preface ix

SESSION I 1

1

The U.S. External Deficit: Its Causes and Persistence 3

Peter Hooper and Catherine L. Mann

Commentary by Rudiger W. Dornbusch 107

Commentary by Alan Reynolds 113

Commentary by Michael R. Darby 125

SESSION II 129

2

The Current Account and Macroeconomic Policy: An Econometric Analysis 131

John B. Taylor

Commentary by Ray C. Fair 187

3

The Impact of the U.S. Current Account Deficit on Other OECD Countries 193

Jeffrey R. Shafer

Commentary by Richard D. Haas 231

SESSION III 237

4

Trade Deficits in the Long Run 239

Barry J. Eichengreen

Commentary by Anna J. Schwartz 279

5
An Evaluation of Policies to Resolve the Trade Deficit 287
Sven W. Arndt

Commentary by William Poole 309

Contributing Authors

Professor Sven W. Arndt
Department of Economics
University of California-Santa Cruz
Santa Cruz, California 95064

Mr. Michael R. Darby
Assistant Secretary for Economic Policy
U.S. Department of the Treasury
1500 Pennsylvania Avenue, N.W.
Washington, D.C. 20220

Professor Rudiger W. Dornbusch
Department of Economics
MIT
E52–357
Cambridge, Massachusetts 02139

Professor Barry J. Eichengreen
Department of Economics
University of California-Berkeley
Berkeley, California 94720

Professor Ray C. Fair
Cowles Foundation
Box 2125
Yale Station
New Haven, Connecticut 06520

Mr. Richard D. Haas
Advisor, Research Department
International Monetary Fund
Washington, D.C. 20431

Mr. Peter Hooper
International Finance Division
Board of Governors of the Federal Reserve System
Washington, D.C. 20551

Ms. Catherine L. Mann
Economist
World Bank
1750 Pennsylvania Avenue, N.W.
Washington, D.C. 20433

Professor William Poole
Department of Economics
Brown University
Providence, Rhode Island 02912

Mr. Alan Reynolds
Vice President
Polyconomics, Inc.
86 Maple Avenue
Morristown, New Jersey 07960

Ms. Anna J. Schwartz
National Bureau of Economic Research
269 Mercer Street, 8th Floor
New York, New York 10003

Mr. Jeffrey R. Shafer
Economics and Statistics Department
Organization for Economic Cooperation and Development
2, rue Andre'-Pascal
75775 Paris Cedex 16
France

Professor John B. Taylor
Department of Economics
Stanford University
Stanford, California 94305

Preface

On October 23 and 24, 1987, the Federal Reserve Bank of St. Louis hosted its twelfth annual economic policy conference, "The U.S. Trade Deficit: Causes, Consequences, and Cures." This book contains the papers and comments delivered at that conference.

A sharp decline in the value of the dollar against major foreign currencies began in March 1985 and continued through December 1987. Despite this decline, the U.S. trade deficit experienced considerable growth during this time. Many consider the simultaneous occurrence of these two events over so long a period to be a problem requiring a policy response. The conference addresses this issue. Various papers discuss the cause of the trade deficit, the reason for its size and persistence, its relationship with other macroeconomic variables, its impact on other industrialized countries, and various policy proposals aimed at reducing the deficit.

Session I

Peter Hooper and Catherine L. Mann provide an analytical setting for the conference with their "The U.S. External Deficit: Its Causes and Persistence." Their observation that the unprecedentedly large U.S. trade imbalance is striking in both its size *and* its persistence could well be the subtitle of each of the papers presented. The macroeconomic studies, which Hooper and Mann summarize in their review of the existing literature, uniformly conclude that the deficit has not responded to fundamental macroeconomic determinants—relative U.S. income growth and the dollar's exchange rate—in the way that earlier, smaller U.S. external imbalances did. Hence, the explanatory power of U.S. monetary and fiscal policies is not adequate to rationalize the magnitude and durability of the external imbalance. The research strategy of these authors, therefore, is to examine the microeconomic aspects of U.S. international trade as a possible explanation of the persistence issue.

The macroeconomic analysis is accomplished in an expectations-augmented Mundell-Fleming framework. A partial equilibrium model for the external sector is obtained from an open economy macroeconomic model and balance of payments accounting identities. Price adjustment is modeled as a markup over marginal cost of production, and the markup process takes account of market imperfections such as entry costs and home firms in the import market. Given their two-part research strategy, however, the imperfections and pricing aspects are more tractable within the microeconomic analysis. Basically, the macroeconomic results simply present evidence that the persistence of the deficit has microeconomic roots:

> The overprediction of nonagricultural export volumes and nonoil import prices suggests that foreign competitors were reducing their export prices in terms of their own currencies (hence their profit margins) more than they would have in the past in response to the appreciation of their currencies against the dollar. The model's overprediction of U.S. nonagricultural export prices is also symptomatic of more intense price competition from abroad than had been observed in the past, on average, under similar circumstances.

The macroeconomic roots of the deficit in the Hooper-Mann analysis are a combination of tight U.S. monetary policy and expansive U.S. fiscal policy, both taken relative to the other major industrial economies throughout the 1980s. Yet, the combination of these two contemporaneous shifts explains only two-thirds of the rising external deficit and the strengthening dollar during the 1980–1985 period. Moreover, Hooper and Mann find little *macroeconomic* explanation for the slowness of the external deficit adjustment during the dollar's decline beginning early in 1985:

> These estimates suggest that while the combination of fiscal expansion at home and fiscal contraction abroad accounted for as much as two-thirds of the current account deficit, they can explain at most one-third of the rise in the real interest differential and an even smaller portion of the rise in the dollar. Evidently, the changes in fiscal policy influenced the current account to a substantial degree through their impacts on relative growth of GNP and domestic demand in the United States.

To account for the remaining one-third and the deficit's persistence, they turn to microeconomic analysis of U.S. tradeable goods' pricing.

The microeconomic aspects of the trade imbalance are financial deregulation, agricultural policy, export controls, and foreign trade barriers (quotas, licensing, product characteristics, and the like). At the industry level, they find substantial evidence of foreign producers' price adjustment lagging changes in the dollar's exchange rate during both its appreciation up to March 1985 and its depreciation since then.

The discussion remarks of Darby and Dornbusch focus primarily on the macroeconomic issues—the unaccounted-for one-third of the U.S. trade imbalance. Dornbusch finds this to be evidence of market inefficiency—that is, the failure of exchange markets to adjust rates incorporating full information about the ultimate financial implications of ill-conceived U.S. fiscal policy. Darby found this lacunae—"...the dog that didn't bark"—to be evidence of the strength of the U.S. economy, brought about by fiscal and regulatory policies which have made U.S. assets more attractive to investors than current U.S. output.

In contrast, Reynold's discussion focuses on the microeconomic explanation of slow-to-adjust U.S. import prices. He challenges the Hooper-Mann hypothesis that foreign producers have squeezed profit margins to maintain U.S. market shares. Fundamentally, his critique focuses on another implication of the falling dollar: lowered input costs for foreign producers. These lowered costs are energy prices and the prices of some raw materials and inputs produced by newly industrialized countries which peg to the dollar. Complementary with this, Reynolds emphasizes the improved competitiveness of U.S. producers, a resultant of the high level of investment financed, ironically, by foreign capital.

Session II

The macroeconomic effects of the U.S. current account deficits are the focus of the chapters by John Taylor and Jeffrey Shafer. Both authors use multicountry models and counterfactual assumptions to study the effects of the U.S. current account deficit on the United States and on other countries. John Taylor focuses more on effects on the United States and on issues concerning alternative domestic and international policies to eliminate the real current account deficit. Shafer focuses more on the effects on other countries. Shafer, like Taylor, incorporates fairly strong fiscal restraint in his counterfactual analysis, but his emphasis is more heavily on an assumed absence of exchange rate movements and on changes in private sector behavior.

The chapters of part II differ in other important respects. For example, Taylor's paper focuses more heavily on interest rate and exchange rate effects of the deficit, while Shafer focuses somewhat more on the real side of the economy and income effects. Also, Taylor's model is smaller, based on rational expectations with sticky wage-price behavior. Shafer's model is a much larger, Keynesian, structural model, but with a more detailed aggregate supply sector. Both chapters explore the trade-offs involved in reducing the U.S. current account, however, and complement each other well.

In chapter 2, Taylor examines the effects of the trade deficit on the U.S. economy, especially on the saving-investment balance. The basic question posed by Taylor is, given that domestic saving would rise relative to investment if the trade balance were reduced, what would happen to each individually—would the levels of saving and investment be higher or lower? The answer arises from his model, in which there is a high degree of capital mobility and an unusual pair of key assumptions: rational expectations yet differing real rates of interest across countries.

The fundamental scenario in the Taylor chapter is a phased 3% cut in U.S. government purchases as a share of real GNP. Taylor shows that, in real terms, the expected crowding-in from such a policy falls most heavily on the current account deficit, which declines by 2.1 percent of real GNP. Taylor's simulation also shows the effects on German and Japanese prices and output. He finds that inflation declines abroad, but by less than in the United States. While there are real GNP gains abroad, they are smaller than the loss in U.S. real GNP.

The Taylor chapter also addresses the issue of whether the elimination of the U.S. trade deficit can be brought about through growth differentials or must be accompanied by dollar depreciation. Taylor shows that the "best" case is for domestic monetary policy to be more expansionary when purchases are cut, where best refers to greater price stability and output stability, both domestically and abroad. In the short run, output falls less abroad and does not fall at all in the United States in this case; prices fall less abroad and rise less in the United States. The trade-off in this case is greater exchange rate volatility, with the nominal value of the dollar falling relatively more than without monetary accommodation. Taylor shows that less exchange rate volatility and greater output and price volatility occur when foreign monetary growth accompanies the domestic purchases reduction. This scenario shows that the U.S. real trade deficit can be reduced with exchange rate stability. The stability is accomplished largely at the expense of greater inflation abroad and slightly less price level pressure in the United States.

Chapter 3, by Jeffrey Shafer, also examines a counterfactual scenario intended to examine the U.S. and foreign implications of the U.S. current account deficit. Shafer uses the Organization for Economic Cooperation and Development (OECD) model for these purposes. Shafer concentrates more heavily on the effects on other countries and less on the adjustments of interest rates and exchange rates across countries than Taylor does. He is even more explicit in arguing that a counterfactual analysis does not provide a scientific answer to the question of the effects of the U.S. current account deficit. Shafer argues that such an answer is impossible, because the question requires an analysis of a unique event and because the current account is the endogenous response to a number of interactions in the world economy.

The emphasis in Shafer's simulation is that outcomes are more sensitive to private behavior, especially saving. The central assumption is to keep household saving at 7% of household income, the rate in the late 1970s, rather than letting it fall to 4% in 1986. The principal fiscal policy change in the simulation is to set nonwage government spending at levels where the total government expenditure share would have been unchanged over the period, given the historical path of GNP. On the tax side, direct taxes were raised slightly to offset a 0.5 percentage point decline from 1981 to 1986 in the share of direct tax receipts in household income.

These counterfactual changes wipe out the growth of the U.S. *nominal* current account deficit from 1980 to 1986, actually leaving it in surplus as it was in 1980. The reader will be struck by Shafer's description of the counterfactual simulation, because the general pattern of the counterfactual macroeconomic developments remain similar to actual history, especially slowing inflation and relatively low real growth.

The effects of the rise in the U.S. current account deficit, in Shafer's results, were largely redistributive for output, employment, and domestic demand. Overall, however, Shafer's results indicate that the U.S. deficit (or departures from the counterfactual) raised prices, increased world income and employment, and generally raised world economic growth and trade. The incidence by country is markedly different, as are the year-by-year developments. Despite the increase in net foreign lending to the United States associated with the U.S. deficit, overall investment outside the United States would not have been consistently higher in the absence of actual conditions in the 1980s.

Ray C. Fair discussed the Taylor chapter. Fair's discussion focuses on the rational expectations restrictions imposed in the model and whether they could be successfully tested. His belief, based on his model, is that the restrictions can be rejected and that these restrictions are the source of the large initial changes that arise in Taylor's simulations.

Richard Haas discussed chapter 3, by Shafer. Haas stresses that two of

Shafer's major conclusions are open to doubt. First, he questions the result that investment and growth would not have been higher outside the United States in the absence of the current account deficit. According to Haas, this conclusion may arise from peculiarities of large-scale models which are more short-run oriented and, therefore, of limited value for such a long-run issue. Second, he regards the conclusion about EMS tensions to be significant and unexpected; he questions the source of this result.

Both discussants applaud the use of empirical macro models for addressing such counterfactual questions and the skill of the authors in doing so. However, both raise some questions about the structure of the models and the sensitivity of some of the conclusions to the specifications.

Session III

The final conference session considers the uniqueness of the U.S. trade deficit with respect to both previous U.S. experience and that of other countries and evaluates policies aimed at resolving the deficit problem.

In chapter 4, "Trade Deficits in the Long Run," Barry Eichengreen analyzes merchandise trade deficits by examining the period 1870–1985. The analysis is not restricted to the United States but includes Canada, Japan, and the United Kingdom. This historical/cross-country comparison leads Eichengreen to conclude that U.S. trade deficits reached unprecedented levels in the mid-1980s. Unlike the experiences of other countries that have run comparable deficits in the past, the U.S. deficit has not been financed by interest earnings on prior foreign investment or by the large-scale export of services. Furthermore, Eichengreen concludes that the resources the United States has obtained from foreign trade have not been funneled into investment projects that would expand future U.S. export capability. Given these conditions and barring a fortuitous shock to the terms of trade or a reallocation of resources toward investment in export-oriented sectors, Eichengreen suggests that U.S. merchandise trade deficits will not be eliminated quickly or at low cost in terms of foregone output.

In chapter 5, Sven Arndt evaluates various policies to resolve the U.S. trade deficit. Arndt points out that the policy proposals differ because each is based on different beliefs about the cause of trade deficits. In one instance, the U.S. trade deficit is attributed to excess domestic aggregate demand which is largely a result of a substantial increase in the federal deficit. This views the trade deficit as a macro problem and suggests that resolving the trade problem hinges on balancing the federal budget.

Alternatively, others emphasize that the U.S. trade deficit is a result of unfair trade practices by foreigners and/or the declining competitiveness of U.S. export industries. The alternative explanation views the U.S. trade deficit as a micro problem and suggests that macroeconomic policies cannot be used to solve the underlying problem and would prove to be costly in terms of reduced output and employment.

Arndt's evaluation of the above explanations makes it clear that the rise in the U.S. trade deficit during the early 1980s is a macro phenomenon. In Arndt's view, the budgetary policies of the federal government played the key role in raising the U.S. trade deficit. Though less significant, monetary policy and the global economic environment of the time contributed importantly to the problem. Accordingly, Arndt suggests that an appropriate policy for reducing the U.S. trade deficit is one directed at balancing the federal budget.

Arndt and Eichengreen take for granted that the U.S. trade deficit is a problem. This assumption is criticized in the comments of both Anna Schwartz (chapter 4) and William Poole (chapter 5). Poole, for example, argues that "the capital flow that is the counterpart of the current account deficit involves purchases and sales of assets by consenting adults." Poole suggests that Arndt is mistaken in assuming that capital flows are a completely passive source of financing for the trade deficit in a world of floating exchange rates. If the increase in the trade deficit is a result of increased foreign demand for U.S. capital, it is not clear that the deficit problem has much economic content.

SESSION I

1 THE U.S. EXTERNAL DEFICIT: ITS CAUSES AND PERSISTENCE

Peter Hooper and Catherine L. Mann*

1.1 Introduction and Summary

The emergence and persistence of an unprecedented U.S. trade deficit during the 1980s has become a matter of central concern to economic policymakers. With each month's announcement of another record imbalance, pressure to "do something" about the deficit mounts. Policy solutions range from fiscal and monetary reform to trade policy reform, both at home and abroad. This chapter analyzes the U.S. external deficit

* The authors are, respectively, members of the staff of the Division of International Finance, Board of Governors of the Federal Reserve System and the World Bank. The views expressed in this chapter are our own and do not necessarily reflect the views of the Board of Governors, the World Bank or other members of their staffs. Catherine L. Mann worked on this project while on leave at the National Bureau of Economic Research and thanks the Ford Foundation for financial support. We have benefited from comments and suggestions by William L. Helkie, David H. Howard, Ellen Meade, Jaime R. Marquez, Kathryn A. Morisse, and Lois Stekler. We also thank Virginia Carper, Lucia Foster, and Kathryn A. Larin for their excellent research assistence.

with the view that any policy action that is taken, if it is to be effective and appropriate, should be based on a clear understanding of the causes of the deficit and its persistence.

Much has been written on the causes of the deficit, considerably less on the reasons for its persistence. We begin with a review of the literature in section 1.2. We see several distinct perspectives on the causes and persistence that are, in fact, complementary; to a certain extent these perceptions reflect different levels of analysis from within an internally consistent model. (We say more about this model in section 1.3.)

At one level, a number of studies have attributed the deficit to the decline in U.S. price competitiveness (associated with the appreciation of the dollar during the early 1980s), the relative strength of domestic growth in the United states, and the international debt situation. The relative importance of these factors in explaining the origin of the deficit varies across the studies, as do the roles these factors may play in resolving the deficit.

At a more fundamental level, the origin of the deficit has been attributed to shifts in monetary and fiscal policies that reduced the national savings rate in the United States as compared to that in other countries, while raising U.S. real interest rates, domestic growth, and the dollar relative to their foreign counterparts. Several studies stress the importance of the U.S. fiscal expansion as the major causal factor; some even claim that the external deficit will persist until the federal budget deficit is reduced. Others stress the importance of the U.S. monetary contraction in the early 1980s, and exogenous shifts in international preferences for dollar assets.

While the literature focuses predominantly on macroeconomic causes, bilateral deficits with certain countries (Japan in particular) have been examined from the microeconomic standpoint as well. These studies find microeconomic distortions, such as financial deregulation, agricultural policy, export controls, and foreign trade barriers, to be of secondary importance as *causes* of the deficit. However, the role of trade barriers in the *persistence* of the deficit may be more important. In view of the attention being given to microeconomic—particularly protectionist—solutions to the deficit, microeconomic reasons for the deficit and its persistence are given considerable attention in this paper.

Section 1.3 presents our own framework for macroeconomic and microeconomic analysis, which is general enough to encompass the various perspectives outlined in the literature review. The basic macroeconomic framework is drawn from an expectations-augmented Mundell-Flemming model. We outline the partial-equilibrium net export sector—as well as various accounting identities related to the external balance—that can be extracted from the underlying macroeconomic model. We also describe the model of exchange rate determination that is used in our empirical analysis.

In section 1.4, we briefly review data on the widening and persistence of the external deficit in both real terms and nominal terms. This review covers trends in the overall deficit and its major trade and service account components since 1980, as well as some details on key developments in the trade account by commodity and region, and by quantity and price.

Our empirical analysis of the partial-equilibrium "causes" of the deficit—that is, the roles of relative economic growth and changes in relative prices—is presented in section 1.5. We find, based on an analysis of conventional trade equations, that the change in relative prices associated with the rise in the dollar between 1980 and early 1985 was the most important partial-equilibrium factor. The relatively rapid growth through 1986 of GNP and especially of domestic expenditures ($C + I + G$) in the United States, as compared to the rest of the world, also contributed significantly to the deficit. In empirical tests we find little basis for choosing between GNP and domestic expenditures as the determinant of trade volumes; and we conclude, largely on a priori grounds, that a combination of the two is appropriate. Using either measure of growth, the widening of the deficit between 1980 and 1986 can be more than accounted for by changes in relative prices and relative growth in the United States and the rest of the world.

However, we also find that a conventional macro trade model that reflects the experience of the past two decades cannot fully explain the persistence of the real trade deficit to mid-1987. While the real trade deficit was substantially smaller in mid-1987 than it would have been if the dollar had not declined from its peak (ceteris paribus), that deficit was adjusting more slowly to the fall in the dollar than the model predicted it would. The model's prediction error reflected in part overprediction of aggregate import prices, which were rising substantially less rapidly than past experience would have suggested. Import prices were slow to adjust partly because of a squeezing of foreign profit margins, and partly because of a reduction in foreign production costs which is not adequately picked up in movements in aggregate foreign prices.

We analyze the causes of the deficit at the more fundamental level of the domestic and foreign policy mix, in section 1.6. This section begins with an analysis of the contribution of changes in long-term real interest rates to movements in the dollar in real terms (based on an open-interest parity model). We find that this primary channel through which macroeconomic policies influence real exchange rates can explain much, but not all, of the longer-term movements in the dollar in real terms. We then draw on the results of simulations with a wide range of macroeconometric models in an effort to quantify the effects of shifts in policies. The simulation results suggest that the fiscal expansion in the United States and fiscal contraction in other industrial countries during the first half of the 1980s can explain about two-thirds of the U.S. external deficit, but that they explain a much smaller portion of the rise in the interest differential and the dollar. According to the models, the shift in relative fiscal policies alone (holding money growth at home and abroad unchanged) would have widened the current account deficit primarily through a substantial increase in U.S. GNP growth relative to growth abroad. However, when the shifts in fiscal policies are combined with the relative tightening of U.S. monetary policy that took place in the early 1980s, we can explain roughly two-thirds of both the rise in the dollar and the widening of the external deficit. The remainder of the deficit we attribute to debt problems in developing countries, agricultural policies, and a significant appreciation of the dollar during 1984 that was not related to economic fundamentals (and which some studies have suggested reflected speculative behavior in foreign exchange markets).

In section 1.7, we turn to an analysis of microeconomic factors that may have contributed to the deficit and its persistence. In particular, we examine the pricing behavior of U.S. and foreign exporters, and possible structural changes in the pass-through relationship that may help to explain the presistence of the deficit. We also investigate the contribution to the external deficit of protectionist policies and other barriers to trade at home and abroad.

We find evidence of a shift in the pricing of U.S. imports and exports that has tended to dampen the effects of the dollar's decline and prolong the deficit. We also find that barriers to trade, both at home and abroad, probably contributed only marginally to the initial widening of the deficit. However, protection abroad, along with quantitative restraints on U.S. imports and restrictions at home on U.S. exports, may have become a more significant factor underlying the recent persistence of the deficit in the face of the dollar's sharp decline.

Our conclusions, including the implications we draw from this study of the past and present for possible courses of action in the future, are given in section 1.8.

1.2 Literature Review

The magnitude of the U.S. current account deficit is nearly matched by the volume of material that has been produced to explain its existence. But, just as the current account has yet to improve, so too has the literature lagged somewhat in its efforts to explain the persistence of the deficit. Our objective in this section is not so much an exhaustive review of the literature, as it is an attempt to generalize the literature and place it within a common framework, which is further developed in the next section. From this common framework, we can then focus on how the similarities and differences of emphasis and results from these analyses can yield quite different views on appropriate and effective policy for reducing the deficit.

There are three relatively distinct, but nevertheless related, approaches to analyzing the causes of the deficit; two are macroeconomic in focus, and the third is microeconomic. These approaches are distinct in that they can lead to different policy prescriptions, but they are related in that they all are more or less derived from the basic open-economy IS-LM model. The features that distinguish the approaches are essentially the degree to which they (1) focus on the partial-equilibrium current account per se, (2) explain the movements in the variables that are taken as exogenous in the partial-equilibrium approach by analyzing the deficit within a full general-equilibrium model, (3) focus on accounting identities that are derived from a general-equilibrium model, or (4) factor microeconomic incentives into the analysis.

The partial-equilibrium "elasticities" approach usually ascribes the widening of the deficit to the appreciation of the dollar and the differences in growth rates of economic activity between the United States and the other industrial countries. The debt crisis is often given a separate role. This is partial analysis in that the movements in the dollar, the differences in economic activity, and the debt crisis are taken as given. The theoretical foundations for this approach are outlined in, for example, Laursen and Metzler [1950], which examines the conditions for a successful devaluation, and Dornbusch [1980].

The representatives within this strand of the literature do not necessarily agree on the allocation of the deficit to the two major factors of dollar and growth, and they therefore may not agree on policy prescriptions. For example, even though Bryant and Holtham [1987], Bergstrand [1987], Helkie and Hooper [1987], Krugman and Baldwin [1987], Marquez [1987], Marris [1985], and Reinhart [1986] all agree that the rise in the dollar accounts for the majority of the deterioration of the current account, they interpret this result with different policy perspectives.

The specification for the volume equations varies between Helkie-Hooper (HH), Krugman-Baldwin (KB), Marquez, and Marris, who provide perhaps the most comprehensive sets of estimates. HH use GNPs as activity variables and includes a proxy for secular shifts in relative supplies in a model of the U.S. current account, whereas KB use domestic expenditures and do not include proxies for supply shifts in a model of the partial trade balance. The result is that HH attribute substantially less of the deficit to the income growth differentials (since the GNP growth differentials were much less than the growth differentials of domestic expenditure and since the inclusion of supply proxies tends to reduce the income elasticity of imports). Nevertheless, even the KB specification suggests that if the growth gap were closed, we would still be left with a sizeable deficit. Marquez uses GNP with no supply proxies in a global bilateral model of merchandise trade and attributes about two-thirds of the U.S. deficit to appreciation of the dollar and one-third to relative GNP growth. In a model of the U.S. current account (with imposed coefficients, and in which aggregate trade volume equations are a function of GNPs and relative prices), Marris concludes that the growth gap accounts for about one-fourth of the $103 billion widening of the current account deficit between 1980 and 1984, while the strong dollar accounts for about two-thirds. The debt crisis and the decline in net investment income accounts for the rest.

Bergstrand and Reinhart both estimate bilateral trade equations. Bergstrand covers bilateral trade between the United States and the United Kingdom, France, Germany, Japan, and Canada; Reinhart covers just U.S.-Japan trade. Bergstrand's results corroborate the results of HH and KB's work. Reinhart attributes a significantly larger amount of the bilateral U.S.-Japan trade deficit to the slow growth of income in Japan relative to the United States, suggesting a greater role for jaw-boning the Japanese into expanding their economies.

Bryant and Holtham (BH) reflect on the results of a January 1987 Brookings workshop on the U.S. current account in which a number of partial-equilibrium models of the U.S. current account (including the HH model) reported on comparative simulations involving changes in exchange rates and in U.S. and foreign growth. One implication they draw from the results is that only coordinated macroeconomic policy—expansion overseas and contraction in the United States—along with a moderate further decline in the dollar, will significantly reduce the deficit. Excessive dependence on the dollar for adjustment is likely to result in too much inflation in the United States and deflation abroad. Failure of the foreign economies to expand in conjunction with a fiscal contraction in the United States is a recipe for world recession.

A somewhat different tack is taken by representatives of the accounting approach to the balance of payments. Total domestic savings minus investment equals the current account deficit. Proximate causes of the deficit therefore are either booming investment in the United States relative to overseas, as suggested by Darby [1987], or a U.S. savings rate that is too low relative to foreign savings rates, especially that in Japan (a view expoused by many, including Bergsten and Cline [1985]). Mundell [1987] and McKinnon and Ohno [1986] both outline a savings-investment link to the current account which suggests the irrelevance of the exchange rate to current account equilibrium. As KB point out, however, this result apparently rests on the strong assumption that changes in nominal exchange rates do not have a lasting influence on relative prices. Persson and Svensson [1985] also examine these linkages in a theoretical framework that focuses on how the current account evolves when shocks to the terms of trade and real interest rates are transmitted through savings and investment. They reach very different conclusions about the efficacy of using exchange rate changes to achieve current account equilibrium.

Of course, most of these authors recognize that the exchange rate, income, savings, and investment are all endogenous, and many of them either appeal to or have themselves authored articles that link the partial-equilibrium elasticities explanation for the deficit with the general-equilibrium policy-fundamentals approach. This linking tends to focus on one or another of the proximate causes—what moves the dollar, causes the growth gap, or affects savings and investment rates—and then proceeds to explain that variable using the policy fundamentals—fiscal policy, monetary policy, or the policy mix in the United States by itself or in concert with (or in contradiction to) the other major industrial countries. Within this literature, there are widely varying views about the fundamental causes of the deficit.

Those who lean more or less towards "budget deficit" or fiscal policy explanations include Branson, Fraga, and Johnson [1985], BH, Feldstein [1986a], HH, Hooper [1985], Hutchinson-Piggot [1984], Laney [1984], and Marris [1985]. The general idea is that the U.S. fiscal expansion (in many cases in conjunction with fiscal contraction abroad), led to an increase in U.S. relative growth, an increase in the long-term real interest rate differential, and an appreciation of the dollar, all of which caused the current account to deteriorate. A good survey of the theoretical underpinnings of these and counter arguments (which essentially asks under what conditions Ricardian Equivalence holds) is in Leiderman and Blejer [1987].

Darby [1987] points to tight money in the United States as the fundamental cause of the deficit. Basically, this argument suggests that there has been little empirical evidence supporting the notion that budget deficits and real interest rates are linked, whereas money growth and interest rates are clearly linked. Thus, it was the tightening by the Fed that led to increases in real interest rates, which along with tax-cut-induced declines in the cost of capital, made investment in the United States more attractive, and caused the dollar to appreciate and the current account to plunge.

Some studies have stressed the role of "micro-incentives" to save, invest, or diversify investment portfolios. Darby, et al. [1987] view the cut in U.S. tax rates as contributing to the attractive investment opportunities in the United States. Haynes, Hutchison, and Mikesell [1986a] (HHM) and others look to the structure of Japanese society for an explanation of high Japanese savings rates. Friedman and Sinai [1987], Bergsten and Cline [1985], Saxonhouse [1983], and HHM suggest that changes in financial regulations affected the demand for U.S. and dollar assets, contributing to the appreciation of the dollar and deterioration of the trade balance.

A relatively small set of authors cannot find one villain, but instead assert that it was the "policy mix"—fiscal expansion and monetary contraction in the United States, in combination with the opposite mix overseas—that led to the speed and degree of deterioration of the deficit. Authors taking this line include, Sachs [1985], Obstfeld [1985], HHM [1986b], and Feldstein [1986b].

To complete the macroeconomic viewpoints, there are the full-scale general-equilibrium models that are specified in terms of the policy fundamentals and structural attributes of the economies. One theoretical foundation for this school is in Dornbusch and Fischer [1980]. Authors that use quantitative macroeconomic models to analyze the causes of the deficit include Sachs and Roubini [1987] (using the McKibben-Sachs Global Model, MSG2), Masson and Blundell-Wignall [1985] (using the OECD's MINILINK model), and HH (using the Federal Reserve Board Staff's Multi-Country Model as well as the results of simulations by a group of models that participated in a March 1986 Brookings conference reported in Bryant et al. [1988]). These models often differ in their policy conclusions in large part because of different treatment of expectations and intertemporal constraints. In part also, these authors have tended to focus on the policy experiment that they believe is most relevant to explain the existence of the deficit (for backward-looking analysis) or is the most likely policy to be followed (for forward-looking analysis). Sachs and Roubini focus relatively more on fiscal experiments (as do Masson and Blundell-Wignall), as their model shows the U.S. external balance to be relatively more sensitive to shifts in fiscal policy than do other models. The work of HH and Hooper [1987], who average the results of a diverse set of models, is reviewed and extended in section 1.6 below.

While most of the literature on the deficit has a macroeconomic focus, a growing portion addresses microeconomic factors underlying the deficit. To a certain extent, this literature reflects, more broadly, the growing interest in productivity and competitiveness. On the whole, however, most studies in this area suggest that microeconomic factors contributed only marginally to the widening of the deficit.

One notable exception to that general finding is in agriculture. Thompson [1987] and Tucker [1987] both argue that the halving of agricultural exports between 1981 and 1984 (which nevertheless accounts for only about $10 billion of the $160 billion deficit) was overwhelmingly due to the price supports written into the 1981 Farm Bill. The support prices were set well above world price levels for much of the first half of the decade. This choice of domestic policy instrument, along with the international debt crisis, the appreciation of the dollar, and the "success" of the Common Agricultural Policy, apparently doomed U.S. agricultural exports.

Trend movements in productivity and technological competitiveness are the focus of Marston [1986], KB, and Krugman and Hatsopoulos [1987]. These authors argue that the severity of the deterioration of the deficit was the result of macroeconomic factors in combination with an underlying decline in the technological leadership of the United States and a slowdown in U.S. productivity growth relative to that in other major industrial countries, especially Japan and Germany. In part, these factors are to be expected as the U.S. economy matures. (Japan itself may well be slowing down relative to Korea.) But, these authors argue that the general trend in productivity growth masks a significant deterioration in relative productivity in the United States in key traded goods, particularly capital goods. Since capital goods represent more than one-third of U.S. trade, any significant change in the competitiveness of these products will have a substantial effect on overall trade volumes, and therefore the deficit. These analyses suggest that the dollar must fall substantially further than is suggested by Purchasing Power Parity calculations that use overall wholesale price indexes (such as in McKinnon and Ohno [1987]) before the current account will improve.

A related topic is whether the appreciation of the dollar led to a structural loss in the competitiveness of U.S. manufactured exports that can only be regained at a much lower level of the dollar. This argument, and some empirical investigation, is in Baldwin and Krugman [1986], KB, Krugman [1986, 1987], and Baldwin [1987]. U.S. exporters may have retreated from international markets because of the strong dollar. Because the costs of entering a market are quite high, the dollar will have to fall much lower before it is worthwhile for U.S. exporters to reenter the foreign markets. A similar calculation faces foreign suppliers of imports to the U.S. market.

A number of authors have investigated the role of trade barriers; U.S.-

Japan bilateral trade flows are a frequent focus. As a rule, these analyses (BC, HHM (1986a), Christelow [1986], Bergstrand [1986], Saxonhouse [1983, 1986], HHM, and Bergsten and Williamson [1983]) find only a small role for trade barriers. For example, a figure of about $10 billion is frequently mentioned as the maximum improvement in the deficit if all Japanese trade barriers were removed. Moreover, many of these authors point out that relaxing U.S. export controls, expecially on certain agricultural products and crude oil, would lead to an improvement in the deficit of about the same magnitude. Another set of authors, Darby [1987] and Kaempfer and Willet [1984], argue that macroeconomic forces determine the magnitude of the deficit, and microeconomic elements determine the composition of trade.

Some authors have looked to the theoretical literature on industry structure to see how external shocks might be transmitted through the economy to contribute to the deficit. Once again, these authors (Woo [1984], Berner [1987], Mann [1986], and Baldwin [1987]) find only a small role for microeconomic structure in causing the deficit. Pricing strategies associated with an imperfectly competitive industry structure (which may be a consequence of product type, production technology, or trade barriers—see Dornbusch [1987]) lead to foreign firms absorbing exchange rate movements into profit margins, thus offsetting to some degree the relative price signals that change trade volumes. While these changes were probably overshadowed by macroeconomic factors causing the deficit to widen, imperfect competition and trade barriers might play a significant role in the persistence of the deficit.

That persistence (in the face of a sharp fall in the dollar) is a more recent issue, and until quite recently has received less direct attention in the literature than the initial causes of the deficit. HH and KB both address the persistence of the deficit and conclude that it reflects for the most part normal lags in the adjustment to a depreciation of the dollar that followed a long period of appreciation. These studies also note that the deficit, while persistent, was considerably smaller in real terms by late 1986 than it would have been in the absence of the depreciation of the dollar, ceteris peribus. Berner [1987] and others have argued that the dollar really hasn't fallen as much in real terms as some aggregate exchange rate indexes would suggest, particularly against the currencies of key developing countries. Berner also cites reductions in foreign profit margins and various structural factors (such as off-shore migration of U.S firms and rapid growth of industrial capacity in certain developing countries) as reasons for the persistence of the deficit. Loopesko and Johnson [1987] analyze the persistence of Japan's trade surplus, and note that the surplus has been much slower to respond to the rise in the yen than past experience would predict (based on a model of the Japanese trade balance). They also find that Japanese export prices (and by implication profit margins) have declined substantially more in response to the rise in the yen than they did under similar circumstances in the past.

We turn now to a description of our own framework for analyzing the causes and persistence of the U.S. external deficit, a framework that draws heavily on the work that has been reviewed here.

1.3 Analytical Framework

Our analysis of the causes and persistence of the U.S. external deficit adopts several of the approaches covered in our review of the literature in section 1.2. We consider macroeconomic factors, employing both partial-equilibrium analysis and general-equilibrium analysis; we also consider microeconomic factors. This section outlines these approaches in more detail than was done in section 1.2, and illustrates the extent to which they can be derived from a consistent analytical framework.

1.3.1 Partial-Equilibrium Analysis

The partial-equilibrium approach we adopt involves analyzing the contributions of "proximate determinants" in a structural model of the external balance. The standard structural model includes behavioral equations for the volumes and prices of imports and exports of goods and services, plus identities defining the overall balance. An example of a fairly complete partial-equilibrium model of the U.S. external balance is provided by HH. The reduced form of this model can be written:

$$X - M = f(Y, Y^*, EP/P^*, Z) \tag{1.1}$$

where $X - M$ is nominal net exports, Y and Y^* are home and foreign income, EP/P^* is the real exchange rate (or the nominal rate times the ratio of home to foreign prices), and Z is a vector of other factors (such as oil prices, interest rates, asset stocks, and so on) that directly affect the value of trade in goods and services.

Analyzing the causes of the deficit under this approach entails quantifying the contributions of changes in each of the major proximate determinants on the right-hand side of equation (1.1), based on estimates of the structural relationships underlying this reduced-form equation. In section 5, we review the calculations made by others and add our own, based on a respecification of some of the import and export volume equations estimated by HH and KB.

1.3.2 General-Equilibrium Analysis

The general-equilibrium approach involves identifying the contributions of changes in policies and other fundamentally exogenous factors through simulations with a complete model of the world economy. Our empirical analysis in section 1.6 draws on the results of simulations with a number of multicountry macroeconomic models. A least common denominator for the theoretical structure of most of these models is the extended (expectations-augmented) two-country Mundell-Flemming model, as described by Frankel [1988].[1] These models specify behavioral sectors for the supply of and demand for goods and services, money and other assets in the United States and the rest of the world, with varying degrees of aggregation and coverage of foreign countries. Current incomes (outputs), prices, interest rates, exchange rates, and capital stocks are determined endogenously. Thus, the behavioral relationships underlying the reduced-form equation above enter into the determination of U.S. and foreign demand for goods and services, and the major proximate determinants on the right-hand side of (1.1) are all determined endogenously.

A more thorough description and presentation of the structure of these macro models is beyond the scope of this paper. However, it would be instructive to review some of the basic GNP and balance of payments identities pertaining to the external balance that can be derived from these models. We also briefly review the process of exchange rate determination.

To begin with, the external balance, or net exports ($X - M$), can be viewed as the difference between domestic supply of goods and services or domestic output (Y) and domestic demand or expenditures ($C + I + G$):

$$X - M = Y - (C + I + G) \tag{1.2}$$

By rearranging (1.2), the external balance can also be viewed as the difference between domestic saving (income minus private and government consumption) and domestic investment:

$$X - M = (Y - C - G) - I \tag{1.3}$$

This relationship can be refined by adding and subtracting from the right hand side of (1.3) taxes (T) and transfers (TR) between the government and private sector. The external balance can then be defined as the difference between domestic investment and the sum of government saving and private saving:

$$X - M = [(T - G - TR) + (Y + TR - T - C)] - I \quad (1.4)$$

As can be seen from (1.4), in the special case where private saving $(Y + TR - T - C)$ is equal to investment, the external balance will be equal to the government budget surplus.

From the balance of payments identity, the current account, which is essentially equal to net exports minus net unilateral transfers to foreigners (TF), equals (ex post) the change in net domestic demand for foreign assets (ΔFA) minus the change in net foreign demand for domestic assets (ΔDA^*):[2]

$$X - M = \Delta FA - \Delta DA^* + TF \quad (1.5)$$

In a global context, U.S. net exports are the rest of the world's combined net imports:[3]

$$X - M = M^* - X^* \quad (1.6)$$

Thus, the identities (1.2)–(1.4) can also be viewed from the rest of the world's perspective. By adding asterisks to, and reversing the signs of the right-hand side variables of (1.2)–(1.4), U.S. net exports can be defined as the excess of foreign demand or expenditure over foreign supply or output:

$$X - M = -Y^* + (C^* + I^* + G^*) \quad (1.7)$$

or the excess of investment abroad over saving abroad:

$$X - M = -(Y^* - C^* - G^*) + I^* \quad (1.8)$$

$$X - M = -[(T^* - G^* - TR^*) + (Y^* + TR^* - T^* - C^*)] + I^* \quad (1.9)$$

In brief, U.S. net exports can be viewed as (a) U.S. excess demand (or foreign excess supply) of goods and services, (b) U.S. private and government savings net of investment (or the excess of domestic investment abroad over private and government savings abroad), or (c) U.S. net demand for foreign assets minus foreign net demand for U.S. assets. In the global general-equilibrium models we make use of in section 1.6, all of these factors are jointly determined by exogenous monetary and fiscal policy variables at home and abroad, as well as by other fundamentally exogenous factors (such as autonomous shifts in private consumption or investment behavior).

1.3.3 Exchange Rate Determination

Since the behavior of exchange rates is central to our analysis of the external deficit, we outline here the model of exchange rate determination that will be used later in the chapter. The model we use is real open-interest parity, which is either included explicitly or approximated fairly closely in most of the global models to which we will be refering.[4] The basic assumptions of this model are: (1) perfect substitutability of assets denominated in different currencies, (2) absence of foreign exchange risk (or risk aversion), and (3) a constant expected long-run equilibrium level of the real exchange rate (q_t^e). Under assumptions (1) and (2), open interest parity holds:

$$s_t^e - s_t = \gamma(i_t^* - i_t) \tag{1.10}$$

where

s_t = log of the nominal spot exchange rate (foreign currency/home currency) in period t.
s_t^e = expected value of s γ years ahead.
i_t = log of 1 plus the annual rate of interest on home-currency bonds with a term of γ years.[5]

and denotes foreign variable, e denotes expectations.

Under assumption (3), above, the expected value of the nominal spot exchange rate (s_t^e) in the long run (γ years ahead) is defined:

$$s_t^e = p_t^{*e} - p_t^e + q_t^e \tag{1.11}$$

where p_t^{*e} and p_t^e are log values of expectations in the current period about the levels of foreign prices and home prices, respectively, γ years ahead. Substituting current price levels and expected average annual rates of inflation (π) for expected future prices levels in equation (1.11), we have

$$s_t^e = p_t^* + \gamma\pi_t^{*e} - (p_t + \gamma\pi_t^e) + q_t^e \tag{1.12}$$

Substituting the right-hand side of (1.12) for s_t^e (1.10), and rearranging yields

$$s_t - p_t^* - p_t = q_t^e + \gamma(i_t - \pi_t^e - i_t^* + \pi_t^{*e}) \tag{1.13}$$

which expresses the log of the real exchange rate as a function of the expected real exchange rate in the long run and the real interest rate differential. The horizon γ is defined as being long enough for q_t^e to be considered constant. We will return to an empirical analysis of this model in section 1.6.

1.3.4 Price Determination

One factor contributing to the persistence of the current account deficit is the behavior of nonoil import prices in dollar terms. In this subsection we set out a simple model of price determination in imperfectly competitive markets that allows for variation in profit margins and that incorporates the possible effects of protection.

Equation (1.14) shows, in an accounting sense, the relationship between dollar import prices, foreign prices, and the exchange rate:

$$P_i^{\$} = P_i^{*}/E_i \tag{1.14}$$

where, P_i^* is the foreign-currency price of a product produced by a foreign firm and exported to the United States, $P_i^{\$}$ is the import price in dollars, and E_i is the product-specific foreign-currency/dollar exchange rate. If the foreign price remains unchanged, a change in the exchange rate will be fully passed through to the dollar import price.

Next, assume that the foreign-currency price of the product equals the marginal cost of production. C_i^*, in foreign currency, times a markup factor, λ, which is equal to one plus a percentage profit margin:

$$P_i^{\$} = C_i^{*} \cdot \lambda_i/E_i \tag{1.15}$$

Under perfect competition, where the foreign firm faces infinitely elastic demand, λ_i equals 1.0. But, perfect competition is unlikely to accurately reflect the market structure of most traded goods, because of the heterogeneity of many products (particularly manufactured goods), and because of the presence of quantitative restraints on some of the products.

A plausible behavioral characterization of (1.15) can be written

$$P^{\$} = C^{*}[I(w, r, k), E, Q)] \cdot \lambda(E, Q, Y)/E \tag{1.16}$$

where the product subscript i has been suppressed. Marginal cost is a function of input costs (I), which is a function of productivity-adjusted wages (w), raw material costs (r), and capital costs (k); the exchange rate E, to the extent that imported intermediates are used in the production process; and the quantity produced (Q), to the extent that there are economies of scale or scope. The markup is a function of (1) the exchange rate E, which proxies for the degree of competition from home firms in the import market; (2) the quantity produced, which in the presence of quantitative import restraints may differ from the equilibrium quantity demanded; and (3) shifts in demand, Y, associated with changes in income, tastes, and so on.[6]

Log differentiation of (1.16) yields (1.17), which expresses the percent change in the dollar import price as a function of changes in the input costs, the exchange rate, the quantity produced, and exogenous shifts in demand, given the elasticities of marginal cost and the markup with respect to the exchange rate, quantity produced, and demand shifts:

$$\hat{P}_i^\$ = \{\eta_c^I\}\hat{I} + \{\eta_c^e + \eta_\lambda^e - 1\}\hat{E} + \{\eta_c^q + \eta_\lambda^q\}\hat{Q} + \eta_\lambda^y\hat{Y} \quad (1.17)$$

where,

$\eta_c^I = (\delta C/\delta I)(I/C)$ measures the responsiveness of marginal cost to changes in input costs, which may depend on institutional structure in the labor and capital markets.

$\eta_c^e = (\delta C/\delta E)(E/C)$ varies with the importance of imported inputs.[7]

$\eta_\lambda^e = (\delta\lambda/\delta E)(E/\lambda)$ is the elasticity of the markup (measured in foreign currency) with respect to exchange rate changes.

$\eta_c^q = (\delta C/\delta Q)(Q/C)$ measures the slope of the marginal cost curve.

$\eta_\lambda^q = (\delta\lambda/\delta Q)(Q/\lambda)$ measures changes in the markup along the demand curve.[8]

$\eta_\lambda^y = (\delta\lambda/\delta Y)(Y/\lambda)$ measures changes in the markup as the demand curve shifts.[9]

This simple model points to several sources for "persistence" in the U.S. external deficit. One aspect of persistence is a slower than expected adjustment of import prices and import volumes to the fall in the dollar.[10] In this model of imperfect competition, any given decline in the foreign exchange value of the dollar, will lead to less of an increase in dollar import prices to the extent that foreign profit margins or production costs are reduced. on the other hand, if at the same time that the exchange rate moves, quantitative restraints are tightened, there may be no apparent relationship between exchange rate changes and dollar import prices, and from there to import volumes.

Some of these effects are illustrated in the top panel of figure 1–1, which shows price determination for a foreign firm selling a differentiated product in the U.S. market. Initially the firm is selling the quantity Q_0 at a foreign-currency price P_0. Suppose the foreign currency appreciates against the dollar. This exchange rate change shifts the U.S. demand curve facing the foreign firm to the left, from D_0 to D_1. The firm can now continue to sell the quantity Q_0 at a substantially lower price (and profit margin), P_1, or it can sell less (Q_1), with a smaller reduction in profits, at price P_2. The exchange rate change will also induce U.S. competitors to enter the market, thereby increasing the elasticity of demand for the foreign firm's product, and flattening the demand curve to D_2. This would lead to a further reduction in price (and profit margins) if the firm con-

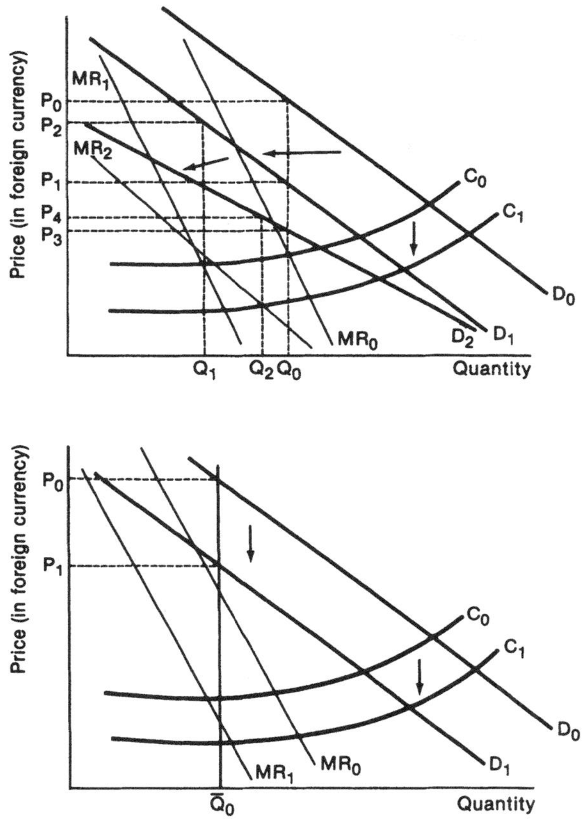

Figure 1–1. Dollar Depreciation and Foreign Price Determination

tinued to sell quantity Q_0. The exchange rate change may also reduce the firm's raw material input costs, moving the marginal cost curve from C_0 to C_1. In this case, the firm may either regain some of its lost profits or further reduce its price and regain some of its lost market share. Overall, any reduction in the foreign-currency price means that some portion of the exchange rate change is absorbed, yielding a smaller increase in the dollar import price than would be predicted by the simple relationship in equation (1.14). The degree of such absorption can vary widely, depending on the circumstances.

Next, suppose that imports of the foreign product are subject to a quantitative restriction at the time of the exchange rate change, as illustrated in the bottom panel of the figure. If the restriction was binding and the foreign firm had set its price well above the unrestricted profit maximizing level, it could be in a position to absorb the full amount of the exchange rate change, reducing its foreign-currency price from P_0 to P_1, and leaving the dollar price and the quantity sold unchanged. If the quantitative restrictions were tightened while the exchange rate change was taking place, it should be clear that the price would be higher and the quantity sold lower than the final outcome shown in the bottom panel of the figure. Finally, if U.S. demand were rising, due to an increase in income for example, the price would be higher than the final outcome shown in the bottom panel of the figure, and both the price and quantity would be higher than the final outcome shown in the top panel of the figure.

We turn next to our empirical analysis.

1.4 The Anatomy of the External Deficit: Data Review

This section reviews the facts about the emergence of the external deficit and its persistence in the 1980s. Chart 1–1 provides an historical perspective. After fluctuating well within a range of plus or minus 1% of GNP during most of the preceding three decades, the current account plunged to a deficit of more than 3.5% of GNP during the first half of the 1980s. The rate of decline was greatest during 1982–1984 as U.S. growth recovered strongly from the 1982 recession. The deficit continued to widen through mid-1987, although at a noticeably slower pace than had been the case earlier. As indicated in the bottom panel of the chart, the bulk of the decline in the current account reflected a widening of the trade deficit. Net services and transfers, shown as the shaded area, narrowed from a comfortable surplus in the early 1980s to about a zero balance in 1986 and the first half of 1987, contributing significantly further to the widening of the current account deficit.

1.4.1 Nominal and Real Net Exports

The widening of the deficit between 1980 and 1986 can be more than accounted for by a fall in real net exports. This is illustrated in the top panel of chart 1–2, which compares movements in the current account with those in nominal and real net exports of goods and services. While the difference between the current account and nominal net exports has been fairly stable over time, real net exports declined substantially more be-

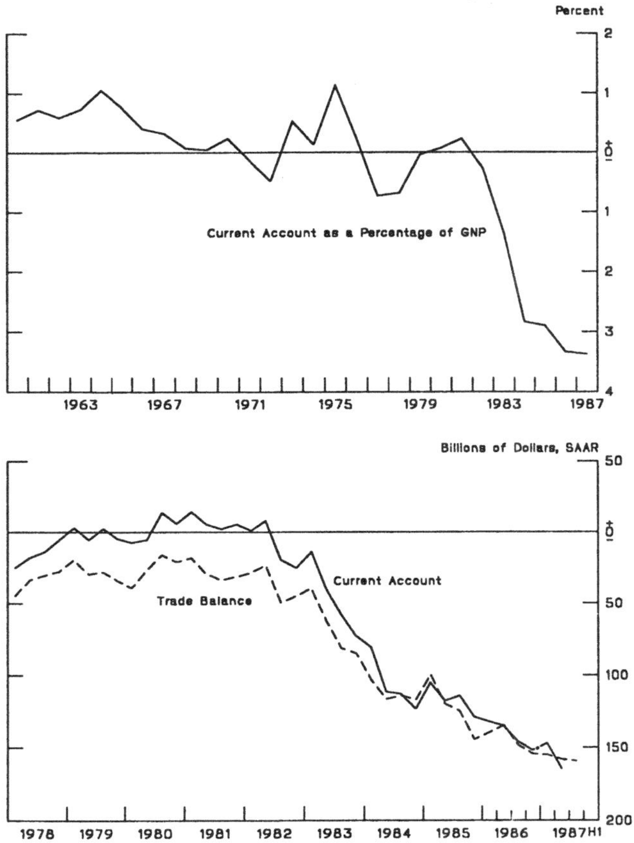

Source: U.S. Department of Commerce, Survey of Current Business

Chart 1–1. U.S. External Balances

tween 1980 and 1986 than either of the two nominal balances. As indicated in the bottom panel, the U.S. terms of trade improved over this period, as export prices rose moderately, on average, while import prices were reduced by the sharp fall in oil prices and the additional depressing effect of the rise in the dollar on the prices of nonoil imports (see also table 1–1).

More recently, the real deficit has begun to deviate from the nominal deficit in a different direction. That is, real net exports have begun to trend up from a low point in the third quarter of 1986, whereas the nominal deficit has persisted and even widened further. Most of the rise in real net

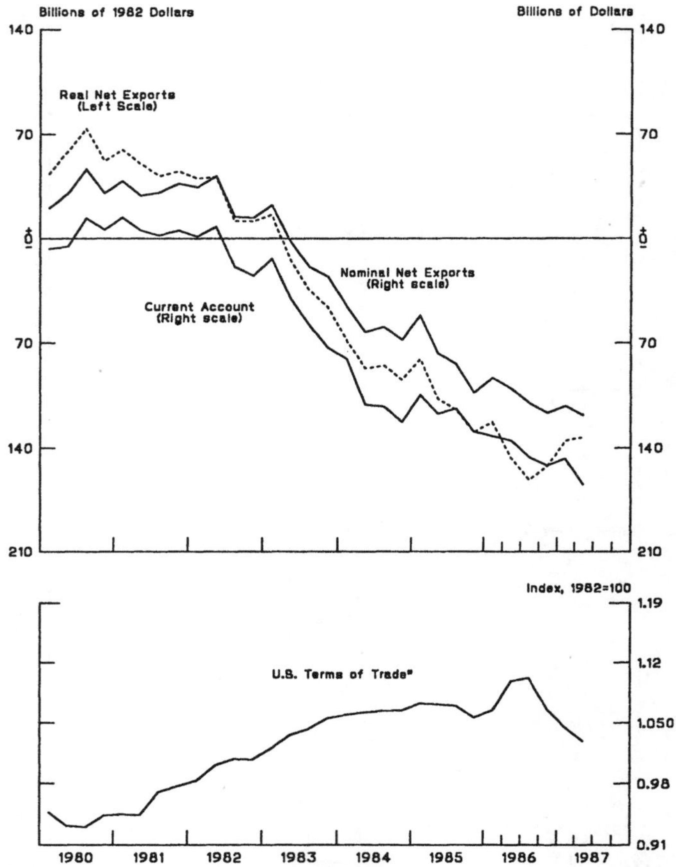

Source: U.S. Department of Commerce, Survey of Current Business

* GNP deflator for exports of goods and services divided by the GNP deflator for imports of goods and services.

Chart 1–2. U.S. Nominal and Real External Balances (S.A.A.R)

exports between the third quarter of 1986 and the second quarter of 1987, reflected a drop in the volume of oil imports, which had risen to unusually high levels in the summer of 1986 as oil import prices bottomed out, and were depressed thereafter as prices rebounded. Thus, excluding oil imports, the recent quarterly pattern of real net exports shows only a slight

Table 1–1. U.S. Trade Prices and Quantities by Major Component (seasonally adjusted annual rates)

					Change 1980–1986		*Change 1986H1–1987H1*	
	1980	*1986*	*1986H1*	*1987H1*	*Billions of $*	*Percent*	*Billions of $*	*Percent*
Imports								
Total Goods and Services:								
1. Value (bil. $)	319	482	470	520	+163	+51	+50	+11
2. Quantity (bil. 1982 $)	332	523	505	535	+191	+58	+30	+6
3. Price (1982 = 100)	96	92	93	97		−4		+4
Goods:								
Nonoil								
4. Value (bil $)	170	335	323	353	+165	+97	+30	+9
5. Quantity (bil 1982 $)	173	345	340	353	+172	+99	+13	+4
6. Price (1982 = 100)	99	97	95	100		+2		+5
Oil								
7. Value (bil $)	79	34	36	37	−45	−58	+1	+3
8. Quantity (bil 1982 $)	83	72	65	70	−11	−13	+5	+8
9. Price (1982 = 100)	96	47	55	53		−51		−4
Exports								
Total Goods and Services:								
10. Value (bil $)	351	376	372	404	+25	+7	+32	+9
11. Quantity (bil 1982 $)	389	376	372	404	−13	−3	+32	+9
12. Price (1982 = 100)	90	100	100	100		+11		0
Goods:								
Nonagricultural								
13. Value (bil $)	182	197	195	207	+15	+8	+12	+6
14. Quantity (bil 1982 $)	202	212	210	225	+10	+5	+15	+7
15. Price (1982 = 100)	90	93	93	92		+3		−1
Agricultural								
16. Value (bil $)	42	27	27	27	−15	−36	0	0
17. Quantity (bil 1982 $)	39	30	28	32	−9	−23	+4	+14
18. Price (1982 = 100)	108	90	95	84		−17		−12
Net Services:								
19. Value (bil. $)	55	37	38	37	−18	−33	−1	−3

Source: Bureau of Economic Analysis, *Survey of Current Business*; all value data are from the U.S. Balance of Payments Accounts. Prices are deflators from the National Income and Product Accounts. Components may not sum to totals due to rounding.

upward movement (as we will see in chart 1–5). The nominal deficit has continued to widen, however, because the terms of trade have turned down over the recent period, as oil prices have rebounded and the prices of nonoil imports have begun to respond to the depreciation of the dollar, while export prices have remained relatively stable. Although not shown on the table, the nominal and real trade deficits appear to have widened somewhat further in the third quarter—based on data for July and August—due largely to an apparently transitory reemergence of strong oil imports related to domestic stockbuilding.

The data in table 1–1 indicate that the fall in real net exports between 1980 and 1986 was accounted for by a doubling of the volume of nonoil imports (line 5), while the volume of exports (lines 11, 14 and 17) remained little changed. Of the $204 billion (1982 prices) decline in real net exports over that period, a fall in the real partial trade balance (merchandise excluding agricultural exports and oil imports) accounted for 80% of the total, and a decline in real net services accounted for the remainder. The volumes of agricultural exports and oil imports both declined by $9 billion. Both the real trade balance and real net exports of goods and services were about unchanged between the first half of 1986 and the first half of 1987. This leveling-off of the deficit in real terms reflects a substantial pickup in export growth, while import growth slowed significantly (but remained positive).

1.4.2 Trade by Area

The widening of the deficit between 1980 and 1986 was dispersed across major U.S. trading partners (see table 1–2). All regions increased their nonoil exports to the United States at substantial rates, with those from Japan and other Asian countries (lines 10 and 12 in the table) showing the most spectacular growth. The growth of U.S. exports to most areas was stagnant by comparison, with exports to Latin American countries and other developing countries (particularly those with international debt problems), as well as Western Europe, showing noticeable net declines. Only in the case of trade with Canada did the growth rate for U.S. exports approach half the rate of growth of imports. Exports to Japan also rose, but much of this increase between 1980 and 1986 reflected a temporary bulge in gold shipments in mid-1986.[11]

In the past year, the growth of imports from industrial countries has slowed substantially, while imports from developing countries have continued to advance at healthy rates, and in some cases have actually

Table 1–2. U.S. Merchandise Trade by Region 1980–1987H1

	Levels (Billions of $, SAAR)				*Average Annual Rates of Change (%)*	
	1980	*1986*	*1986H1*	*1987H1*	*1980–86*	*1986H1–87H1*
Total Exports						
To:						
1. All Regions	224.3	224.4	221.6	234.0	0	5.6
Selected Industrial Countries:						
2. Canada	41.6	57.0	57.9	60.4	6.2	4.3
3. Japan	20.8	26.4	26.0	24.3	4.5	−6.5
4. Western Europe	67.6	60.7	59.5	66.9	−1.7	12.4
Selected Developing Countries:						
5. Asia*	14.2	17.3	16.5	20.1	3.6	21.8
6. Latin America	38.8	30.9	29.5	31.6	−3.4	7.1
7. Rest of World	41.3	32.1	32.2	30.7	−3.7	−4.7
Nonoil Imports						
From:						
8. All Regions	170.5	334.9	322.8	353.1	16.1	9.4
Selected Industrial Countries:						
9. Canada	38.8	65.9	66.4	68.6	11.6	3.3
10. Japan	31.2	80.7	76.6	81.4	26.4	6.3
11. Western Europe	42.7	85.0	83.3	87.7	16.5	5.3
Selected Developing Countries:						
12. Asia*	17.7	45.7	40.7	53.2	26.4	30.7
13. Latin America	18.9	30.6	30.7	32.7	10.3	7.2
14. Rest of World	21.2	27.0	25.1	29.3	4.5	16.7

Source: Bureau of Economic Analysis, *Survey of Current Business*; U.S. Balance of Payments Accounts.

* Asia includes Hong Kong, Singapore, Taiwan, and Korea.

accelerated. This pattern is consistent with the much greater decline in the dollar in real terms that has occurred against the currencies of industrial countries than against the currencies of developing countries over the past two and a half years (as we will be discussing in section 1.6). The rebound in exports since the first half of 1986 has been concentrated in shipments to Western Europe and developing countries in Asia, while shipments to Canada have continued to grow steadily.

1.4.3 Trade by Commodity Group

By major end-use commodity group (table 1–3), business machinery was the only category to show any noticeable export growth in real terms over the 1980–1986 period, and has continued to grow strongly over the past year. Most other categories of exports showed declines in real terms over the first half of the 1980s. Some categories of industrial supplies (notably paper and wood products), agricultural goods, and consumer goods have contributed, along with machinery, to the strengthening of exports more recently.

Among nonoil imports, capital goods showed the strongest growth, tripling in volume between 1980 and 1986, with business machinery accounting for a significant portion of the total. Consumer goods and autos doubled in volume, while imports of food and nonoil industrial supplies grew at somewhat slower rates. The growth in real imports of all categories has slowed substantially in the past year, although imports of capital goods and to a lesser extent consumer goods (significantly business machinery and consumer goods from Asian countries other than Japan) have continued to grow fairly briskly. Industrial supplies and materials is the only major import category to have shown a decline in the past year.

1.4.4 Net Services

While most of the decline in real net exports is accounted for by the fall in the real merchandise trade balance, a decline in net services also contributed. In real terms, net services fell by about $39 billion at an annual rate between 1980 and 1986.[12] As indicated in line 19 of table 1–1, the decline in current dollars was somewhat less, and the balance on net services has remained significantly positive. Movements in the major components of net services are shown in the top panel of chart 1–3. The investment income accounts have shown divergent movements. Net portfolio income

Table 1–3. U.S. Merchandise Trade Volumes and Prices by Major Commodity Group

	Levels				Average Annual Rate of Change	
Volumes	*1980*	*1986*	*1986H1* (billions of 1982 $)	*1987H1*	*1980–1986*	*1986H1–1987H1* (percent)
Exports						
Foods, feed, and beverages	33.0	25.7	24.5	27.6	−3.7	12.7
Industrial supplies and materials	68.1	63.5	60.8	68.9	−1.1	13.3
Capital goods	87.1	94.2	90.9	100.6	1.4	10.7
Business machines	8.3	35.0	32.6	40.8	53.6	25.2
Automotive	21.6	22.7	23.9	22.9	0.9	−4.2
Consumer goods	17.7	14.0	13.3	16.2	−3.5	21.8
Nonoil Imports						
Foods, feed, and beverages	16.1	22.9	22.3	23.7	7.0	6.3
Industrial supplies and materials	47.2	72.8	71.6	73.0	9.0	2.0
Capital goods	31.2	93.3	89.7	100.3	33.2	11.8
Business machines	4.1	35.0	31.6	41.7	125.6	32.0
Automotive	33.2	66.3	64.2	67.4	16.6	5.0
Consumer goods	34.9	74.1	71.7	76.3	18.7	6.4
Prices[a] (1982 = 100)						
Exports						
Foods, feed, and beverages	108.1	88.0	92.4	81.5	−3.1	−11.8
Industrial supplies and materials	99.5	91.6	93.3	93.1	−1.3	0.2
Capital goods	86.7	98.2	97.9	99.8	2.2	1.9
Business machines	109.4	47.9	47.3	45.1	−9.4	−4.7
Automotive	81.5	112.4	111.6	113.7	6.3	1.9
Consumer goods	95.0	103.0	102.3	105.6	1.4	3.2
Nonoil Imports						
Foods, feed, and beverages	112.8	105.0	105.3	101.9	−1.1	−3.2
Industrial supplies and materials	103.1	84.4	84.3	86.8	−3.0	3.0
Capital goods	100.2	92.5	90.4	98.6	−1.3	9.1
Business machines	109.4	46.9	47.3	45.1	−9.5	−4.7
Automotive	84.1	117.7	114.8	123.6	6.7	7.7
Consumer goods	98.7	104.9	102.9	111.5	1.1	8.4

Source: Bureau of Economic Analysis, *Survey of Current Business*, National Income and Product Accounts; Business Machines: Bureau of Economic Analysis. All volume data at a seasonally adjusted annual rate.

[a] Prices are GNP fixed-weight deflators.

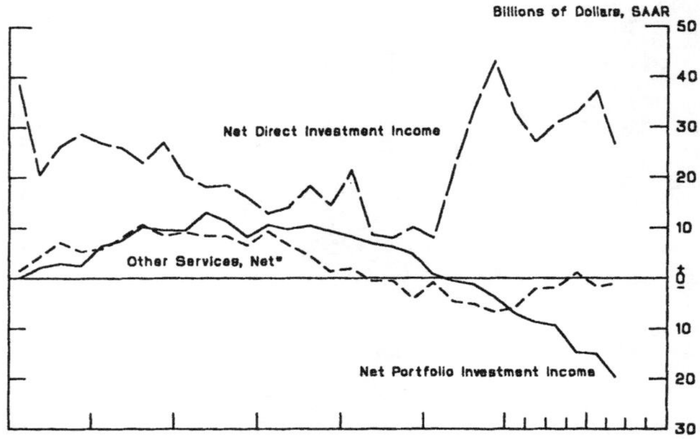

Chart 1–3a. U.S. Service Account Transactions

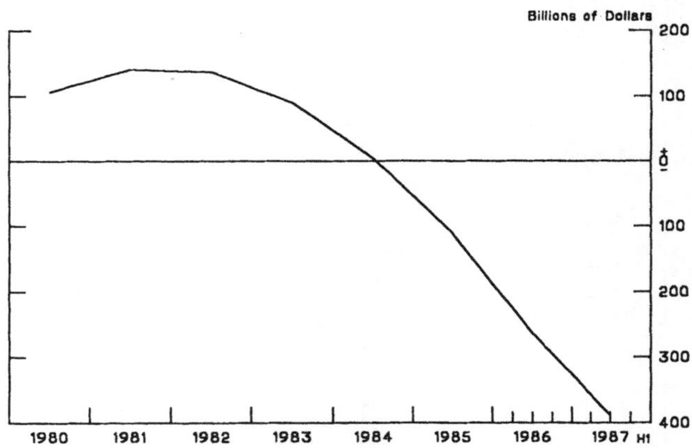

Source: U.S. Department of Commerce, Survey of Current Business

* Includes net military transactions as well as travel, transportation, and other services.

** Stock position; 1987H1 is an estimate based on the recorded position as of end-1986 plus the U.S. current account balance during 1987H1.

Chart 1–3b. U.S. Net Foreign Investment Position**

fell off noticeably between 1980 and 1986, while net direct investment income actually rose, despite an $80 billion deterioration in the U.S. net direct investment stock position over that period.[13] Changes in net direct investment income have been dominated by changes in capital gains associated with the impact of swings in the dollar's exchange rate on the valuation of assets and liabilities denominated in foreign currencies. In addition, the dollar value of U.S. income flows denominated in foreign currencies was falling as the dollar appreciated over the first half of the 1980s and has risen sharply since the dollar began to depreciate in early 1985.

The decline in net portfolio income has followed more closely the pattern of decline in the U.S. overall net foreign investment position, shown in the bottom panel of the chart 1–3. More than three-fourths of the $370 billion deterioration in the U.S. net investment position between 1980 and 1986 reflected increasing net foreign portfolio claims on the United States. This shift occurred as U.S. banks reduced their net claims on foreigners, as foreign private residents invested heavily in U.S. government and corporate securities, and, more recently, as foreign official agencies have increased their holdings of dollar assets in the United States due to intervention to support the dollar. Nevertheless, the decline in net portfolio income between 1980 and 1986 (a little over $10 billion at an annual rate) was small relative to the nearly $300 billion decline in our net portfolio investment position. This apparent discrepancy reflects the fact that the average recorded rate of return on U.S. portfolio liabilities to foreigners is less than that on U.S. assets held abroad and that both assets and liabilities have continued to grow during this period. The combination of higher gross stocks and differential rates of return was apparently enough to more than offset the effects of a declining *net* foreign asset position.[14]

Other services, net, including travel, transportation, and so on, fell by roughly ($10) billion dollars between 1980 and 1985, but have rebounded since 1985, reflecting the effects of the decline in the dollar, among other factors.

1.5 Macroeconomic Causes: Partial-Equilibrium Analysis

As we noted in the preceding section, the widening of the U.S. external deficit during 1980–1986 was more than accounted for by the decline in real net exports over that period. In this section we first consider the factors that contributed to the decline in real net exports, in a partial-equilibrium framework. We then analyze the extent to which this analytical framework can explain the persistence of the deficit more recently, focusing in particular on the recent behavior of aggregate import prices.

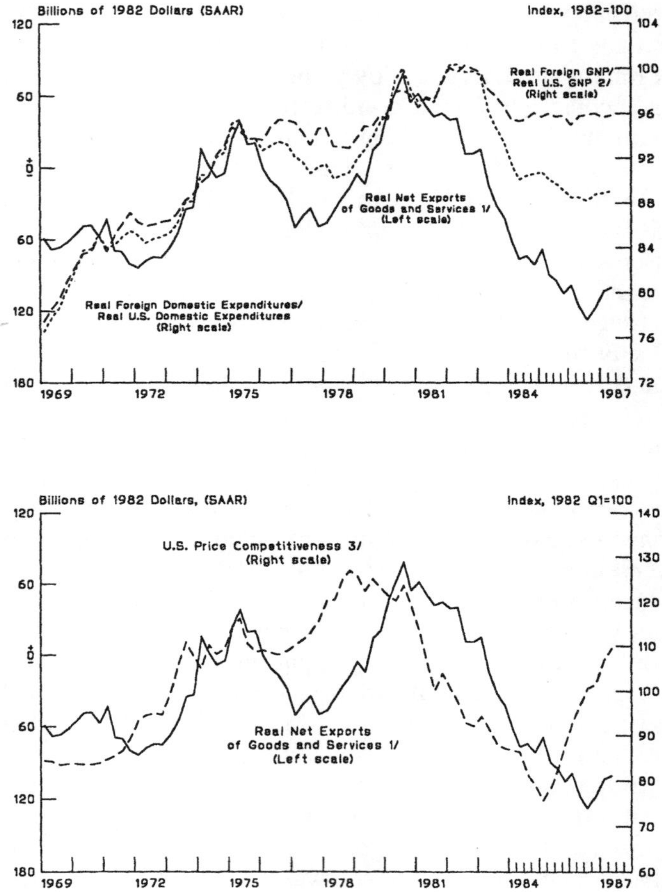

Source: Federal Reserve Board USIT model database

[1] Adjusted for trend growth in U.S. trade volume between 1969 and 1987.

[2] Foreign GNP includes all OECD countries, OPEC and non-OPEC developing countries.

[3] Ratio of consumer prices in 10 industrial countries and 8 developing countries (in dollars) to U.S. consumer prices. Foreign prices are weighted by multilateral trade shares.

Chart 1–4. Determinants of U.S. Real Net Exports of Goods and Services

1.5.1 Income and Relative Prices

As was discussed in section 1.4, the major determinants of changes in real net exports are the relative growth of real income or expenditure at home and abroad, and the relative prices of goods and services produced at home and abroad. Chart 1–4 shows a comparison of real net exports with various measures of relative growth and relative prices over the past two decades. The top panel shows two measures of relative activity compared with net exports, and the bottom panel shows a measure of relative prices compared with net exports. In order to make net exports comparable with the other indicators in the chart over the entire period shown, they have been normalized by trend growth in real U.S. trade during 1969–1986.[15]

The two measures of relative real activity in the top panel are GNP and domestic expenditures $(C + I + G)$.[16] Foreign and U.S. GNPs (or total outputs) are the more appropriate activity variables for the nearly 50% of U.S. exports and imports that can be classified as intermediate goods. Total domestic expenditures (or final demand) may be more appropriate for the rest of U.S. trade, which can be classified as finished goods. As indicated by the chart, in the early 1970s and again in the late 1970s, significant increases in real net exports coincided with substantial increases in foreign activity relative to U.S. activity. The increase in the level of U.S. activity relative to foreign activity since 1980 contributed to the decline in real net exports over that period.

The measure of relative prices shown in the bottom panel is the ratio of an index of consumer prices in dollars of major foreign industrial and developing countries to U.S. consumer prices. (As is discussed in section 1.6 below, movements in this index of relative prices have been dominated by swings in the dollar's exchange rate against the currencies of G-10 countries over the past two decades.) The chart indicates that the increases in real net exports in both the early 1970s and latter 1970s followed significant increases in this crude measure of U.S. international price competitiveness with a lag of about one to two years. The decline in net exports after 1980 followed a dramatic decline in price competitiveness that had peaked about a year and a half earlier. More recently, the apparent bottoming-out of real net exports in the third quarter of 1986 came about a year and a half after the peak in the dollar and the low point in U.S. price competitiveness.

This chart provides a qualitative indication of the relative contributions of the factors shown to the widening of the deficit after 1980. Movements in relative prices clearly have been strongly correlated with that in net exports (with a lag); between the activity variables, the ratio of domestic expenditures appears to have been more closely correlated than that of GNPs. The latter comparison is potentially misleading, however, inasmuch as GNPs and domestic expenditures are both influenced by net exports, and in opposite directions. A fall in net exports stimulated by a decline in U.S. price competitiveness, for example, will tend to increase U.S. domestic expenditures relative to foreign domestic expenditures, and at the same time reduce U.S. GNP relative to foreign GNP. In these instances, the expenditure ratio in the top panel of the chart will be more closely correlated than the GNP ratio with net exports (as it was during 1981–1986), but only because the direction of causation has been reversed from that intended in the chart. This example illustrates the pitfalls of partial-equilibrium accounting exercises to assign causation among jointly determined variables. It also signals potentially significant simultaneous-equation bias in the estimation of standard trade equations during periods when trade volumes are responding significantly to factors other than income. Having confessed our sins in advance, we now turn to our quantitative analysis using these very same techniques.

Table 1–4 quantifies changes in the income and relative price determinants of the key components of real net exports that took place from 1980 to 1986 and from 1986H1 to 1987H1. The increase in U.S. GNP exceeded that in foreign GNP over the 1980–1986 period by only 2 percentage points, whereas the difference in total growth of real domestic expenditures was on the order of 10 percentage points. Over the past year, U.S. growth by either measure has been slightly below foreign growth. The

Table 1–4. Changes in the Volume of Imports (average annual rates, percentage points)

	12 Quarters *1986Q3/1983Q3*	*2 Quarters* *1987Q1/1986Q3*
1. Total imports	15	−5
2. Oil	7	−36
3. Nonoil	18	4
4. Food	8	−1
5. Industrial supplies	10	8
6. Capital goods	32	1
7. Business machines	56	13
8. Other capital goods	23	−6
9. Automotive	21	0
10. Consumer goods	18	6

price of U.S. nonagricultural exports relative to foreign consumer prices in dollars actually fell between 1980 and 1986, largely because of the dollar's depreciation during 1985–1986. The relative price of exports had risen by about 30% between 1979 and the dollar's peak in early 1985. (Given that export volumes respond with a significant lag to relative price changes, the increase in relative prices over the earlier interval is more appropriate for analyzing what happened to exports through 1986.) Meanwhile, the price of nonoil imports fell by 30% relative to the U.S. GNP deflator over both 1980–1986 and 1979–1985Q1. In the past year the falling dollar has had a significant impact on the relative price of exports, but it has had very little effect on the relative price of imports.

Table 1–5 presents estimates of the implications of the changes in

Table 1–5. Sources of the Real Trade Deficit

	Real Trade Balance (billions of 1982 $)	
	Total	*Excl. Ag. Exports and Oil Imports*
1. Helkie-Hooper (1987)		
Contribution to change in real trade balance 1980–1986 of:		
A. Changes in the levels of U.S. and foreign real GNP 1980–1986	−42	−18
B. Changes in relative prices of exports and nonoil imports 1980–1986	−131	−121
C. Changes in other (secular) supply factors	−26	−26
D. Lagged response to oil-price shock (conservation and increased production)	+37	—
E. Other	−4	0
F. Total (change 1980–1986)	−166	−165
2. Krugman-Baldwin (1987)		
Contribution to level of real trade balance in 1986Q4 of:		
A. Deviation of U.S. and foreign domestic demand growth from an average annual rate of 2.5% 1980Q1–1986Q4	—	−49
B. Change in the dollar in real terms from its 1980Q1 level	—	−63
C. (Other factors)	—	(−26)
D. Total (level 1986Q4)	—	−138

relative economic activity and relative prices over the first half of the 1980s for the decline in U.S. real net exports. These estimates were obtained from the Helkie-Hooper and Krugman-Baldwin studies. HH found that the $165 billion decline in the real partial trade balance (excluding oil imports and agricultural exports) between 1980 and 1986 can be attributed largely to the decline in U.S. price competitiveness. They used GNPs as the key activity variables in their import and export equations, and found that the U.S.-foreign growth difference explains only a relatively small part of the widening of the partial trade deficit. In contrast KB, who used domestic expenditure variables, attributed a substantially larger amount of the deficit to the growth difference. KB did find that nearly half of the real trade deficit at the end of 1986 can be attributed to movements in the dollar's real exchange rate, but their quantitative estimate of that effect appears to be only a little over half as large as the HH estimate. Part of this difference might be due to the fact that KB considered a more recent period (1986Q4, compared with HH's 1986 year average), over which the dollar was falling and offsetting some of the estimated contribution of its earlier rise. Moreover, the KB model has shorter lags in the response of real net exports to relative prices than does the HH model. This means that in the KB esitmate the depreciation of the dollar since early 1985 would have had a greater positive impact on net exports, offsetting more of the negative effect of the earlier appreciation.

1.5.2 GNP versus Domestic Expenditures

The choice between GNP and domestic expenditure in this exercise is important, not just for historical accounting purposes, but also in its implications for possible "cures" to the deficit. A prescription based on relative GNP growth targets could imply a significantly more painful adjustment process than one based on domestic expenditure targets. If GNPs are what move export and import volumes, the widening of the deficit to date apparently has not been due to any significant degree to a cyclical widening of the growth gap that could be readily reversed. GNPs at home and abroad were at or near cyclical peaks in 1980, and average growth rates since then have been quite similar.[17] Also, to the extent that policy makers rely on changes in relative growth rates to reduce the deficit, U.S. GNP would have to fall significantly relative to foreign GNP, and U.S. domestic expenditures would have to decline relative to domestic expenditures abroad by an even greater amount (reflecting the resulting increase in net exports). However, if it is domestic expenditures that move trade volumes, growth factors have been quantitatively important in "causing" the widening of the deficit to date. Moreover, significant adjustment could be achieved by reversing the domestic expenditure gap that has emerged over the past seven years, and leaving relative GNP growth rates unchanged. Of course, changing the domestic expenditure gap implies structural adjustment at home and abroad as the U.S. economy shifts to the production of tradable goods and as foreign growth (which has until recently been export-led) is focused inward.

In view of the implications of this issue for ongoing debates about cures to the deficit, we have reestimated the partial trade balance equations reported by HH using alternative activity variables, including GNPs, domestic expenditures, and a mix of the two. A priori, we would expect a mix of the two to outperform expenditures alone. As noted earlier, demand for intermediate goods, which account for nearly half of U.S. trade, are more plausibly considered a direct function of output or GNP than of final domestic demand. With respect to imports and exports of finished goods, which account for a little over half of U.S. trade, plausible theoretical cases can be made for either total incomes (GNPs) or expenditures as the appropriate determinants, although final expenditures would seem, to us, to be the more closely related variable.

The partial trade balance equations from the model reported by HH are listed in table 1–6 in their implicit functional form. The equations for both the nonagricultural export and the nonoil import volume include, in addition to the activity variables, relative prices, a relative capital stock variable (to capture shifts in the supply of traded goods that are not adequately captured in relative price data), and a variable that quantifies the trade volume effects of dock strikes.[18] In the import equation the activity variables are included with a one-quarter distributed lag (both the current and lagged coefficients are reported), and in both the import and export equations the relative price variables are included with eight-quarter distributed lags (for which only the sum of lagged coefficients is reported). (Table 1–6 also shows the import and export price equations used by HH, which will be further analyzed at the end of this section.)

We estimated the volume equations over the period 1969Q1–1984Q4, in a double-log functional form. In-sample simulations were run over the period 1980Q1–1984Q4 and post-sample simulations were run over 1985Q1–1987Q2. The simulations were static (autoregressive residuals were excluded); the percentage root-mean-squared prediction errors are reported for all the simulations.

The results of our regressions are shown in table 1–7. In both the export and import equations the domestic expenditure variables yield slightly

Table 1–6. Partial Trade Balance Equations

Nonagricultural Export Price

$$P_{xna} = f(PD, (P^*/E)_{L4})$$

Nonagricultural Export Volume

$$X_{na}/P_{xna} = f[Y^*, (P_{xna}/E_m \cdot P_m{}^*)_{L9}, K^*/K, DS_{xna}]$$

Nonoil Import Price

$$P_{mno} = f[P_b^*, (E_b)_{L8}, (PC)_{L4}]$$

Nonoil Import Volume

$$M_{no}/P_{mno} = f[Y, (TR \cdot P_{mno}/P)_{L8}, K/K^*, CU^*/CU, DS_{mno}]$$

Definitions

CU = U.S. manufacturing capacity utilization.
CU^* = deviation from potential output in foreign G-10 countries.
DS_{mno} = dock strike variable specific to nonoil imports.
DS_{xna} = dock strike variable specific to nonagricultural exports.
E_b = exchange rate (foreign currency/dollar), 18 currencies, bilateral nonoil import weights.
E_m = exchange rate (foreign currency/dollar), 18 currencies, multilateral trade weights.
K = U.S. private fixed-capital stock.
K^* = private fixed-capital stock in foreign OECD + 10 major developing countries.
M_{no} = nonoil import volume.
P = U.S. GNP deflator.
P_b^* = foreign CPI, 18 countries, bilateral nonoil import weights.
P_m^* = foreign CPI, 18 countries, multilateral trade weights.
P_{mno} = nonoil import deflator (GNP accounts).
P_{xna} = nonagricultural export deflator (GNP accounts).
PD = weighted average of U.S. producer prices, nonagricultural export weights.
TR = index of tariff rates on nonoil imports.
X_{na} = nonagricultural export value.
Y = U.S. real GNP (or real domestic expenditures).
Y^* = foreign real GNP (or real domestic expenditures), all countries, weighted by shares in U.S. nonagricultural exports.
$(\ )_{L9}$ = denotes, for example, a nine-quarter distributed lag on the term inside the parentheses.

higher coefficients than the GNP variables, while the coefficients on the mixed-activity variables (which are 50/50 combinations of the other two) are intermediate. These differences are not statistically significant, however. The different activity variables influence other coefficients as well. Notably, both the level and the significance of coefficients on the relative price, capacity utilization, and relative capital stock variables fall when the expenditure variable is used in the import equation. In terms of overall equation fit and recent in-sample behavior, the mix variable has at best only a slight edge over either of its two components. The differences in in-sample standard errors and corrected R-squares are small, however, reflecting the extent to which GNPs and domestic expenditures moved together over most of the sample period. In terms of post-sample prediction accuracy, the mix does slightly better than the others in the export equation, but clearly comes in second to GNP in the import equation.

In brief, the results in table 1–7 provide little empirical basis for choosing among the alternative activity variables. In constructing our own estimates of the partial-equilibrium "causes" of the deficit below, we have chosen on a priori grounds (as described earlier) to use the mix specification.

1.5.3 Partial-Equilibrium Accounting

Table 1–8 presents our estimates of the contributions of each of a number of partial equilibrium factors to the widening of the partial real trade deficit (nonagricultural-nonoil), the total real trade deficit, and the deficit on real net exports of goods and services, between the fourth quarter of 1980 and the fourth quarter of 1986. These estimates were calculated as in HH, using essentially the same model, but with the nonagricultural export and nonoil import volume equations using the "mix" version of the activity variables substituted for those using GNP variables.[19] The difference between columns 1 and 2 reflects the impact of contributing factors on oil imports and agricultural exports. The decline in oil imports in lagged response to the 1979–1980 oil price hike made a significant positive contribution to the real trade balance. The difference between columns 2 and 3 reflects impacts on the various components of the service account. For example, changes in GNP influence both direct investment income (through its impact on resource utilization and profits) and demand for other services (travel, transportation, and so on). And changes in relative prices (or exchange rates) influence both the demand for other services and the valuation of net direct investment income receipts. The decline in real net portfolio investment income is due largely to the increase in U.S. net

Table 1–7. Regression Results for U.S. Import and Export Volume Equations with Alternative Economic Activity Variables (*t* ratios in parentheses)

	Nonoil Imports			*Non-agricultural Exports*[a]		
	Real GNP	*Real Domestic Expenditures*	*Mix*[b]	*Real GNP*	*Real Domestic Expenditures*	*Mix*[b]
1. Constant	−2.21	−7.28	−5.55	−2.57	−13.80	−12.59
	(−0.48)	(−1.21)	(−1.09)	(−0.52)	(−1.99)	(−1.84)
2. Activity variable	1.11	1.24	1.19	1.91	2.09	2.03
	(2.85)	(3.27)	(3.08)	(4.33)	(4.67)	(4.57)
3. Activity variable (−1)[c]	0.96	1.07	1.06	—	—	—
	(2.38)	(2.45)	(2.54)	−0.95	−0.80	−0.88
4. Relative prices (0–7)[d]	−1.13	−0.84	−0.98	(−6.39)	(−5.23)	(−5.90)
	(−10.34)	(−5.73)	(−8.20)	—	—	—
5. Relative capacity utilization	−0.30	−0.03	−0.13	0.76	1.01	−0.93
	(−1.41)	(−0.13)	(−0.56)	(−1.25)	(−1.62)	(−1.50)
6. Relative capital stocks	−0.84	−0.47	−0.59	0.75	0.75	0.75
	(−2.25)	(−0.98)	(−1.45)	(7.73)	(7.88)	(7.80)
7. Dock strike dummy	0.80	0.83	0.81			
	(5.65)	(5.90)	(5.70)			
8. Rho	0.46	0.50	0.46	0.72	0.73	0.72
	(4.09)	(4.57)	(4.07)	(8.00)	(8.03)	(7.96)
9. Durbin Watson	1.91	1.92	1.91	2.07	2.09	2.08
10. R^2 (corrected)	0.9862	0.9858	0.9863	0.9874	0.9879	0.9877
11. Standard error %	3.12	3.16	3.11	2.84	2.77	2.80
Model prediction errors[e]						
12. In-sample: RMSE (1980:1–1984:4)%	2.47	2.49	2.38	3.37	3.75	3.49
13. Post-sample: RMSE (1985:1–1987:2)%	2.66	4.61	3.70	5.79	5.72	5.60
Sample Period: 1969:1 to 1984:4						

[a] Foreign GNP and Domestic Expenditures measures cover all foreign countries (see text).
[b] Mix is calculated by equally weighting GNP and Domestic expenditures.
[c] Denotes one-quarter lag.
[d] Denotes 8-quarter distributed lag for both imports and exports; sum of lagged coefficients is reported.
[e] Based on in-sample and post-sample simulations excluding autoregressive residual. Root mean squared prediction errors are reported.

portfolio indebtedness. In principle, this decline could be allocated among the other causal factors that contributed to the increasing indebtedness (by reducing net exports), but we have not done so in the table.

The estimates in table 1–8 are broadly similar to those in the previous studies. First, they suggest that partial-equilibrium macroeconomic factors can fully account for the widening of the deficit between 1980 and 1986. (In fact, the residual item near the bottom of the table suggests that the other factors shown more than account for the deficit.) Second, changes in relative prices and the associated depreciation of the dollar are still the dominant contributing factors. However, the growth factor also has a substantial impact, contributing nearly $80 billion, or roughly 40% of the total

Table 1–8. Partial-Equilibrium "Causes" of the Real External Deficit (billions of 1982 dollars, annual rates)

	Contributions to Change in Real Net Exports and Its Major Components 1980:4–1986:4		
Contributing Factor	*Partial Real Trade Balance (1)*	*Total Real Trade Balance (2)*	*Net Exports of Goods and Services (3)*
Changes in U.S. and foreign GNP and domestic demand[b]	−48	−69	−77
Changes in relative prices of exports and nonoil imports	−98	−105	−113
Changes in relative capital stocks	−20	−20	−20
Lagged responses to oil-price shock (conservation and increased production)	—	+26	+26
Decline in net investment income	—	—	−25
Other factors	0	−4	+5
Total	−166	−172	−204

[a] Calculated as contribution due to total change in the contributing factor over the period 1980:4–1986:4, except for relative prices, which are lagged.

[b] Based on 50/50 mix of GNP and domestic expenditures for both U.S. and foreign variables.

decline in net exports of goods and services over the period in question. These results suggest that a reversal of the U.S.-foreign GNP and domestic demand gaps that emerged during the first half of the 1980s would contribute substantially to a resolution of the U.S. trade deficit. Nevertheless, if a resolution were to be achieved without a significant drop in U.S. GNP relative to foreign GNP, it would most likely involve a reversal of the relative price shock that took place over the first half of the decade. In view of the substantial reversal of the dollar's earlier appreciation that *has* taken place already over the past two and a half years, we now ask why the external deficit has persisted to mid-1987.

1.5.4 The Persistence of the Deficit: Macro Explanations

Most measures of the dollar's real exchange rate indicate that as much as three-fourths of the appreciation over the first half of the decade has been reversed since early 1985. (This subject is considered in more detail in the next section.) Yet the nominal deficit apparently has continued to widen through the third quarter of 1987, and absent some sharp fluctuations in oil imports, real net exports have begun to show only moderate signs of a turnaround. HH and KB have attributed the persistence of the deficit to the pattern of exchange rate changes (notably the fact that the dollar was appreciating strongly before it started to fall) and normal lags (including J-curve effects) in the adjustment of the deficit to these swings in the dollar. They also note that significant adjustment *has* taken place in that the deficit is smaller than it would have been if the dollar had not depreciated.

Does this explanation still hold up? Our answer is partly yes, partly no. There are now clear signs that the adjustment process is taking longer than would be predicted on the basis of historical experience, particularly for certain components of the external deficit.

1.5.4.1 Persistence of the Partial Trade Deficit. Chart 1–5 shows predictions of the real and nominal partial trade balance (nonagricultural export − nonoil import) equations discussed earlier, using our "mix" specification for activity variables. Two predictions were made, one using actual values of nonoil import and nonagricultural export prices, and a second using the model's predictions of those prices. A third simulation is also included, showing the model's prediction of where the deficit would be if the relative prices of nonoil imports and nonagricultural exports had remained at their values in the first quarter of 1985 when the dollar was at its peak.

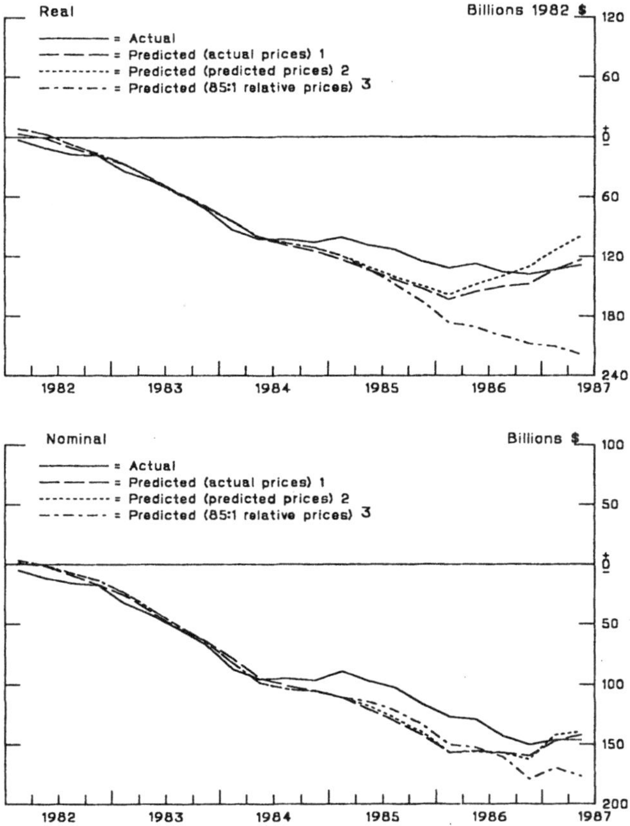

[1] Model prediction using actual values of relative prices.
[2] Model prediction using model's prediction of import and export prices.
[3] Model prediction holding relative prices unchanged at their 85Q1 values.

Chart 1–5. Partial Trade Balance

The chart suggests that the decline in the dollar has clearly had a substantial impact to date, particularly on the real trade balance (as indicated in the top panel). The model's prediction of the *real* partial trade balance in 1987:2 was slightly more than half as large as it would have been if the dollar had not declined and relative prices had remained at their 1985:1 values.[20] At the same time, the predicted real balance fell below the actual balance in 1985, but has been rising noticeably faster since early 1986 (particularly when predicted import and export prices are used). Thus, while the real deficit *has* responded significantly to the fall in the dollar, it has done so more slowly than past experience would have predicted, particularly in recent quarters.

The bottom panel of the chart shows that the model's prediction of the *nominal* trade balance was only slightly above the actual balance in the second quarter of 1987. Although the predicted nominal balance had been rising for several quarters, it had fallen below the actual earlier. The fall in the dollar has had a much smaller positive impact on the model's prediction of the nominal trade balance than its prediction of the real balance because of J-curve effects. The steady depreciation of the dollar has led to a predicted steady increase in import prices (in fact, an over-prediction, as discussed below), which has offset much of the predicted gain in real net exports. In any event, the results in chart 1–5 suggest that the persistence of the deficit, in real terms at least, cannot be fully explained by partial-equilibrium macroeconomic factors.

The prediction errors of the major components of the partial trade balance are shown in table 1–9. The most striking errors are for nonoil import prices, and to a lesser extent nonagricultural export prices, both of which were being overpredicted by the model. (These prediction errors are also illustrated in chart 1–6 as the difference between the predicted and actual values of the nonoil import and nonagricultural export deflators shown.) The model also began to overpredict the volume of nonagricultural exports in the first half of 1987 (especially when the actual value of nonagricultural export prices was used in the volume equation), and to underpredict nonoil import volumes when predicted values of nonoil import prices were used.

The overprediction of nonagricultural export volumes and nonoil import prices suggests that foreign competitors were reducing their export prices in terms of their own currencies (hence their profit margins) more than they would have in the past in response to the appreciation of their currencies against the dollar. The model's overprediction of U.S. nonagricultural export prices is also symptomatic of more intense price competition from abroad than had been observed in the past, on average, under similar circumstances. Moreover, the model's underprediction of real net exports during 1984 and 1985 suggests the possibility that competition abroad was less intense than expected during the latter stages of the rise in the dollar. Profit margins of foreign competitors may well have been built up more during this earlier period, providing a cushion that could be squeezed later. This cause of persistence in the U.S. external deficit, particularly in real terms, will be the focus of much of our discussion of microeconomic factors underlying the deficit in section 1.7. In the remainder of this section

Table 1–9. Partial Trade Balance Equations: Post Sample Prediction Errors[a]

	1985				1986				1987	
	Q1	*Q2*	*Q3*	*Q4* (percent)	*Q1*	*Q2*	*Q3*	*Q4*	*Q1*	*Q2*
Volume equations (using actual prices)										
Nonag. export volume	−6.96	−6.78	−6.92	−6.32	−6.61	−5.14	−4.59	−2.30	3.55	5.89
Nonoil import volume	3.19	3.98	5.38	4.63	5.50	4.76	1.31	1.32	2.32	2.25
Price Equations										
Nonag. export price	−0.33	−0.09	0.29	1.18	2.08	2.19	3.91	5.48	6.17	6.94
Nonoil import price	1.17	0.05	0.17	0.77	2.42	3.35	5.34	9.02	8.23	10.81
Volume equations (using predicted prices)										
Nonag export volume	−6,51	−6.29	−6.40	−5,85	−6.31	−5.17	−4.98	−3.16	2.03	3.58
Nonoil import volume	2.07	3.21	4.86	4.07	4.27	2.74	−1.94	−3.95	−4.24	−5.79

[a] Error = predicted minus actual.

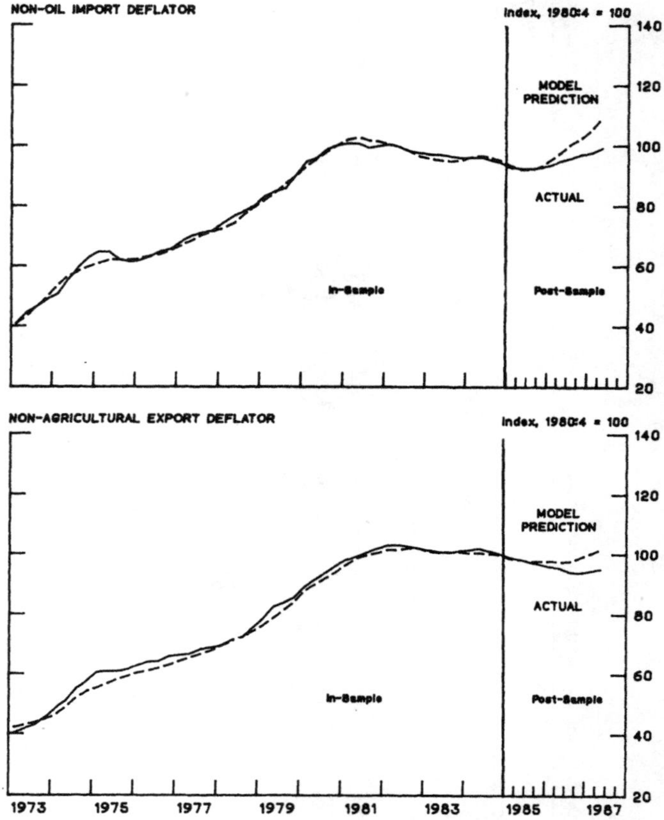

Chart 1–6. Trade Prices

we review evidence on the behavior of profit margins that can be gleaned from macro data.

5.4.2 Aggregate Data on Prices and Profit Margins. Chart 1–7 shows the two most important components of the import price equation discussed earlier: the nonoil import deflator and a weighted average of foreign consumer prices in dollars (as a proxy for foreign production costs). It is clear that after having moved quite closely together during 1973–1984, the two series began to diverge in 1985, as the import deflator fell substantially relative to this particular proxy for foreign costs in dollars.[21] These data

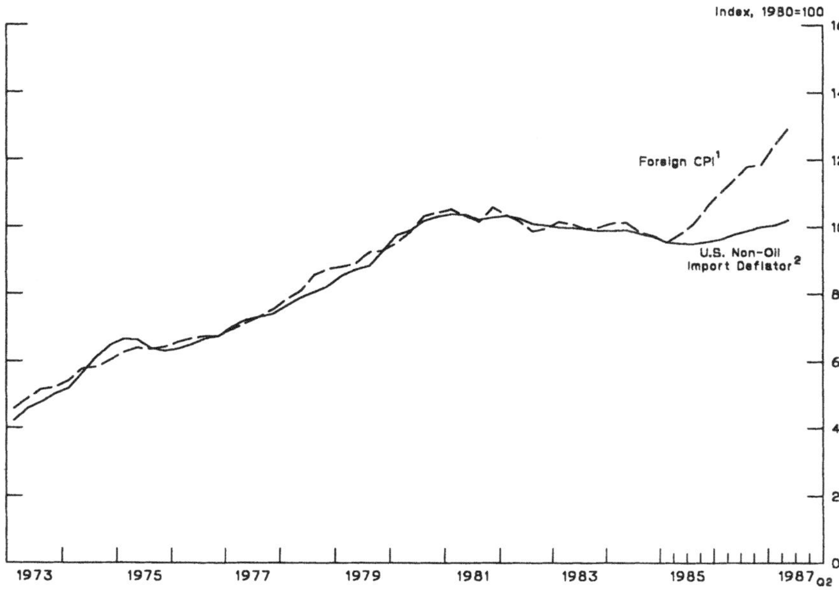

Source: Federal Reserve Board USIT model database

[1] CPI's in dollars for 10 industrial countries and 8 developing countries weighted by shares in U.S. nonoil imports during 1978–1983.

[2] Implicit deflator from the GNP accounts.

Chart 1–7. U.S. Import Prices and Foreign Prices

appear to support the hypothesis that foreign profit margins have been squeezed significantly over the past two years as foreign firms have strived to maintain their shares of the U.S. market in the face of a falling dollar. At the same time, however, these aggregate data provide little evidence to suggest that profit margins on goods exported to the United States widened significantly while the dollar was rising. This chart suggests that even if foreign producers had delayed the pass-through of exchange rate changes thus far, they cannot continue to do so, and further adjustment of import prices must be in the pipeline.

There are several other possible explanations for the emerging gaps between import prices and foreign prices shown in these charts, which have different implications for the movement in import prices. To begin with, consumer prices are not ideal proxies for foreign production costs. Some evidence on this point is presented in chart 1–8, which shows CPIs com-

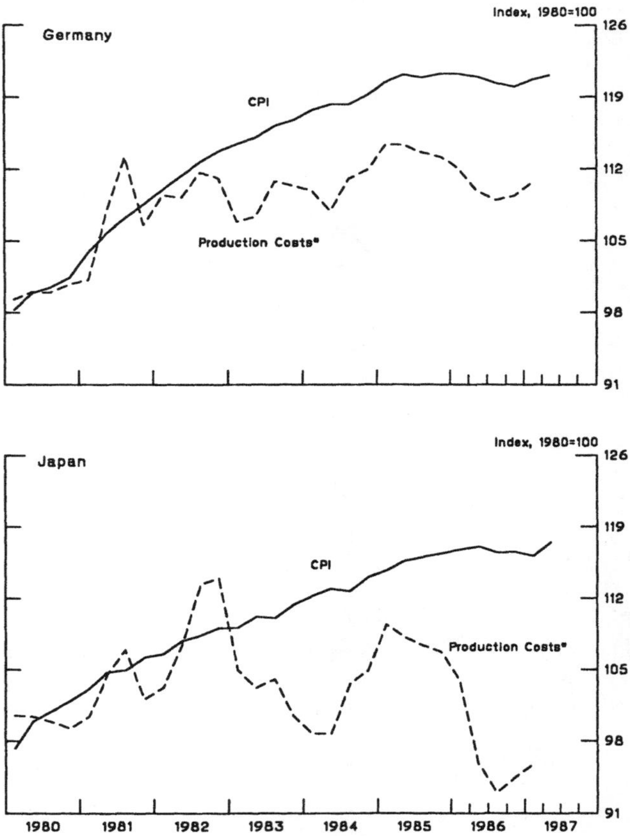

Source: CPI: National sources, ULC and raw materials prices see chart 1–9

* Weighted average of manufacturing unit labor costs (65%) and raw materials (including petroleum) prices (35%).

Chart 1–8. Consumer Prices and Manufacturing Production Costs (In local currencies)

pared with local production costs for Germany and Japan. The measure of production costs shown is a weighted average of unit labor costs in manufacturing and the local wholesale price index for raw materials and fuels. The components of the cost index are shown in chart 1–9, along with the combined index. (The weights used in constructing the combined index

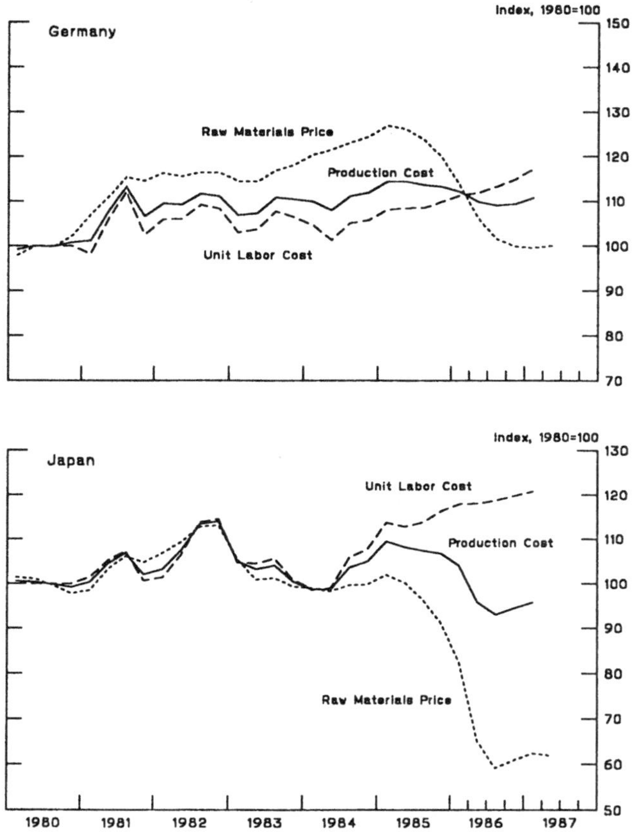

Source: ULC: OECD; Raw materials price: National sources

Chart 1–9. Manufacturing Cost Indexes and Their Components (In local currencies)

were based on the relative shares of labor compensation and raw material plus fuel inputs in manufacturing in the 1977 U.S. input-output table.) It is clear from chart 1–8 that after having fluctuated more or less in line with the CPIs historically, the cost indexes have declined noticeably relative to the CPIs since 1984, particularly in Japan. As indicated in chart 1–10, this decline reflects a sharp decline in the local currency prices of raw materials and fuels in those countries.

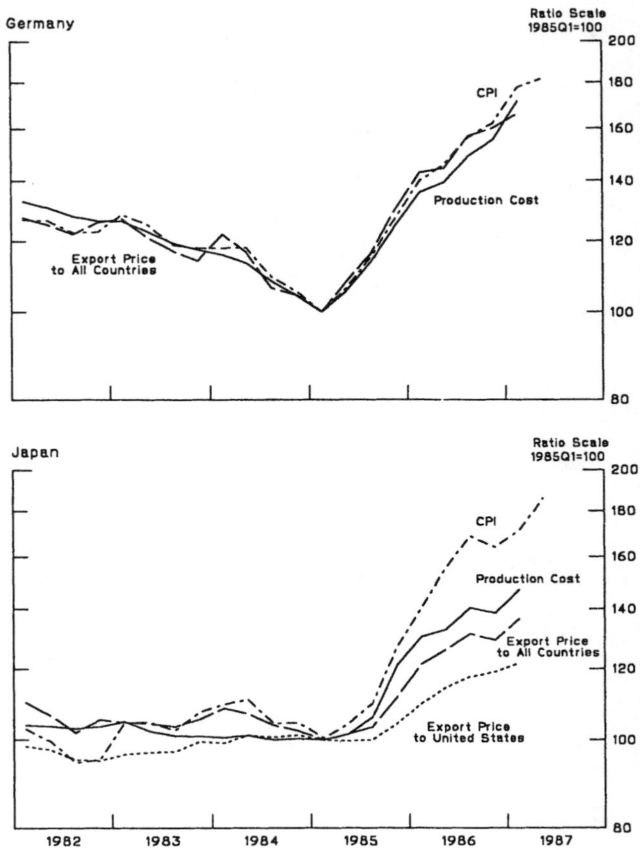

Source: CPI: National sources; Export prices: BLS

Chart 1–10. Foreign Export Prices and Production Costs (all Indexes in U.S. dollars)

To the extent that CPIs overstate the rise in foreign production costs they understate the increase in profit margins earned while the dollar was rising and overstate the decline in foreign profit margins that has occurred with the decline in the dollar. To gauge the possible significance of this bias, we compare production costs and CPIs with German and Japanese export prices for manufactured goods in chart 1–10. Also shown for Japan is the BLS price index for that country's manufactured exports to the United States. In the Japanese case, the gap that has emerged between export prices and production costs is substantially smaller than that between export prices and the CPI. By 1987:1, the apparent squeeze in profit margins on Japan's exports to the United States based on the index of production costs was about half as large as that based on the CPI as a proxy for costs. (It is also noteworthy that Japanese exporters appear to have squeezed their profits on exports to the United States more than they have on exports to other countries—a point we will return to later.) In the German case, the production cost measure appears to eliminate any decline in profit margins on total exports over the past two years. This still leaves open the possibility of a squeezing of profits on exports to the United States, however.

Another possible explanation for the emerging gap between import prices and foreign prices concerns a key component of the import deflator. The prices of business machinery, which account for over 10% of imports in 1982 dollars, have been estimated by the Department of Commerce (Bureau of Economic Analysis) to have declined at roughly a 15% annual rate over the past four years. The effect of this component on the overall deflator is shown in chart 1–11, which plots the nonoil deflator and the deflator for nonoil imports excluding business machines. The decline in business machine prices almost has the effect of creating a break in the series for the total deflator beginning in about 1983.[22] It is unlikely that foreign CPIs or even aggregate production costs adequately reflect the importance to the U.S. import deflator of the decline in the cost of producing business machinery. Therefore, some of the apparent decline in aggregate profit margins probably reflects instead the unusual behavior of business machinery prices.[23]

In sum, the evidence based on aggregate data appears to suggest that foreign profit margins on exports to the United States have been squeezed somewhat more than might have been expected over the past two years. However, various measurement problems with available aggregate data render this evidence somewhat less than conclusive. It seems likely, for example, that foreign production costs have risen somewhat less than foreign consumer prices, on average. Nevertheless, using more refined estimates of production costs for Japan, we do find evidence of a significant squeezing of profit margins on Japanese exports to the United States since 1985. We will return to the subject of foreign pricing behavior and an analysis of the behavior of U.S. import prices at the industry level with our discussion of microeconomic factors in section 1.7. First, however, we turn to macroeconomic causes of the deficit at a more fundamental level.

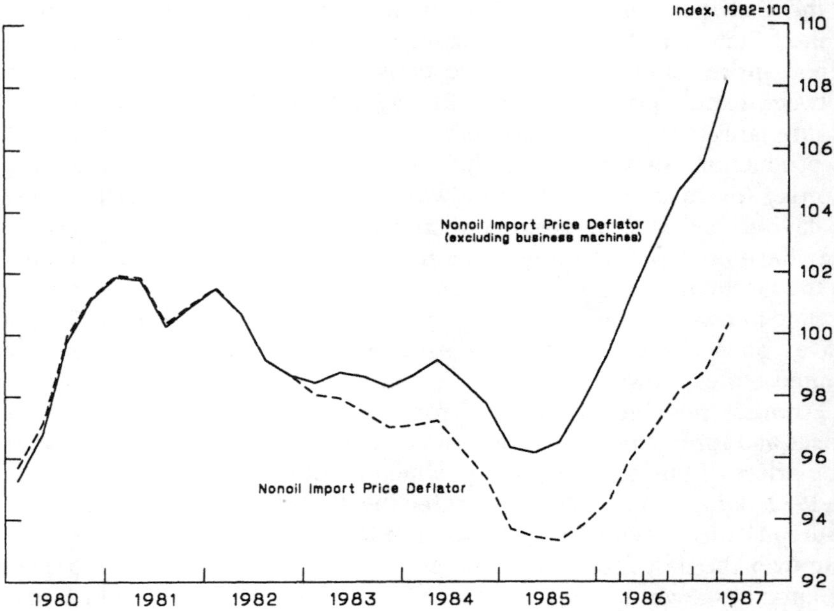

Source: FRB macro database

Chart 1–11. Nonoil Import Deflators

1.6 Macroeconomic Factors: Policy Shifts and Other Fundamentals

In the preceding section we established that partial-equilibrium macroeconomic factors, including relative prices (or real exchange rates) and relative growth rates, can account for the widening of the external deficit between 1980 and 1986, though not for all of its more recent persistence. We now consider the extent to which the contributions of these proximate determinants can be explained by shifts in fiscal and monetary policies at home and abroad during the 1980s. We begin with an analysis of factors underlying movements in the dollar's exchange rate, and then turn to a quantitative analysis of the effects of shifts in fiscal and monetary policy, drawing on the results of policy simulations with a number of international macroeconomic models.

1.6.1 Factors Underlying Movements in the Dollar

Movements in the dollar's average real (CPI-adjusted) foreign exchange value against the currencies of several different groups of countries are shown in chart 1–12. The indexes shown include ten industrial countries, eight developing countries, and the eighteen countries combined. The currencies are weighted by each country's share in world trade. The G-10 and 8-Developing country indexes show divergent movements. While the dollar has fallen sharply against the G-10 currencies over the past two years, developing countries, on average, have kept their currencies from appreciating in real terms against the dollar over this period. This divergence of rates has important implications for certain categories of U.S. imports, as we will discuss in the next section. Overall, however, the 18-country index is dominated by movements in the G-10 index, and in the rest of this section we will focus on factors that have led to swings in the dollar's exchange rate against the currencies of industrial countries.[24]

Our analysis of movements in the dollar's real exchange rate draws on the model of exchange rate determination that was discussed at the end of section 1.3—the long-term real open-interest parity relationship. The essence of this model is that the dollar will move to equate the expected rate of return on assets denominated in different currencies. An empirical representation of this relationship is given in chart 1–13.

The top panel of chart 1–13 shows the real dollar against G-10 currencies and a measure of the difference between U.S. and foreign (G-10) long-term real government bond yields. The bottom panel shows the U.S. and foreign components of the real interest differential. In calculating the real bond yields, a three-year centered moving average of CPI inflation rates (i.e., ranging from six quarters in the past to six quarters in the future) was used as a proxy for inflation expectations. (The countries and weights in the foreign interest rate index are the same as in the exchange rate index.)

It is clear from the chart that movements in the dollar's real exchange rate have been at least roughly correlated with the long-term real interest rate differential over much of the floating-rate period. Movements in the dollar over the 1980s can be broken into three stages. The first stage, which lasted through 1983, was a rapid appreciation (with several interruptions) that followed a sharp (6 percentage-point) increase in the real U.S. bond rate relative to the average foreign rate. The second stage, beginning in early 1984, was a further rapid appreciation that took place despite a sharp decline in the U.S. real interest rate relative to foreign rates. The third stage was the rapid depreciation beginning in March 1985 that coincided

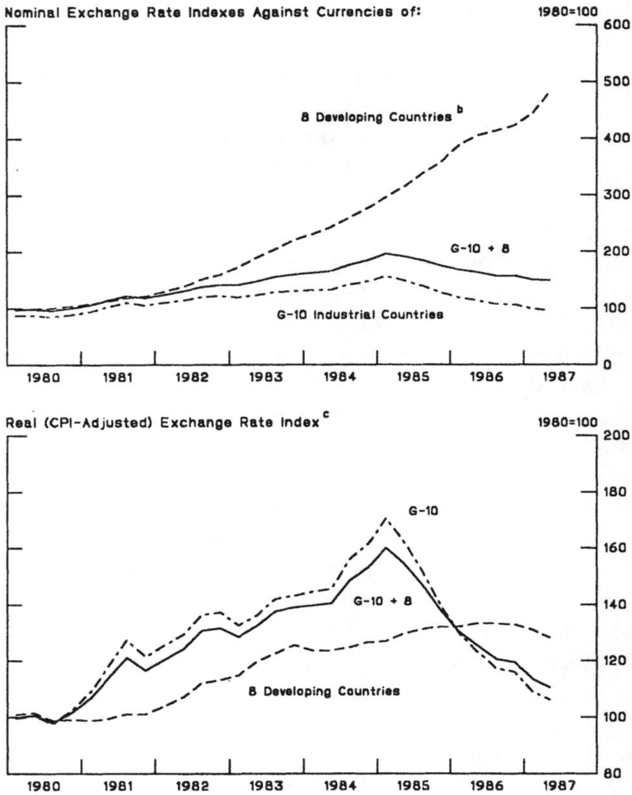

Source: Federal Reserve Bulletin

[a] Foreign currency/dollar indexes weighted by each country's share in world trade during 1978–83.

[b] Includes Brazil, Hong Kong, Malaysia, Mexico, Philippines, Singapore, South Korea, and Taiwan.

[c] CPI-adjusted index is equal to nominal index times the ratio of US CPI to weighted average foreign CPI (using same countries and weights as in nominal index).

Chart 1–12. Foreign Exchange Value of the Dollar[a]

with a continued decline in the interest differential through early 1987.

Given the assumptions underlying the long-run open-interest parity model (close substitutability of assets, absence of exchange risk aversion, and a constant expected long-run equilibrium real exchange rate), a 1

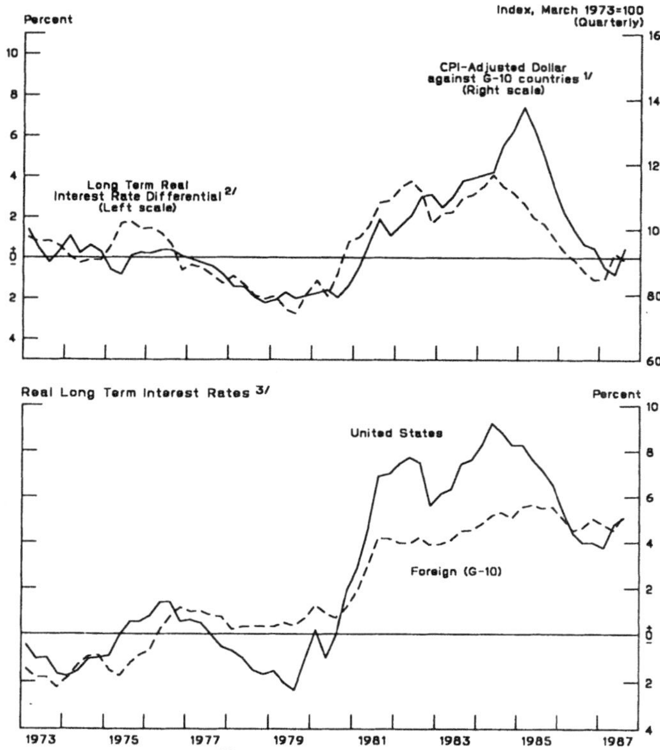

Source: Federal Reserve Board macro data base

[1] The CPI-adjusted dollar is a weighted-average index of the exchange value of the dollar against the currencies of the foreign Group-of-Ten countries plus Switzerland, where nominal exchange rates are multiplied by relative levels of consumer price indexes. Weights are proportional to each foreign country's share in world exports plus imports during 1978–1983.

[2] Long-term real U.S. interest rate minus weighted average of long-term real foreign-country interest rates.

[3] Long-term government or public authority bond rates adjusted for expected inflation estimated by a 36-month centered calculation of actual inflation. Foreign index uses the same trade weights as described in note 1.

Chart 1–13. The Dollar and Long-Term Real Interest Rates Using 3-Year Centered Moving Average Inflation Expectations percentage-point increase in real dollar interest rates relative to foreign rates on bonds maturing in x years will induce an immediate $x\%$ appreciation of the dollar. In this case, the dollar can be expected to depreciate by 1% per year for x years, returning to its long-run equilibrium level. The scaling of the top panel of chart 1–13 is consistent with about a six-year expectations horizon. That is, a 1 percentage-point increase in the interest differential (left scale) induces roughly a 6% appreciation of the dollar (right scale). In principle, the horizon could be significantly longer, given that the interest rates used in the chart pertain to bonds with terms to maturity ranging between five and ten years. (The terms to maturity vary across countries, depending on data availabilities.) On purely empirical grounds, however, the six-year horizon appears to fit best.[25]

This relationship suggests that the roughly 35% appreciation of the dollar during stage 1 (1980–1982) can be fully explained by the 6 percentage-point increase in the interest differential over that period. During stage 3 (1985–1986), however, the dollar fell considerably more than this relationship would suggest. (We will return to this point, as well as a discussion of stage 2, below.)

The bottom panel of the chart illustrates clearly that the stage 1 increase in the real interest differential reflected a very large (nearly 10 percentage-point) increase in U.S. real rates that was only partly offset by an increase in average foreign rates. The more recent decline (through early 1987) has been largely the result of a decline in U.S. rates, while foreign rates have been much more stable. As it emerges from the literature, the consensus explanation for the rise in U.S. real interest rates in the early 1980s includes a combination of monetary tightening beginning with the shift in the Federal Reserve's operating procedures in November 1979, and fiscal expansion following the passage of the federal tax cuts in 1981.[26] The more recent decline in U.S. real rates has been linked to both the adoption of a more accommodative monetary policy stance by the Federal Reserve after 1982, and improved prospects for a significant reduction of the federal budget deficit following the passage of the Gramm-Rudman legislation in 1985.[27] We will return to a discussion of the quantitative effects of shifts in U.S. (and foreign) fiscal and monetary policy on the dollar (and the external deficit) at the end of this section.

The long-term real interest parity relationship, and more fundamentally, the shifts in policies underlying the changes in real interest rates, still leave a significant portion of the dollar's movement during the 1980s unexplained. Deviations between the dollar and the interest differential in chart 1–13 can be traced to the failure of one or more of the assumptions underlying the interest parity model. Consider, for example, the assumption of a constant expected equilibrium real exchange rate. The long-run equilibrium real rate is often defined as the rate that is consistent with a sustainable level of the current account in the long run.[28] Views about what level of the current account (and therefore the dollar) is politically sustainable appear to have changed over time. By mid-1985 the unprecedented level of the U.S. current account deficit and prospects for even larger deficits had become a matter of central concern to economic policymakers. Mounting protectionist pressures in the United States, and official pronouncements (such as the September 1985 "Plaza Accord") that the dollar would have to be brought down, may well have induced a significant shift in market expectations about the equilibrium real exchange rate. Such a shift would have caused the dollar to fall faster than the rate predicted by movements in the real interest differential, as it did in stage 3 (early 1985–early 1987).

Movements in the dollar and the interest differential could also differ significantly if the assumption that financial assets denominated in the different currencies are close substitutes does not hold. In this case the risk premium on dollar assets would rise (and the dollar would fall, with unchanged interest rates) as the U.S. current account deficit required foreign residents to hold increasing amounts of dollar-denominated claims. This effect could help to explain the rapid fall in the dollar since 1985, but it should also have been holding the dollar below the interest differential when U.S. net external debt was beginning to rise substantially during 1983–1985. In any event, a number of empirical studies have suggested that this effect has not been empirically significant in the past, and that the assumption of close substitutability does hold to a reasonable approximation.[29]

Finally, stage 2 (early 1984–early 1985) remains a puzzle. The dollar rose more than 20% over a twelve-month period in which the U.S. interest rates were falling rapidly relative to foreign rates and the current account deficit was in excess of $100 billion. Frankel and Froot [1986] observe that survey data suggested that even market participants expected the dollar to fall during this period. They conclude that the rise in the dollar in 1984 reflected irrational speculative behavior. Other studies have suggested that financial deregulation in Japan and elsewhere loosened pent-up demand for dollar assets that contributed to the continued rise in the dollar.[30] Whatever its cause, the rise in the dollar over this period, which had important implications for the U.S. external balance, apparently cannot be traced to the effects of shifts in macro policies through their impacts on real interest rates. We turn next to a quantitative analysis of the extent to which changes in fiscal and monetary policies *did* affect real interest rates, the dollar and the external deficit.

1.6.2 The Contribution of Shifts in U.S. and Foreign Macroeconomic Policies

Table 1–10 presents a combination of OECD and IMF estimates of the exogenous shifts in fiscal policy that occurred over the first half of the 1980s. These data suggest that changes in U.S. fiscal policy resulted in an expansion of the structural (exogenous) federal deficit by an amount equal to about 3.5% of GNP between 1980 and 1985. Over the same period changes in policies in other industrial countries resulted in contractions of structural government budget deficits equal to about 2.5% of GNP on average. Although not shown in the table, since 1985 the United States has made some progress in reducing its structural deficit, while the position of the other countries, *on average* remains little changed.

Quantitative estimates of the effects of these fiscal policy shifts can be obtained from the results of policy simulations reported by a group of 12 multicountry models in a March 1986 Brookings conference.[31] The models were asked to simulate the effects of sustained exogenous shifts in government spending equal to 1% of baseline GNP both in the United States and in other OECD countries combined, while holding the growth of monetary aggregates exogenous. They were also asked to simulate the ef-

Table 1–10. Fiscal Policy: Cumulative Exogenous Changes in Budget Balances 1980–85[a] (as percent of GNP/GDP)

	IMF Fiscal Impluse		*OECD Change in Structural Budget Balance*
	Central/ Federal Government	*General Government*	*General Government*
Germany	2.9	4.4	3.2
Japan	1.5	3.5	3.6
United Kingdom	3.0	3.8	4.1
France	0.0	3.2	0.6
Italy	−0.5	0.8	−2.8
Canada	−2.4	−2.9	−3.4
Average of 6 above	1.2	2.8	2.0
United States	−3.7	−2.3	−2.4

Source: IMF estimates: *World Economic Outlook*, April 1986; OECD estimates: *Economic Outlook*, various issues.

[a] A positive number indicates a fiscal contraction, an increase in the structural budget surplus, or a reduction in the structural deficit.

fects of an exogenous 4% increase in the U.S. M1 money stock. The average longer-run impacts on several key variables reported by 9 of these models are shown in table 1–11.[32] The data shown are averages of wide ranges of results. However, all of the estimates in the ranges were generally consistent with the qualitative predictions of conventional macroeconomic theory as embodied in the extended Mundell-Flemming model. The mean estimates suggest that the U.S. fiscal expansion causes U.S. GNP to rise, and eventually leads to 0.5 percentage-point increase in U.S. long-term real interest rates relative to foreign rates, a 2–2.5% appreciation of the dollar in real terms against OECD currencies on average, and a $14 to $20 billion decline in the current account balance. The foreign fiscal contrac-

Table 1–11. Simulated Impacts of Fiscal and Monetary Policy Shocks, Average of 9 Models (deviations from baseline)

	U.S. Fiscal Expansion Equal to 1% of GNP		*Foreign Fiscal Contraction Equal to 1% of GNP*		*4% Decline in U.S. M1 Money Stock*	
	After 3 Years	*After 5 Years*	*After 3 Years*	*After 5 Years*	*After 3 Years*	*After 5 Years*
Impact on:						
U.S.-foreign long-term real interest rate differential (percentage points)	$\frac{1}{2}$	$\frac{1}{2}$	0+	0+	$\frac{1}{2}$	0
OECD dollar real exchange rate (percent)	2	$2\frac{1}{2}$	1	$1\frac{1}{2}$	4	$2\frac{1}{2}$
U.S. current account balance (billions of $, AR)	−14	−20	−8	−8	0	0
U.S. CPI level (percent)	1	2	$-\frac{1}{2}$	−1	$-1\frac{1}{2}$	$-2\frac{1}{2}$
U.S. real GNP level (percent)	1	$\frac{1}{2}$	$-\frac{1}{4}$	−0	−1	$-\frac{1}{2}$
Foreign (OECD) real GNP level (percent)	$+\frac{1}{4}$	$+\frac{1}{4}$	$-1\frac{1}{2}$	$-1\frac{1}{4}$	$-\frac{1}{4}$	$-\frac{1}{4}$

Source: Calculated from Bryant et al. (1988); see text.

tion also leads to an appreciation of the dollar and a decline in the U.S. current account balance. The average effect of the foreign fiscal shock on the real interest rate differential is negligible, however, and the exchange rate and current account effects are substantially smaller than in the case of the U.S. shock. A U.S. monetary contraction raises the real interest rate differential and the dollar's exchange rate, but it also reduces U.S. real income. With the rise in income tending to raise imports and the decline in the dollar working in the opposite direction to stimulate net exports, the U.S. monetary contraction has a negligible impact on the current account balance.

The results in the first and third columns of table 1–11 suggest that the U.S. fiscal expansion (equal to 3.5% of GNP) and the foreign fiscal contraction (2.5% of GNP) combined, accounted for less than one–third (or 3.5×0.5 percentage points $+2.5 \times 0$ percentage points $= 1.75$ percentage points) of the 6 percentage-point increase in the long-term real interest rate differential between late 1979 and early 1984 (seen in chart 1–13). Similar calculations suggest that these shifts in U.S. and foreign fiscal policy accounted for about 10 percentage points or roughly one-fifth of the rise in the dollar and as much as $90 billion (or nearly two-thirds) of the widening of the current account deficit over that period.[33]

These estimates suggest that while the combination of fiscal expansion at home and fiscal contraction abroad accounted for as much as two-thirds of the current account deficit, they can explain at most one-third of the rise in the real interest differential and an even smaller portion of the rise in the dollar. Evidently, the changes in fiscal policy influenced the current account to a substantial degree through their impacts on relative growth of GNP and domestic demand in the United States and elsewhere. Based on the estimates in columns 1 and 3 of table 1–11, the shifts in U.S. and foreign fiscal policy raised the level of U.S. GNP by as much as 6 percentage points relative to foreign (OECD) GNP during the first half of the 1980s, substantially more than the actual GNP growth differential during the period (see table 1–4).[34]

If, by process of elimination, we attribute the remaining two-thirds (or 4 percentage points) of the rise in the long-term real interest rate differential to a significant tightening of U.S. monetary policy relative to monetary policy abroad, beginning in late 1979, that shift in monetary policy can explain a substantial part of the rise in the dollar. The estimates in table 1–11 suggest that for every ½ percentage-point rise in the real interest rate differential in the case of a U.S. monetary tightening, the dollar rises by 4% in real terms, or a ratio of 8 to 1. (This impact is somewhat greater than the roughly 6 to 1 ratio illustrated in chart 1–13.) Applying this 8 to 1 ratio to the 4 percentage-point rise in the interest differential that is not "explained" by fiscal policy, the monetary tightening would account for something more than a 30% rise in the dollar.

At the same time, the average results of an model simulation suggest that the U.S. monetary tightening by itself does not explain any of the widening of the current account deficit. This is because the change in monetary policy induces a change in income that offsets the current account effect of the induced exchange rate change. A U.S. monetary tightening eight times as great as that shown in table 1–11 would have reduced the level of U.S. GNP relative to foreign GNP by 6%. According to the models, the positive current account effects of this shift in relative GNPs were large enough to offset the negative effects of the rise in the dollar caused by the monetary restraint. On this basis, the monetary tightening also reduced the level of U.S. consumer prices by something on the order of 20% below where it would otherwise have been in the mid-1980s.[35]

In brief, based on the average predictions of a group of international macroeconomic models, the U.S. monetary tightening beginning in the latter part of 1979 resulted in a sharp runup in the real interest rate differential and the dollar; it also contributed significantly to the 1982 recession. As the fiscal stimulus took hold in 1982 and 1983 there was a strong recovery from the recession, which contributed further to the rise in the interest differential and the dollar. The current account did not fall substantially into deficit until 1983, when the recovery in GNP growth was under way and the lagged effects of the earlier appreciation of the dollar were beginning to have strong effects.

Our quantitative estimates suggest that, taken separately, neither the shift in monetary policy alone nor the shift in fiscal policies alone can adequately explain the changes in the U.S. external sector that took place during the first half of the 1980s. Taken *together*, however, the combined effects of these policy changes can explain something approaching two-thirds of the increases in both the dollar and the current account deficit. They also appear to have reduced U.S. GNP growth somewhat, foreign GNP growth by a greater amount, and the U.S. inflation rate by a substantial amount.[36] Explanations for the remaining one-third of the rise in the dollar and the widening of the current account deficit may be found in exchange market bubbles, the debt crisis (which interrupted the flow of new lending to, and therefore the growth of major U.S. markets among, developing countries), and other exogenous factors (animal spirits?) that may have raised U.S. growth relative to foreign growth.

Some words of caution about the interpretation of these results are in order. First, with respect to our estimates of the effects of shifts in fiscal policy, there is some inconsistency between the policy shifts that took place and the model simulations that were used. Perhaps most importantly, the model simulations were based on an increase in U.S. government spending, whereas the actual U.S. fiscal expansions was due primarily to a cut in taxes. Several of the models whose results we employ participated in a Brookings workshop in September 1985, for which they were asked to simulate a lump-sum federal tax cut and an increase in spending, both equal to 1% of baseline GNP. The tax cut had a 15% smaller impact on GNP, the dollar, and the current account than the spending increase, on average. A cut in tax rates could well have a somewhat smaller impact than a lump-sum tax cut in many of these models. FRB Multicountry Model simulations of the tax law changes in the Economic Recovery Tax Act of 1981 and the Tax Equity and Fiscal Responsibility Act of 1982, reported by Hooper [1985], show estimated impacts on the dollar and the current account that are about two-thirds as large as estimates based on the average multipliers reported above.[37]

Second, the unexplained portion of the current account deficit could well be greater than indicated in our estimates, inasmuch as developments in oil markets, including both oil price declines and the continuing response of U.S. consumption (hence imports) to earlier price increases, were working to reduce the deficit.

Finally, the quantitative estimates outlined above are based on averages of a wide range of results obtained from a variety of different models. These averages should be taken as no more than very crude indicators of the possible orders of magnitude of the quantitative effects of monetary and fiscal policy shifts. A recent study by Sachs and Roubini [1987] for example, finds that the U.S. current account deficit can be fully explained by a combination of changes in fiscal policy and the reduction of lending to developing countries. The model they employ was included in the March 1986 Brookings conference, and its estimate of the current account effects of a U.S. fiscal expansion was at the high end of the range, more than double the average estimate shown in table 1–11.

1.7 Microeconomic Factors: Pricing Behavior and Protection

We turn now to the microeconomic factors contributing to the widening and persistence of the current account deficit. In the previous sections, we argued that macroeconomic factors could explain the initial but not all of the widening of the deficit, nor the persistence of the deficit. Indeed, at the end of section 1.5 we found evidence in aggregate data (despite significant problems with those data) that changes in the pricing and profit-setting behavior of importers and exporters were contributing to the persistence of the deficit. In this section, we begin (in section 1.7.1) by investigating microeconomic (or industry-level) evidence of changes in the behavior of prices and profit margins. Recalling the simple model of price determination presented earlier, we will, in section 1.7.2, select industries that illustrate how the relationship between exchange rates and dollar import prices can be affected by (1) differences between products with respect to their sources or destinations, and (2) specific characteristics of the products and their marketplace. In section 1.7.3 we review the spread of protectionist policies at home and abroad, and consider the extent to which these policies may have contributed to the persistence of the deficit by prolonging the process of adjustment to the lower dollar. A summary of the material in this section is contained in section 1.7.4.

1.7.1 Prices and Profit Margins

We found, at the end of section 1.5, that the equation for the nonoil import deflator significantly overpredicted in recent quarters, suggesting that import prices are adjusting more slowly to changes in the exchange rate than they have in the past. However, this macro analysis was clouded to some extent by data problems: foreign consumer prices, used as a proxy for the costs of production, probably understate movements in the cost of production, and the import deflator may understate increases in import prices due to shifts in commodity composition (particularly involving the increasing share of business machinery). Our micro model showed how the failure to account for changes in input costs, or quantitative restraints, could overstate the estimates of the pass-through of an exchange rate change to dollar import prices. In an effort to get around some of these data problems, and to more closely examine industry pricing behavior and exchange-rate pass-through, we turn now to an investigation of micro (industry-level) data.

Our analysis of disaggregated data uses a relatively small sample of industries. Table 1–12 lists the industries, which accounted for about 15% of U.S. imports and exports in 1980. These industries were chosen because they have the longest available series for import and export transactions prices. While not a large sample, it is representative of the predominant categories of imports and exports of the United States.

In the past, an analysis of the behavior of trade prices at the industry

Table 1–12. SIC Code Number and SIC Product Category Name

	IMPORTS
2311	men's and boy's suits and coats (certain apparel)
2621	paper mill products
2221	weaving mill products, synthetics, silks (certain textiles)
2033	canned fruits and vegetables
314	men's and women's leather footwear (3313 + 3314)
331	rolling mill and electrometalurgical steels (3312 + 3313)
3531	construction machinery
	EXPORTS
2611	pulp mill products
2011	meat packing and preparations
3494	valves and pipe fittings
3519	internal combustion engines
3523	farm machinery and equipment
3533	oilfield and gasfield equipment
3546	power-driven hand tools
3555	printing trades machinery
3674	semiconductor devices

level has depended on unit-value data as proxies for price movements. However, the Bureau of Labor Statistics has recently begun publishing transactions prices for imports and exports disaggregated according to the four-digit SIC, the five-digit SITC, and the four-digit end-use classification.[38] These prices, which are transactions prices obtained from a survey of a selected sample of industries, are available quarterly, one observation per quarter (usually the observation is the third month of the quarter). Both the import and the export prices are indexed in dollar terms.

Unfortunately, most of the series start only in 1980 or later. For the analysis in this paper, we wanted to compare periods of appreciation and depreciation, and compare the current depreciation with an earlier depreciation. Thus, we wanted a sample that included at least the depreciation in the late 1970s. The industries in table 1–12 are the only ones that go back that far.

1.7.1.1 Constructing Indexes of Industry-Specific Profit Margins. An index of profit margins for U.S. exports of each SIC category was calculated in dollar terms, as the ratio of each product's BLS export price index to its matched U.S. producer price index. We used the industry-specific producer price index as a proxy for the costs of production of the good in the United States. Since producer price indexes include a profit margin at the wholesale level, they overstate the true costs of production. Thus, the constructed index of exporter's profit margins captures both price discrimination—the extent to which profit margins differ between exporting versus selling the same product in the United States—and movements in price-cost margins. We will be unable to distinquish between the two. However, to the extent that we are interested in the differential margin applied to the international market, and the possible consequence of changes in this margin for international competitiveness, the extra margin embodied in the producer price index is not a problem. But, it should be noted that nothing can be inferred from the level of this index because the choice of base year was arbitrary.

For imports, the study examines foreign currency profit margins on the assumption that a foreign firm maximizes profits measured in its own currency. Therefore, each product's BLS import price index must be converted to foreign currency units. An index of nominal exchange rates weighted by import shares was created for each product.[39] Multiplying this index by the BLS index of dollar import prices yields an index of import prices in foreign currency terms. Multiplying the import-share weights by each country's proxy for the product's production costs creates an index of foreign currency costs of production for each imported good. Since foreign countries have their own industry disaggregation schemes, there is no breakdown for foreign costs of production that exactly match the disaggregated SIC-based import price data. Thus, the analysis relies on the producer price index from national sources most nearly equivalent to the four-digit SIC scheme.[40] The ratio of the indexes of foreign currency import prices and of foreign currency costs of production forms an index of foreign currency profit margins for each import.

1.7.1.2 Behavior of Prices and Profit Margins of Specific Industries. Chart 1–14 shows the behavior of prices and profit margins for the *imported* products. Table 1–13 shows the level and percent change in the index of profit margins calculated in foreign currency terms for the periods of dollar appreciation and depreciation over the last 10 years.[41] The general pattern that emerges is that profit margins bear the brunt of changes in exchange rates and foreign costs, leaving U.S. dollar prices of imports less variable than they would be if prices were set simply as a mark-up over costs. This evidence for specific industries contrasts with the evidence from aggregate data, which suggested relatively small changes in profit margins until quite recently. The difference between the aggregate and the disaggregate may be due in part to the difference between consumer price and wholesale price indexes, as noted earlier.

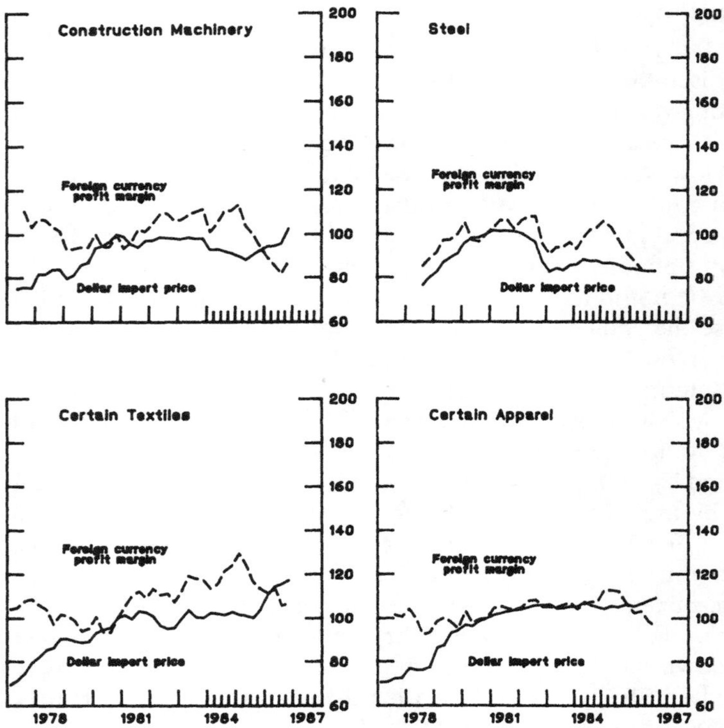

Chart 1–14. Prices and Profit Margins—Imports (index 1980:4 = 100)

Chart 1–14 and table 1–13 also suggest that during both periods of dollar depreciation, importers squeezed profit margins in their own currency, while during the long appreciation of the dollar, profit margins widened. This behavior of foreigner's profit margins is quite important for the persistence of the deficit. As foreign importers cut profit margins and delay the pass-through of exchange rate changes to increases in dollar import prices, the turnaround in the current account is also delayed.

The vital question is, how long can the foreigners continue to squeeze margins? In other words, is this source of persistence in the U.S. external deficit likely to be temporary or sustained? For some products (steel, construction machinery, certain apparel, and certain textiles), the index of foreign currency profit margins has reached or fallen below levels seen in the beginning of the sample period, during the last dollar depreciation

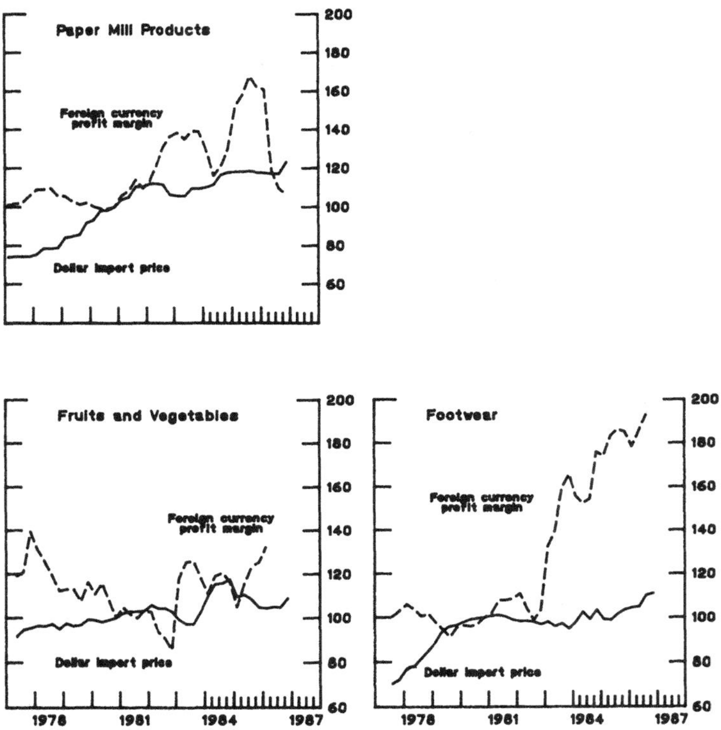

Chart 1–14. (continued).

in the late 1970s. (See table 1–13, top panel.) Whether that level represents a lower bound for margins cannot be determined from these data. But, since margins overall increased during the years of appreciation, foreign suppliers might be able to endure abnormally low margins for awhile during the current depreciation. The recent squeezing of profits may also be due to relatively slack demand and low levels of resource utilization abroad, which has induced foreign firms to try harder to maintain their shares of the U.S. market. To the extent that such cyclical factors are at work, we can expect margins eventually to rebound to normal levels, thus leading ultimately to a rise in import prices. This suggests that significant adjustment of the U.S. external deficit—in real terms—to the depreciation that has already taken place is still in the pipeline.

Alternatively, it may be that foreign firms are reducing export prices

Table 1–13. Index of Profit Margins—Imports (1980:4–100)

		Index				*Percent Change in Index*		
SIC	*Name*	*1977*[a]	*1980*[a]	*1985:2*[b]	*1986:4*[c]	*77–80*	*80–85:2*	*85:2–86:4*
314[d]	footwear	101.62	97.34	178.47	192.77	−4.2	83.3	8.0
2033[e]	fruit & vegs.	126.41	108.51	110.21	132.21	−14.2	1.6	20.0
222	textiles	106.36	96.87	126.70	106.28	−8.9	30.8	−16.1
3531[f]	construction mach.	106.92	97.19	108.50	84.64	−9.1	11.6	−22.0
262	pulpmill	102.56	99.50	155.13	107.79	−3.0	55.9	−30.5
231[g]	apparel	101.04	100.11	112.76	97.28	−1.0	12.6	−13.7
331[h]	steel	87.06	99.71	104.51	85.95	2.7	4.8	−17.8

[a] Average of 4 quarters in 1977, 1980.
[b] Average of 1985:1 and 1985:2.
[c] Average of 1986:3 and 1986:4.
[d] 314, average of 1977:3, :4, and point estimate 1986:3.
[e] 2033, average of 1977:2, :3, :4, and point estimate 1986:1.
[f] 3531, average of 1977:3, :4.
[g] 231, average of 1977:3, :4.
[h] 331, average of 1978:3, :4.

to the U.S. market, while enjoying a normal level of profits on exports to other countries (or on other, nonmanufacturing activities). If so, then these firms could continue to essentially subsidize prices to the U.S. market until the dollar stabilizes. We saw in chart 1–10 some evidence that Japanese exporters have been reducing their profits on exports to other countries less than those on exports to the United States. Or, there is evidence in table 1–13 that for certain industries, profit margins have not yet reached their lowest levels. Either of these scenarios suggests that the change in the dollar to date has completed its impact on dollar import prices, and that further changes in the dollar would be necessary to reduce margins or raise import prices.

The overall picture presented by the microeconomic data we have reviewed shows a willingness of foreign firms to reduce profit margins significantly to maintain market share. A delay in the adjustment of U.S. import prices to the dollar's decline has important implications for real net exports, but a much smaller impact on nominal imports in the longer run (given a price elasticity in the neighborhood of unity). If foreign firms are reducing their margins on exports to third markets as well, this affects the competitiveness of U.S. exports and could be adding significantly to the persistence of the nominal deficit as well as the real deficit.

Chart 1–15 shows the behavior of prices and profit margins for the sample of U.S. *exports*. Table 1–14 shows the level and percent change in the profit margin index for U.S. exports for the periods of dollar appreciation and depreciation. Profit margins are remarkably stable, apparently unaffected by external developments.[42] This corroborates the finding of a stable coefficient of 1 on the domestic price term in the equation for the nonagricultural export deflator: U.S. exporters do not price-discriminate in international markets, and price their exports off of domestic costs.

Because profit margins do not move very much, we can infer that movements in U.S. export prices have been dominated by movements in costs of production, rising rapidly during the relatively high inflation 1970s and then stabilizing in the 1980s. U.S. exporters adjusted export prices and profit margins very little in the face of the significant dollar appreciation. Not only did U.S. exporters (except for semiconductors) fail to absorb any of the rise in the dollar, in most cases the dollar export price rose as the dollar appreciated. Although no different from historical experience, this myopic behavior resulted in a significant loss of competitiveness as foreign currency prices shot up. This may have contributed to the widening of the deficit, especially as foreign growth sagged.

However, over the last year, there may have been some change in the pricing policy of U.S. exporters. In particular, there is some evidence that

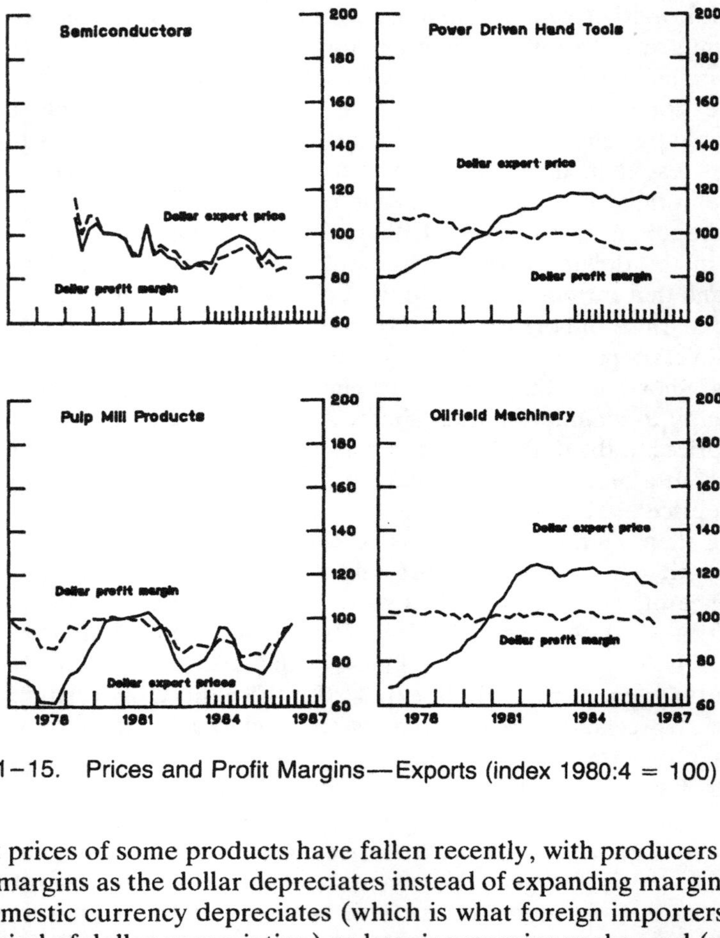

Chart 1–15. Prices and Profit Margins—Exports (index 1980:4 = 100)

export prices of some products have fallen recently, with producers *cutting* profit margins as the dollar depreciates instead of expanding margins when the domestic currency depreciates (which is what foreign importers did in the period of dollar appreciation) or keeping margins unchanged (which is the historical pattern for U.S. exporters). In the case of semi-conductors, power-driven hand tools, and oil-field machinery, the cuts in margins are particularly pronounced. This behavior could reflect persistent competition from foreign producers who have been willing to sacrifice profits for a time at least. It could also signal a more aggressive pricing strategy on the part of U.S. producers, or quite differently, cyclical weakness in particular industries (oil and computers, in particular).

In summary, there are two stylized facts about the behavior of prices and profit margins. First, because foreign producers use profit margins to buffer changes in the exchange rate, dollar import prices are not now

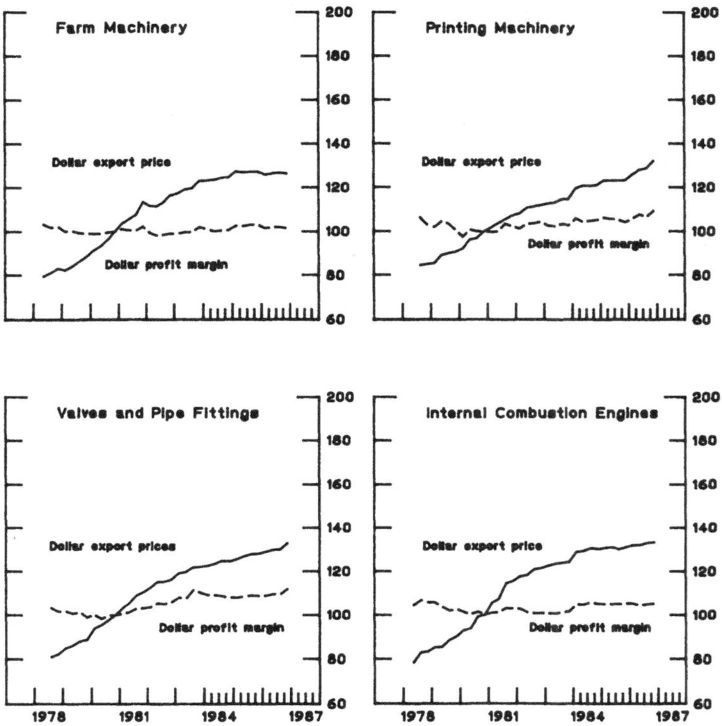

Chart 1–15. (Continued).

rising very quickly. Second, U.S. export prices have been unaffected by movements in the exchange rate and profit margins have been stable; but this behavior might be changing. These stylized facts and deviations from them suggest the importance of product source and destination (the $I(w, r, k)$ and E in equation (1.16)), market structure and competition (the λ in equation (1.16)), and protection (the $\hat{Q}$ in equation (1.17)).

1.7.2 Explaining the Behavior of Prices and Profit Margins

1.7.2.1 Geographical Explanations, and the "Real" Real Exchange Rate. One explanation for the deviation in the behavior of prices and profit margins on some products from the stylized facts is that some of these imports and exports have actually faced little change in real exchange rates. That

Table 1–14. Index of Profit Margins—Exports (1980:4–100)

		Index				Percent Change in Index		
SIC	*Name*	*1977*[a]	*1980*[a]	*1985:2*[b]	*1986:4*[c]	*77–80*	*80–85:2*	*85:2–86:4*
261	paper	96.06	100.30	82.67	95.91	4.4	−17.6	16.0
2011[d]	meat packing	96.62	92.83	110.79	124.74	−3.9	19.3	12.6
3494[e]	valves etc.	102.32	99.57	108.24	110.71	−2.7	8.7	2.3
3519[f]	engines	105.61	100.77	104.97	105.10	−4.6	4.2	0.0
3523[g]	farm mach.	102.34	99.38	102.37	101.52	−2.9	3.0	−1.0
3533[h]	oil mach.	102.65	99.61	99.98	97.93	−3.0	0.4	−2.1
3546[i]	power tools	106.61	101.33	94.43	93.13	−5.0	−6.8	−1.4
3555[j]	printing mach.	104.55	99.51	105.93	107.92	−4.8	6.5	1.9
3674[k]	semiconductors	108.68	102.25	93.55	83.89	−5.9	−8.5	−10.3

[a] Average of 4 quarters in 1977, 1980.
[b] Average of 1985:1 and 1985:2.
[c] Average of 1986:3 and 1986:4.
[d] 2011, average of 1977:2, :3, :4.
[e] 3494, average of 1978:3, :4.
[f] 3519, average of 1978:2, :3, :4.
[g] 3523, average of 1978:2, :3, :4.
[h] 3533, average of 1977:2, :3, :4.
[i] 3546, average of 1977:2, :3, :4.
[j] 3555, average of 1978:3, :4.
[k] 3674, average of 1979:2, :3, :4.

is, in some cases prices and profit margins have not "responded" to real exchange rate changes because the real exchange rate for the product has not moved. In the structure of the micromodel, everything else equal, small changes in $\hat{E}$ would lead to small changes in $\hat{P}^{\$}$. If, in the aggregate equations, we overstate the real exchange rate movement, we would estimate a larger change in dollar import prices than we would actually observe.

Table 1–15 shows the source of imports and the destination of exports for each for the products in the sample. These shares are used to construct product-specific real and nominal exchange rates.[43] For each imported good, we constructed a source-weighted real exchange rate index using IMF data for the nominal exchange rates and consumer price indexes from national sources to deflate to obtain the real exchange rate. For each exported product, we constructed a destination-weighted real exchange rate using the same methodology. We assumed that the region "rest-of-world" behaved as the simple average of all regions, except Brazil.[44]

The top panel of table 1–15 shows the degree to which Canada and Western Europe are major destinations for manufactured exports. Latin America (represented by Brazil) is also a major export trading partner.[45] On the other hand, Japan is not well represented in any of the export categories—a fact frequently used to support notions of "unfair" trading practices. The unallocated part of the world is quite large for certain categories—oil-field machinery, farm machinery, and printing machinery. Thus averaging all countries to represent the residual may mask the effect of the destination-weighted exchange rate on the export price. The bottom panel suggests the importance of Asia (represented by Korea) and Western Europe as import trading partners. It also suggests that the source of imports is more concentrated than is the destination for exports. It is important to note that these weights are, in some cases, quite different from the weighting schemes used in the aggregate equations.[46]

In chart 1–12 (section 1.6) we noted that the currencies of industrial countries had moved quite differently from those of developing countries, on average. In fact, significant differences can be observed within the G-10 index as the Canadian dollar has remained much more stable than other currencies against the dollar. If movement in the real exchange rate is an important determinant of pricing strategies of foreign exporters, we might not observe large changes in prices or profit margins on products sourced primarily from countries whose currencies have not risen against the dollar.

For the same reason, the competitiveness of U.S. exports in the domestic markets of Canada, Latin America, and Asia, for example, has not changed nearly as much over the last six years as would be suggested by

Table 1–15. Sources of Imports and Destination of Exports (share in 1986, value terms)

	Canada	*Brazil*[a]	*Korea*[b]	*G-6*[c]	*U.K.*	*Germany*	*Japan*	*ROW*[d]
				EXPORTS				
2611	.059	.108	.136	.208	.072	.095	.209	.118
2011	.140	.060	.061	.057	—	—	.390	.292
3494	.299	.126	.065	.088	.059	0.41	.123	.199
3546	.254	.148	.050	.130	.083	.058	—	.277
3674	.140	.062	.069	.236	.124	.105	.088	.176
3523	.438	.137	—	.072	—	—	—	.353
3533	.065	.216	.112	.058	.071	—	—	.478
3519	.929	—	—	—	—	—	—	.071
3555	.153	.148	—	.203	.097	.070	—	.329
				IMPORTS				
2033	—	.586	.138	—	—	—	—	.276
2221	—	—	.270	.240	.050	—	.300	.150
231	—	.085	.665	.075	—	—	—	.175
3531	.195	—	—	.135	.090	.230	.195	.155
2621	.795	—	—	—	—	—	—	.205
314	—	.148	.463	.220	—	—	—	.169
331	.110	.065	.058	.155	.040	.100	.370	.102

Source: FT990.

[a] Represents Latin America.
[b] Represents Asia nec.
[c] G-6 is Belgium, France, Italy, Netherlands, Sweden, Switzerland.
[d] Rest-of-World.

an *aggregate* real exchange rate index. Thus, even if some U.S. exporters are becoming more strategic in their response to exchange rate movements, we may not observe much in the way of changes in export prices and margins of products destined primarily for these markets.

Table 1–16 pulls together, for *exports*, a variety of information on destinations, changes in prices, profit margins, and destination-weighted real exchange rates. This table concentrates on the most recent period of dollar depreciation in order to focus on the persistence of the deficit looking at the export side. Column 1 shows the change in the destination-weighted real exchange rate for the specific product; the products are ranked according to the change in this variable. Column 2 shows the share of exports destined for areas where the dollar has not fallen in real terms; this ranking is not too dissimilar from the one based on the real exchange

Table 1–16. The Behavior of Prices, Profit Margins, and Exchange Rates Between 1985:2 and 1986:4

SIC	*Name*	$\%\Delta RXR$[a] *(1)*	*Share*[b] *(2)*	*Exports* $\%\Delta PX$[c] *(3)*	$\%\Delta V$[d] *($)*	$\%\Delta PX/\%\Delta RXR$[e] *(5)*	$\%\Delta V/\%\Delta RXR$[f] *(6)*
3519	engines	−3.6	93%	1.7	0.0	−0.47	−0.03
3523	farm mach.	−12.9	57%	0.0	0.8	0.0	0.06
3546	power tool	−16.8	45%	1.1	−1.3	−0.07	0.08
3533	oil mach.	−17.5	39%	−4.8	−2.1	0.27	0.12
3494	valves etc.	−17.6	50%	4.1	2.3	−0.23	−0.13
3555	printing mach.	−21.1	30%	5.8	1.9	−0.27	−0.09
3674	semiconductor	−22.7	27%	−9.4	−10.2	0.69	0.45
261	paper	−24.9	31%	4.4	15.9	−0.87	−0.64
2011	meat pkg.	−25.1	28%	19.4	23.9	−0.77	−0.95

[a] $\%\Delta RXR$ = percent change destination-weighted real exchange rate.
[b] Share = share of exports of SIC category destined for Canada, Korea, Brazil.
[c] $\%\Delta PX$ = percent change in BLS export price.
[d] $\%\Delta V$ = percent change in profit margin.
[e] $\%\Delta PX/\%\Delta RXR$ = percent change export price divided by percent change real exchange rate.
[f] $\%\Delta V/\%\Delta RXR$ = percent change profit margin divided by percent change real exchange rate.

rate.[47] Column 3 shows the change in the export price, column 4 the change in the profit margin, column 5 the ratio of the change in price to change in real exchange rate, and column 6, the ratio of the change in margin to change in real exchange rate.

It appears from all this information that export prices have risen relatively little in general, which is consistent with the behavior of the non-agricultural deflator. However, it appears that export prices may have risen relatively less on certain products (farm machinery, internal combustion engines, and power-driven hand tools) destined for markets where the dollar has not fallen as much in real terms. This supports the hypothesis that pricing is now more attuned to international competitiveness. That is, where U.S. exporters have not gained in competitiveness simply on account of changes in the exchange rate, they are trying to improve competitiveness through their export pricing strategy. We support this story by noting that margins, column 4, have risen only a little or have been squeezed on these products. Thus the movement in export prices cannot be fully accounted for by stable costs of production.

In markets where U.S. exporters have gained competitiveness substantially on account of movements in the real exchange rate, price increases are still modest, although somewhat larger (valves and pipe fittings, printing trades machinery, meat packing, and pulp mill products). Margins have increased on these products.

Column 5 of table 1–16, which shows the ratio of the change in the price to the change in the real exchange rate, is a point estimate of the product-specific pass-through observed to date.[48] For some exports, (printing, valves, and engines) this point estimate of pass-through is close to the estimated coefficient in the aggregate equation. Other producers (especially meat packing and pulp mills) are apparently using the exchange rate change to increase prices in domestic currency terms without any deterioration of the competitive position when measured in foreign currency terms—the same strategy used by the foreign importers during the dollar appreciation. But, for other producers (farm machinery, hand tools, oil machinery, and semiconductors) the point estimate for pass-through is much lower than, or of the opposite sign from, the coefficient as estimated with aggregate data.

The behavior of import prices, profit margins, and the product-specific source-weighted exchange rate for *imports* is displayed in table 1–17. As in the table on exports, this table concentrates on the most recent period of dollar depreciation so as to focus on the persistence of the deficit looking at the import side. Column 1 shows the change in the source-weighted real exchange rate for the specific product; the products are ranked according to the change in this variable. Column 2 shows the share of imports destined

Table 1–17. The Behavior of Prices, Profit Margins, and Exchange Rates Between 1985:2 and 1986:4

SIC	Name	$\%\Delta RXR$[a] (1)	*Share*[b] (2)	*Imports* $\%\Delta PM$[c] (3)	$\%\Delta V$[d] (4)	$\%\Delta PM/\%\Delta RXR$[e] (5)	$\%\Delta V/\%\Delta RXR$[f] (6)
314	footwear	3.1	61%	11.9	8.1	3.8	2.6
2033	fruits & vegs.	0.1	73%	−3.0	28.4	−30.0	284.3
261	paper mill	−6.0	80%	1.0	−30.6	−0.17	5.1
231	apparel	−7.6	75%	3.6	−13.7	−0.47	1.8
3531	construction mach.	−24.0	20%	11.5	−21.6	−0.48	0.9
222	textiles	−24.7	27%	14.9	−17.3	−0.60	0.7
331	steel	−27.6	23%	−4.3	16.6	0.16	0.6

[a] $\%\Delta RXR$ = percent change in source-weighted real exchange rate.
[b] Share = share of product sourced from Canada, Brazil, Korea.
[c] $\%\Delta PM$ = percent change in BLS import price.
[d] $\%\Delta V$ = percent change profit margin.
[e] $\%\Delta PM/\%\Delta RXR$ = percent change import price divided by percent change real exchange rate.
[f] $\%\Delta V/\%\Delta RXR$ = percent change profit margin divided by percent change real exchange rate.

for areas where the dollar has not fallen in real terms; again, this ranking is not too dissimilar from one based on sources. It also appears that there may be a distinction in the behavior of the real exchange rate and sourcing patterns for consumer-type goods and capital-type goods. (If we eliminate textiles from the capital-goods group, it is a perfect match.) Column 3 shows the change in the import price in dollars, column 4 the change in the foreign currency profit margin, column 5 the ratio of the change in price to change in real exchange rate, and column 6, the ratio of the change in margin to change in real exchange rate.

It appears that dollar import prices have risen relatively more on products sourced from countries where the dollar has fallen the most in real terms (construction machinery, certain textiles). But, profit margins in foreign currency terms have fallen the most on these same products, suggesting that producers in both Europe and Japan have needed to, and made the greatest effort to offset the loss in competitiveness coming from the appreciation of their currencies.

Dollar prices of some products sourced from countries against which the dollar has stayed relatively flat in real terms (fruits and vegetables, certain apparel, and paper products) have changed only a little, and foreign currency profit margins of some of these foreign importers in their own currencies have continued the rising trend observed during the period of strong dollar appreciation (fruits, shoes). For these goods, since there has been little or no loss in competitiveness coming directly from changes in the dollar, there has been little need to adjust margins. Since these margins have continued to expand, it appears that these producers also have been able to more than pass on changes in their costs of production. On the other hand, the margin on certain apparel has fallen despite an increase in the price, suggesting that in this case producers may not have been able to fully pass on increases in the cost of production.

Looking at the point estimate of the pass-through of the real exchange rate change into dollar prices (column 5, table 1–17), we see that in most cases it is well below the coefficient in the aggregate import unit-value equation.[49] This corroborates other evidence that suggests that pass-through has been delayed.

1.7.2.2 Explanations Based on Product and Market Characteristics. In this section we consider the possibility that the characteristics of the product (i.e., the extent to which it is homogeneous or heterogeneous) and the characteristics of the market (i.e., whether it is a market with a substantial degree of foreign competition) might help explain the stylized facts about pricing behavior outlined earlier. Essentially, we are looking for examples where the relationship between the mark-up (λ) and the exchange rate (E) in equation (1.17) might have changed. For example, movements in the exchange rate may affect the introduction into the market of new products that are substitutable for the product in question. Or, exchange rate changes may affect the pricing behavior of other firms or alter the number of firms in the market, thus changing the perceived elasticity of demand of the industry in question.

The stylized fact that U.S. export prices historically have been determined mostly by movements in internal prices and very little by external events is consistent with the fact that United States is a large domestic market with most competition occurring among domestic firms who are subject to, more-or-less, the same changes in costs of production. In this view, exports are a residual market and, therefore, developing a separate pricing policy dependent on movements in the exchange rate is not worth the menu costs.

Deviations from this scenario might be due to a change in the importance of the international market for some U.S. industries. A these industries become more dependent on international sales, producers may become more attuned to the effect of exchange rate changes on the price of their product in overseas markets. Moreover, if the product is relatively homogeneous, or does not enjoy brand loyalty, export prices might become more sensitive to exchange rate movements as exports become a larger share of industry output.[50] And, as the international market becomes more important, domestic producers must consider the pricing policies of their foreign competitors in third markets when choosing their own pricing strategy.

Table 1–18 shows an index for each industry of exposure of domestic production to export sales. Each SIC-based export exposure index is calculated as the ratio of the SIC-based export volume index to the SIC-based industrial production index.[51] Column 4 shows the implied average annual change in the exposure index. High average annual changes suggest that the export market is consuming an increasing percentage of domestic production. (The index says nothing about whether export volume is or is not increasing.) A negative average annual change suggests that the export market is becoming relatively less important as an outlet for domestic production.

Industries with high average annual increases in exposure can be expected to be relatively more attuned to changes in the international environment. In particular, these industries might give more consideration to the role of the exchange rate in their pricing policies. In fact, the industries with the greatest exposure are semiconductors and oil-field machinery, which are also industries where export prices have been squeezed (refer to table 1–16).[52]

On the other hand, industries where the average annual change in the

Table 1–18. Index of Export Exposure[a] (1980–100)

SIC *(1)*	*Name*	*1977* *(2)*	*1986* *(3)*	*Average Annual Change* *(4)*
3674[b]	semicond.	87.7	137.6	6.2
3533	oil mach.	58.4	86.2	2.8
3494[b]	valves etc.	87.8	68.7	−2.1
2611	paper	78.1	96.4	1.8
3519[b]	engines	96.6	82.9	−1.5
3555[b]	printing mach.	76.5	66.6	−1.1
2011	meat pkg.	102.1	109.2	0.7
3523[b]	farm mach.	76.7	74.3	−0.3

[a] Export volume index divided by industrial production index.
[b] Figures shown are for 1978 not 1977.

Note: (No index of industrial production, so export exposure index could not be constructed for SIC 3546 power-driven hand tools.)

index of international exposure is low or negative can be expected to remain unconcerned with movements in the exchange rate. We would expect to see stable margins as export prices key directly off of domestic prices. Farm machinery, printing trades machinery, and internal combustion engines, have low or negative annual averages for changes in export exposure (table 1–15), they also are industries with stable margins.[53]

The inherent heterogeneity of many manufactured products may partially explain why U.S. exports in general do not respond much to exchange rate movements. Ceteris paribus, the more heterogeneous the good, the larger price changes can be before the customer will incur the menu costs required to move to a new supplier. This assumes no new entrants producing similar goods, and no strategic pricing on the part of existing competitors. On the other hand, the more foreign producers introduce new goods with characteristics similar to the products currently in the market, the more existing domestic producers need to adjust prices to take into account exchange rate changes. In addition, if existing competitors take into account exchange rate changes in their pricing decisions, but U.S. producers do not, then the U.S. producer effectively become relatively less competitive when the dollar appreciates.

Strategic pricing by existing suppliers, or the introduction of new products, must be considered in the pricing decision of the U.S. exporter. Chart 1–16 shows how U.S. export prices and German and Japanese export prices in domestic currency terms for similar product categories

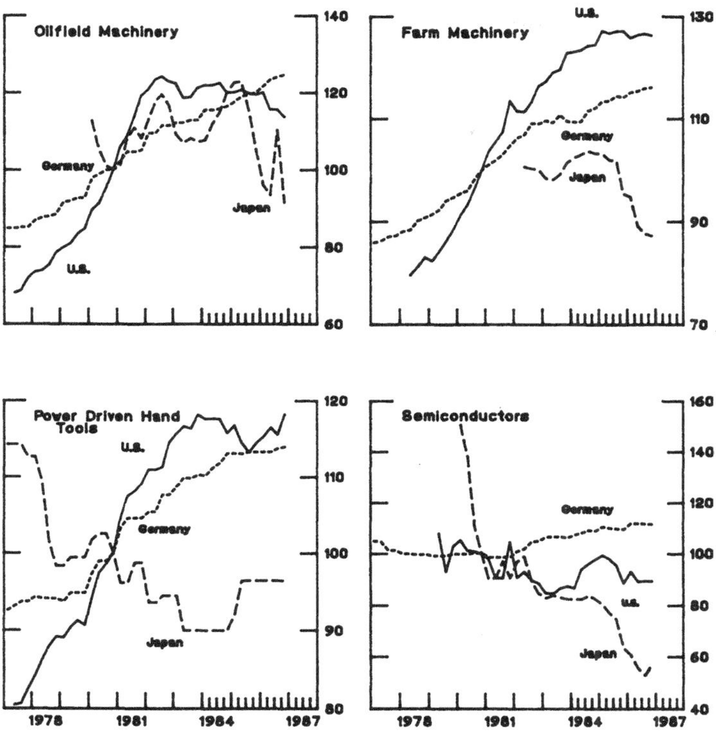

Chart 1–16. U.S., German, Japanese Export Prices expressed in local currency; index 1980:4 = 100)

have moved over the sample period. The chart suggests that in certain products, where the export stake (as measured by export exposure) is high (semiconductors, power tools, and oil-field machinery), U.S. exporters cut prices when their competitors (especially the Japanese) cut prices. Where the stakes are lower (valves and printing machinery), there appears to be less price competition.

In general, export prices of German producers moved more in line with U.S. export prices. When adjusted for the exchange rate change, this suggests that the competitiveness of German exports vis-a-vis U.S. exports in third markets increased during the dollar appreciation and is declining now. The data for German export prices also suggest somewhat less cutting of profit margins, which is consistent with the aggregate evidence in chart

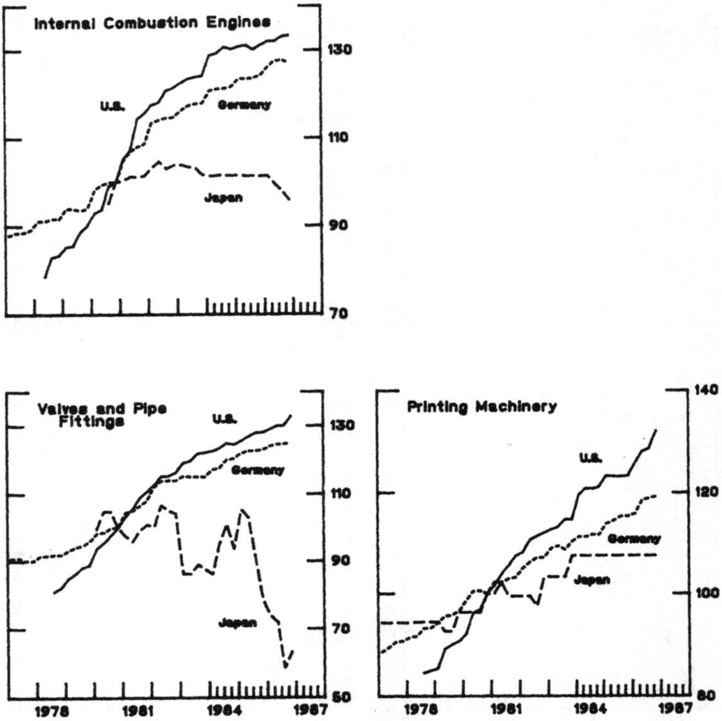

Chart 1–16. (Continued).

1–10. In part, this behavior stems from the European market focus of German exports—if we were to create a trade-weighted exchange rate for the Deutsche mark, it would move much less than the bilateral DM-$ rate.

The behavior of Japanese export prices is rather different. Export prices in yen terms have fallen on oil-field machinery, power-driven hand tools, and semiconductors. These are also the industries where U.S. producers' dependence on export sales have grown, and where U.S. producers are pricing more aggressively (table 1–18). In other cases, such as printing trades machinery and internal combustion engines, Japanese price competition appears to be less stiff. Along with low export exposures (table 1–18), this may explain the limited attention these U.S. producers apparently pay to the effects of the exchange rate on the price of their products in overseas markets. Overall, this suggests that where the stakes are high and there is competition for market share, U.S. export prices are falling.

The stylized fact that *import* prices in dollar terms have on the whole remained stable with the profit margin acting as a buffer for changes in the exchange rate, is consistent with the notion that foreign importers are pricing to market in the United States, or are pricing sufficiently below the market to increase market share in the United States. The degree to which pricing-to-market or pricing-below-market strategies are important depends on the degree of heterogeneity of the product and the current status of the product in the market. If the imported product is relatively new to the market and the market is relatively brand-loyal (as might be expected in a market of heterogeneous products), then the importer must price below the market to make inroads today and profits tomorrow. On the other hand, if the import is well established in the marketplace, or is homogeneous, then simply pricing to the market price will be the profit-maximizing strategy. In either case, to the extent that foreign suppliers are pricing to market or pricing below market, they are not allowing the change in the exchange rate to pass-through to import prices, thereby contributing to the adjustment delay and the persistence of the deficit.

We now consider evidence relating product heterogeneity, foreign pricing strategy, and changes in market shares. Table 1–19 shows data on the exposure of domestic producers of import-competing goods to import volume. The index shown is calculated as the ratio of the index of import volume to the industrial production index, matched by SIC code. Consistent with the widening deficit, all the values for average annual changes are positive; imports have increased market share in virtually all product categories. But, the figures for several of these categories are quite large. If foreign producers are just pricing to market, the share of imports relative to domestic production should be about stable. But, if foreign

Table 1–19. Import Exposure Index[a] (1980–100)

SIC	*Name*	*1977*	*1986*	*Average Annual Change*
314	footwear	100.6	444.2	34.4
3531	constr. mach.	79.5	372.2	29.3
231	apparel	99.6	247.2	14.8
2221	textiles	86.7	213.7	12.7
331[b]	steel	117.3	198.8	9.1
2033	fruits & veg.	91.2	181.4	9.0
2621	pulp mill	96.5	116.1	2.0

[a] Figures are for 1978.
[b] Import volume index divided by industrial production index.

producers are pricing below the market to increase market share, imports as a share of domestic production would increase.

A good example of a pricing-below-market product is construction machinery. The average annual increase in exposure is quite large and starts from the lowest base among the industries in the sample. Import prices for construction machinery were kept well below the domestic producer price index for the same SIC category (see chart 1–17).

Examples of the pricing-to-market strategy of foreign suppliers are steel and apparel. In these markets, imports prices move relatively more in line with exchange rate changes to keep the ratio between the dollar price of import and the domestic cost proxy more stable (see chart 1–17). Moreover, in these three industries, the ratio of import volume to domestic

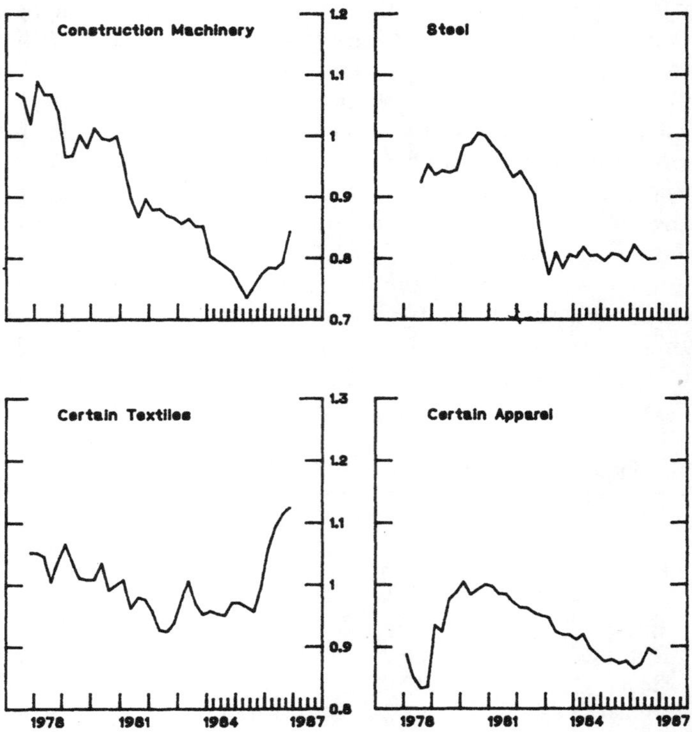

Chart 1–17. Ratio of BLS Import Prices to Matched U.S. Producer Prices (ratio of two series indexed to 1980:4 = 100)

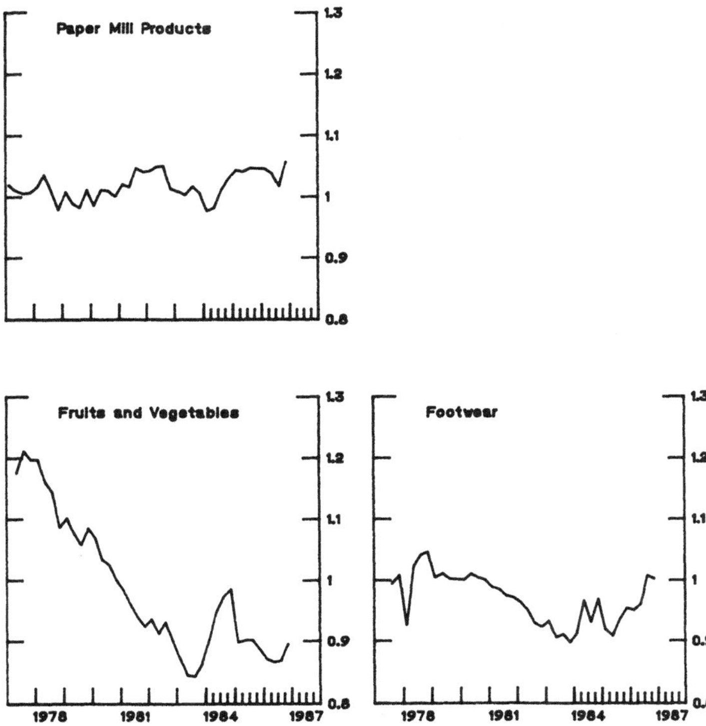

Chart 1–17. (Continued).

production was greater than 100% in 1977, indicating the extent to which imports had already captured the domestic market (table 1–19).

To summarize, the degree of product heterogeneity and the competitive characteristics of the marketplace appear to interact to affect the pricing behavior of U.S. and foreign firms. On the export side, the greater the dependence of domestic production on international sales and the greater the degree of international competition, the more U.S. producers apparently incorporate international factors into the pricing strategy. On the import side, foreign suppliers seeking to establish a market in the United States appear to price below market, varying profit margins as necessary to keep dollar import prices well below U.S. producer prices. Foreign importers already established in the U.S. market appear to price to market, with somewhat greater increases in profit margins during the period of dollar appreciation, and reductions in profit margins only sufficient to keep out other foreign competitors. Taken all together, this pricing behavior points to a delay in the adjustment of prices to exchange rate changes, and thus to a persistence in the deficit.

1.7.3 Protection

In this subsection, we consider the role trade barriers might have played in the widening and persistence of the deficit. In the past 15 years, both the United States and other countries have increased their use of nontariff barriers to protect domestic industry. On the export side, trade barriers imposed by other countries and export controls imposed by the United States may have contributed to the widening of the deficit, and led to its persistence, by keeping growth of export volume below what would be expected on the basis of historical experience.

On the import side, an increased reliance in the United States on bilateral quantitative restraints has contributed to the creation of world cartels. As U.S. demand increased, this policy allowed some foreign suppliers to keep prices from falling when the dollar was appreciating and to build up profit margins that are now being reduced. While there is little evidence to support the view that trade restraints contributed significantly to the initial widening of the deficit, they may well have added to the persistence of the deficit by slowing the process of adjustment to the fall in the dollar. Moreover, bilateral quantitative restraints may continue to bind as the dollar falls, leading import volume to not respond to a change in exchange rates and prices. Trade restraints break the link between international price and exchange rate developments and the value or volume of U.S. imports, and thus contribute to stubbornly high imports and a persistent deficit.[54]

We examine the role of export barriers first. Since most analyses of trade barriers facing U.S. exporters focus on foreign barriers, the impact of U.S. export controls is perhaps less appreciated. U.S. exporters are subject to extensive licensing and regulation by the U.S. government. Table 1–20 shows that in 1985, $57 billion of nonmilitary manufactured goods were exported under license; this represents somewhat more than one-quarter of total exports.

Many licenses are valid for more than one year, and products destined for Canada do not require a license. Adjusting for these two factors leaves about $31 billion in exports, or about one-quarter of nonagricultural, non-Canadian-destined products, required to apply for a new license in 1985.

Licensing is designed to restrict the availability overseas of nonmilitary,

Table 1–20. U.S. Export Licensing

1. Value of U.S. exports under license (1985)	$57 billion
2. Share of total U.S. exports under license (1985)	27 percent
3. Value of U.S. exports applying for new license (1985)[a]	$31 billion
4. Share of "licensable" U.S. exports (1985)	24 percent
Memo: Value of total exports, 1985: $213 billion	
Value of non-agricultural, non-Canadian exports: $125 billion	

[a] Author's estimate.

Source: National Academy of Sciences, Department of Commerce.

but so-called "dual use," products that could be diverted to military purposes. The Toshiba-Kongsberg case illustrates the complexity of the export control problem—on the one hand, the government would like to promote exports, on the other hand, it needs to restrict the availability overseas of potentially harmful military technology.

In some cases, such as crude oil, regulations prohibit exports, altogether. A variety of sources suggest that if the United States simply lifted this ban, exports to Japan alone would increase by about $8 billion.

License requirements also act like a tax on U.S. exports, reducing the price competitiveness of U.S. producers of high-technology products. While the appreciation of the dollar was undoubtably the most significant "tax" on exports during the first half of the 1980s, as U.S. technology advanced, more products were added to the export control list. At the margin, this may have added to the deficit.

The restrictiveness of the licensing process, and the tax implicit in that restriction, depends on a number of factors. In 1985, license processing by the Commerce Department took 54 days on average (it takes 2 days in Japan). Small firms, high-tech products, and Eastern Bloc destinations face longer delays, sometimes up to months or years. Moreover, on average, 7% of license applications are returned to the applicant without action because of problems ranging from lack of a signature to incomplete technical information about the product, thus requiring the applicant to resubmit and wait again.[55]

U.S. export controls are also tighter than controls imposed on exports from other allied-western nations. Many U.S. products must be licensed even though similar technology available from foreign suppliers need not be. Moreover, foreign producers using U.S. licensed exports in their products must obtain re-export licenses from the U.S. government before they sell their products abroad—no other nation requires re-export licensing.

Improvements instituted in 1987 purport to significantly reduce the delay, complexity, and uncertainty associated with the licensing process. But, as U.S. exports expand with the decline in the dollar, the licensing procedure will likely bind more tightly. More firms will apply for licenses to sell new products to new destinations, thus incurring the more burdensome costs of the new license. Export controls act as a tax on a significant fraction of U.S. exports and the burden is greater on high-tech products where the United States still holds comparative advantage. Thus, to a certain degree export controls offset movements in the exchange rate, contributing to the persistence of the deficit.

Increases in trade barriers overseas may also have contributed, marginally, to the widening of the deficit. Once in place, trade barriers add to the persistence of the deficit. Table 1–21 shows that U.S. exporters face a world-trading environment where nontariff barriers (NTBs) are increasingly important. Line 1 shows that the value-share of nonfuel exports to industrial markets protected by a broad measure of NTBs increased from 20% in 1981 to 23% in 1986.[56] The bulk of this increase is accounted for by increased use of quantitative restrictions, most notably on iron and steel.

By destination, NTBs covering exports to developing countries are only slightly higher than those imposed by the industrial-country destination. But, the average tariff rate imposed on imports of the developing countries is about 10 times higher than the 3% average tariff rate imposed on imports

Table 1–21. Exports to Industrial Markets Covered by Nontariff Barriers (percent of value)

	Type of Restriction			
	All NTBs		*ORS*	
Product	*1981*	*1986*	*1981*	*1986*
All items, excluding food	19.6	23.1	12.2	14.4
All food	40.8	42.6	27.3	27.4
Ores & metals	12.7	24.7	4.5	16.8
Iron & steel	29.0	64.2	7.8	47.3
Nonferrous	3.8	6.4	0.4	0.4
Chemicals	13.2	12.7	8.1	7.6
Manufactures (nonchemical)	18.6	20.5	11.7	12.2
Electrical machinery	n.a.	12.0[a]	n.a.	n.a.

[a] Figure for 1983.

Source: UNCTAD *TB/B*/1126 add. 1.

of the industrial countries. Thus, in the case of developing countries, tariff barriers may be a significant deterrant to U.S. exports.

None of the previous statistics include barriers like "health, safety, and technical standards," which may be even more important than quantitative restraints. Quantitative restraints are at least observable policy instruments with less opportunity for so-called "administrative guidance." For example, only 11% of Japanese nonfuel imports from industrial countries are covered by the NTBs measured in table 1–21. But, "health, safety, and technical standards" are imposed on over 50% of Japanese imports from industrial countries.[57]

A greater dependence by foreign nations on nontariff barriers to protect their domestic markets reduces the effectiveness of the depreciation of the dollar in making U.S exports competitive and restricts the potential growth in volume of U.S. exports. Moreover, to the extent that the NTBs are relatively more frequently imposed, or are tightened on those products in which the United States has a comparative advantage, U.S. export growth is further hampered, thus contributing to the widening and the persistence of the deficit.

In recent years, the United States also has depended to an increasing degree on bilateral quantitative restraints for the conduct of its trade policy. Chart 1–18 shows this rise. To the extent that the U.S. market for a product continues to grow, bilateral quotas guarantee a limited set of importers a share of an expanding market. With import supply thus constrained, import prices would likely rise along with increasing demand for the product in the United States, especially if U.S. producers of import-competing products could not (because of production costs) or choose not to (because of short-term profit-maximizing strategies) capture the unserved part of the market.

There is some evidence that the period of appreciation and the relatively robust U.S. economy, together with quantitative restraints, allowed foreign suppliers to raise foreign currency export prices and fatten margins. At the same time, these factors allowed import prices in dollars to remain below the domestic producer's costs of production, thus preventing the domestic supplier from capturing increases in demand for the product. (See chart 1–17.) With profit margins and market share thus built up, the foreign producers are in an excellent position to eat into those margins and keep market share, even as the dollar falls. The bilateral restraints may continue to bind even at quite low levels of the dollar. In both cases, quantitative restraints break the link between exchange rate movements and prices and volumes, preventing adjustment and adding to persistence.

We would expect to see the strongest interaction between a measure

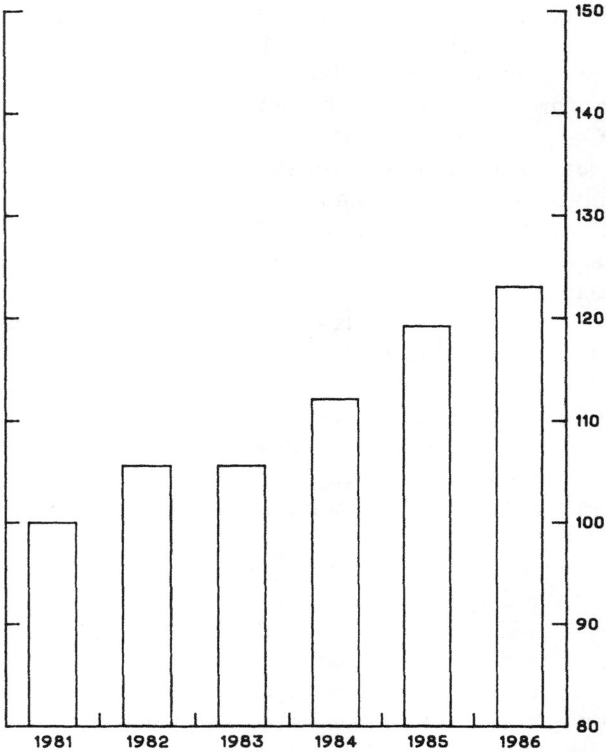

Source: World Bank, "World Development Report," 1987

Chart 1–18. Index of U.S. Non-oil Imports Covered by Nontariff Barriers (1981 = 100)

of U.S. demand and import prices on those products with the tightest bilateral quotas. Table 1–22 shows the share of U.S. imports covered by nontariff barriers by broad product category and source for 1983. First, it is interesting to note the imports from the developing countries are relatively more constrained.[58] By product, textiles have significant nontariff barriers, reflecting the quotas under the Multi-Fiber Arrangement (MFA) and other quantitative restraints on textile and apparel trade. The renegotiation of the MFA in 1986 (which broadened and tightened it) as well as tighter bilateral arrangements reached in the latter part of 1986 with Japan, Korea, Taiwan, and Hong Kong suggests that the figure in table 1–22

Table 1–22. U.S. Imports Covered by Nontariff Barriers (percent of value; 1983)

	Imports from	
Imports of	*Industrial Countries*	*Developing Economies*
All, less fuels	16.6	18.9
Agriculture	23.5	25.1
Manufacturers	16.5	18.6
textiles	31.1	64.0
footwear	0.0	16.7
iron & steel	35.6	48.9
electrical machinery	5.2	5.3
vehicles	34.7	0.0
rest of manufactures	6.4	5.4

Source: Nogues, Olechowski, and Winters.

understates the share of textiles and apparel that is covered by NTBs. Steel restraints were quite high already in 1983, but were tightened further in 1985 with the bilateral voluntary restraints covering 18 major supplying countries. Restraints on footwear are rather high also.

Table 1–23 shows changes in the prices and values of steel mill products and consumer textile products over recent periods. Despite the sharp fall in the dollar, prices of both categories rose only moderately during 1986. In the first half of 1987, however, these prices accelerated sharply. As can be inferred from the similarity of value and price changes for steel, the volume of steel imports has remained fairly flat over this period. Given that capacity utilization in the domestic industry was rising sharply in the first

Table 1–23. Changes in Imports of Steel Mill Products and Consumer Textiles

	Percent Changes (AR)	
	1986Q4 / 1985Q4	*1987Q2 / 1986Q4*
Textile and apparel		
Import value	18.5	25.7
Import price	2.3	16.0
Steel mill products		
Import value	5.4	11.3
Import price	4.1	10.0

half of 1987, the import restraints would appear to have been binding.[59] The continued rise in the volume of imports of textiles and apparel suggests that the import restraints are somewhat less binding overall than in the case of steel. Nevertheless, the sharp rise in the prices of textile and apparel products undoubtedly reflects the tightening of NTBs in the second half of 1986 and the fact that U.S. textile mills were running at very high utilization rates in the first half of 1987.[60]

Another approach to the question of the effect of NTBs on import prices is to more explicitly model the inverse demand curve for imports. Essentially we would like to model equation (1.17) more explicitly. Table 1–24 outlines a simple regression of import prices in dollars against the source-weighted product-specific exchange rate, the source-weighted product-specific foreign cost of production, and a disaggregated component of real U.S. expenditure. We expect a positive correlation between foreign costs and import prices, and a negative correlation between changes in the exchange rate (as defined here). If restraints are important, with no offsetting increase in supply from the domestic market, there should be a positive sign on the demand term.

Table 1–25 shows the results. It appears that for shoes, textiles, and steel, the hypothesis is borne out: import prices in dollar terms are positively affected by foreign currency costs of production, negatively

Table 1–24. Outline of Regression of Import Prices

Basic Functional Form of Regression

log (dollar import price) = a_0 + a_1 log (source-weighted nominal exchange rate)
+ a_2 log (source-weighted industry-specific foreign wholesale price index)
+ a_3 log (real expenditure-broad product group)

Selected Disaggregations of U.S. Expenditure

- Real personal consumption expenditure
  - Consumer durables
  - Consumer nondurables
    - Clothing and shoes (used for 314, 222, 231)
    - Foods and beverages (tried on 2033)
- Real Business Fixed Investment (used for 3531) (tried for 262)
  - Structures
    - Residential
    - Nonresidential (used for 33)
  - Plant and durable equipment, nonresidential

Table 1–25. Regressions for Industry-Specific Import Prices (t statistics in parentheses)

SIC	*Name*	*Foreign Cost*[a]	*Source-weighted Nominal Exchange Rate*	*Real Expenditure Broad Product Group*	$\bar{R}^2$	*Rho*	*DW*
314	footwear	0.170797	−0.182013	0.371729	.224	.80	—
		(2.56675)	(2.56062)	(1.77464)[b]			
222	textiles	0.359349	−0.279614	0.417937	.627	.62	—
		(2.09563)	(2.88496)	(2.65659)			
331	steel	1.55485	−0.017625	0.300111	.567	1.0	—
		(5.35644)	(0.418374)	(2.49286)			
231	apparel	0.410084	−0.055316	−0.314462	.222	1.0	—
		(1.95866)	(−1.35055)	(−1.44265)			
3531	construction machinery	0.591566	−0.278898	−0.319724	.860	—	1.5
		(10.4882)	(4.85328)	(−7.2494)			
				Industry specific U.S. producer price			
262	pulpmill	0.009167	0.096071	1.01313	.946	.54	—
		(0.227527)	(0.842444)	(11.357)			
2033	fruits & veg.	0.133882	−0.141845	1.322798	.353	.67	—
		(2.89641)	(−2.8572)	(2.48106)			

[a] Source-weighted industry-specific foreign producer price index.
[b] Two lags.

affected by movements in the dollar, and positively affected by U.S. real expenditure on the broad product group appropriate to the specific import. On the other hand, for construction machinery, import prices are affected by costs of production and the exchange rate. In the absence of barriers to entry, an increase in U.S. real business fixed investment leads to an incipient rise in price, which attracts new supply and keeps prices from rising.[61] Despite the Multi-Fiber Arrangement, apparel prices do not appear to react to demand pressures.[62] The World Bank has described the MFA as "porous," suggesting that there is enough variation in the product and in suppliers that bilateral quantitative restraints in fact do not restrain imports much at all.

Pulp mill products and fruits and vegetables appear to follow pricing-to-market strategies. The primary determinant of pulp mill import prices is the cost of production of the domestic substitute. In the case of fruits and vegetables, foreign costs, exchange rate, and U.S. domestic prices are determinants of the import prices.

One final note on the pricing equations. In several cases, surprisingly little of the variation in import prices can be attributed to movements in costs, the exchange rate, or demand. It appears the import prices for footwear, apparel, and fruits and vegetables, are close to being a random walk. What might be causing movements in these import prices that is neither a cost nor a demand effect is unclear.

1.7.4 Microeconomic Factors: Summary

In this section we have examined industry-specific behavior of import and export prices, as well as changes in protectionist policies, and have related these factors to the widening and persistence of the U.S. external deficit. On the import side, the deficit may have continued to widen somewhat, and is surely persisting, as a result of the pricing behavior of foreign suppliers, at least in a number of key areas. Import prices have risen slowly relative to the decline in the dollar, in part because foreign exporters have been willing to sustain significant reductions in profit margins, at least temporarily, and in part because production costs have been falling abroad. For some commodity categories, import price stability has reflected little change in the real exchange rates of some major supplying countries; in others, prices have risen not because of dollar depreciation but because of quantitative restrictions.

The ability of foreign exporters to price to the U.S. market is related in some cases to the geographic pattern of exchange rate changes, in other cases to the particular characteristics of the products, and in still other cases to quantitative restraints on U.S. imports that tend to reduce the degree of competition in the marketplace. Suppliers in some key U.S. trading-partner countries have not yet had to contend with significant appreciation of their currencies. Where products are quite homogeneous, it appears that foreign exporters price to market, changing foreign currency prices and margins sufficiently to keep the dollar price of imports competitive. On the other hand, where quantitative restraints are most prevalent, the relationships between exchange rate movements and the price and quantity of imported products have been particularly tenuous. To the extent that foreign profit margins adjust to exchange rate changes and demand conditions, import prices do not adjust. And, to the extent that quotas remain binding as the dollar falls, import volumes will not fall even as import prices rise, so long as the quantity constraints bind. Overall, this behavior delays the adjustment process, leading in the short run to persistence of the deficit by stretching out the J-curve.

On the export side, U.S. producers appear to be taking a more strategic view toward developments in international markets than has been the case historically. Where exports have become an important part of domestic production, U.S. exporters are taking into account price competition from other foreign suppliers in third markets, and are trimming their prices. In addition, exporters are maintaining lower export prices for products destined primarily for markets where the U.S. has gained little in competitiveness because of only small movements in the dollar. Subdued price increases on exports in the short run will keep export value down, thus contributing to persistence in the nominal deficit. The failure of export volumes to expand rapidly enough to begin to reduce the nominal deficit, especially given these signs of more aggressive pricing by U.S. firms, must rest with lags, quality, or trade restraints.

It is difficult to argue that changes in trade barriers had more than a marginal impact on the widening of the deficit. However, they may well have contributed more significantly to its persistence. Increasing quantitative restrictions on imports at home and abroad undoubtedly have slowed the process of adjustment of real net exports to gains in U.S. price competitiveness. And U.S. export restrictions may well have inhibited export growth to some degree, particularly in high-tech areas.

1.8 Conclusions

Our empirical analysis suggests that the widening of the U.S. external deficit between 1980 and 1986 can be accounted for by macroeconomic factors. At one level of analysis, the excess of growth in both domestic expenditures and GNP in the United States, relative to that in the rest of the world, accounts for a little over one-third of the deficit. The decline in U.S. international price competitiveness associated with the rise in the dollar through early 1985 accounts for most of the rest of the deficit. At a more fundamental level, drawing on the accumulated (and averaged) wisdom of a group of global macroeconomic models, roughly two-thirds of the external balance effects of these changes in relative growth and real exchange rates can be explained by the mix of fiscal expansion and monetary tightening in the United States, along with fiscal contraction in other major industrial countries during this period. We attribute the rest of the widening of the deficit to the unexplained rise in the dollar during 1984, to debt problems in developing countries, and to policies at home and abroad that have depressed U.S. agricultural exports.

While macroeconomic analysis can account for the initial widening of the deficit, it cannot fully explain the persistence of the deficit two and a half years after the peak in the dollar. As of the third quarter of 1987, import prices were clearly rising less rapidly than historical experience suggested they should, and exports, though expanding briskly, were doing so at a pace that fell short of conventional model predictions. Our assessment of available microeconomic evidence suggests that changes in the pricing behavior of foreign exporters, and the gradual spread of protectionist measures at home and abroad, were contributing significantly to this persistence. Foreign exporters on average, and of a number of products in particular, were reducing their profit margins. They were also benefiting from a reduction in costs associated with the appreciation of their currencies. Moreover, quantitative trade restrictions may well have slowed the adjustment of trade volumes to changes in relative prices.

What implications do we draw from these results for possible solutions to the deficit problem? First, some of the factors underlying the persistence of the deficit are likely to be transitory, and significant further adjustment is probably in train. However, we suspect that a substantial deficit would remain even after full adjustment to the level of exchange rates prevailing in the third quarter of 1987 has taken place. In the absence of a significant adjustment of relative growth rates, the continuation of a sizable deficit seems likely, in view of: (1) the persistence of the growth gap that emerged over the first half of the 1980s; (2) the decline in the U.S. net foreign asset position (and related fall in net investment income receipts); (3) the fact that the dollar in the third quarter of 1987 was still above its 1980 level in real terms; and (4) the apparent willingness of foreign suppliers to squeeze their profits for a sustained period.

The closing of the U.S. current account deficit will require a significant reduction in the growth of U.S. domestic spending relative to that abroad, and probably a further decline in the dollar at some point. Our analysis of recent history suggests that a policy scenario to achieve this outcome probably would have to include a U.S. fiscal contraction, accompanied by a temporary easing of monetary policy (to keep GNP growth from falling unduly), and a fiscal expansion abroad. This mix of policies would close the growth gap, reduce U.S. real interest rates relative to those abroad, and lead to some further downward adjustment in the dollar. In addition, the difficulties evident in the adjustment process that can be traced to trade barriers, suggest that any progress that can be made in the current Uruguay Round of trade talks to roll back quantitative restrictions on world trade, would be highly desirable.

Notes

1. Frankel [1988] analyzes the results of simulations with the same set of models that we employ in section 16, and concludes that they are for the most part consistent with the predictions of the standard Mundell-Flemming model augmented to allow for varying exchange rate expectations. Frenkel and Razin [1987] present a recent review of the Mundell-Flemming model.

2. The difference between the current account and GNP net exports of goods and services reflects several minor differences in statistical definitions between the balance of payments and national income accounts (in addition to the exclusion of unilateral transfers from the latter), as will be discussed in section 1.4.

3. This "identity" abstracts from FOB-CIF differences (transportation cost, etc.), and expresses foreign imports and exports in dollars.

4. See, for example, Shafer and Loopesko [1983] and Hooper [1985] for descriptions of this model.

5. The interest rates in (1.10)–(1.13) are implicitly divided by 100, given that the exchange rates are expressed as logarithms and the scale factor γ is expressed in number of years.

6. For a more formal derivation of the model, see Mann [1984].

7. In the case of Cobb-Douglas production, this would be the share of imported intermediates into the production process.

8. The elasticity of the demand curve can be affected by the number of firms in the market, which may in itself be a function of the exchange rate—see Baldwin [1986], and by the rate of change in demand for the product—see Mann [1986].

9. In the case of constant elasticity of demand, both this elasticity and the one above are zero, since by definition, the elasticity of demand does not change.

10. Slow adjustment of import prices does not necessarily explain persistence of the *nominal* trade deficit, since the weakness in import prices, if anything, tends to depress the nominal deficit initially. Moreover, even if import prices were rising, with a price elasticity of demand in the neighborhood of unity, volumes would eventually fall enough to offset the rise in price, leaving nominal imports about unchanged. Nevertheless, the slow adjustment of

import prices is an important factor underlying the persistence of the deficit in real terms. It may also be indicative of foreign pricing behavior in U.S. export markets, which has important implications for exports in both real terms and nominal terms.

11. In the first half of 1986 Japan trans-shipped nearly $5 billion (at an annual rate) in gold through the United States. These transactions had the effect of raising recorded U.S. exports of gold to Japan by that amount, while raising recorded U.S. imports of gold from other countries by about the same amount.

12. On a GNP basis, real net services were $68.7 billion in 1980, $29.7 billion in 1986, and $30.2 billion (at an annual rate) in 1987Hl.

13. Foreign direct claims on the United States rose by about $125 billion between 1980 and 1986, while U.S. direct claims on foreigners rose by only about $45 billion on a book value basis. See U.S. Department of Commerce, *Survey of Current Business*, June 1987, p. 40.

14. The discrepancy in average rates of return reflects several factors. First, U.S. bank-reported claims and liabilities account for a significant portion of gross U.S. claims and liabilities, and banks are intermediaries who make income on their portfolios by charging higher rates of interest on their loans to foreigners than they do on their liabilities to foreigners. In addition, receipts include substantial fee income earned by U.S. banks for services provided to foreigners. Second, the recorded return on corporate stocks does not include capital gains and therefore is relatively low (primarily reflecting dividend payments). Foreign holdings of U.S. stocks are more than three times as great as U.S. holdings of foreign stocks. Moreover, increases in foreign holdings of U.S. stocks net of U.S. holdings of foreign stocks accounted for about one-fourth of the total decline in the U.S. net portfolio investment position over the 1980–1986 period. See Helkie and Stekler [1987] or Helkie and Hooper [1987] for more on the relative rates of return on U.S. international claims and liabilities.

15. Between 1969 and 1986 (the period covered in the chart), the U.S. total trade increased by about 250% in real terms. Without scaling for this trend growth, a given percentage change in relative activity or relative prices would be associated with a substantially greater change in net exports at the end of the period shown than it would be at the beginning.

16. Foreign domestic expenditures were not measured directly, but were approximated by adding U.S. net exports to aggregate rest-of-world GNP.

17. Various indicators, including unemployment rates and crude measures of potential output, do suggest that U.S. GNP is presently as much as several percentage points closer to potential output than is foreign GNP. However, this gap is substantially smaller than the domestic expenditure gap discussed below.

18. The supply developments in question, including, for example, the dramatic entry of Japan and subsequently a number of developing countries into world markets of various manufactured goods over the past two decades, tend to be spuriously correlated with income variables. Thus, the relative supply proxy has the effect of reducing the estimated income elasticity for U.S. imports and raising the estimated elasticity for U.S. exports. See Helkie and Hooper [1987] for a more detailed discussion of this issue.

19. These calculations were made in some cases by simulating the model with the contributing factors listed in table 1–7 (U.S. and foreign GNP and domestic expenditures, relative prices, and relative capital stocks) each alternately held unchanged at their 1980:4 values, through 1986:4. In other cases, the estimates were made judgmentally as described below.

20. The decline in the dollar has had a much smaller impact on the model's prediction of

the nominal trade balance to date because of J-curve effects. The gradual depreciation of the dollar causes a gradual increase in import prices, which initially offsets much of the gain in real net exports. Note that these simulations were run with income and other "exogenous" determinants of the partial trade balance held unchanged. Factors that might have induced the alternative relative price paths could also have influenced the trade balance through its other determinants.

21. Foreign wholesale prices in dollars show a qualitatively similar picture. We prefer to use consumer prices because the coverage of available aggregate wholesale price indexes is much more variable across countries. In some cases they reflect a fairly narrow set of tradable commodities, and do not adequately represent movements in domestic labor costs. Of course, CPIs have their problems too as proxies for costs, as we note below.

22. One could also raise more fundamental questions about the use of deflators to measure prices and profit margins, given their sensitivity to shifts in the composition of imports. However, as suggested by charts 1–7 and 1–8, the problem that has arisen is a fairly recent one. We find that the deflator does about as well as a fixed-weight import price index in aggregate import price equations over the historical sample period through 1984. Moreover, the fixed-weight index is also affected noticeably by the decline in business machinery prices (though not as much as the deflator).

23. This does not pertain to the apparent squeezing of Japanese profit margins illustrated in the bottom panel of chart 1–12, since the BLS export price date shown there does not incorporate a strong negative trend in business machinery prices.

24. This is also true of indexes weighted by bilateral import shares. See Helkie and Hooper [1987] and Pauls [1987].

25. This empirical result is confirmed in regression analysis reported in Hooper [1985], and can probably be explained by the flatness of yield curves at terms of more than five years.

26. See Blanchard and Summers [1984] for an analysis of factors underlying the rise in real interest rates in the early 1980s. Branson, Fraga, and Johnson [1985]; Feldstein [1986]; and Hooper [1985] all provide empirical analyses linking the rise in the dollar to the 1981 tax cut through its impact on real interest rates.

27. See Johnson [1986].

28. See, for example, Krugman [1987].

29. See, for example, Danker et al. [1985] and Frankel [1982].

30. See, for example, Friedman and Sinai [1987]; and Haynes, Hutchison, and Mikesell [1986a].

31. The conference was entitled "Empirical Macroeconomics for Interdependent Economies: Where Do We Stand?" The simulation results are reported and analyzed in detail in Bryant et al. [1988].

32. The models included in these averages are: the DRI model, the EC COMET model, the FRB Multicountry Model, Project LINK, the IMF staff's MINIMOD, the McKibben-Sachs Global model, the OECD staff's INTERLINK model, the Taylor rational expectations multicountry model, and the Wharton model. Also participating in the exercise were the Japanese EPA World Econometric Model, the Minford Liverpool model, and the Simms-Litterman World VAR model. The latter three models are not included in the averages shown in table 1–11 either because they were unable to run the simulations as specified or because the results were clearly outliers.

33. That is, the U.S. fiscal expansion led to an estimated 3.5 × 2% = 7% rise in the dollar, and a 3.5 × \$14 billion = \$49 billion decline in the current account. The foreign fiscal contraction led to an estimated 2.5 × 1% = 2.5% rise in the dollar, and a 2.5 × \$8 billion = \$20 billion fall in the U.S. current account. The combined effects after three years are 9.5%

and \$69 billion, respectively. As indicated in table 1-11, these estimates would be somewhat larger if the five-year impacts were used instead of the three-year effects. The three-year horizon is probably more pertinent to the dollar and the interest differential, both of which had peaked by early 1985. The longer horizon may be more pertinent to the current account deficit, which continued to widen through 1986. On a five-year horizon the current account effects are equal to $3.5 \times 20 + 2.5 \times 8 =$ \$90 billion.

34. The estimate of a 6% growth gap resulting from the shift in fiscal policies was computed as follows. The U.S. fiscal expansion equal to 3.5% of GNP was multiplied by the 0.75% increase in U.S. minus foreign GNP that the average model simulations shown in table 1–11 indicate would be the impact of a fiscal expansion equal to 1% of GNP. This product was then added to the product of a foreign fiscal contraction equal to 2.5% of GNP times the 1.25% increase in U.S. minus foreign GNP that would be induced by a 1% foreign fiscal contraction (also from table 1–11).

35. This estimate is equal to 8 times the 5-year impact of the U.S. money shock on the CPI shown in table 1–11. Since most of the models appear to show some tendency toward neutrality of money in the longer run, the full price effect of the shock may well be somewhat greater in the longer run.

36. The net negative impact on U.S. GNP growth is consistent with the shortfall of GNP growth relative to potential during the 1980s. Between 1980 and 1987 U.S. growth averaged only about 2.0% per year, well below most estimates of potential growth.

37. The MCM simulations took into account, inter alia, the effect of the tax changes on the user cost of capital, estimated to be something in the neighborhood of −1 percentage point, on average.

38. We used the SIC disaggregation primarily because most U.S. data at the industry level are available according to the SIC scheme. In particular, U.S. producer price indexes are available according to the SIC. In addition, U.S. indexes of industrial production and some annual trade value data are disaggregated according to the SIC. On the other hand, obtaining trade data for country-industry pairs on an SIC basis remains quite difficult. We have used several different schemes to construct matched country-industry trade data.

39. In concept, the import-share weights are the share each foreign country has in the total imports into the United States of a particular four-digit SIC category of product. However, disaggregated trade data by individual countries are available only on a Schedule A disaggregated basis. Therefore, the import-share weights are based on Schedule A, with a concordance between Schedule A and the SIC used to determine which six-digit Schedule A categories to aggregate to get the four-digit SIC category. The share weights were calculated for the top three to five supplying countries for 1980 and 1984, interpolating for the intervening years. This technique accounted for an average of 80% of the imports of each four-digit SIC category, ranging from a low of 66% for steel to a high of 89% for footwear. The average values for the exchange rate index were used for the fraction not allocated to any particular country.

40. The following sources were used: For Canada: industry selling price indexes based on 1970 Standard Industrial Classification, Statistics Canada, *Canadian Statisitical Review*. For Japan: wholesale price indexes (by products and sectors), Bank of Japan, *Statistical Bulletin*. For Brazil: precos por atacado (nova classificacao), offerta global, *Conjuntura Economica, National Economic Indexes*. For United Kingdom: index numbers of wholesale (producer) prices, price indexes of output of broad sectors of industry, Central Statistical Office, Government Statistical Service, *Monthly Digest of Statistics*. For Germany: priese und Priesindizer fur gewerbliche produkte (erzeugerpreise), W. Kohlhammer GMBH, *Statistisches Bundesamt Wiesbaden*. For Italy: Numeri indici prezzi all ingrosso, indici por settori e

branche, indici alcuri gruppi, Institutio Centrale de Statistica, *Bollettino Mensile Da Statistical*. For South Korea: wholesale price indexes (by commodity by subgroup), Bank of Korea, *Monthly Statistical Bulletin*. For Taiwan: indexes of wholesale prices in Taiwan area, Executive Yuan Republic of China, Directorate-Generale of Budget Accounting and Statistics, *Monthly Statistics of the Republic of China*.

41. Generally speaking, 1977 to mid-1980, and 1985:2 to the present were periods of dollar depreciation, and mid-1980 to 1985:2 the period of dollar appreciation. See the top panel of chart 1–6.

42. Charts 1–14 and 1–15 have the same scales, to facilitate comparison between industries.

43. These shares are based on a relatively more aggregated set of Schedule A data than are the shares used in the construction of the foreign currency profit margins. These shares are based on data that are available for some individual trading parters and some regions of the world. In particular, industry-specific data are not broken out for individual trading partners in Latin America and Asia n.e.c (comprised primarily of South Korea, Hong Kong, Singapore, and Taiwan). For these regions, we chose the nominal exchange rate and consumer price index for a representative country—Brazil represents Latin America and Korea represents Asia.

Data for Canada, Japan, Germany, and United Kingdom are available. But, other countries in Western Europe are not broken out. Thus, for the rest of Western Europe, we used a multilateral trade-weighted average of data for Belgium, France, Italy, the Netherlands, Sweden, and Switzerland—the G-10 countries less the big four.

The line-item "rest-of-world" is the share of trade in the product that was not allocated to any of these regions or countries.

44. Brazil's exchange rate and consumer price performance have been so spectacular that we did not want to accord it any greater weight than was appropriate based on the share data. This also brings up the argument over multilateral versus bilateral weighting schemes. No doubt multilateral schemes are superior on the export side because of the importance of competition from third countries. To a certain extent we have accounted for that though the average weighting on the residual world.

45. The importance of Brazil as a destination for exports may be understated somewhat because the year chosen for the fixed-share weights is 1986. In any case, the potential impact of the debt crisis is clear from the breadth of the trading relationship.

46. See Pauls [1987] for a more thorough discussion of weighting schemes.

47. The two rankings are not identical because the weights on other countries will vary, and movements in the real exchange rates of those destinations can be quite different.

48. The coefficient in the aggregate equation is the sum of about eight lags, although almost all of the pass-through occurs in the first two quarters. This point estimate takes the average for two quarters, thus to some extent accounting for lagged affects.

Another very important difference is that the nominal exchange rate is used in the aggregate equations, while the point-estimate calculated here uses the real exchange rate.

49. The problems noted in the previous note also apply here.

50. Aggressive export pricing leads to a greater share of domestic production sold in the export market. A greater share of domestic production sold as exports encourages aggressive export pricing. Clearly a chicken and egg problem.

51. Trade volume is constructed from annual trade value data that are available by SIC (it is only for industry-country pairs that SIC data are not available in a time series form) and the matched SIC-based BLS transactions price data. Trade volume is indexed to 1980 to match the index of industrial production.

52. There could be spurious correlation between export exposure and export pricing. For example, the behavior of export prices for semiconductors and oil-field machinery could simply be a result of industry slump.

53. The stable margins and low annual change in export exposure could be a result of long-term contracts. For example, contracts or accounting issues may affect the prices of internal combustion engines traded between subsidiaries of the major car companies in the United States and Canada more than does the exchange rate or export exposure.

54. Consider the effect of a simultaneous change in E, Q, and Y in equation (1.17).

55. See National Academy of Sciences [1987].

56. The statistic in the table pertains to all trade between industrial countries. Therefore, U.S. trade barriers are included in these averages. These statistics only measure the presence of nontariff barriers, not the degree to which they bind. The nontariff barriers included in these statistics are: measures that control price (variable levies, countervailing duties, administered prices), and volume (quotas, prohibitions, voluntary export restraints), and surveillance of these measures.

57. See UNCTAD [1986].

58. On the one hand, these countries might benefit from the restraints if they lead to higher prices. On the other hand, resource misallocations and unproductive activities related to allocation of the quota right within the developing country most likely lead to welfare losses overall.

59. The Federal Reserve's index of capacity utilization in the steel industry rose from 62% in 1986:4 to 73% in July 1987.

60. The Federal Reserve's index of capacity utilization for textile mill products reached 97% in 1987:2; unfilled orders were also rising sharply.

61. The strong negative sign in the domestic expenditure variable suggests that importers price below market to gain a hold of an expanding market.

62. Note however, that the material in table 1–23, which shows a substantial increase in textile import prices, with much less change in import volume, suggests that the new MFA and the bilateral agreements are binding.

Bibliography

Baldwin, Richard. 1987. "Empirical Evidence on Hystereisis in Trade." Presented at the NBER Summer Institute, "International Issues/Real Side," July.

Baldwin, Richard, and Krugman, Paul. 1986. "Persistent Trade Effects of Large Exchange Rate Shocks." NBER Working Paper 2017. Cambridge: National Bureau of Economic Research, January.

Bergsten, C. Fred, and Cline, William R. 1985. *The U.S.-Japan Economic Problem*. Washington: Institute for International Economics, October.

Bergsten, C. Fred, and Williamson, John. 1983. "Exchange Rates and Trade Policy." In William R. Cline (ed.), *Trade Policy in the 1980s*. Cambridge: MIT Press.

Bergstrand, Jeffrey H. 1986. "U.S.-Japan Trade: Predictions Using Selected Economic Models." *Federal Reserve Bank of Boston New England Economic Review*, May–June.

———. 1987. "The U.S. Trade Deficit: A Perspective from Selected Bilateral

Trade Models." *Federal Reserve Bank of Boston New England Economic Review*, May–June.
Berner, Richard. 1987. "The Structural Problem in U.S. Trade and the Likely Policy Response." Salomon Brothers Bond Market Research, April 10.
Blanchard, Olivier J., and Summers, Lawrence. 1984. "Perspectives on High World Interest Rates." *Brookings Papers on Economic Activity*. Vol. 2.
Branson, Richard; Fraga, Arminio; and Johnson, Robert A. 1985. "Expected Fiscal Policy and the Recession of 1982." International Finance Discussion Paper 272. Washington: Board of Governors of the Federal Reserve System.
Bryant, Ralph C., and Holtham, Gerald. [BH]. 1987. "The U.S. External Deficit: Diagnosis, Prognosis, and Cure." Brookings Discussion Papers in International Economics 55. Washington: Brookings Institution, March.
Bryant, Ralph C., Henderson, Dale W; Holtham, Gerald, Hooper, Peter; and Symansky, Steven (ed.). 1988. *Empirical Macroeconomics for Interdependent Economies*. Washington, D.C.: Brookings Institution.
Bryant, Ralph C., Holtham, Gerald, and Hooper, Peter. 1988. *External Deficits and the Dollar: The Pit and the Pendulum.* Washington, D.C.: Brookings Institution.
Christelow, Dorothy. 1986–1987. "Japan's Intangible Barriers to Trade in Manufactures." *Federal Reserve Bank of New York Quarterly Review* 10(4).
Clarida, Richard, "Current Account, Exchange Rates, and Monetary Dynamics in a Stochastics Equilibrium Model." Cowles Foundation Discussion Paper 694. New Haven: Yale University.
Danker, Deborah J.; Haas, Richard D., Henderson, Dale W.; Symansky, Steven; and Tryon, Ralph. 1985. "Small Empirical Models of Exchange Market Intervention: Applications to Germany, Japan and Canade." Board of Governors of the Federal Reserve System, Staff Study no. 155, April.
Darby, Michael R. 1987. "The Current Account Deficit, Capital Account Surplus, and National Investment and Saving." Washington, D.C.: U.S. Department of the Treasury, May.
Darby, Michael R., Gillingham; Robert, and Greenlees, John S. 1987. "The Impact of Government Deficits on Personal and National Savings Rates." U.S. Treasury Research Paper 8702. Washington, D.C.: U.S. Treasury.
Dornbusch, Rudiger. 1987. "Exchange Rates and Prices." *American Economic Review* 77.
———. 1980. *Open Economy Macroeconomics*. New York: Basic Book Publishers.
Dornbusch, Rudiger; and Fischer, Stanley. 1980. "The Exchange Rate and the Current Account." *American Economic Review* 70.
Feldstein, Martin. 1986a. "The Budget Deficit and the Dollar." NBER Working Paper 1898. Cambridge: National Bureau of Economic Research, April.
———. 1986b. "Correcting the World Trade Imbalance." Cambridge: National Bureau of Economic Research, December.
Frankel, Jeffrey. 1982. "In Search of the Exchange Risk Premium: A Six-Currency Test Assuming Mean-Variance Optimization." *Journal of International Money and Finance*. 1.

———. 1988. "Ambiguous Macroeconomic Policy Multipliers in Theory and in Empirical Models." In Ralph Bryant et al. 1988.

Frankel, Jeffrey, and Froot, K. 1986. "The Dollar as an Irrational Speculative Bubble: A Tale of Fundamentalists and Chartists." NBER Working Paper #1854. Cambridge: NBER, March.

Frenkel, Jacob A., and Razin, Assaf. 1987. "The Mundell-Flemming Model: A Quarter Century Later." IMF Working Paper 87/46. Washington, D.C., July, 2.

Friedman, Edward, and Sinai, Allen. 1987. "The Dollar and the Financial Markets." Prepared for the 62nd Annual Conference of the Western Economic Association, July 9.

Gylfason, and Risager. 1984. "Does Devaluation Improve the Current Account?." *European Economic Review*.

Haynes, Stephen E.; Hutchinson, Michael M.; and Mikesell, Raymond R. [HHM]. 1986a. "Japanese Financial Policies and the U.S. Trade Deficit." *Essays in International Finance 162*. Princeton: International Finance Section, April.

———. 1986b. "U.S.-Japan Bilateral Trade and the Yen-Dollar Exchange Rate: An Empirical Analysis." *Southern Economic Journal*, April.

Helkie, William H., and Hooper, Peter. [HH]. 1987. "The U.S. External Deficit in the 1980s: An Empirical Analysis." International Finance Discussion Paper 304. Washington: Board of Governors of the Federal Reserve System (also in Bryant, Holtham, and Hooper. 1988).

Helkie, William H., and Stekler, Lois. 1987. "Modeling Investment Income and Other Services in the U.S. International Transactions Accounts." Federal Reserve Board (forthcoming).

Hooper, Peter. 1987. "The Dollar, External Imbalance, and the U.S. Economy." Presented at Western Economics Association, July.

———. 1985. "International Repercussions of the U.S. Budget Deficit." Brookings Discussion Papers in International Economics 27. Washington, D.C.: Brookings Institution, February.

Hufbauer, Gary Clyde, and Rosen, Howard F. 1986. *Trade Policy for Troubled Industries*. Washington, D.C.: Institute for International Economics, March.

Hutchinson, Michael, and Piggot, Charles. 1984. "Budget Deficits, Exchange Rates, and the Current Account: Theory and U.S. Evidence." *Federal Reserve Bank of San Francisco Review*, Fall.

Johnson, Robert A. 1986. "Anticipated Fiscal Contraction: The Economic Consequences of the Announcement of Gramm-Rudman-Hollings." International Finance Discussion Paper 291. Washington: Board of Governors of the Federal Reserve System.

Kaempfer, William H., and Willet, Thomas D. 1984. "Why an Import Surcharge Wouldn't Help America's Trade Deficit." *World Economy* 10(1).

Krugman, Paul. 1987a. "Sustainability and the Decline of the Dollar." *Brookings Discussion Papers on International Economics*, #57 Washington D.C.: Brookings Institution, March.

———. 1987b. "Long Run Effects of the Strong Dollar." In Richard Marston (ed.), *Exchange Rate Misalignment and International Competitiveness*. Confer-

ence Report, May. Cambridge: NBER.
———. 1986. "Pricing-to-Market When the Exchange Rate Changes.", Massachusetts Institute of Technology, (mimeo.) January.
Krugman, Paul, and Baldwin, Richard. [KB]. 1987. "The Persistence of the U.S. Trade Deficit." *Brookings Papers on Economic Activity*. Vol. 1.
Krugman, Paul, and Hatsopoulos, George N. 1987. "The Problem of U.S. Competitiveness in Manufacturing." *Federal Reserve Bank of Boston New England Economic Review*. January–February, 1987.
Laney, Leroy O. 1984. "The Strong Dollar, the Current Account, and Federal Deficits: Cause and Effect." *Federal Reserve Bank of Dollas Review*. January.
Laursen, Stephen, and Metzler, Lawrence. 1950. "Flexible Exchange Rates and the Theory of Employment." *Review of Economics and Statistics* 32.
Leamer, Edward E., and Stern, Robert M. 1970. *Quantitative International Economics*. Newton, MA: Allyn and Bacon.
Liederman, Leonardo, and Blejer, Mario I. 1987. "Modeling and Testing Ricardian Equivalence: A Survey." IMF Working Paper WP/87/35, April 29.
Loopesko, Bonnie E., and Johnson, Robert A. 1987. "Realignment of the Yen-Dollar Exchange Rate: Aspects of the Adjustment Process in Japan." International Finance Discussion Paper 311. Washington D.C.: Board of Governors of the Federal Reserve System, August.
Mann, Catherine L. 1984. "Employment and Capacity Utilization in Import Sensitive U.S. Industries." PhD Thesis "Trade and Finance Relations Between the Industrial and Developing Countries." MIT.
———. 1986. "Prices, Profit Margins, and Exchange Rates." *Federal Reserve Bulletin*, June.
———. 1987. "Prices, Profit Margins, and Exchange Rates: After the Fall." Presented at the NBER Summer Institute," International Issues/Real Side," July.
Marquez, Jaime R. 1987. "The Global Repercussions of Reducing the U.S. Trade Deficit: An Econometric Analysis." Federal Reserve Board (unpublished).
Marris, Stephen. 1985. *Deficits and the Dollar: the World Economy at Risk*. Washington D.C.: Institute for International Economics, December.
Marston, Richard C. 1986. "Real Exchange Rates and Productivity Growth in the United States and Japan." NBER Working Paper 1922. Cambridge: National Bureau of Economic Research, May.
Masson, Paul, and Blundell-Wignall, Adrian. 1985. "Fiscal Policy and the Exchange Rate in the Big Seven: Transmission of U.S. Government Spending Shocks." *European Economic Review* 28.
McKinnon, Ronald I. 1987. "Money Supply versus Exchange Rate Targeting in Open Economies," mimeo, Standford University, June.
McKinnon, Ronald I., and Ohno, Kenichi. 1986. "Getting the Exchange Rate Right: Insular versus Open Economies." Paper presented at the American Economic Association, December.
———. 1987. "Purchasing Power Parity as a Monetary Standard," mimeo, Stanford University, August.
Mishkin, F. S. 1986. "U.S. Macroeconomic Policy and Performance in the 1980s:

An Overview," NBER Working Paper #1929. Cambridge: National Bureau of Economic Research, May.

Mundell, Robert A. 1987. "A New Deal on Exchange Rates." Paper presented at Japan-United States Symposium on Exchange Rates and Macroeconomics, Tokyo Japan, January.

National Academy of Sciences. 1987. *Balancing the National Interest U.S. National Security, Export Controls and Global Economic Competition*. Washington, D.C.: National Academy Press.

Nogues, Julio; Olechowski, Andrez; and Winters, L. Alan. 1986. "The Structure of Non-Tariff Barriers Facing the Exports of the Industrial Countries." World Bank Staff Working Paper.

Obstfeld, Maurice. 1985. "Floating Exchange Rates: Experience and Prospects." *Brookings Papers on Economic Activity*. Vol. 2.

Pauls, B. Dianne. 1987. "Measuring the Foreign-Exchange Value of the Dollar." *Federal Reserve Bulletin*, June.

Persson, Torsen, and Svensson, Lars. 1985. "Current Account Dynamics and the Terms of Trade: Harberger-Laursen-Metzler Two Generations Later." *Journal of Political Economy* 93: February.

Reinhart, Vince. 1986. "Macroeconomic Influences on U.S.-Japan Trade Imbalances." *Federal Reserve Bank of New York Quarterly Review*. Spring.

Richardson, Peter. 1987. "Tracking the U.S. External Deficit: 1980–1985: Experience with the OECD Interlink Model." OECD Working Paper 38. Washington, D.C.: Office of Economic Cooperation and Development, February.

Sachs, Jeffrey D. 1985. "The Dollar and the Policy Mix: 1985." *Brookings Papers on Economic Activity*. Vol. 1.

Sachs, Jeffrey, D., and Rubini, Noriel. 1987. "Sources of Macroeconomic Imbalances in the World Economy: A Simulation Approach." Prepared for the Third International Conference sponsored by the Institute for Monetary and Economic Studies of the Bank of Japan, June.

Saxonhouse, Gary R. 1983. "The Micro- and Macro-economics of Foreign Sales to Japan." In William R. Cline (ed.), *Trade Policy in the 1980s*. Cambridge: MIT Press.

———. 1986. "Japan's Intractable Trade Surpluses in a New Era." *World Economy* 9(3): September.

Shafer, Jeffrey R., and Loopesko, Bonnie E. 1983. "Floating Exchange Rates After Ten Years." *Brookings Papers on Economic Activity* 1.

Thomas, Charles. 1987. "U.S. International Transactions in 1986." *Federal Reserve Bulletin*, May.

Thompson, Robert L. 1987. "Agriculture in the Uruguay Round." Presented at NBER Summer Institute, August 14.

Tucker, Stuart K. 1987. "Reforming U.S. Agricultural Trade Policy." *Policy Focus 2*. Washington, D.C.: Overseas Development Council.

Turner, Philip, and Tuveri, Jean-Pierre. 1984. "Some Effects of Export Restraints on Foreign Trading Behavior." OECD Economic Studies 2, Spring.

UNCTAD. 1983, 1986. "Problems of Protectionism and Structural Adjustment." TD/B/1039 Part I, TD/B/1126 Add. 1, TD/B/940.

Woo, Wing T. 1984. "Exchange Rates and the Prices of Non-Food, Non-Fuel Products." *Brookings Papers on Economic Activity*. Vol. 2.

World Bank. 1987. *World Development Report.* Washington, D.C.: World Bank.

COMMENTARY

by Rudiger W. Dornbusch

Hooper and Mann have offered a scholarly, definitive autopsy of the U.S. trade problem. Their presentative stands out in the care for detailed exploration of alternative hypotheses and explanations. It is particularly refreshing that they do not skirt issues: they ask just how much of the deficit can be explained by U.S. fiscal policy and do not even show temptation for preposterous supply-side theories of deficits. There is much to be learned from this chapter and little with which one can disagree. But there are some areas where some comments are in order. I will touch in my comments on two points: one is the relationship between exchange rates and interest rates and the question of market rationality, the other is the role of the NICs in U.S. trade.

Exchange Rates and Interest Rates

Exchange rate economics in chapter 1 is built around an expectations-augmented Mundell-Fleming model. Capital is perfectly mobile in the sense that assets are perfect substitutes and portfolio balance is sustained continuously. In such a setting, interest differentials, for whatever maturity, must equal expected currency depreciation over the matching horizon. The relation can be expressed in real terms by stating that the *real* interest differential over a given horizon equals the anticipated rate of real depreciation, d, over that same horizon:

$$R - R^* = d \tag{1}$$

Noting that the long-run real exchange rate $\bar{q}$ (in logs) is equal to the current rate plus accumulated depreciation over δ years,

$$\bar{q} = q + \delta d \tag{2}$$

we have, combining (1) and (2),

$$q = \bar{q} - \delta(R - R^*) \tag{3}$$

Hooper and Mann show in their chart 1–13 a quite striking performance for this relationship. They note that up to 1984–1985 the relationship held, but that subsequently a "bubble" in the real exchange rate caused real interest differentials to mispredict the direction of the dollar. In 1985 the dollar should have been going down; in fact it took a trip up.

In fact the relationship between interest rates and movements in exchange rates is very poor, much more so than the Hooper-Mann picture would let on. This can be more immediately verified by asking whether nominal short-term interest differentials predict well the depreciation occurring over the period to maturity as stated in the equation

$$i - i^* = e\cdot \tag{4}$$

Equivalently, we can write the same relationship in real terms, denoting by r and r^* the short-term real rates and by α the reciprocal of the mean lag with which real rates exchange rates adjust to their long-run equilibrium level.

$$q = \bar{q} - \alpha(r - r^*) \tag{5}$$

Neither (4) nor (5) captures in any manner the direction or turns of the dollar. This fact is well established from the work of Mussa and, more recently, Meese and Rogoff. The failure of theoretical exchange rate models to perform well empirically is tantamount to a failure of equations (4) and (5). Of course, (4) and (5) are stated in terms of expectations. Where there models break down is in one of two possible directions. Either there are large and unexplained risk premia, or there is a dominance of surprises and these surprises cannot be explained in terms of the variables used in our models.

There is an increasing tendency, in exchange rate economics as well as in the economics of asset pricing more generally, to question whether markets are deadly efficient. In work by Shiller and others this question is posed in terms of excess volatility. In a growing literature, it is referred to as plain irrationality or fads. Summers [1985] has gone furthest in the direction of questioning efficiency of asset markets; and the Chicago conference on rational choice reported in Hogarth and Reder [1986] makes it clear that the hypothesis of plain and simple rationality is under fire.

At present there are three plausible directions of research on the apparent departures from rationality. One possibility, as already noted, is fads. Asset market participants entertain theories of the principal determinants of an asset price that are not necessarily the true model, but cannot be statistically rejected. Moreover, asset holders may shift from one theory to another—current account theories, safe haven theories, etc.—and thus bounce around asset markets according to the fashion of the day. The outcome is inevitably excess volatility and the possibility of departures from fundamentals, the simplest form of which would be a bubble.[1]

The second possibility, perhaps complementing that above, relies on an institutional explanation. If markets are dominated by asset holders who have a very short planning horizon, cumulative departures from fundamentals become a clear possibility. The explanation for the short horizon is the hard part. The fact is, though, that financial institutions and even manufacturing corporations live by the quarterly horizon of their financial statements and by the very short-term race for comparative performance. In such a situation, it becomes almost impossible to take positions that rely on long-run fundamentals. While *ultimately* such a position would be vindicated, the portfolio manager would long be out of a job. Of course, there is some long-term speculation, but it is impressive to hear, from fund managers and manufactures investing in innovation, that their horizon is the quarter not the year or the two-year span.

The third direction of research, even less comfortable in terms of traditional economics, is the notion that simple rationality is just not enough. This is, of course, the direction of research emphasized in psychology.[2] A particularly interesting application of this approach is the idea of "disaster myopia" advanced in Guttentag and Herring [1986]. They advance the proposition that asset holders (in their case commercial banks) systematically underestimate the objective probability of occurrence of a disaster (in their case commercial banks underestimating the possibility of sovereign debt default). One supposes there is also the counterpart: when a major adjustment comes underway, it is perceived as a full-fledged crisis, which leads to overshooting.

My own inclination is to believe that this last approach, which probes more deeply into subjective perception of risks, will be the most promising in helping us understand why people hold on so comfortably to obviously overpriced assets. The striking fact, in real estate, in the stock market, and in the exchange market is that assets prices either do not move or they skyrocket or plunge.

The NICs

In trade equations and current account models for the United States close attention is paid to competitiveness relative to other industrial countries and to levels of spending here and in other OECD countries. For data reasons there is only a very limited inclusion of the newly industrializing countries (NICs) of Latin America and Asia. Thus the debt problem that turned around Latin America's noninterest current account. In the same way there is no very satisfactory treatment of the massive expansion of export capacity throughout South East Asia. In the 1970s the U.S. exported capital goods to these countries, and today that capital is used to produce for export to the United States. This kind of structural change is not well captured in models of the U.S. current account. Nor do we capture well the dramatic change in the ability of countries like Japan to sustain competitiveness even in the face of dramatic Yen appreciation. One means of doing so is to shift sourcing for components to Korea or Taiwan. These possibilities are relatively new, but they are already of first-order importance.

Just how important the NICs are in U.S. trade is brought out by the shift in our manufacturing trade balance. In 1980–1981 we had a $28 billion bilateral manufacturing-trade surplus with the NICs, today we have a deficit of that amount.

The size of the swing in manufacturing is a third of our trade deficit and

Table 1. U.S. Trade with Developing Countries (billion $)

	All Goods			*Manufactures*		
	Imports	*Exports*	*Balance*	*Imports*	*Exports*	*Balance*
1980	122.6	79.6	−43.0	29.5	55.6	26.1
1981	121.3	87.4	−33.9	35.1	61.5	26.4
1985	122.2	69.7	−52.5	65.5	46.0	−19.5
1986	124.8	68.3	−56.5	77.3	49.4	−27.9

Source: GATT and U.S. Department of Commerce.

hence certainly deserves attention. This is all the more the case in that manufacturing exports from these countries will show trend growth rates far in excess of those from established industrialized countries. U.S. political interests dictate that we allow relatively easy market access to countries from South East Asia and Latin America. That will imply a major shift in real exchange rates over the next few years. We will have to gain competitiveness relative to Japan and Europe to make room for exports from the NICs.

It used to be said that the NICs are not an issue for two reasons. One, whatever they earn from extra exports they will spend on extra imports. That is now seen as a fallacy. On one side they save a large fraction of their extra incomes; on the other side they tend to sell to the United States, but buy from Japan. In the short and medium run the U.S. is thus left out! The other argument that used to be advanced is that low wages in the NICs reflect low levels of productivity. That, too, is now understood to be wrong in many cases. Productivity levels in many industries are at the U.S. levels, but wages are only one-tenth our level. Moreover, with capital accounting for a large fraction of costs expressed as a share of value added, the much longer working hours and much better control of downtime for machinery help reduce costs even below U.S. levels. All this will make the NICs awesome competitors in the years ahead.[3]

Notes

1. See Dornbusch [1986, ch. 2] for such models.
2. See the introductory essay in Hogarth and Reder [1986].
3. See Shaiken [1987] for a very interesting comparison of manufacturing costs in Mexico and the United States.

References

Dornbusch, R. 1986. *Dollars, Debts and Deficits*. Cambridge: MIT Press.

Guttentag, J. M., and Herring, R. J. 1986. *Disaster Myopia in International Banking*. Essays in International Finance, No. 164, International Finance Section, Princeton University, September.

Hogarth, R. M., and Reder, M. W. 1986. *Rational Choice*. Chicago: University of Chicago Press (also appeared as a supplement to the *Journal of Business*, October 1986).

Shaiken, H. 1987. *Automation and Global Production*. University of Southern California, San Diego, U.S. Mexico Center.

Summers, L. 1985. "On Economics and Finance." *Journal of Finance* 40:633–635.

COMMENTARY

by Alan Reynolds

Popular discussions of trade have become extremely emotional, leaving innocent policymakers wandering through a maze of contradicitions and paradoxes. Back in 1985, we heard that budget deficits supposedly made the dollar go up, yet only two years later the same economists were warning that the dollar would surely go into a precipitous "free fall" unless the budget deficit (which had already fallen by a third) was dramatically reduced. Trade deficits were supposedly caused by a rising dollar, yet trade deficits were later cited as the cause of a falling dollar. The gap between U.S. and foreign interest rates was at first said to be the reason the dollar went up, yet that same gap was later used as proof that the dollar must come down.

Hooper and Mann courageously sort through such conceptual confusion in a conciliatory manner, assigning percentages of the truth to various explanations of trade. One conclusion is that U.S. economic growth has been too fast, so they suggest "a substantial U.S. fiscal contraction," and "a significant decline in the growth of U.S. domestic spending" to close the gap between U.S. and foreign economic growth. Hooper and Mann also imply that U.S. inflation has been too low. In their chart 1–4, competitiveness is defined as the ratio of U.S. to foreign consumer prices, so that, by definition, the United States was most "competitive" when it had the highest relative inflation rate.

The authors propose to separate these "macroeconomic" causes of the U.S. current account deficit from "microeconomic" explanations of why the deficit persists, thus giving the impression that the causes of trade gaps are largely unrelated to the cure. Theories of trade and capital flows could instead be more instructively categorized as "real" or "monetary" theories. The real theories emphasize either relative economic growth or gaps between real investment and domestic savings. Monetary theories emphasize exchange rates. All relevant microeconomic policies could then be integrated into this taxonomy by asking, for example, how tax rates or trade barriers affect investment and savings or the relative growth of real output.

Hooper and Mann survey the real and monetary approaches and conclude that each is partly right. Yet it is quite difficult to reconcile the two approaches. If the relative-growth theory is correct, then a lower dollar could only reduce the trade deficit by slowing economic growth in the United States or by increasing economic growth abroad. Yet Japan and Germany certainly do not believe that rising currencies have boosted their economic growth since 1985. And U.S. advocates of a weaker dollar rarely boast that their policy is intended to weaken the U.S. economy. On the contrary, the idea of sinking the dollar has been sold as a way to increase U.S. GNP at the expense of other countries. Yet if relatively faster growth is the cause of the trade deficit, then any method of improving U.S. growth at the expense of other countries must increase, not reduce, the U.S. trade deficit.

Alternatively, suppose the analysis is in terms of savings exceeding domestic investment in trade-surplus countries, and vice versa for deficit countries. In that case, a weaker dollar could only help by reducing investment or raising savings in the United States, or by reducing savings or raising investment in countries with appreciating currencies. Yet advocates of a weaker dollar rarely complain of "excessive" capital formation in the United States. And nobody even attempts to argue that Americans are more likely to accumulate dollar-denominated assets if the dollar is expected to fall. On the contrary, Americans would then hold *foreign* stocks, bonds, and CDS in order to get an exchange rate gain.

On the foreign side of investment-savings imbalances, why would a rising currency stimulate investment or discourage savings in, say, Japan or Germany? After all, the whole point is to render industries less competitive in foreign countries, and people do not invest in uncompetitive industries. With profit margins falling and employment prospects reduced by a rising yen or mark, there is likely to be less investment and more precautionary savings in those countries. Since a weaker dollar would seem to discourage domestic investment abroad and discourage domestic savings in the United States, it might well increase, rather than reduce, the trade deficit. In short, the real and monetary theories are blatantly incompatible.

Exchange Rates Theories

Hooper and Mann correctly point out that "excessive dependence on the dollar for adjustment is likely to result in too much inflation in the United States and deflation abroad." Indeed, any devaluation that results in inflation in the United States and/or deflation abroad could be considered "excessive," unless trade is arbitrarily given priority over price stability. Inflation at home is not going to make it easier to sell U.S. products, and deflation abroad is not going to make it easier for other countries to buy. The combination of U.S. inflation and foreign deflation would tend to restore purchasing power parity and leave the real terms of trade more-or-less unchanged.[1] Hooper and Mann likewise acknowledge that since the dollar fell, or was pushed, foreign countries "have also benefitted from a reduction in costs associated with the appreciation of their currencies." That observation contradicts the belief that a weaker dollar necessarily makes U.S. costs more "competitive." More likely, a country with a falling currency will face higher costs of raw materials, as well as of credit and equity finance, and could only have lower labor costs if workers, like many economists, had a bad case of money illusion. In fact, the entire microeconomic section of the Hooper-Mann paper could be viewed as an explanation of why the exchange rate theory of trade does not work, even though the authors accept the exchange rate theory.

Inflation could, of course, weaken the U.S. economy—partly by raising the tax rate on real profits and real capital gains, and partly by provoking a tighter Federal Reserve policy. But that is actually a monetary variation on the real theories of trade. Indeed, it is no coincidence that the alleged success of previous dollar devaluations in reducing trade deficits just happened to coincide with the recessions of 1974–1975 and 1980–1982. Inflation and deflation do have real effects, including effects on the prices and profit margins of domestic farmers and oil producers, so there may well be a secondary role for monetary analysis *within* the "real" theories. For policy purposes, however, it would greatly simplify things if we would assign to monetary policy the one task that it is best suited to accomplish—that of leaning against inflation or deflation—and use other instruments such as tax and regulatory policy to affect relative growth rates and investment rates, and therefore trade. If monetary policy were instead subordinated to trade considerations, then there would be no effective policy tools remaining with which to minimize disruptive price gyrations.

In assigning greater importance to monetary rather than real developments, the authors rely on the authority of "the accumulated (and averaged) wisdom of a group of global macroeconomic models." Yet these simulation results are only as credible as the relationships embodied in econometric models. An OECD study by Chan-Lee and Kato observes that, "most models remain broadly income/expenditure systems of a fundamentally Keynesian inspiration. . . few embody fully specified stock or wealth effects in the expenditure functions, and none seems to embody the latest theoretical thinking on expectations or supply-side effects" [2]. Despite the models' common biases, Frankel notes that there is nonetheless considerable disagreement among them even about the direction of effect, such as "whether a monetary expansion worsens or improves the current account" [3]. Averaging such contradictions does not help.

Hooper and Mann note that the dollar has been fairly stable against the currencies of Canada and the Asian NICs. So, why did the U.S. trade deficit widen from 1982 through 1984 with these countries? Why did the trade deficit later remain most persistent with precisely those countries whose currencies had risen most sharply?

To grasp how tenuous the commonly assumed links between exchange rates, budget deficits, and trade really are, it is merely necessary to turn the story around. Suppose, for example, that the Federal Reserve were to engage in a severe tightening of monetary policy at a time of little inflation. The dollar would surely go up, but the economy—and imports—would surely go way down. The budget deficit would likewise increase, due to the recession, even as the trade deficit was reduced. In this uncontroversial example, we find a rising dollar and a larger budget deficit combined with a falling trade deficit. The lesson is that trade imbalances are *real*, and exchange rates and budgets are only relevant to the extent that they may affect relative real growth and investment in complex ways.

Microeconomic Theories

It is only because the authors espouse the theory that exchange rates dominate trade that they feel obliged to add ad hoc microeconomic explanations of why a much lower dollar has had little or no effect. Hooper and Mann thus seem surprised to discover that stubborn Japanese producers actually take account of competition before pricing their products out of both the

U.S. and the Japanese markets (prices have to fall in yen in order to not rise in dollars, or else Japanese exporters would be sued for "dumping"). The authors suppose that the reluctance of foreigners to raise prices in dollars when the dollar falls is just a temporary setback in the exchange rate theory, as though Japanese producers had any choice except to be price takers or go bankrupt. Yet if prices of Japanese exports are going to go up anyway, sooner or later, then to claim that Japanese exporters are temporarily holding prices down implies irrationality. If Japanese producers knew they were going to lose market share eventually, after their prices later rise in dollars, why would they forego profit margins in the meantime?

Sufficient bankruptcy among Japanese exporters probably would reduce that country's exports to the United States (and also its imports from the World), but, like shipping Alaskan oil to Japan and replacing it with Mexican oil, this simply changes the location of trade imbalances. The United States might import fewer Japanese cars, for example, and replace them with Mercury Tracers from Mexico or Volkswagen Foxes from Brazil. Should the United States then devalue the dollar against the Mexcian peso and Brazilian cruzado? Could that be done without the U.S. adopting a Latin American inflation rate?

If the trade deficit is instead explained by changes in the relative performance of real economies, then we do not need complex microeconomic explanations of why Japanese steel cannot sell for much more than any other country's steel, or why a Toyota Corolla cannot sell for much more than the similar Chevrolet Nova. There is much less mystery about the persistence of trade surpluses when we realize that industrial production in Japan *fell* in 1986, or that real GNP in Germany rose only 0.8% between the second quarters of 1986 and 1987, or that investment rates have fallen since 1980 in almost all countries except the United States.

Under the two "real" theories of trade, the solutions are absolutely clear–either the U.S. economy slows down, or other economies speed up; either the U.S. invests less, or others invest more. In conclusion, Hooper and Mann revert to the "real" theory, and advocate "a significant decline in the growth of U.S. domestic spending." But the case for weakening the U.S. economy must rest on its own merits, whatever those might be, not on elevating trade balance to be the sole concern of economic policy. It may sound reasonable to suggest that the United States should slow down while others speed up, but the export-dependent economies are quite unlikely to be able to expand domestic output, employment, and income rapidly enough to make up for a deep cutback in exports to the Untied States (or to other countries that export to the U.S.). Moreover, real U.S.

imports have never declined significantly except during recessions. It is by no means clear that anyone is sufficiently expert at fine tuning to engineer a U.S. slowdown that would not, in fact, turn into a recession at home and a depression in all the trade-surplus countries that rely on having a large net importer somewhere in the world in order to maintain what few jobs they still have.

"Twin Deficits"

Hooper and Mann describe, but do not evaluate, the "twin deficits" theory: viz., that the U.S. budget deficit was the cause of trade deficits, so higher taxes would actually expand the economy by cutting the trade deficit. This theory rests on the accounting misconception that all government borrowing is for consumption and is, therefore, disaving. It also involves the really curious idea that taxes are the same as savings, because taxes supposedly do not reduce private savings.[2] Yet countries with budget deficits much larger than those of the United States (relative to GNP)—such as the Netherlands, Belgium, Canada, Italy, and Spain—have often experienced trade surpluses. Countries with budget surpluses—such as Denmark, Finland, Switzerland, Ecuador, and Hong Kong—have instead had sizable trade deficits.

In 1987, the general government deficit was 2.3% of GNP in the United States, 2.9% in the other G-7 countries [5]. It could be argued that the U.S. "structural" deficit is nonetheless higher than those of Europe, because unemployment rose in Europe and fell in the United States. But that begs the question of why budget deficits did *not* stimulate economic growth or attract foreign capital in other countries, such as Italy or the Netherlands, as smaller deficits are alleged to have done in the United States. The supply-side answer is that the detailed structure of marginal tax incentives is much more conducive to economic expansion in the United States.[3] The Keynesian answer is to ignore the question.

The main theoretical dispute is between Robert Mundell's 1960 global Keynesian approach, and Mundell's post-1971 global monetarist and supply-side approach. Some global Keynesians have recently become quite sympathetic to supply-side concerns about tax incentives, but only when applied to Europe, rather than the United States. Buiter writes of Europe that "a positive response is even more likely if the compostion of fiscal stimulus in investment and supply-side friendly" [7]. Blanchard and Summers likewise write, about Europe, that "A decrease in tax rates [shifts]. . . aggregate supply. . . . Tax cuts are likely to be very effective. . . .

It is conceivable that they could be self-financing without any accomodating [monetary] policy changes. . . .The end result would be increases in employment and real wages without increases in government budget deficits" [8]. Such supply-side effects have the potential of narrowing gaps between U.S. and foreign growth rates and investment rates in a positive way, without a U.S. contraction, yet that option is ruled out, by assumption, in the econometric models.

The actual cause of trade deficits is easier to find if we recall when the trade deficit first appeared. As Hooper and Mann point out, "the current account did not fall substantially into deficit until 1983." Yet their comparisons of relative growth rates begin in 1980, which is a somewhat misleading base year. To explain change, something has to have changed dramatically *since 1982*. There was no such dramatic change in foreign trade barriers, or in U.S. budget deficits, or in slower money growth. The changes were, a sharp reduction of marginal tax rates and, by no coincidence, a relative increase in both economic growth and investment rates. Something similar happened in the United Kingdom, which also experienced relatively rapid growth and investment, and a sizable trade deficit. It is no secret that "tax havens" attract foreign capital, or that high tax rates are evaded by capital flight.

Since 1980–82, the United States has been the only industrial country that increased fixed investment, even relative to its rapid 25% increase in real GNP. From 1982 to 1986, real fixed capital formation increased by 38% in the United States, compared with less than 18% in Japan and 7% in Germany [9]. But that comparison understates the difference, because Japan and Germany include investment in government infrastructure (public works), while the United States does not. Excluding government plant and equipment exaggerates U.S. consumption and understates both investment and savings. Excluding consumer durables also understates relative U.S. investment, because most other countries use more business capital (such as rented autos and laundries) for the same purposes as we use consumer capital.[4]

As Jurg Niehans put it, "countries are debtors if their investment opportunities exceed their wealth and are creditors if their wealth exceeds their investment opportunities" [12]. Financing plant and equipment in the United States became more attractive to both Americans and foreigners, while the value of U.S. assets abroad (mainly loans to developing countries) became much less attractive.

From the fourth quarter of 1982 to the second quarter of 1987, industrial production increased by 27.7% in the United States, 21.9% in Japan, and 16.1% in Germany. Yet comparisons of industrial production actually understate a 36% increase in U.S. manufacturing output over the same period, because total industrial production in the U.S. was uniquely depressed by oil and gas and other mining industries, where (unlike manufacturing) reduced domestic output implies larger imports. Real disposable income per capita in the United States also rose by 12% over this period, but that understates the improvement because it excludes capital gains while nonetheless subtracting the income tax on those gains (household net worth increased by 39%).[5] An economy that is rapidly expanding will devote most of its output to domestic uses, leaving few resources available for export, and will also need to import industrial supplies, components, and business machines.

The United States is also the only major country that has reduced its unemployment rate since 1982. Many European countries, with an average unemployment rate of 11%, and nearly all developing countries, have been in a seven-year recession. It is not the fault of U.S. policy that unemployed foreign workers are unable to buy more U.S. exports, or that bankrupt foreign companies and countries either cannot profitably use U.S. capital goods or do not yet merit the credit to pay for them.

Single-Entry Bookkeeping

Much of the anxiety about foreign debt comes from extrapolating unchanged current account deficits over the next five years. That implies that the rest of the world never catches up to U.S. growth, and that fixed capital keeps piling up in the United States despite its growing scarcity elsewhere. In that unlikely case, it is said that the U.S. foreign debt might get as large as $1 trillion by 1992, which would then be about 16% of GNP. That 16% could be compared with the foreign debt of Korea, which has been 50% of GNP until very recently, or of Canada, where it is still 40% of GNP. As in those cases, the enormous increase in real fixed capital in the United States makes it easy to service even a $1 trillion foreign debt. There are tangible assets to match the financial liabilities. Paying interest and dividends to those who supplied productive capital is no more onerous simply because they happen to live in Tokyo or Melbourne rather than St. Louis.

The conclusion usually drawn from the "net debtor" scare is that the U.S. is "mortgaging its future," which is no better argument in this case than it is against mortgages. What it means is that the "problem" with low exports today is that they imply high exports tomorrow. "The point is fast approaching," warns Norman Jonas of *BusinessWeek* (November 16,

1987), "when [foreigners] will want to be paid in U.S. goods." If expanded U.S. exports are such a bad thing, then why does everyone assume that the same situation has been good for Japan and Germany? Expanded future exports would imply reduced domestic consumption in the future—lower living standards—only if we assume both full employment in U.S. export industries (which is surely not a bad thing), and also *zero* growth of capacity in the rest of the economy. Even under those assumptions, housing and durables bought earlier would continue to yield services. If an American buys a Japanese car and borrows the money from a Japanese bank, does that mean his future living standard has to go down as he pays interest on the loan? Only if we do not count the car as part of his living standard.

The anxiety about U.S. *domestic* debt is also single-entry bookkeeping—such as worrying about more mortgages and forgetting that there are more houses. The fixed capital of U.S. businesses, households, and governments increased from $16.8 trillion to $19.8 trillion between 1983 and 1986, while the debt of those sectors merely increased proportionately, from $6.4 trillion to $9.3 trillion.[6]

The total U.S. *net* capital stock, in 1982 dollars, rose 9.8% from 1983 to 1986. Net investment looks weaker than it really is, however, because of the rapid expansion of high-tech business equipment that saves space and therefore does not require building larger offices and plants. The more such equipment is added, the shorter the average depreciation period becomes, therefore depreciation estimates soar and the gap between net and gross investment get wider.[7] If the U.S. bought fewer computers, net investment might well look better, thanks to the gradual depreciation of obsolete factory buildings. The amount spent on high-tech equipment is also misleading, since there is no way to adjust prices of new technological equipment for the staggering increases in quality per dollar. Indeed, some of the most important capital—computer software—is counted as consumption. In any case, it is gross investment that has to be financed through capital inflows, not net investment.

From 1982 to 1986, the U.S. current account deficit increased by 3.3% of GNP, while gross fixed investment, even aside from government and consumer investment, increased by 3.5 percentage points of GNP. Niehans' "investment opportunity" theory of trade and capital flows is the only theory we need to explain why the U.S. current account swung from balance to deficit. The same theory correctly predicts that real fixed investment has declined relative to GNP in all the countries where current accounts have moved from deficit or balance into surplus. In Taiwan, for example, the domestic investment rate dropped from about 32% to 17% of GDP since 1980, while the savings rate remained very high. The gap between the two is Taiwan's current account surplus. In Latin America, investment rates fell from 24% to 15% of GDP.[13] The same thing happened to a lesser extent in Japan, Europe, and Africa. Declining capital formation in most other countries meant that surplus savings moved to the United States, where the after-tax rewards looked brighter. Countries with growing current account surpluses, and falling investment rates, have been consuming their capital, exporting their "seed corn."

We don't need microeconomic theories or exchange rate theories to explain why countries with negligible economic growth and weak investment have relied on exports to generate what few jobs they have. If the weakest economies will reduce tax and regulatory barriers to provide incentives to utilize their slack capacity and invest in more, then the world will once again be able to afford the U.S. exports which our very sizable real investments have made possible. The added U.S. income from added exports would provide savings to displace foreign capital, and world trade would come into reasonable balance at a higher level of world output.

The alternative of curing the trade deficit through a "policy mix" of rising tax rates and a falling dollar has been tried before, from 1972 to 1974 and again from 1978 to 1980. It simply produces stagflation, followed by world recession. The alternative of protectionism has also been tried before, in 1921 and 1930, and it produces world depression. There are worse things than trade deficits.

Notes

1. There have been frequent and massive nominal devaluations in Latin America in recent years, but real effective exchange rates nonetheless were virtually unchanged. Inflation wiped out the devaluations [1].

2. "A rise in. . . net taxes lowers the ratio of disposable income to the net national product, but personal saving is reduced proportionately much more than disposable income" [4].

3. "These calculations showed that a 10% revenue neutral reduction in marginal tax rates would yield a 12.8% increase in per capita income for LDCs and a 6.1% increase in per capita income for non-LDCs." [6]

4. Recent studies suggest that U.S. accounting practices vastly understate both investment and savings. [10] [11].

5. See Joint Economic Committee, *Economic Indicators* (September 1987); U.S. Department of Commerce, *Business Conditions Digest*; Congressional Budget Office, *The Economic and Budget Outlook* (August 1987) p. 27.

6. Both assets and debts are nominal, because debt figures are usually reported that way. See U.S. Department of Commerce, *Survey of Current Business* (August 1987); Board of Governors, Federal Reserve System, "Flow of Funds Summary Statistics" (September 25, 1987).

7. "In the United States there appears to have been a shift in investment in favor of

machinery and equipment, which tends to reduce the average age of the capital stock and to raise the share of depreciation. . ." [Bank for International Settlements, "Fifty-Sixth Annual Report," Basle (June 9, 1986) p. 24.]

References

1. Inter-American Development Bank. 1984. *Economic and Social Progress in Latin America*, p. 14.
2. Chan-Lee, J. H., and Kato, H. 1984. "A Comparison of Simulation Properties of National Econometric Models." *OECD Economic Studies*, Spring, 146.
3. Frankel, Jeffrey A. 1987. "The Sources of Disagreement Among International Macro Models, and Implications for Policy Coordination." University of California, Berkeley, Working Paper no. 8725, January.
4. Von Furstenberg, George. 1981. "Saving." In Henry J. Aaron and Joseph A. Pechman (eds.). *How Taxes Affect Economic Behavior.* Washington, D.C.: Brookings Institution.
5. IMF. 1987. *World Economic Outlook.* Washington, D.C.: International Monetary Fund, October, 56.
6. Koester, Reihard B., and Kormendi, Roger C. 1987. "Taxation, Aggregate Activity and Economic Growth: Cross-Country Evidence on Some Supply-Side Hypotheses." University of Michigan, October.
7. Buiter, William H. 1987. "The Right Combination of Demand and Supply Policies: The Case for a Two-Handed Approach." NBER Working Paper no. 2333. Washington, D.C.: National Bureau of Economic Research, August, p. 35.
8. Blanchard, Oliver J., and Summers, Lawrence H. 1986. "Fiscal Increasing Returns, Hysteresis, Real Wages and Unemployment." NBER Working Paper no. 2034, October, p. 23.
9. OECD. 1987. *Querterly National Accounts* no. 1.
10. Lipsey, Robert E., and Kravis, Irving B. 1987. "Is the U.S. a Spend-thrift Nation?" *Tax Notes*, September 7.
11. Hendershott, Patric H., and Peek, Joe. 1987. "Private Saving in the United States." NBER Working Paper no. 2294. Washington, D.C.: National Bureau of Economic Research, June.
12. Niehans, Jurg. 1984. *International Monetary Economics*. Baltimore: Johns Hopkins University Press, p. 107.
13. Inter-American Development Bank. 1987. *Economic and Social Progress in Latin America*, p. 24.

COMMENTARY

by Michael R. Darby

It's good to be here with so many old friends, colleagues, and students. It's better to be the last discussant because the other two have covered the main points and I can be idiosyncratic—or just plain quirky in what I talk about. It's best to be here in St. Louis where at least baseball fans think this week of October 19, 1987 been a good week.

The first thing that I always ask myself is what have I learned from reading the work I am supposed to discuss. The key insight for me is that Alan Greenspan is an incredibly patient man. This chapter exceeds all bounds on length. I seriously believe that economists have a responsibility to each other as well as to any policymakers we serve to emphasize what's new and important and not bury it in old stuff. At UCLA we had a rule that points would be deducted for correct but irrelevant material, and I would be remiss in my deterrent duties to not do so here.

I want to take the bulk of my time to raise some issues we're thinking about at Treasury and correct some misapprehensions about those views expressed in the paper. In doing so, I shall be talking about the fundamental causes which work through relative incomes and especially exchange rates. I concentrate on this area because I have no quarrel with what I believe is the substance of their contribution—the examination of why the adjustment in the trade deficit has been slower than would be predicted given the movements in these fundamentals.

Before doing so, I think that I should note that it is outrageous to talk about U.S. restraint (monetary or fiscal) to reduce the growth gap when we still have substantial unemployed resources and other countries should grow both for their own interests as well as the interests of the world trading system.

Fundamental Causes

We believe that foreign factors promoting capital flows into the United States have played at most a secondary role in the increase in national investment—saving gap or trade deficit. This is because real interest rates and the dollar began to rise in late summer 1980 with the real after-tax interest rate in the 1980s returning from less than zero to the levels averaged in the 1950s and 1960s. Thus secondary roles must be ascribed to factors that would lower real interest rates, such as relaxation of foreign capital controls, safe-haven capital flight, and the LDC debt crisis.

Therefore, we would focus on factors decreasing desired U.S. national saving or shifting upward U.S. investment demand.
The budget deficit story seems to me totally unconvincing:

1. In 1980, increases in the deficit under not-yet President Reagan were unexpected but hardly unprecedented. In the 1970s we saw larger structural deficits and dollar depreciation going hand-in-hand.
2. Until 1984, the increase in budget deficit was essentially all in the net interest and cyclical components with substantially no change in the structural noninterest deficit. Even at 1985–1986 peak the federal structural deficit was not large relative to the 1960s and 1970s, and the general government structural deficit was negligible in both absolute and comparative terms. This could not be an *independent cause* of the rise in interest rates and exchange rates until the last year of the appreciation and even then it is too small.
3. Our simulations say that private saving is right on track with my 1975 vintage consumer expenditure function and would have been lower if taxes were higher. It is really hard to account for more than 0.3%–0.7% of GNP national saving decrease by the rise in deficit.

Moreover, the deficit is a terrible measure of the effect on consumption and government spending of fiscal policy. Our research indicates that a $1 cut in government spending on goods and services increases national saving at a given level of income by 80 cents while in the first year compared to a 20 cent increase for a $1 tax increase or transfer-payment reduction. Given this 4 to 1 ratio in effect on consumption and government spending as a function of income, it is easy to develop "antideficit" programs in which consumption and government spending change so as to decrease national savings.

Investment works much better and we believe that an upward shift in the investment demand function for 1981–1985 explains the bulk of the dollar appreciation and hence the trade deficit. Our estimates indicate about a 5% upward shift. Note that this is not exactly the same thing as an investment boom as claimed by Hooper and Mann. It's more a question of the dog that didn't bark: Why didn't investment fall with saving during the 1981–1982 recession and subsequent period of rising but substantially underemployed resources? That's what happened before when transitory income and capacity utilization fell. Especially, why didn't this happen when after-tax real interest rates were rising so dramatically?

We think we have some useful ideas about why investment did not fall given these pressures. Beginning in late summer 1980, it became apparent that the next President would be Ronald Reagan and that this reflected a profound shift from an antibusiness political climate. Here we see the beginning of an upward shift in investment demand, real interest rates, and the dollar. Part of this reversal of climate has been in reducing the threat of arbitrary regulatory change to the value of an American factory. Perhaps more important has been the convergence of disinflation and tax law changes to substantially lower the corporate tax rate. I might add that the dollar decline started when the Treasury I Tax Reform proposal was submitted and continued as probability of a corporate tax increase rose to 1.

Thus we see a rather different micro rather than aggregative channel through which fiscal policy can play a major role in the appreciation and subsequent depreciation of the dollar.

One final note on the shaky foundation of the twin towers: of the 20 OECD countries only 9 over the 1970s and 80s had budget deficits and trade deficits with the same sign. One would ask that such an article of faith do at least as well as chance or my mother's astrology.

SESSION II

2 THE CURRENT ACCOUNT AND MACROECONOMIC POLICY: AN ECONOMETRIC ANALYSIS*

John B. Taylor

Introduction

Beginning in late 1982, a huge gap between domestic saving and domestic investment began to develop in the U.S.; and this gap has remained large through 1987. Investment recovered rapidly after the 1981–1982 recession and has remained abnormally high by U.S. standards in the five years since the recession ended. Domestic saving also recovered rapidly after the 1981–1982 recession, but starting in late 1982, saving fell as a ratio to income. Paralleling this saving-investment gap has been the much-discussed U.S. trade deficit. At the same time, trade surpluses and corresponding saving-investment surpluses developed and persisted in Germany and Japan. (See figures 2–1 through 2–4).

---

* Prepared for the conference "The U.S. Trade Deficit—Causes Consequences, and Cures," Federal Reserve Bank of St. Louis, October 23 and 24, 1987. This research was supported by a grant from the National Science Foundation at the National Bureau of Economic Research. I am grateful to Tam Bayoumi, Jonathan Eaton, Peter Klenow, Paul Lau, Andrew Levin, Ellen McGrattan, Ronald McKinnon, Kenichi Ohno, and Peter Hooper for helpful assistance, discussions, and advice.

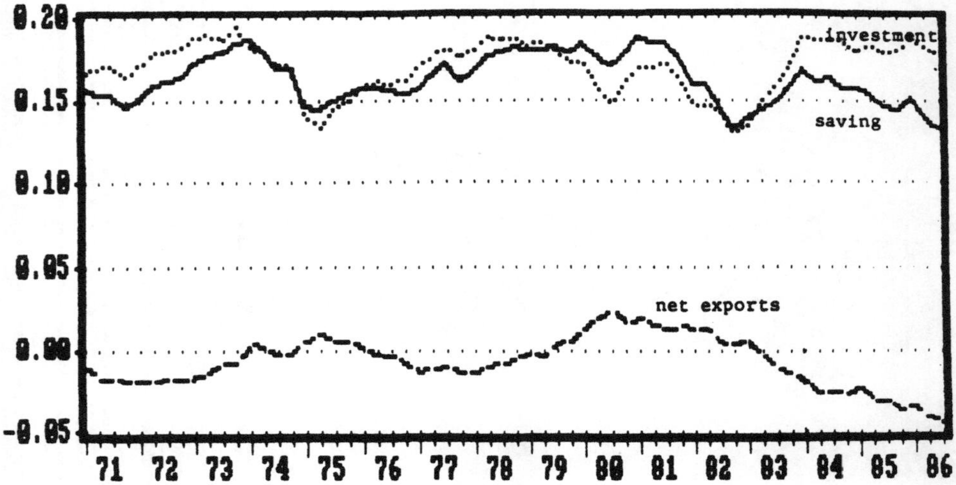

Figure 2–1. U.S. real net exports (X), real investment (I), and national saving ($S = Y - C - G$) as a fraction of real GNP (Y)

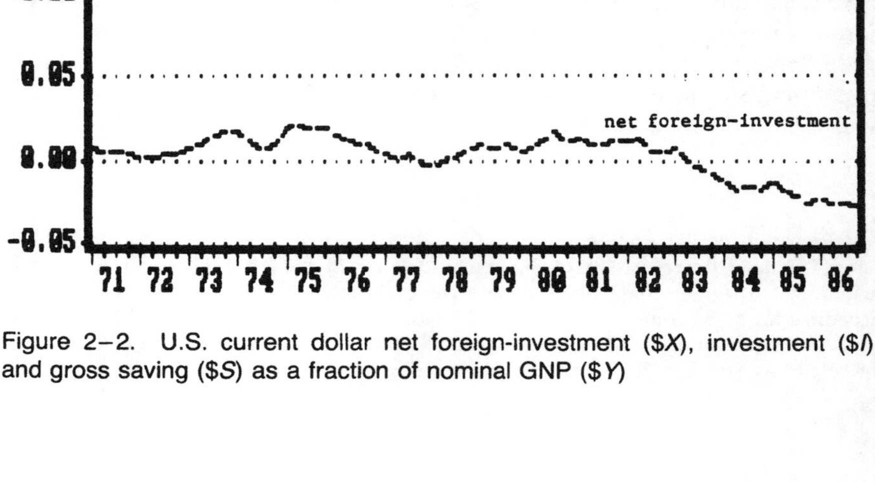

Figure 2–2. U.S. current dollar net foreign-investment ($\$X$), investment ($\$I$), and gross saving ($\$S$) as a fraction of nominal GNP ($\$Y$)

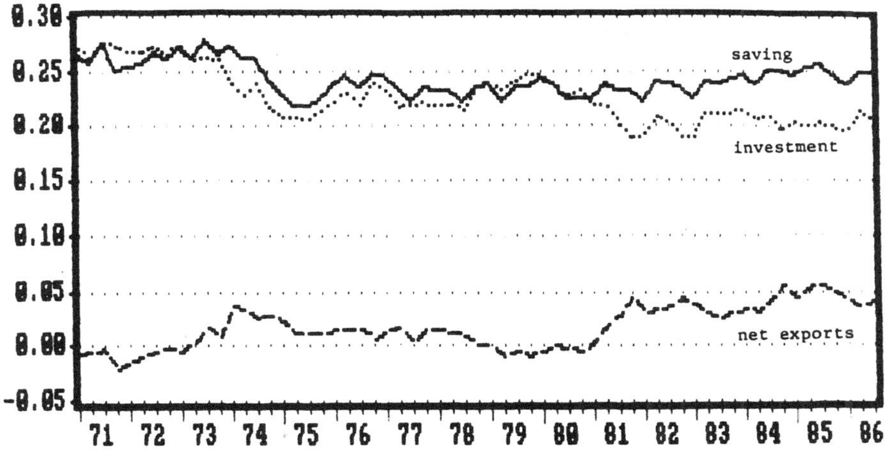

Figure 2–3. German real net exports, real investment, and real national saving as a fraction of real GNP

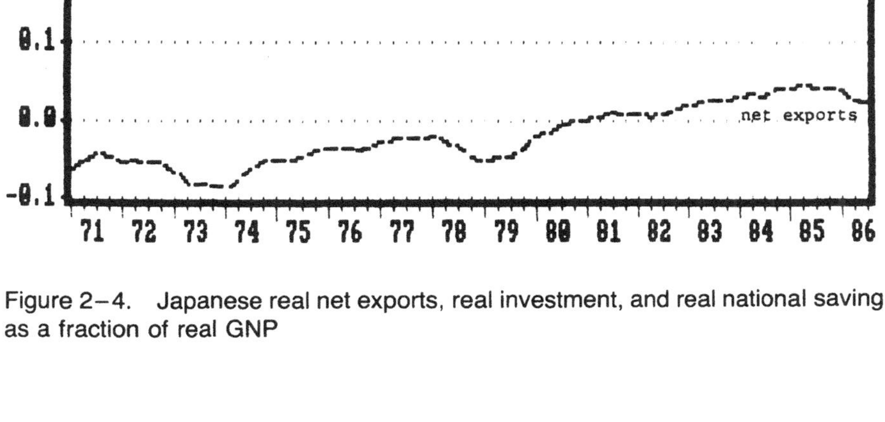

Figure 2–4. Japanese real net exports, real investment, and real national saving as a fraction of real GNP

My purpose here is to examine what would have happened to saving and investment in the United States if the United States had followed policies that would have prevented the trade deficit from growing as rapidly as it did in the post-1982 period. The simple accounting identity that the trade deficit is equal to the difference between domestic saving and domestic investment tells us that saving would have been higher compared to investment if the trade deficit had been reduced. But whether the levels of saving and investment would have been higher or lower depends on the source of the change in the deficit as well as on a host of empirical magnitudes such as interest rate elasticities of investment, exchange rate elasticities of exports and imports, the degree of international capital mobility, and the impact of a change in U.S. interest rates on interest rates in the rest of the world.

I measure the impact of the trade deficit on saving and investment by performing counterfactual simulations of smaller trade deficits using a multicountry econometric model. The model incorporates the high degree of international capital mobility characteristic of the 1980s and uses econometric estimates of the elasticities and lags based on data from the 1970s and 1980s. By using the rational-expectations assumption, the model permits real interest rates to differ among the advanced industrial countries by the amount of the expected changes in real exchange rates. The model also permits long-term interest rates and exchange rates to move in anticipation of future changes in monetary and fiscal policy. There is wide agreement that these interrelationships between real interest rates, real exchange rates, and expectations are a key feature of any explanation of the trade deficit during the 1980s (see, for example, Feldstein [1987] and McKinnon and Ohno [1986]). Hence, an econometric model that is fit to the data *and* incorporates capital mobility with rational expectations seems particularly suited to assessing the quantitative impact of the trade deficit on saving and investment, and the real economy in general.

Because the trade deficit itself is an endogenous variable, it is misleading to provide counterfactual simulations of what the world would have looked like without the trade deficit by simply manipulating the trade deficit as if it were exogenous. Rather, it is necessary to first retreat a step and provide an explanation for the trade deficit in terms of more fundamental exogenous causes. Once these causes are identified, then counterfactual simulations of alternative scenarios for the trade deficit, as generated by these exogenous factors, are possible.

Several studies have been reported during the last year concerning the "proximate" causes of the U.S. trade deficit. These studies have explored whether movements in exchange rates, U.S. GNP, or foreign GNP can explain the movement in the U.S. trade deficit (see Bryant and Holtham [1987]) who summarize of the partial equilibrium results from the trade sectors of several large econometric models, and Krugman and Baldwin [1987] and Hakkio and Roberts [1987] who focus on more rudimentary models). However, these "proximate" factors, such as exchange rates and GNP, are just as endogenous as the trade deficit. They are certainly endogenous to saving and investment behavior, which is the issue examined here. Hence, it is necessary to look for more fundamental causes in order to address these issues.

The focus of this chapter is on U.S. fiscal policy as the exogenous forcing variable behind the trade deficit. In particular, the chapter examines the effects of a counterfactual fiscal policy in the United States during the 1982–1986 period, in which government purchases are reduced relative to their historical path so as to eliminate the government deficit. According to the model, this counterfactual change in U.S. fiscal policy results in smaller trade deficits and hence generates the kind of counterfactual trade balance needed to address the above question.

Most of the following analysis focuses on the real trade deficit (real net exports), as well as on real investment and real saving—the latter simply defined as the excess of real GNP over real consumption and real government purchases. For the purpose of looking at the effects of the trade deficit on the real economy, real net exports is the appropriate measure, as emphasized by Bryant and Holtham [1987]: "it is the deficit in constant prices that is relevant for assessing influences on real GNP and jobs, both in the U.S. economy and abroad." But it should be emphasized that the trade deficit in current dollars is more relevant for assessing future burdens of the deficit (see Denison [1981]). As will be clear below, the model suggests that changes in government purchases have a much larger effect on the real deficit than on the current dollar deficit and the current account.

For the purpose of this exercise, there are two potential problems with identifying fiscal policy as the cause of the trade deficit. First, fiscal policy may be endogenous and simply responding to developments in the economy that make it appear to have a role in causing the trade deficit. It is assumed that this is not the case for U.S. government purchases during 1982–1986. The shift in government purchases that began in 1982 is largely identified with an exogenous increase in defense expenditures, and U.S. government purchases show almost no counter-cyclical behavior in the entire post-war period. The second problem is perhaps more serious. Focus on fiscal policy ignores the possibility that some other forces may have been responsible for the trade deficit. For example, some have argued that attractive investment opportunities in the United States compared to Germany and Japan are the cause of the U.S. trade deficit. This possibility is not examined here. Similarly, I do not try to address questions about what would have happened had the United States run a large fiscal deficit and there was no trade deficit, perhaps because of restrictive trade legislation. It is possible that as part of the political process of trading off one special interest against another, Congress would have been able to enact more spending cuts if it had given in to more restrictive trade bills, and thereby reduced the fiscal deficit. In this round-about way, fiscal policy could become endogenous to the trade deficit. It is also possible that interest rates would have risen, choking off investment and eliminating the saving-investment deficit by another route. These possibilities are not examined here, but they are clearly good subjects for future research.

This chapter is organized as follows: Section 2.1 describes the counterfactual simulation experiments. Section 2.2 briefly describes the model, which is listed in detail in the appendix (tables 2A–1 through 2A–4). Section 2.3 describes the results of the simulations, detailing how much of the change in the trade deficit results in a change in investment and a change in saving in both the short run and the long run. Section 2.4 steps back from the particular model used here and examines the robustness of the key results to different modeling assumptions. Section 2.5 discusses the policy implications.

2.1 A Description of the Counterfactual Hypotheses

U.S. real net exports began to turn negative in early 1983. In order to bring about a counterfactual reversal of this decline, it is supposed that real U.S. government purchases of goods and services grew less rapidly than the historical record starting in the first quarter of 1982. In particular, it is assumed that by 1986:1 this cut resulted in real government purchases lower than reality by an amount equal to 3% of historical real GNP. The full amount of the cut does not occur immediately, however. It is phased in gradually from 1982:1 through 1986:1 in equal increments. The gradual phase-in, much like the Gramm-Rudman-Hollings type of phase-in for budget deficit reductions, is meant to mitigate the real output effects of a cut in government purchases. Three percent of real GNP gives a cut in government expenditures that approximately balances the combined fiscal deficit at the federal, state, and local levels. No changes in taxes or other components of government expenditures are assumed. Instead, the cut in government purchases results in a counterfactual reduction in the outstanding stock of government bonds, as the government needs to borrow less to finance the smaller budget deficit.

With a forward-looking model it is important to describe the counterfactual-expectations assumption that underlie this counterfactual change in government spending. The implicit assumption made here is that as of 1982:1 (but not before) people became aware of the cut in government spending. They knew, that, starting in that quarter, real government spending would be eventually lowered by 3% of real GNP, and they knew that the cut would be phased in gradually. As we will see, this expectation begins to have immediate and large effects on interest rates and exchange rates as soon as the cut is announced and before most of the cut takes place.

An important policy controversy relating to the trade deficit/saving-investment deficit identity has arisen during the last few years. As discussed in Krugman and Baldwin [1987] and McKinnon and Ohno [1986], the debate is over whether exchange rate adjustments are necessary to bring about adjustments in the trade deficit, or whether shifts in the saving-investment balance (perhaps brought on by a decrease in government spending) can bring about the adjustments without exchange rate adjustments. In order to investigate the empirical significance of these issues, three alternatives to the simple reduction in government purchases in the United States were also examined. All these alternatives assume that U.S. government purchases are cut by 3% of real GNP as in the scenario described above. They differ in the degree of monetary accommodation by the Fed or the other central banks or in the degree to which the trade surpluses are reduced in Germany and Japan. These alternatives along with the scenario (scenario 1) described above are summarized as follows:

1. No other change.
2. Expansionary U.S. monetary policy (U.S. money supply increased by 8%).
3. Expansionary foreign monetary policy (money supply is increased in all the non-U.S. G-7 countries by 8%).
4. Expansionary fiscal policy in Japan and Germany (government purchases are raised by 2% of baseline GNP in Germany and Japan).

As will be seen below, the 8% money supply expansion (which is also phased in gradually) was chosen to roughly offset the deflationary effects of the cut in U.S. government purchases. Whether this occurs in the United States or abroad has implications for exchange rate behavior. The expansionary fiscal policy (scenario 4) is meant to examine the effects of reducing the trade deficits in Japan and Germany.

2.2 Brief Description of the Model

The econometric model is built to explain short-run economic fluctuations in the Group of Seven countries: the United States, Canada, France, Germany, Italy, Japan, and the United Kingdom. It is a quarterly model fit to data mostly from the quarterly OECD national income accounts. The parameters of the model are based on quarterly observations from 1971 through 1986 with the exact starting and ending quarters depending on the type of equation (number of leads and lags).

The definition of the variables used in the model and the notation is described in appendix 2A. A listing of the model equations is found in appendix 2B. The estimated coefficients are found in appendix 2C, and summary elasticities are found in appendix 2D.

Although a multicountry model necessarily involves many equations and variables, this particular model is quite simple in structure and the size of the model for any one country is quite modest. The model is simply an empirical multicountry version of a Mundell-Fleming two-country model with rational expectations and sticky wages as modeled via the staggered wage-setting hypothesis.

The rational-expectations assumption is a highlight of the model. Expectations are assumed to be rational in all markets—labor markets as well as financial markets. Hence, wages are both "sticky" and "forward-looking." Monetary policy has an effect on real output, though of a qualitatively different type than in Keynesian models without rational expectations.

The financial side of the model is a disaggregated version of the Mundell-Fleming approach to international financial markets with perfect capital mobility and with perfect substitution between assets. The nominal interest rate spread between each pair of countries is equal to the expected rate of change in the exchange rate between the same two countries. In the classic Mundell-Fleming model, the interest rates are equalized because expectations of exchange rates are not considered. In this model, expectations of exchange rate changes are forward looking—computed using the entire model—and permit interest rate differentials between countries as discussed in the introduction. Although capital flows between countries may be quite large, with the perfect capital mobility approximation, the accumulated capital stocks need not be calculated explicitly. According to the model, aggregate demand determines output in the short run, as the aggregate wage and price level are essentially predetermined in each quarter—only a fraction of the workers adjust their wages each quarter. Aggregate demand is built up from disaggregated spending decisions—consumption, investment, government, and net exports. The important price variables in these demand equations are the real interest rate (rational expectations of future inflation are a factor here) and the relative price of domestic goods to foreign goods (the exchange rate is a factor here).

Consumption is disaggregated into durables, nondurables, and services in most of the countries, and is assumed to depend on expected future income and on the real interest rate. A lagged dependent variable in these equations captures the partial adjustment of consumption to changes in these variables. Negative real interest rate effects are found for durables in the United States, Canada, France, and Japan; for nondurables in the United States, Canada, and the U.K.; and for total consumption in Germany and Italy.

Investment depends, with a lag, on expected demand and on the real interest rate. For the United States, fixed investment is disaggregated into equipment, nonresidential structures, and residential structures. For France, Japan and the United Kingdom, total nonresidential is considered separately from total residential. Only total fixed-investment equations were estimated for Canada, Germany, and Italy. The real interest rate has a negative impact on fixed investment for every country except France, and a negative impact on inventory investment in all countries.

Real exports depend on the ratio of the price of imports to the price of exports, and real imports depend on the ratio of import prices to the domestic deflator. In addition, imports depend on domestic output, and exports depend on a weighted average of output in the other countries. Imports and exports are not disaggregated by type of good; they correspond to the definition of exports and imports in the NIPA accounts. The equations are in logarithmic form for each country. For each country, an increase in the relative price of exports to imports decreases real net exports. These equations are dynamic (lagged dependent variables are included in the estimated equations). In the short run, the elasticities are much less than in the long run.

Wages in the model are determined according to the staggered-contract approach. That is, wages are assumed to be bid up relative to expected future wages and prices if aggregate demand (as measured by actual output) is above potential output. The distribution of contracts by length is assumed to vary by country and is estimated using aggregate data. In Japan synchronized wage setting is permitted and the estimates suggest that a relatively large fraction of workers have annual wage adjustments at the time of the Shunto. Potential output is assumed to grow at a constant rate, and there is no impact of increases in the capital stock on potential output.

Output prices are set according to a markup over wages and import prices with an allowance for trend increases in productivity and demand effects in some countries. A lagged dependent variable allows for slow adjustment so that margins fall in the short run after an increase in wages or import prices. Eventually the full wage and import price increase is passed through.

For each of the seven countries, import prices are assumed to depend directly on an average of prices in the rest of the world converted into domestic currency units using the exchange rate between each country. The effect of exchange rates on domestic prices occurs through this channel in that domestic prices are affected by import prices as described above. Export prices, on the other hand, are assumed to move in response to domestic prices and foreign prices. In the United States, Canada, and France, the impact of foreign prices in export prices was small and insignificant and was omitted from these equations.

To see how interest rates are determined in the model, suppose that the money supply is exogenous in each country. The partial adjustment money demand equations for each country are inverted to give an equation for the short-term interest rate. The short-term interest rates are then used to determine long-term rates through a forward-looking term structure equation: the long rate is assumed to be a geometric distributed lead of the short rate. Finally, the exchange rate is related to the differential between interest rates in each country according to uncovered interest rate parity.

Taking the money supply and government spending in each country as exogenous, the model consisting of the above equations can be solved in each period for the endogenous variables. Rational expectations of future variables appear throughout the model: expectations of future prices and income appear in the consumption equations, expectations of future output and prices appear in the investment equations, expectations of future exchange rates appear in the exchange rate equations, expectations of future interest rates appear in the term structure equations, and expectations of future wages, prices, and output appear in the wage equations. The solution is performed numerically using the extended-path algorithm discussed in Fair and Taylor [1983].

2.3 Results

The simulation results are summarized in tables 2–1 through 2–4. These four tables correspond to the four different scenarios described in section 1. Of course much more information can be extracted from the simulations

Table 2–1. Effects of a Reduction in the U.S. Trade Deficit Induced by a Reduction in U.S. Government Purchases—1982–1987.

The counterfactural decline in real government purchases is equal to 3 percent of real GNP. The decline is phased in gradually in equal percentage increments each quarter starting in 1982.1 and finishing in 1986:1. Although the model is quarterly, only the first quarter of each year is reported. Figures are in percent difference from historical values (or percentage point difference for interest rates and ratios).

	82:1	*83:1*	*84:1*	*85:1*	*86:1*	*87:1*
SHORT-TERM RATES						
US-Fed. funds	−.45	−1.67	−2.12	−2.40	−2.48	−2.35
Germany-call money	.15	−.65	−.79	−.80	−.70	−.58
Japan-call money	−.05	−.55	−.99	−1.19	−1.10	−.84
EXCHANGE RATES						
D-Mark	13.10	12.50	11.20	9.61	7.80	5.92
Yen	11.10	10.30	9.08	7.85	6.48	4.96
LONG-TERM RATES						
US-gov't bonds	−1.10	−1.93	−2.26	−2.43	−2.41	−2.31
Germany-gov't bonds	−.38	−.71	−.79	−.77	−.66	−.54
Japan-gov't bonds	−.34	−.80	−1.09	−1.12	−.94	−.69
REAL SPENDING						
US consumption	−0.05	−0.21	−0.38	−0.54	−0.57	−0.51
US investment	0.00	0.48	1.00	1.56	2.38	3.89
German investment	−0.19	0.10	0.98	2.10	2.86	2.88
Japan investment	−0.13	−0.43	0.05	1.18	2.38	3.42
US exports	0.13	1.58	3.61	5.47	6.87	7.73
US imports	−0.47	−3.86	−6.27	−8.13	−9.34	−8.77
US real GNP	0.03	−0.26	−0.39	−0.72	−0.97	−0.58
German real GNP	−0.20	−0.44	−0.39	−0.25	−0.06	0.07
Japan real GNP	−0.10	−0.48	−0.51	−0.24	0.16	0.38
PRICES						
US GNP deflator	−0.10	−1.12	−2.50	−3.85	−5.02	−5.95
German GNP deflator	−0.02	−0.51	−0.95	−1.24	−1.37	−1.35
Japan GNP deflator	−0.01	−0.42	−1.10	−1.72	−2.02	−1.93
US import price	1.21	4.72	6.38	6.73	6.24	5.26
US export price	−0.04	−0.78	−2.06	−3.41	−4.65	−5.65
RATIOS TO REAL GNP						
US real nat. saving	0.06	0.67	1.42	2.01	2.58	2.85
US real investment	−0.00	0.10	0.26	0.42	0.63	0.78
US real net exports	0.06	0.57	1.16	1.59	1.94	2.07
RATIO TO GNP						
US net exports	−0.07	0.03	0.15	0.35	0.48	0.46

Table 2–2. Effects of a Reduction in the U.S. Trade Deficit by a Simultaneous Reduction in Government Purchases and an Increase in the Money Supply—1982–1987.

The decline in purchases is 3 percent of real GNP and is phased in gradually starting in 1982:1 and ending in 1986:1. The money increase is 8 percent, phased in the same way. Figures are in percent differences from historical values.

	82:1	*83:1*	*84:1*	*85:1*	*86:1*	*87:1*
SHORT-TERM RATES						
US-Fed. funds	.63	−0.30	−1.19	−0.23	−3.41	−1.79
Germany-call money	−0.11	−0.52	−0.61	−0.61	−0.55	−0.49
Japan-call money	−0.05	−0.54	−0.87	−1.01	−0.90	−0.01
EXCHANGE RATES						
D-Mark	19.80	19.90	19.90	18.70	16.20	14.40
Yen	17.50	17.60	17.70	16.90	14.80	13.40
LONG-TERM RATES						
US-gov't bonds	−0.27	−0.80	−1.84	−2.54	−2.17	−1.90
Germany-gov't bonds	−3.19	−0.56	−0.61	−0.59	−0.53	−0.46
Japan-gov't bonds	−0.00	−0.01	−0.01	−0.01	−0.01	−0.01
REAL SPENDING						
US consumption	0.55	1.53	1.56	1.21	0.74	0.42
US investment	4.96	13.30	9.77	9.85	7.45	6.22
German investment	−0.23	0.07	0.87	1.80	2.41	2.39
Japan investment	−0.13	−0.35	0.17	1.19	2.17	2.96
US exports	0.22	2.14	4.15	5.69	6.72	7.24
US imports	0.80	1.43	−0.50	−2.79	−5.43	−6.46
US real GNP	1.02	2.12	1.84	1.25	0.29	0.05
German real GNP	−0.16	−0.25	−0.21	−0.12	−0.03	0.01
Japan real GNP	−0.10	−0.43	−0.40	−0.14	0.18	0.30
PRICES						
US GNP deflator	0.10	1.40	2.48	2.83	2.60	2.06
German GNP deflator	−0.01	−0.52	−0.86	−1.06	−1.12	−1.08
Japan GNP deflator	−0.01	−0.43	−1.03	−1.53	−1.72	−1.61
US import price	1.83	7.49	11.10	13.00	13.50	13.00
US export price	1.03	1.05	1.08	1.14	1.18	1.18
RATIOS TO REAL GNP						
US real nat. saving	0.50	1.54	1.99	2.49	2.76	2.76
US real investment	0.57	1.47	1.47	1.53	1.34	1.06
US real net exports	−0.07	0.07	0.53	0.96	1.42	1.70
RATIO TO GNP						
US net exports	−0.27	−0.56	−0.47	−0.19	0.10	0.25

Table 2–3. Effects of a Reduction in the Trade Deficit by a Simultaneous Reduction in U.S. Gov't Purchases and a Rise in the Money Supply in 6 Other Countries (1982–1986).

The decline in purchases is 3 percent of real GNP and is phased in gradually starting in 1982:1 and ending in 1986:1. The money increase is 8 percent, phased in the same way. Figures are in percent differences from historical values (or percentage point difference for interest rates and prices).

	82:1	*83:1*	*84:1*	*85:1*	*86:1*	*87:1*
SHORT-TERM RATES						
US-Fed. funds	−0.34	−1.28	−1.60	−1.79	−1.82	−1.64
Germany-call money	0.48	0.51	0.70	0.42	−0.33	−0.15
Japan-call money	0.22	−0.08	0.71	0.90	0.12	0.12
EXCHANGE RATES						
D-Mark	12.00	10.90	8.63	6.13	4.03	2.33
Yen	9.42	8.79	6.89	4.20	1.67	−0.42
LONG-TERM RATES						
US-gov't bonds	−0.84	−1.46	−1.70	−1.79	−1.72	−1.60
Germany-gov't bonds	0.34	0.61	0.61	0.21	0.16	−0.25
Japan-gov't bonds	−0.01	0.40	0.80	0.61	0.18	−0.42
REAL SPENDING						
US consumption	−0.04	−0.17	−0.33	−0.49	−0.53	−0.46
US investment	0.04	0.33	0.66	0.94	1.52	2.70
German investment	0.89	4.90	6.61	7.49	6.63	4.02
Japan investment	0.99	5.80	8.31	7.89	5.10	1.84
US exports	0.29	2.73	5.47	7.61	8.90	9.35
US imports	−0.34	−3.19	−5.54	−7.67	−9.35	−9.26
US real GNP	0.05	−0.20	−0.32	−0.64	−0.89	−0.51
German real GNP	0.53	1.76	1.93	1.63	1.05	0.23
Japan real GNP	0.41	1.80	2.09	1.34	0.11	−1.16
PRICES						
US GNP deflator	−0.08	−0.86	−1.91	−2.91	−3.76	−4.38
German GNP deflator	0.10	1.05	2.91	4.80	6.22	7.00
Japan GNP deflator	0.05	1.21	3.73	6.56	8.51	8.91
US import price	0.97	4.03	6.11	7.43	8.12	8.28
US export price	−0.03	−0.60	−1.58	−2.59	−3.49	−4.18
RATIOS TO REAL GNP						
US real nat. saving	0.07	0.69	1.45	2.04	2.61	2.87
US real investment	−0.00	0.07	0.19	0.29	0.46	0.56
US real net exports	0.07	0.62	1.26	1.76	2.15	2.32
RATIO TO GNP						
US net exports	−0.04	0.16	0.34	0.53	0.61	0.52

Table 2–4. Effects of a Reduction in the Trade Deficit by a Simultaneous Reduction in U.S. Gov't Purchases and an Increase in German and Japanese Gov't Purchases 1982–1987.

The decline in U.S. purchases is 3 percent of real GNP. The increase in Germany and Japan is 2 percent of GNP. All are phased in gradually starting in 1982:1 and ending in 1986:1.

	82:1	*83:1*	*84:1*	*85:1*	*86:1*	*87:1*
SHORT-TERM RATES						
US-Fed. funds	−0.30	−1.02	−1.37	−1.63	−1.73	−1.66
Germany-call money	−0.09	−0.24	−0.00	0.25	0.52	0.54
Japan-call money	−0.04	−0.41	−0.37	−0.05	0.42	0.57
EXCHANGE RATES						
D-Mark	19.40	19.00	17.80	16.00	13.60	11.10
Yen	18.60	18.20	17.30	15.90	13.80	11.30
LONG-TERM RATES						
US-gov't bonds	−0.67	−1.22	−1.51	−1.68	−1.69	−1.67
Germany-gov't bonds	−0.20	−0.14	0.11	0.35	0.52	0.53
Japan-gov't bonds	−0.24	−0.37	−0.17	0.20	0.50	0.54
REAL SPENDING						
US consumption	−0.01	−0.09	−0.22	−0.35	−0.36	−0.30
US investment	0.16	0.40	0.67	0.94	1.56	2.80
German investment	−0.16	0.37	0.82	0.80	0.13	−0.58
Japan investment	−0.11	−0.07	0.56	1.19	1.18	0.59
US exports	0.20	2.21	4.80	7.09	8.78	9.69
US imports	−0.49	−4.04	−6.58	−8.58	−9.93	−9.48
US real GNP	0.09	−0.11	−0.19	−0.49	−0.71	−0.32
German real GNP	−0.18	0.05	0.14	0.27	0.44	0.27
Japan real GNP	−0.14	−0.26	−0.04	0.32	0.69	0.25
PRICES						
US GNP deflator	−0.07	−0.68	−1.58	−2.51	−3.37	−4.07
German GNP deflator	0.01	−0.35	−0.29	−0.01	0.33	0.64
Japan GNP deflator	−0.00	−0.36	−0.58	−0.44	0.05	0.59
US import price	1.51	6.10	8.77	10.00	10.20	9.70
US export price	−0.03	−0.47	−1.29	−2.21	−3.09	−3.84
RATIOS TO REAL GNP						
US real nat. saving	0.08	0.72	1.48	2.08	2.65	2.93
US real investment	0.01	0.07	0.16	0.26	0.43	0.54
US real net exports	0.07	0.65	1.32	1.82	2.22	2.39
RATIO TO GNP						
US net exports	−0.09	0.01	0.15	0.37	0.50	0.47

than is reported in these tables. Even though the model is quarterly, only the first quarter of each year from 1982 through 1987 is reported. The variables in the tables are selected because they are key to explaining the behavior of the trade deficit, investment, and consumption. For simplicity, the focus here is on only two other countries, Germany and Japan, in addition to the United States. Figures 2–5 and 2–6 give some plots for the major variables in each quarter for scenario 1. It is apparent from these quarterly charts that the yearly summaries in tables 2–1 through 2–4 are sufficient for assessing the effects on these alternative scenarios.

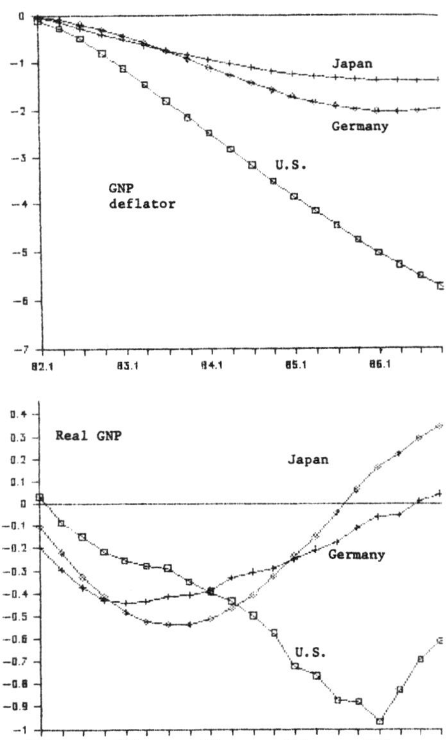

Figure 2–5. Effects on real GNP and GNP deflators in U.S., Germany, and Japan of a reduction in U.S. government purchases (percent deviation from historical value). Simulation corresponds to that reported in table 2–1.

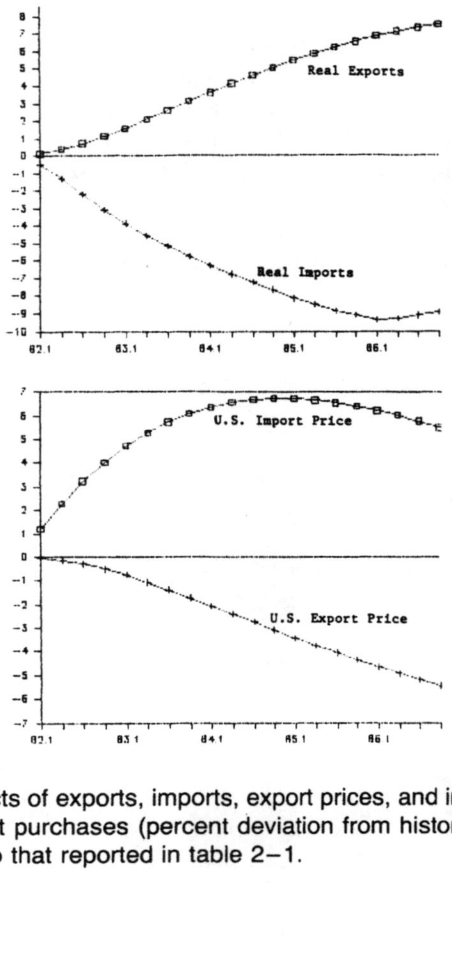

Figure 2–6. Effects of exports, imports, export prices, and import prices of a cut in U.S. government purchases (percent deviation from historical values. Simulation corresponds to that reported in table 2–1.

2.3.1 Theoretical Prediction

What are the theoretical long-run effects of a cut in government purchases equal to 3% of real GNP in a model like this? The model satisfies the natural rate property so that the long-run effects on output should be zero. Hence, the decrease in government purchases should lead to a increase (crowding in) for consumption, investment, and/or net exports (recall that durable consumption depends on interest rates in this model). In the long run, prices and exchange rates will have settled down to a new equilibrium so that real interest rates in all countries must be equal. Thus, the amount by which investment, consumption, and net exports change depends on how much the world real rate of interest declines, on the interest rate elasticities of investment and consumption, and on the elasticities of import and export demand. In theory, real net exports could rise by the full amount of the cut in government expenditures (3% of real GNP), domestic saving could rise by 3% of real GNP (if the interest rate elasticity of consumption was zero) and investment could remain unchanged (if the interest rate elasticity of investment was zero). With high interest rate elasticities there might be a very small increase in net exports. Hence, even in the long run, the theoretical implications are ambiguous. In the short run, where output can change as a result of the spending cut, the results are even more ambiguous.

2.3.2 Simulation Results

Consider first scenario 1, the cut in U.S. government spending with no other changes. Table 2–1 shows how real output and prices fall in the United States relative to their historical values (see also figure 2–5). Note that the government spending multiplier is very small (between 0.3 and 0.5), because the bulk of the spending cut is anticipated due to the fact that it is known to be phased in gradually. In fact, the output effects of a fully unanticipated 3% decrease in government spending would be much larger. In scenario 1, long-term interest rates fall immediately with the start of the budget cuts, and this begins to stimulate investment and consumer durables. Note how long-term rates drop more than short-term rates in the first years of the simulation. This is due to the forward-looking term structure assumptions of the model. In addition, the dollar exchange rate depreciates by a fairly large amount in the first quarter and then appreciates slowly, permitting a differential to exist between U.S. interest rates and foreign interest rates. Prices fall throughout the simulation forcing nominal interest rates to fall and stimulate investment given the unchanged U.S. money supply. Because of the slow adjustment of wages, however, prices do not adjust instantaneously.

Surprisingly, the output effects in Germany and Japan are larger than in the United States in the first few years of the simulation. Again, this is because of the anticipated aspects of the policy change: the exchange rates in Japan and Germany appreciate by a large amount and this reduces exports and increases imports in these countries. Moreover, with the dollar expected to appreciate after the initial fall, interest rates do not fall as much abroad as in the United States. A fully unanticipated increase in government spending in the United States has much larger effects on United States output than on foreign output.

Consider now the effects on the trade deficit and the saving-investment deficit. As shown in table 2–1, by 1987, five years after the start of the cut in government purchases and one year after the cut has reached the new steady level in terms of real GNP, the level of real net exports has risen by 2.1 percentage points as a fraction of real GNP. This improvement in the real trade deficit has resulted in an increase in saving ($Y - C - G$) of 2.9 percentage points and a rise in real investment of 0.8 percentage points. Stated differently, virtually all of the cut in government purchases has generated a rise in saving, and about 3/4 of this rise in saving has been an increase in net exports. In "crowding out" language, the government spending cut has crowded in much more net exports than investment.

Note that the long-run effects of the government spending change have not yet been reached, however. The real lont-term interest rate in the United States is still greater than the real long-term interest rate in Japan and Germany, because the real dollar exchange rate is still appreciating. In real terms, the U.S. long interest rate is about 1.5 percentage points below history and the long yen interest rate is about 0.8 percentage points below history, leaving a differential of about 0.7%. After a further period of time, the U.S. interest rate will rise a bit and the Japanese interest rate will fall a bit, until they reach equality (in terms of deviations from the baseline). This will tend to raise the measured saving rate (as consumption falls), and lower the investment ratio.

2.3.3 The Role of the Exchange Rate

Now consider what happens if this same change in government purchases is matched by an increase in the money supply in the United States, as in scenario 2. The increase in the money supply is approximately the same order of magnitude as the decline in prices in scenario 1. In this case the dollar depreciates much more than in scenario 1—about 20% against the Mark and 18% against the yen. The reason is that the expansionary monetary policy tends to raise prices in the United States, and this requires a depreciation of the dollar.

In this scenario, the increase in net exports in the short run is much smaller than in scenario 1 because the expansionary effects of money on U.S. output increase imports more than the depreciation of the dollar decreases imports. Note that this is an example where a depreciation of the dollar can actually make the trade deficit worse.

Eventually the short-run output effects wear off, however, and the effects on the trade deficit are much like those in scenario 1. (In the very long run the effects should be the same because money is completely neutral in the long run in this model.) It is important to note, however, that there is a large difference in the nominal exchange rate although the change in the real trade deficit is about the same in scenarios 1 and 2. In nominal terms the dollar is about 8% lower in scenario 2 than in scenario 1, but in real terms the dollar is almost identical in the two scenarios. In scenario 1, U.S. prices fell by about 6% and the dollar depreciated by 6% against the D-Mark; in scenario 2, the dollar fell by 14% against the D-Mark and U.S. prices rose by 2%. Since German prices are about the same in both scenarios, the change in the real exchange rate is about the same.

Can we say which of the two scenarios is better on policy grounds? In terms of domestic price stability, scenario 2 is better in that the GNP deflator does not fall as much (note that an even better policy in terms of price stability could be designed). Moreover, in terms of output, scenario 2 seems better. The decline in output is less in Germany and Japan, and there is no output decline in the United States. In terms of nominal exchange rate stability, scenario 2 is worse, however, in that the nominal exchange rate has fluctuated more. However, this fluctuation in the nominal exchange rate has relatively small effects on the economy. This seems to be a case where one would prefer that the nominal exchange rate rather than domestic prices absorb the burden of the adjustment to a higher level of net exports.

Scenario 3 provides another perspective on the role of the exchange rate in the adjustment of net exports, investment, and saving to a change in government expenditures. In this case the foreign central banks (all the non-U.S. G-7 countries) increase their money supplies by 8%, again phased in over a four-year period. In other words, the foreign central banks rather than the Fed provide the expansion to offset the downward pressure on prices caused by the fiscal contraction in the United States. In this case, the longer-term effects on the real U.S. trade deficit are about the same as in scenarios 1 and 2. In this case, however, the nominal dollar exchange rate depreciates by less than in scenario 1. In effect, this type of policy is what would be required to keep the dollar in a target zone during a fiscal contraction. By 1987:1, the adjustment to the improved trade balance has occurred with a smaller fluctuation in nominal exchange rates than in scenario 1 and especially scenario 2. Note that the real exchange rate has moved about the same amount as in scenarios 1 and 2 by 1987:1 (11%). In this case, price level has been less stable in Germany than in scenarios 1 and 2, increasing by 8% rather than falling slightly. There has been more price stability in the United States than in scenario 1 but less price stability than in scenario 2. There is clearly less output stability in the rest of the world in scenario 3 compared with scenarios 1 and 2. Compared to scenario 1, the attempt to keep exchange rates within a narrower band in scenario 3 has led to much less output and price stability abroad. The effects in the U.S. have been rather small.

2.3.4 Fiscal Expansion Abroad

As noted in the introduction, there has been a saving-investment surplus in Germany and Japan during the period that there has been a saving-investment deficit in the United States. Scenario 4 attempts to look at the impact on the U.S. deficit of a fiscal expansion in these two countries of 2% of their real GNP, again phased in gradually, and on top of the contraction in the United States. As is clear in table 2–4, the impact of the fiscal contraction in these two countries on the U.S. trade deficit and the saving-investment deficit is very small. Comparing tables 2–1 and 2–4 shows how a fiscal expansion in Japan and Germany of this magnitude only improves the U.S. trade balance by a few tenths of a percentage point in 1987:1. It is unlikely that the pressure on these governments to expand fiscal policy will have an effect on the U.S. trade deficit, though it does have a significant effect on the trade surplus in those countries (not shown in table 2–4).

2.3.5 Real versus Nominal Net Exports and the Current account

Thus far focus has been entirely on real net exports. Also shown in tables 2–1 through 2–4 are the changes in nominal net exports, as well as the changes in export prices and import prices which are the source of the different between real and current dollar measures of net exports. As is clear in tables 2–1 through 2–4, the change in current dollar net exports (measured as a fraction of nominal GNP) is very small for all the scenarios when compared with real net exports. The reason for this is that for all scenarios, import prices rise more than export prices. As a close approximation, the fall in the ratio of export prices to import prices is about the same for all scenarios, around 11% by 1987:1. The fall in the terms of trade is, of course, what stimulates real net exports, but this same fall offsets this increase when computing current dollar net exports. The offset is made worse in this scenario by the fact that for the historical values imports are much larger than exports.

The fact that current dollar net exports fall much less than real net exports has pessimistic implications for the ability for the United States to make significant inroads into the current account simply by reducing government expenditures. In fact the actual change in the trade deficit since mid-1986 is consistent with this finding. The dollar appreciation has changed import prices by enough that the large decline in real net exports since 1986 has not led to any decline in current dollar net exports (through the second quarter of 1987).

2.3.6 The Saving-Investment Imbalance in Current Dollars

What is the effect of the change in current dollar net exports on current dollar investment and current dollar saving? The answer depends on the behavior of the prices of investment, consumption, and government purchases in comparison with the GNP deflator. The behavior of investment and consumption deflators in response to changes in the exchange rate has been difficult to analyze during the last five years because the change in exchange rates has occurred at the same time that technological change affected the prices of many durable goods. Rather than estimating equations for investment and consumption goods deflators, I provide some simple alternative calculations in table 2–5. The effects of the increase in current dollar net exports are calculated under the assumption that in scenario 1 the government purchases deflator moves along with the GNP deflator and that the investment deflator moves 50% with the GNP deflator and 50% with the import deflator. Changes in the consumption deflator can then be calculated implicitly. These rough calculations are based on the behavior of investment deflators and consumption deflators during the 1982–1986 period. The 50-50 split, for example, corresponds to what happened in the 1982–1986 period when producer durable deflators followed the import deflator essentially 1 to 1, the residential structures deflator followed the GNP deflator, and the nonresidential structures deflator was somewhere in between.

Table 2–5 shows that although the cut in government purchases increases nominal net exports and the current account by only 0.5 percentage points as a percentage of nominal GNP, the ratio of investment to nominal GNP increases by a relatively large amount, 1.7 percentage points. And the domestic saving ratio increases by 2.2 percentage points. In other words, the reason that the cut in government purchases does not

Table 2–5. Investment and Saving Effects in 1987:1 of a Reduction in U.S. Government Purchases[a]

	Actual 1987:1	*Change*	*Predicted 1987:1*
	Billions of Constant 1982 Dollars		
National saving $(Y - C - G)$	536.6	103.8	640.4
Investment (I)	671.8	25.4	697.2
Net exports $(EX - IM)$	−135.2	78.4	−56.8
Gov't purchases (G)	759.6	−113.2	646.4
Real GNP (Y)	3772.2	−21.9	3750.3
RATIOS TO REAL GNP			
National saving $(Y - C - G)/Y$	14.2	2.9	17.1
Investment (I/Y)	17.8	0.8	18.6
Net exports $(EX - IM)/Y$	−3.6	2.1	−1.5
	Billions of Dollars		
National saving	554.4	55.0	609.4
Investment[b]	699.9	26.4	726.3
Net exports	−112.2	26.1	−86.1
Transfers + gov't int.	−35.5	2.5	−33.0
Stat. discrepancy	−2.2	0.0	−2.2
Current account	−147.7	28.6	−119.1
Gov't Purchases*	896.2	−169.6	726.6
GNP	4377.7	−282.7	4095.0
RATIOS TO GNP			
National saving	12.7	2,2	14.9
Investment	16.0	1.7	17.7
Net exports	−2.6	0.5	−2.1
Memo items (billions of dollars):		1987:1	
Government deficit		−129.5	
Transfers to foreigners (net)		12.4	
Interest payments by governments to foreigners		23.1	

Note: National saving in current dollars is identical to the BEA definition of gross saving in the NIPA accounts, and equals investment plus the current account minus the statistical discrepancy.

[a] The spending cut is described in table 2–1.

[b] These projections assume that the investment deflator is unchanged and that the gov't purchases deflator moves with the GNP deflator.

raise nominal net exports by more than a fraction of a percentage point, is not that private saving falls to offset the increase in government saving. To be sure, there is a drop in private saving as consumption prices rise a bit relative to the GNP deflator, but not nearly enough to completely offset the increase in government saving. Instead, investment increases as a share of GNP. The reason for the increase is that investment good prices do not fall as much as the GNP deflator. The depreciation of the dollar raises the relative price of tradables compared to nontradables. In the GNP accounts this means an increase in the price of durable goods relative to the price of nondurable goods and especially the price of services.

It is possible that this deterioration of the terms of trade will reduce real consumption, and thereby increase national saving and the trade deficit more than estimated in these simulations. This possibility is not incorporated in the model. An alternative specification that deflates income by the consumption deflator rather than by the GNP deflator in the consumption equation, and which deflates expected output by the investment deflator rather than by the GNP deflator in the investment equation, would (if the estimated coefficients were similar) imply a smaller increase in both real investmant and real consumption in response to the cut in government spending. Real income by these measures would fall as a result of a real depreciation of the dollar and the deterioration in the terms of trade.

2.4 Robustness of the Results

One of the most striking features of the simulation results is that real net exports improve much more than nominal net exports following a reduction in U.S. government spending. This finding does not appear to be unique to the particular formulation of this model, as is suggested by partial simulation exercises conducted for a Brookings conference in January 1987. Partial simulations of the effects of a depreciation of the dollar on the U.S. trade deficit using the trade sector of six econometric models (DRI, Japanese EPA, Federal Reserve MCM, National Institute for Economic and Social Research GEM, the OECD interlink model, and an earlier version of the model used for the analysis here (TAYLOR)) showed that real net exports improved far more than net exports in current dollars. Averaging over the six models gives a 2.2-percentage point improvement in real net exports as a ratio to real GNP five years after the 20% depreciation of the dollar. On the other hand, the current account improves by only 1.0% on average over the six models for the same depreciation over the same span of time. (See "Workshop on the U.S. Current Account Imbalance: Comparative Tables and Charts," Table II–6, Brookings Discussion Papers in International Economics, no. 58.) By comparison, the full simulation results reported above give a real improvement of about 2 percentage points and a nominal improvement of about about 0.5 percentage point.

All the models with the exception of the EPA model showed substantial improvements in real net exports. The MCM and GEM models show a bigger improvement in nominal net exports than the OECD and DRI models, or the model used here. The difference is not due entirely to different elasticity assumptions. Indeed the fact that these models give similar results on real net exports indicates that the elasticities are not the whole story. Another reason that the MCM and the GEM models give a more optimistic result is that import prices move by only a small amount in response to the depreciation—even in the long run. For the GEM model, import prices increase by only 5% five years after a permanent 20% depreciation; in the MCM model the increase is 12%. On the other hand, for the OECD model, import prices increase by 19% after five years.

There is, of course, an apparent inconsistency in models that show only a small change in the terms of trade for valuation purposes and a large change in relative prices in the real import and export demand equations. Helkie and Hooper [1987, p. 21] discuss this inconsistency and attribute it to lags and to the fact that the price variables in import and export demand equations are different than the terms of trade (the ratio of export to import prices). However, in the long run (five years), the behavior of the terms of trade should be very similar to any reasonable measure of relative price (import price relative to domestic price, as in the model used here, or the real exchange rate, or export prices relative to world prices). Hence, it appears that with conventional empirical estimates of import and export elasticities, and with the assumption that import prices eventually rise by about as much as the depreciation, that nominal net exports should be reduced much less than real net exports, much as in the simulations in tables 2–1 through 2–4.

2.5 Concluding Remarks

Three central conclusions emerge from this analysis of the relationship between the trade deficit and the behavior of investment and saving in the United States during the last five years. All have important implications for exchange rate policy and for prospects for a reduction in the trade deficit during the next several years.

1. A reduction in U.S. government purchases by about 3% of real GNP results in an increase in real net exports as a ratio to real GNP of about 2 percentage points, an increase in the real investment ratio of 0.8 percentage points, and an increase in domestic real saving of about 2.8%. In real terms, the major impact of a cut in government purchases is on net exports, rather than on investment.

2. The same reduction in government purchases affects current dollar net exports and investment in reverse proportions: nominal net exports rise by a very small amount, and nominal investment rises by a large amount. The small effect of a government spending cut on the current account occurs because the investment effect is large, rather than because the savings effect is small. This result is a direct empirical implication of the model used in this study, but it is likely to be true for a wider variety of empirical models with consistent modeling of the terms of trade in valuation effects and substitution effects.

3. The process of adjustment of net exports to a change in government spending requires a change in the terms of trade. In real terms, the exchange rate must eventually fall if the trade deficit is to be reduced. This behavior of the real exchange rate occurs regardless of the nominal exchange rate policy followed by the Fed and other central banks. However, a policy that keeps the exchange rate in target zones requires more domestic price instability in order to achieve the real exchange rate change. In the short run, such a policy also requires more output instability as part of the process of adjustment to a smaller trade deficit.

References

Bryant, Ralph C. and Holtham, Gerald. 1987. "The External Deficit: Why? Where Next? What Remedy?" *The Brooking Review* 5 (2):28–36.

Denison, Edward F. 1981. "International Transactions in Measures of the Nation's Production." *Survey of Current Business* May: 17–28.

Fair, Ray C., and Taylor, John B. 1983. "Solution and Maximum Likelihood Estimation of Dynamic Nonlinear Rational Expectations Models" *Econometrica* 51 (4):1169–1185.

Feldstein, Martin. 1987 "Correcting the Trade Deficit." *Foreign Affairs* 65 (4): 795–806.

Hakkio, Craig S., and Roberts, Richard. 1987. "Has the Dollar Fallen Enough?" *Economic Review*. Federal Reserve Bank of St. Louis, July/August, 24–41.

Hansen, Lars P. 1982. "Large Sample Properties of Generalized Method of Moments Estimators." *Econometrica* 50:1029–1054.

Helkie, William L., and Hooper, Peter. 1978. "The U.S. External Deficit in the 1980s: An Empirical Analysis," Brookings Discussion Papers in International

Economics, Discussion paper no. 56, Brookings Institution, March.
Krugman, Paul R., and Baldwin, Richard. 1987. "The Persistence of the U.S. Trade Deficit," *Brookings Papers on Economic Activity* no. 1: 1–43.
McKinnon, Ronald I., and Ohno, Kenichi. 1986. "Getting the Exchange Rate Right: Insular versus Open Economies." Paper presented at the American Economic Association Meeting, New Orleans, December.

APPENDIX 2A
NOTATION AND DEFINITION OF MODEL VARIABLES

Variable Name Conventions

1. An *L* at the beginning of a variable name indicates the logarithm.
2. The numerical subscript indicates the country:
   - *0* = U.S.
   - *1* = Canada
   - *2* = France
   - *3* = Germany
   - *4* = Italy
   - *5* = Japan
   - *6* = U.K.
3. Lags are indicated by a negative number in parentheses.
4. Leads are indicated by a positive number in parentheses.

Financial Variables

RS Short-term interest rate measured as a fraction, that is .06 is 6 percent [U.S.: Fed Funds; Canada: call money; France: call money;

Germany: call money; Italy: 6-mo T-bills; Japan: call money; U.K.: call money]

RL Long-term interest rate [U.S.: Lt-Gov't; [10-yr. composite); Canada: Lt-Gov't; France: Lt-Gov't guar.; Germany: Lt-Gov't; Italy: Lt-Gov't; Japan: Lt-Gov't; U.K.: Lt-Gov't]

RRL Real interest rate—*RL* less expected growth of GNP deflator over next four quarters (scaled by the trend in income growth)

Ei Exchange rates (U.S. cents per unit of each currency):
- *E1*: Canada/dollar
- *E2*: France/franc
- *E3*: Germany/deutche mark
- *E4*: Italy/lira
- *E5*: Japan/yen
- *E6*: U.K./pound

M Money supply (billions of local currency, *M1* definition)

Real GNP (or GDP) and Spending Components

Billions of local currency units; base years are as follows: U.S.: 1982; Canada: 1981; France: 1970; Germany: 1980; Italy: 1970; Japan: 1980; U.K.: 1980. The output measure is GNP for the U.S., Canada, Germany, and Japan; GDP for France, Italy, and the U.K.

Y Real GNP (or GDP)
C Consumption (total)
CD Durable consumption
CS Services consumption
CN Nondurables consumption
INS Nonresidential structures investment
INE Nonresidential equipment investment
IR Residential investment
II Inventory investment
IF Fixed investment (total)
IN Nonresidential investment (total)
IR Residential investment (total)
EX Exports in income-expenditure identity
IM Imports in income-expenditure identity
G Government purchases of goods and services

Variables Relating to GNP and Its Expenditure Components

YP Permanent income, a geometric distributed lead of *Y* over 8 future quarters with a decay factor of 0.9
YW Weighted foreign output (of other six countries)
YT Trend or potential output
T Time trend ($T = 1$ in 1971.1)
YG Percentage gap between real GNP and trend GNP (defined as $YG = LY - LYT$ and coded as a fraction)

Wage and Price Variable

W average wage rate (U.S. ave. hourly earnings index, adjusted for overtime and interindustry shifts, nonfarm, 1977 = 1; Canada: hourly earnings, manufacturing, 1980 = 1; France: hourly rates, manufacturing, 1980 = 1; Germany: hourly earnings, industry, 1980 = 1; Italy: hourly rates, industry, 1980 = 1; Japan: ave. monthly contractural cash earnings, 1980 = 1; U.K.: ave. monthly earnings, all industries, 1980 = 1)
X "Contract" wage rate (constructed from average wage index)
P GNP (or GDP) deflator (see above GNP for base year)
PIM Import price deflator (see above GNP base year)
PEX Export price deflator (see above GNP base year)
PW Trade weighted foreign price (foreign currency units)
EW Trade weighted exchange rate (foreign currency/domestic currency)
FP Trade-weighted foreign price (domestic currency units)

APPENDIX 2B
LISTING OF THE MODEL EQUATIONS

This appendix shows the functional form of the estimated equations and identities. The numerical values of the estimated coefficients and their statistical properties are shown in appendix 2C. The notation and variable definitions are found in appendix 2A.

Money Demand

$$L(M_i/P_i) = a_{i0} + a_{i1}L[M_i(-1)/P_i(-1)] + a_{i2}RS_i + a_{i3}LY_i \qquad i = 0, 1, \ldots, 6$$

Ex Ante Interest Rate Parity

$$LE_i = LE_i(+1) + 0.25^{\circ}(RS_i - RS) \qquad i = 1, \ldots, 6$$

Term Structure Relations

$$RL_i = b_{i0} + (1 - b_i)/(1 - b_i^9)\sum_{s=1} b_i^s RS_i(+s) \qquad i = 0, 1, \ldots, 6$$

Consumption Demand

Consumption is disaggragated by durables, nondurables, and services in the U.S., Canada, France, Japan, and Italy. Only an aggregate consumption equation is estimated for Germany and Italy. The general form for all the consumption equations is:

$$CX_i = c_{i0} + c_{i1}CX_i(-1) + c_{i2}YP_i + c_{i3}RRL_i$$

where

$$\left.\begin{aligned} CX_i &= CD_i \\ &= CN_i \\ &= \mathrm{CS_i} \end{aligned}\right\} \quad \text{for U.S., Canada, France, Japan, U.K.}$$

$$CX_i = \mathrm{C_i} \quad \text{for Germany and Italy}$$

Fixed Investment Demand

Fixed Investment expenditures are disaggregated into nonresidential equipment, nonresidential structures, and residential structures in the U.S., and into total nonresidential, and residential in France, Japan, and the U.K. Only total aggregate fixed investment is estimated for Canada, Germany, and Italy. The general form for all the fixed investment equations is as follows:

$$IX_i = d_{i0} + d_{i1}IX_i(-1) + d_{i2}YP_i + d_{i3}RRL_i$$

where

$$\left.\begin{aligned} IX_i &= INE_0 \\ &= INS_0 \\ &= IR_0 \end{aligned}\right\} \quad \text{in the U.S. } (i = 0)$$

$$\left.\begin{aligned} IX_i &= IN_i \\ & IR_i \end{aligned}\right\} \quad \text{in France, Japan, and the U.K.}$$

$$IX_i = IF_i \quad \text{in Canada, Germany, and Italy}$$

Inventory Investment

$$II_i = e_{i0} + e_{i1}II_i(-1) + e_{i2}Y_i + e_{i3}Y_i(-1) + e_{i4}RRL_i \qquad i = 0, 1, \ldots, 6$$

Real Exports

$$LEX_i = f_{i0} + f_{i1}LEX_i(-1) + f_{i2}(LPEX_i - LPIM_i) + f_{i3}LYW_i \qquad i = 0, 1, \ldots, 6$$

Real Imports

$$LIM_i = g_{i0} + g_{i1}LIM_i(-1) + g_{i2}(LPIM_i - LP_i) + g_{i3}LY_i \qquad i = 0, 1, \ldots, 6$$

Income-Expenditure Identities

$$\begin{aligned}
Y_0 &= CD_0 + CN_0 + CS_0 + INE_0 + INS_0 + IR_0 + II_0 + G_0 + EX_0 - IM_0 \\
Y_1 &= CD_1 + CN_1 + CS_1 + IF_1 + II_1 + G_1 + EX_1 - IM_1 \\
Y_2 &= CD_2 + CN_2 + CS_2 + IN_2 + IR_2 + II_2 + G_2 + EX_2 - IM_2 \\
Y_3 &= C_3 + IF_3 + II_3 + G_3 + EX_3 - IM_3 \\
Y_4 &= C_4 + IF_4 + II_4 + G_4 + EX_4 - IM_4 \\
Y_5 &= CD_5 + CN_5 + CS_5 + IN_5 + IR_5 + II_5 + G_5 + EX_5 - IM_5 \\
Y_6 &= CD_6 + CN_6 + CS_6 + INE_6 + INS_6 + IR_6 + II_6 + G_6 + EX_6 - IM_6
\end{aligned}$$

Wage Determination

$$\begin{aligned}
LX_i = {} & \pi_{i0}LW_i + \pi_{i1}LW_i(+1) + \pi_{i2}LW_i(+2) + \pi_{i3}LW_i(+3) \\
& + \alpha_i[\pi_{i0}YG_i + \pi_{i1}YG_i(+1) + \pi_{i2}YG_i(+2) + \pi_{i3}YG_i(+3)]
\end{aligned}$$

$i = 0, 1, \ldots, 6$ (π weights vary by quarter in Japan)

Aggregate Wage Identities

$$LW_i = \pi_{i0}LX_i + \pi_{i1}LX_i(-1) + \pi_{i2}LX_i(-2) + \pi_{i3}LX_i(-3)$$

$i = 0, 1, \ldots, 6$ (π-weights vary by quarter in Japan)

Aggregate Price Determination

$$\begin{aligned}
LP_i = {} & h_{i0} + h_{i1}LP_i(-1) + h_{i2}LW_i + h_{i3}LPIM_i(-1) \\
& + h_{i4}YG_i + h_{i5}T + U_{pi} \qquad U_{pi} = \delta_{pi}U_{pi}(-1) + V_{pi}
\end{aligned}$$

$i = 0, 1, \ldots, 6$

Import Price

$$LPIM_i = k_{i0} + k_{i1}LPIM_i(-1) + k_{i2}LFP_i + U_{mi} \qquad U_{mi} = \delta_{mi}U_{mi}(-1) + V_{mi} \qquad =i0,1,\ldots,6$$

Export Price

$$LPEX_i = \beta_{i0} + \beta_{i1}LPEX_i(-1) + \beta_{i2}LP_i + \beta_{i3}LFP_i + \beta_{i4}T + U_{xi}$$
$$U_{xi} = \delta_{xi}U_{xi}(-1) + V_{xi}$$
$$i = 0,1,\ldots,6$$

Weighted Price of Other Six Countries (Foreign Currency Units)

$$\begin{aligned}
LPW_0 &= .09LP_1 + .18LP_2 + .26LP_3 + .12LP_4 + .19LP_5 + .16LP_6\\
LPW_1 &= .27LP_0 + .14LP_2 + .21LP_3 + .10LP_4 + .15LP_5 + .13LP_6\\
LPW_2 &= .29LP_0 + .08LP_1 + .23LP_3 + .11LP_4 + .16LP_5 + .13LP_6\\
LPW_3 &= .31LP_0 + .08LP_1 + .16LP_2 + .12LP_4 + .18LP_5 + .15LP_6\\
LPW_4 &= .27LP_0 + .07LP_1 + .15LP_2 + .22LP_3 + .16LP_5 + .13LP_6\\
LPW_5 &= .29LP_0 + .08LP_1 + .15LP_2 + .23LP_3 + .11LP_4 + .14LP_6\\
LPW_6 &= .28LP_0 + .08LP_1 + .15LP_2 + .22LP_3 + .11LP_4 + .16LP_5
\end{aligned}$$

Weighted Exchange Rate (Foreign Currency/ Domestic Currency)

$$\begin{aligned}
LEW_0 &= -.09LE_1 - .18LE_2 - .26LE_3 - .12LE_4 - .19LE_5 - .16LE_6\\
LEW_1 &= LE_1 - .14LE_2 - .21LE_3 - .10LE_4 - .15LE_5 - .13LE_6\\
LEW_2 &= -.08LE_1 + LE_2 - .23LE_3 - .11LE_4 - .16LE_5 - .13LE_6\\
LEW_3 &= -.08LE_1 - .16LE_2 + LE_3 - .12LE_4 - .18LE_5 - .15LE_6\\
LEW_4 &= -.07LE_1 - .15LE_2 - .22LE_3 + LE_4 - .16LE_5 - .13LE_6\\
LEW_5 &= -.08LE_1 - .15LE_2 - .23LE_3 - .11LE_4 + LE_5 - .14LE_6\\
LEW_6 &= -.08LE_1 - .15LE_2 - .22LE_3 - .11LE_4 - .16LE_5 + LE_6
\end{aligned}$$

Weighted Price of Other Six Countries (Domestic Currency Units)

$$\begin{aligned}
LEP_0 &= LPW_0 - LEW_0\\
LEP_1 &= LPW_1 - LEW_1\\
LEP_2 &= LPW_2 - LEW_2
\end{aligned}$$

$$LEP_3 = LPW_3 - LEW_3$$
$$LEP_4 = LPW_4 - LEW_4$$
$$LEP_5 = LPW_5 - LEW_5$$
$$LEP_6 = LPW_6 - LEW_6$$

Weighted Output of Other Six Countries

$$LYW_0 = .09LY_1 + .18LY_2 + .26LY_3 + .12LY_4 + .19LY_5 + .16LY_6$$
$$LYW_1 = .27LY_0 + .14LY_2 + .21LY_3 + .10LY_4 + .15LY_5 + .13LY_6$$
$$LYW_2 = .29LY_0 + .08LY_1 + .23LY_3 + .11LY_4 + .16LY_5 + .13LY_6$$
$$LYW_3 = .31LY_0 + .08LY_1 + .16LY_2 + .12LY_4 + .18LY_5 + .15LY_6$$
$$LYW_4 = .27LY_0 + .07LY_1 + .15LY_2 + .22LY_3 + .16LY_5 + .13LY_6$$
$$LYW_5 = .29LY_0 + .08LY_1 + .15LY_2 + .23LY_3 + .11LY_4 + .14LY_6$$
$$LYW_6 = .28LY_0 + .08LY_1 + .15LY_2 + .22LY_3 + .11LY_4 + .16LY_5$$

Trend Output Paths

	(annual % growth rate)
$LYT_0 = 7.82 + .00602T$	2.4
$LYT_1 = 5.51 + .00795T$	3.2
$LYT_2 = 6.76 + .00607T$	2.5
$LYT_3 = 7.07 + .00508T$	2.0
$LYT_4 = 11.1 + .00557T$	2.2
$LYT_5 = 12.0 + .01026T$	4.2
$LYT_6 = 5.30 + .00373T$	1.5

APPENDIX 2C
ESTIMATED COEFFICIENTS AND STATISTICAL PROPERTIES

Standard errors are reported in parentheses below estimated coefficients. Unless otherwise stated, a constant was included as an instrument in all equations estimated by 2SLS and GMM. The variables are defined as in appendix 2A and the functional form of the equations are as in appendix 2B. In general the country subscript is omitted from the variables and the equations are listed by country. Other symbols are defined as follows:

SE = standard error of the residual where the residual is computed using the actual right hand side variables.
DW = Durbin Watson Statistics
GMM = Generalized Method of Moment (see Hansen (1982))
AR(1) = First order autoregressive error estimated by Cochrane-Orcutt iterative procedure.
RHO = Estimate first order autoregressive coefficient.

Table 2C–1. Money Demand

Dependent variable: *LMP*
Estimation method: 2*SLS*
Instruments: *LM*(−1), *LM*(−2), *LP*(−1), *LP*(−2), *LY*(−1), *LY*(−2), *RS*(−1), *G*

Country	*Constant*	*LMP(−1)*	*RS*	*LY*	*SE*	*RSQ*	*DW*	*Sample*
U.S.	−0.009	0.953	−0.224	0.040	0.009	0.98	1.6	71.3
	(0.413)	(0.036)	(0.055)	(0.031)				86.4
Canada	0.060	0.937	−0.511	0.033	0.019	0.93	2.1	71.3
	(0.225)	(0.039)	(0.106)	(0.026)				86.3
France	0.671	0.683	−0.316	0.167	0.010	0.87	1.7	78.3
	(0.544)	(0.116)	(0.097)	(0.080)				86.2
Germany	−1.241	0.697	−0.646	(0.403	0.020	0.98	2.5	71.3
	(0.497)	(0.090)	(0.120)	(0.133)				86.3
Italy	0.289	0.895	−0.387	0.077	0.016	0.93	1.2	71.3
	(0.386)	(0.037)	(0.068)	(0.030)				86.3
Japan	1.107	0.750	−0.479	0.139	0.016	0.99	1.8	71.3
	(0.194)	(0.059)	(0.090)	(0.043)				86.3
U.K.	−0.778	0.916	−0.778	0.212	0.020	0.97	1.9	71.3
	(0.662)	(0.034)	(0.173)	(0.116)				86.2

Note: TT (a linear trend starting in 1982:1) is included in the U.S. (0.012) (0.0006)) and U.K. (0.0023, (0.0012)) equations.

Table 2C–2. Term Structure

Dependent variable: *RL*
Estimation method: Nonlinear 2*SLS*
Instruments: *RL*(−1), *RL*(−2), *RS*(−1), *RS*(−2), *LY*(−1), *LY*(−2), *LMP*(−1), *LMP*(−1), *LMP*(−1), *G*

Country	*Constant*	*b*	*SE*	*RSQ*	*DW*	*Sample*
U.S.	−0.005	0.753	0.023	0.47	0.1	71.3
	(0.003)	(0.097)				84.4
Canada	0.011	0.464	0.107	0.78	0.4	71.3
	(0.002)	(0.154)				84.4
France	0.015	0.514	0.014	0.78	0.3	71.3
	(0.002)	(0.087)				84.4
Germany	0.015	0.641	0.018	0.49	0.2	71.3
	(0.002)	(0.084)				84.4
Italy	−0.006	−0.182	0.019	0.82	0.4	71.3
	(0.003)	(0.512)				84.4
Japan	0.004	0.738	0.016	0.37	0.2	71.3
	(0.002)	(0.062)				84.4
U.K.	0.023	0.895	0.029	0.01	0.1	71.3
	(0.004)	(0.133)				84.4

Note: The equation estimated is of the form

$$RL = A + ((1 - b)/(1 - b^{**}9)) \cdot (RS + b \cdot RS(+1) + \cdots + (b^{**}8) \cdot RS(+8))$$

The parameter *b* is set to zero for Italy in the model simulations.

Table 2C–3. Durables Consumption

Dependent variable: *CD*
Estimation method: GMM
Instruments: *CD*(−1), *Y*(−1), *Y*(−2), *RL*(−1), *LP*(−1), *LP*(−2), *YT*(−1), *G*

Country	*Constant*	*CD(−1)*	*YP*	*RRL*	*SE*	*RSQ*	*DW*	*Sample*
U.S.	−45.4	0.698	0.040	−29.3	8.37	0.95	1.8	71.3
	(23.7)	(0.072)	(0.013)	(41.2)				84.4
Canada	−5.79	0.632	0.047	−7.53	0.79	0.97	2.1	71.3
	(1.56)	(0.054)	(0.008)	(2.74)				84.3
France	−41.6	0.344	0.079	−34.5	1.51	0.98	1.4	71.3
	(5.9)	(0.077)	(0.010)	(9.1)				80.4
Japan	−4279	0.356	0.041	−4098	284.80	0.98	1.6	71.3
	(459)	(0.065)	(0.004)	(636)				84.3
U.K.	−10.2	0.516	0.073		1.04	0.72	2.1	71.3
	(3.5)	(0.118)	(0.021)					84.3

Table 2C–4. Nondurables Consumption

Dependent variable: *CN*
Estimation method: GMM
Instruments: *CN*(−1), *Y*(−1), *Y*(−2), *RL*(−1), *LP*(−1), *LP*(−2), *YT*(−1), *G*

Country	*Constant*	*CN(−1)*	*YP*	*RRL*	*SE*	*RSQ*	*DW*	*Sample*
U.S.	63.2	0.508	0.098	−24.8	4.66	0.99	1.4	71.3
	(8.4)	(0.055)	(0.012)	(13.1)				84.4
Canada	3.19	0.899	0.015	−3.27	0.67	0.99	2.2	71.3
	(0.84)	(0.037)	(0.008)	(2.24)				84.3
France	25.09	0.330	0.196		2.45	0.99	2.1	71.3
	(4.66)	(0.091)	(0.028)					80.4
Japan	5180	0.822	0.026		821.50	0.98	2.5	71.3
	(1,019)	(0.043)	(0.007)					84.3
U.K.	3.44	0.666	0.090	−5.00	0.708	0.95	1.9	71.3
	(1.57)	(0.072)	(0.020)	(2.00)				84.3

Table 2C–5. Services Consumption

Dependent variable: *CS*
Estimation method: GMM
Instruments: *CS*(−1), *Y*(−1), *Y*(−2), *RL*(−1), *LP*(−1), *LP*(−2), *YT*(−1), *G*

Country	*Constant*	*CS(−1)*	*YP*	*SE*	*RSQ*	*DW*	*Sample*
U.S.	−24.1	0.906	0.038	4.08	0.99	2.7	71.3
	(4.4)	(0.011)	(0.005)				84.4
Canada	−1.2	0.912	0.026	0.449	0.99	2.2	71.3
	(1.2)	(0.037)	(0.012)				84.3
France	−31.4	0.810	0.076	1.33	0.99	2.8	71.3
	(4.9)	(0.026)	(0.010)				80.4
Japan	−1725	0.692	0.093	809.30	0.99	2.4	71.3
	(524)	(0.072)	(0.020)				84.3
U.K.	−2.8	0.913	0.032	0.433	0.99	1.8	71.3
	(1.0)	(0.027)	(0.008)				84.3

Table 2C–6. Aggregate Consumption

Dependent variable: *C*
Estimation method: GMM
Instruments: $C(-1)$, $Y(-1)$, $Y(-2)$, $RL(-1)$, $LP(-1)$, $LP(-2)$, $YT(-1)$, G

Country	*Constant*	*C(−1)*	*YP*	*RRL*	*SE*	*RSQ*	*DW*	*Sample*
Germany	−34.8	0.733	0.177		9.19	0.98	2.5	71.3
	(14.7)	(0.057)	(0.039)	−95.0				84.3
Italy	−388	0.877	0.085	(41.3)	260.30	0.99	1.1	71.3
	(655)	(0.037)	(0.028)	−1204				84.3
				(609)				

Table 2C–7. Nonresidential Equipment Investment

Dependent variable: *INE*
Estimation method: GMM
Instruments: $INE(-1)$, $INE(-2)$, $Y(-1)$, $Y(-2)$, $RL(-1)$, $LP(-1)$, $LP(-2)$, G

Country	*Constant*	*INE(−1)*	*YP*	*RRL*	*SE*	*RSQ*	*DW*	*Sample*
U.S.	−73.6	0.759	0.043	−98.7	7.05	0.96	1.1	71.3
	(15.3)	(0.052)	(0.007)	(23.6)				84.4

Table 2C–8. Nonresidential Structures Investment

Dependent variable: *INS*
Estimation method: GMM
Instruments: *INS*(−1), *INS*(−2), *Y*(−1), *Y*(−2), *RL*(−1), *LP*(−1), *LP*(−2), *G*

Country	*Constant*	*INS(−1)*	*YP*	*RRL*	*SE*	*RSQ*	*DW*	*Sample*
U.S.	−16.2	0.963	0.007	−25.0	3.72	0.95	1.2	71.3
	(6.8)	−0.026	−0.002	(12.2)				84.4

Table 2C–9. Total Nonresidential Investment

Dependent variable: *IN*
Estimation method: GMM
Instruments: *IN*(−1), *IN*(−2), *Y*(−1), *Y*(−2), *RL*(−1), *LP*(−1), *LP*(−2), *G*

Country	*Constant*	*IN(−1)*	*YP*	*RRL*	*SE*	*RSQ*	*DW*	*Sample*
France	11.9	0.812	0.020		3.10	0.95	1.7	71.3
	(3.6)	(0.045)	(0.007)					84.2
Japan	−4755	0.899	0.041	−13454	538.60	0.99	1.5	71.3
	(454)	(0.046)	(0.007)	(1,060)				84.3
U.K.	1.5	0.726	0.034	−4.0	0.921	0.65	2.1	71.3
	(4.1)	(0.142	(0.012)	(3.3)				84.3

Table 2C–10. Residential Investment

Dependent variable: *IR*
Estimation method: GMM
Instruments: $IR(-1)$, $IR(-2)$, $Y(-1)$, $Y(-2)$, $RL(-1)$, $LP(-1)$, $LP(-2)$, G

Country	*Constant*	*IR(−1)*	*YP*	*RRL*	*SE*	*RSQ*	*DW*	*Sample*
U.S.	−132.0	0.614	0.063	−269.5	9.610	0.87	0.9	71.3
	(32.5)	(0.062)	(0.013)	(62.8)				84.4
France	9.2	0.858		−21.5	0.665	0.98	2.2	71.3
	(1.4)	(0.022)		(2.5)				84.2
Japan	2835	0.823		−2578	733.900	0.72	2.1	71.3
	(590)	(0.038)		(865)				84.3
U.K.	2.4	0.728		−1.33	0.429	0.71	2.0	71.3
	(0.7)	(0.075)		(1.03)				84.3

Table 2C–11. Total Fixed Investment

Dependent variable: *IF*
Estimation method: GMM
Instruments: $IF(-1)$, $IF(-2)$, $Y(-1)$, $Y(-2)$, $RL(-1)$, $LP(-1)$, $LP(-2)$, G

Country	*Constant*	*IF(−1)*	*YP*	*RRL*	*SE*	*RSQ*	*DW*	*Sample*
Canada	−2.9	0.933	0.026	−9.70	1.61	0.98	1.4	71.3
	(2.5)	(0.049)	(0.015)	(5.53)				84.3
Germany	−1.3	0.810	0.049	−213.8	10.40	0.74	2.2	71.3
	(13.4)	(0.038)	(0.016)	(80.4)				84.3
Italy	−1128	0.907	0.030	−3016	299.80	0.89	1.1	71.3
	(820)	(0.029)	(0.012)	(848)				84.3

Table 2C–12. Inventory Investment

Dependent variable: *II*
Estimation method: GMM
Instruments: *II*(−1), *II*(−2), *Y*(−1), *Y*(−2), *RL*(−1), *LP*(−1), *LP*(−2), *G*

Country	*Constant*	*II(−)*	*Y*	*Y(−1)*	*RRL*	*SE*	*RSQ*	*DW*
U.S.	−15.4	0.656	0.207	−0.201	−86.3	17.3	0.59	2.1
	(23.6)	(0.047)	(0.083)	(0.084)	(59.2)			
Canada	−8.4	0.715	0.632	−0.605	−24.3	2.7	0.67	2.2
	(3.3)	(0.043)	(0.107)	(0.104)	(7.6)			
France	−0.7	0.699	0.156	−0.151	−45.0	6.8	0.53	1.8
	(13.2)	(0.099)	(0.195)	(0.187)	(21.5)			
Germany	7.7	0.326	0.178	−0.171	−261	13.5	0.30	1.9
	(19.0)	(0.138)	(0.181)	(0.193)	(156)			
Italy	−3462	0.543	0.561	−0.515	−7751	752.0	0.65	1.9
	(1,089)	(0.147)	(0.191)	(0.200)	(2,309)			
Japan	−1064	0.296	−0.306	0.323	−16349	1270	0.31	1.6
	(1,559)	(0.129)	(0.139)	(0.141)	(4,994)			
U.K.	0.65	0.639	0.034	−0.036	−2.52	2.06	0.45	1.9
	(2.6)	(0.123)	(0.144)	(0.144)	(7.6)			

Note: For Sample periods see *IF* and *IR* tables.

Table 2C–13. Export Demand

Dependent variable: *LEX*
Estimation method: OLSQ

Country	*Constant*	*LEX(−1)*	*LPEXPIM*	*LYW*	*SE*	*RSQ*	*DW*	*Sample*
U.S.	−0.70	0.794	−0.151	0.230	0.034	0.98	1.7	71.2
	(0.63)	(0.094)	(0.129)	(0.125)				86.2
Canada	−6.63	0.581	−0.325	1.015	0.033	0.98	2.0	71.2
	(1.34)	(0.088)	(0.104)	(0.205)				86.2
France	−5.69	0.509	−0.376	0.999	0.016	0.99	1.9	71.2
	(0.91)	(0.071)	(0.071)	(0.154)				86.2
Germany	−2.94	0.532	−0.340	0.684	0.024	0.99	2.0	71.2
	(0.66)	(0.080)	(0.103)	(0.129)				86.2
Italy	−1.79	0.704	−0.080	0.595	0.032	0.98	1.8	71.2
	(0.68)	(0.084)	(0.070)	(0.184)				86.2
Japan	−0.82	0.814	−0.153	0.372	0.029	0.99	1.5	71.2
	(0.72)	(0.043)	(0.039)	(0.139)				86.2
U.K.	−6.12	0.131	−0.370	1.129	0.031	0.96	2.1	71.2
	(0.86)	(0.112)	(0.076)	(0.151)				86.2

Table 2C–14. Import Demand

Dependent variable: *LIM*
Estimation method: OLSQ

Country	*Constant*	*LIM(−1)*	*LPIMP*	*LY*	*SE*	*RSQ*	*DW*	*Sample*
U.S.	−7.00	0.440	−0.216	1.275	0.032	0.98	1.7	71.2
	(0.97)	(0.080)	(0.036)	(0.177)				86.4
Canada	−1.48	0.679	−0.100	0.498	0.032	0.98	1.4	71.2
	(0.46)	(0.076)	(0.075)	(0.134)				86.3
France	−3.16	0.688	−0.148	0.698	0.024	0.99	1.6	71.2
	(0.94)	(0.079)	(0.044)	(0.196)				86.2
Germany	−5.39	0.291		1.325	0.024	0.98	2.2	71.2
	(0.81)	(0.100)		(0.191)				86.3
Italy	−7.57	0.414	−0.190	1.777	0.034	0.98	1.5	71.2
	(1.24)	(0.093)	(0.039)	(0.187)				86.3
Japan	−0.35	0.902	−0.081	0.111	0.032	0.97	1.7	71.2
	(0.32)	(0.059)	(0.026)	(0.051)				86.3
U.K.	−2.14	0.651	−0.061	0.657	0.036	0.94	2.0	71.2
	(0.70)	(0.097)	(0.041)	(0.194)				86.3

Table 2C–15. Estimated Coefficients of Wage Equations[a,b]

	U.S.	*Canada*	*France*	*Germany*	*Italy*	*Japan*[c]	*U.K.*
α	0.0298	0.0541	0.0368	0.0393	0.1084	0.2965	0.0528
	(.015)	(.043)	(.012)	(.025)	(.091)	(.111)	(.031)
$\pi(0)$	0.3270	0.4499	0.5117	0.5024	0.4991		0.5272
$\pi(1)$	0.2744	0.3173	0.2883	0.2892	0.3009		0.2728
$\pi(2)$	0.1993	0.1164	0.1000	0.1042	0.1000		0.1000
$\pi(3)$	0.1993	0.1164	0.1000	0.1042	0.1000		0.1000
% annual	79.7	46.6	40.0	41.7	40.0	87.5	40.0
	(5.2)	(18.2)		(16.6)		(7.0)	
% semi-ann.	15.0	40.2	37.7	37.0	40.2	0.7	34.6
% qtr.	5.3	12.3	22.4	21.3	19.8	11.8	25.4
SE	.0027	.0091	.0083	.0061	.0170	.0160	.0160
DW	1.39	1.9	1.7	2.1	1.9	1.9	1.9
Sample	71.4	76.4	71.4	71.4	71.4	71.4	71.4
	86.4	86.4	86.2	86.3	86.3	86.3	86.3
Target Shift	83.1	82.4	81.3	77.3	82.3	76.3	81.2

[a] All equations were estimated with maximum likelihood. In France, Italy, and the U.K. the number of annual contracts was constrained to equal 40%, which is not significantly different than the unconstrained likelihood for these countries. The target shift is the quarter in which it is assumed that the central banks reduce their "target" for wage inflation.

[b] Initial Conditions:

	US	CA	FR	GE	IT	JA	UK
$X(-1)$	−0.4541	−0.4684	−1.2406	−0.7687	−1.3675	−0.8793	−1.3188
$X(-2)$	−0.4031	−0.3628	−1.2491	−0.5475	−1.6123	−1.1033	−1.3935
$X(-3)$	−0.3821	−0.2811	−1.1870	−0.6528	−1.7719	−1.0157	−1.3128

[c] Japanese estimates of π's by quarter allowing for synchronization:

Quarter:	*I*	*II*	*III*	*IV*
$\pi(0)$	0.1533	0.5414	0.3857	0.2815
$\pi(1)$	0.1633	0.0351	0.4232	0.2675
$\pi(2)$	0.2638	0.1597	0.0314	0.4196
$\pi(3)$	0.4196	0.2638	0.1597	0.0314
% of workers in quarter	3	42	26	16

Table 2C–16. Aggregate Price

Dependent variable: *LP*
Estimation method: AR(1) for all countries except Germany.
OLSQ for Germany.

Country	*Constant*	*LP(−1)*	*LW*	*LPIM(−1)*	*T*	*RHO*	*SE*	*DW*
U.S.	−0.163	0.518	0.455	0.027	−0.016	0.57	0.003	2.1
	(0.039)	(0.098)	(0.091)	(0.007)	(0.007)			
Canada	0.017	0.913	0.009	0.078	−0.003	0.60	0.006	2.3
	(0.003)	(0.106)	(0.072)	(0.034)	(0.072)			
France	0.147	0.862	0.102	0.036	−0.077	0.26	0.006	2.0
	(0.038)	(0.049)	(0.032)	(0.017)	(0.024)			
Germany	0.085	0.848	0.132	0.109	−0.074		0.007	2.5
	(0.045)	(0.078)	(0.063)	(0.015)	(0.030)			
Italy	0.210	0.856	0.111	0.033	−0.086	0.33	0.009	2.0
	(0.072)	(0.064)	(0.042)	(0.022)	(0.042)			
Japan	0.033	0.932	0.053	0.015	−0.046	0.85	0.007	2.3
	(0.019)	(0.069)	(0.053)	(0.016)	(0.053)			
U.K.	0.037	0.752	0.160	0.088	−0.072	0.65	0.010	2.2
	(0.010)	(0.101)	(0.072)	(0.029)	(0.033)			

Notes: 1. For Germany, *LFP*3(−1) replaces *LPIM*3(−1).
2. The *T* coefficients are *E*-02 times those shown.
3. The Sample is 71.2 to 86.3 for all countries save the U.S. (86.4) and France (86.2).
4. RSQ = .99 for all seven countries.

Table 2C–17. Import Price

Dependent variable: *LPIM*
Estimation method: AR(1)

Country	*Constant*	*LPIM(−1)*	*LEP*	*RHO*	*SE*	*RSQ*	*DW*	*Sample*
U.S.	−0.284	0.894	0.106	0.59	0.023	0.99	1.9	71.2
	(0.118)	(0.042)	(0.042)					86.2
Canada	0.050	0.987	0.013	0.51	0.016	0.99	2.1	71.2
	(0.087)	(0.033)	(0.033)					86.2
France	1.243	0.318	0.682	0.99	0.026	0.99	1.9	71.2
	(0.288)	(0.078)	(0.078)					86.2
Germany	0.422	0.820	0.180	0.83	0.020	0.99	2.2	71.2
	(0.160)	(0.069)	(0.069)					86.2
Italy	−1.241	0.581	0.419	0.91	0.027	0.99	1.6	71.2
	(0.268)	(0.088)	(0.088)					86.2
Japan	−1.890	0.454	0.546	0.91	0.040	0.99	1.5	71.2
	(0.364)	(0.106)	(0.106)					86.2
U.K.	1.655	0.553	0.447	0.92	0.021	0.99	1.8	71.2
	(0.204)	(0.055)	(0.055)					86.2

Table 2C–18. Export Price

Dependent variable: *LPEX*
Estimation method: AR(1)

Country	*Constant*	*LPEX(−1)*	*LP*	*LFP*	*T*	*RHO*	*SE*	*DW*
U.S.	0.122	0.566	0.434		−0.265	0.93	0.009	1.8
	(0.050)	(0.098)	(0.098)		(0.104)			
Canada	0.111	0.411	0.589		−0.312	0.92	0.015	2.0
	(0.070)	(0.117)	(0.117)		(0.150)			
France	0.011	0.704	0.296		−0.058	0.62	0.016	2.1
	(0.014)	(0.117)	(0.117)		(0.034)			
Germany	0.170	0.798	0.143	0.059	−0.069	0.82	0.007	1.8
	(0.068)	(0.117)	(0.091)	(0.026)	(0.032)			
Italy	−1.324	0.275	0.277	0.448	−0.273	0.88	0.020	2.0
	(0.351)	(0.267)	(0.161)	(0.107)	(0.133)			
Japan	−0.918	0.287	0.386	0.327	−0.431	0.88	0.015	1.5
	(0.187)	(0.145)	(0.087)	(0.058)	(0.105)			
U.K.	0.798	0.601	0.221	0.178	−0.309	0.94	0.013	1.8
	(0.162)	(0.139)	(0.099)	(0.040)	(0.158)			

Notes: 1. The *T* coefficients are *E*-02 times those shown.
2. The Sample is 71.1 to 86.2 for all countries.
3. RSQ = .99 for all seven countries.

APPENDIX 2D
SUMMARY OF ELASTICITIES

Table 2D–1. Money Demand Elasticities

		Short Run	*Long Run*
U.S.	Income	0.04	0.85
	Interest	−0.22	−4.73
Canada	Income	0.03	0.53
	Interest	−0.51	−8.11
France	Income	0.17	0.53
	Interest	−0.32	−0.99
Germany	Income	0.40	1.33
	Interest	−0.65	−2.13
Italy	Income	0.08	0.73
	Interest	−0.39	−3.67
Japan	Income	0.14	0.55
	Interest	−0.48	−1.91
U.K.	Income	0.21	2.52
	Interest	−0.78	−9.24

Table 2D–2. Export Demand Elasticities

		Short Run	*Long Run*
U.S.	Income	0.23	1.12
	Price	−0.15	−0.73
Canada	Income	1.01	2.42
	Price	−0.32	−0.78
France	Income	1.00	2.03
	Price	−0.38	−0.77
Germany	Income	0.68	1.46
	Price	−0.34	−0.73
Italy	Income	0.59	2.01
	Price	−0.08	−0.27
Japan	Income	0.37	2.00
	Price	−0.15	−0.82
U.K.	Income	0.13	1.30
	Price	−0.37	−0.43

Table 2D–3. Import Demand Elasticities

		Short Run	*Long Run*
U.S.	Income	1.27	2.28
	Price	−0.22	−0.39
Canada	Income	0.50	1.55
	Price	−0.10	−0.31
France	Income	0.70	2.24
	Price	−0.15	−0.47
Germany	Income	1.32	1.87
	Price	0.00	0.00
Italy	Income	1.18	2.01
	Price	−0.19	−0.32
Japan	Income	0.11	1.13
	Price	−0.08	−0.83
U.K.	Income	0.66	1.88
	Price	−0.66	−0.18

Table 2D–4. Marginal Propensity to Consume out of GNP

		Short Run	Long Run
U.S.	*CD*	0.04	0.13
	CN	0.10	0.20
	CS	0.04	0.41
	C	0.18	0.74
Canada	*CD1*	0.05	0.13
	CN1	0.01	0.15
	CS1	0.03	0.30
	C1	0.09	0.57
France	*CD2*	0.08	0.12
	CN2	0.20	0.29
	CS2	0.08	0.40
	C2	0.35	0.81
Germany	*C3*	0.18	0.66
Italy	*C4*	0.08	0.69
Japan	*CD5*	0.04	0.06
	CN5	0.03	0.15
	CS5	0.09	0.30
	C5	0.16	0.51
U.K.	*CD6*	0.07	0.15
	CN6	0.09	0.27
	CS6	0.03	0.36
	C6	0.19	0.78

Table 2D–5. Semi-elasticities of Consumption Demand with respect to the Real Interest Rate

		Short Run	*Long Run*
U.S.	*CD*	−0.12	−0.40
	CN	−0.04	−0.08
	CS	0.00	0.00
	C	−0.03	−0.09
Canada	*CD1*	−0.32	−0.88
	CN1	−0.06	−0.59
	CS1	0.00	0.00
	C1	−0.08	−0.38
France	*CD2*	−0.63	−0.96
	CN2	0.00	0.00
	CS2	0.00	0.00
	C2	−0.06	−0.09
Germany	*C3*	−0.15	−0.55
Italy	*C4*	−0.03	−0.23
Japan	*CD5*	−0.62	−0.96
	CN5	0.00	0.00
	CS5	0.00	0.00
	C5	−0.05	−0.07
U.K.	*CD6*	0.00	0.00
	CN6	−0.08	−0.24
	CS6	0.00	0.00
	C6	−0.04	−0.12

Table 2D–6. Marginal Propensity to Invest out of GNP

		Short Run	*Long Run*
U.S.	*INE*	0.04	0.18
	INS	0.01	0.19
	IR	0.06	0.16
	I	0.11	0.54
Canada	*IF1*	0.03	0.38
France	*IN2*	0.02	0.10
	IR2	0.00	0.00
	I2	0.02	0.10
Germany	*IF3*	0.05	0.26
Italy	*IF4*	0.03	0.33
Japan	*IF5*	0.04	0.40
	IR5	0.00	0.00
	I5	0.04	0.40
U.K.	*IN6*	0.03	0.12
	IR6	0.00	0.00
	I6	0.03	0.12

Table 2D–7. Semi-elasticities of Investment Demand with respect to the Real Interest Rate

		Short Run	*Long Run*
U.S.	*INE*	−0.43	−1.79
	INS	−0.23	−6.24
	IR	−2.10	−5.45
	I	−0.85	−3.83
Canada	*IFI*	−0.18	−2.74
France	*IN2*	0.00	0.00
	IR2	−0.62	−4.33
	I2	−0.12	−0.87
Germany	*IF3*	−0.88	−4.62
Italy	*IF4*	−0.28	−2.96
Japan	*IN5*	−0.44	−4.38
	IR5	0.00	0.00
	I5	−0.35	−3.49
U.K.	*IN6*	−0.13	−0.49
	IR6	0.00	0.00
	I6	−0.11	−0.40

COMMENTARY

by Ray C. Fair

This is a remarkably well-written chapter. Taylor has managed in a relatively short space to provide a clear and nearly complete description of his multicountry model, including many of its properties. I think Taylor is right in his choice of experiments, namely fiscal-policy shocks. In a model like this one should shock exogenous variables and not try to look in some more direct way at endogenous variables like the trade deficit. Whether one trusts the results of the experiments as saying something useful about the real world depends on whether one believes that the model is a reasonable approximation of the truth. Thus the following comments will focus on the model.

My main concern about the modeling exercise is that there are not very many tests of alternative specifications. In Taylor's model future predicted values have a very important effect on current predicted values because he has imposed the assumption of rational expectations on many of the equations. It is not clear, however, from my work at least, that the data support Taylor's type of specification. Consider, for example, the consumption equations, where consumption is a function, among other things, of a geometric distributed *lead* of income over eight future quarters. Is this better than using a geometric distributed *lag*? It is possible to test this specification by simply putting in both the distributed lead and the distributed lag and seeing which dominates in a statistical sense. I have done this type of test for many of the equations in my U.S. model [Fair 1987b], and in general the results are not supportive of the use of leads over lags. Since the policy properties of models can be quite sensitive to the use of leads instead of lags, it seems to me that these kinds of tests should be performed. Other equations in Taylor's model where the tests could be performed are the term-structure equations, the fixed-investment equations, and the wage equations.

The following are a few specific comments on the model:

1. The real interest rate (*RRL*) is constructed by subtracting from the nominal rate (*RL*) the expected growth of the GNP deflator over the next four quarters. The maturity length of *RL* is, however, much longer than four quarters (10 years for the United States), and so there is an inconsistency here. Also, in line with the above comments, it would be of interest to test *RRL* against a real rate constructed from the use of lagged values rather than future values of the growth rate of the GNP deflator.

2. There are no wealth variables in the consumption equations. I have found wealth to be an important explanatory variable in consumption equations for many countries.

3. Import demand is treated differently from consumption demand and investment demand in that the income variable is just current income rather than permanent income. Also, the interest rate is not in the import equation. It is not clear why the specification of the import equation should be different in these respects.

4. There are no trade share equations in the model, which means that Taylor has to estimate equations for exports and the price of imports. Some important constraints are being lost by not using trade share equations. Say, for example, that country 1 primarily imports from country 2 and that there is an increase in country 1's demand for imports. This should result in an increase in exports of country 2, but little change in the exports of the other countries. If trade share equations were being used, this effect would be picked up (assuming that the predicted values from the trade share equations are reasonably accurate), but it is not picked up in Taylor's model. Similarly, a country's import price deflator should be an appropriately weighted average of the other countries' export prices, where the weights could be the trade shares, and this constraint is not met in Taylor's model.

Turning now to the properties of the model, in particular the results reported in table 2–1, Taylor has phasedin the reduction in government

Table 1. Properties of Taylor and Fair Multicountry Models (Figures are in percent difference from historical values.)

		Taylor					*Fair*				
		Decrease in real government purchases phased-in over 20 quarters. Reductions are: .15 percent of GNP for quarter 1, .30 percent of GNP for quarter 2, . . . , 3.0 percent of GNP for quarter 20.					*Decrease in real government purchases equal to 1.0 percent of GNP beginning in the first quarter (not phased-in).*				
		Quarters Ahead					*Quarters Ahead*				
		1	*5*	*9*	*13*	*17*	*1*	*5*	*8*	*12*	*16*
Real GNP	US	.03	−.26	−.39	−.72	−.97	−.97	−1.24	−1.10	−.99	−1.00
	GE	−.20	−.44	−.39	−.25	−.06	−.01	−.14	−.18	−.06	.09
	JA	−.10	−.48	−.51	−.24	.16	−.02	−.09	−.11	−.08	−.05
Exchange Rate	GE	13.10	12.50	11.20	9.61	7.80	.00	.63	.72	.55	.57
	JA	11.10	10.30	9.08	7.85	6.48	.01	.24	.20	.06	−.03
GNP Deflator	US	−.10	−1.12	−2.50	−3.85	−5.02	.04	−.19	−.36	−.53	−.66
	GE	−.02	−.51	−.95	−1.24	−1.37	.00	−.04	−.12	−.20	−.19
	JA	−.01	−.42	−1.10	−1.72	−2.02	.00	−.04	−.10	−.16	−.19

spending over five years. The initial reduction is equal to 0.15% of real GNP, and the final reduction is equal to 3% of real GNP. The reduction is phased-in in equal percentage increments. For most experiments with multicountry models in the literature, there is no phasein. A typical experiment is to reduce government spending by 1% of real GNP for each quarter of the horizon. Nevertheless, one can get a general idea of how the properties of Taylor's model compare to other models. Table 1 compares Taylor's results (table 2–1) with results from the model in Fair [1987a, table 1].

Taylor's experiment is one in which the future policy changes are anticipated as of the beginning quarter. Clearly, qutie different results would be generated from his model if the policy changes each quarter were surprises. Since in the Fair model future predicted values do not affect current predicted values, there is no difference between anticipated and unanticipated policy changes. Thus, the changes from the Fair model can be interpreted as anticipated changes and the results compared to Taylor's results.

The properties of the two models are quite different. Consider real GNP. In Taylor's model German GNP is down .20% in the first quarter and .44% in the fifth quarter. Japanese GNP is down .10% in the first quarter and .48% in the fifth quarter. Remember that U.S. government spending fell only .15% of real GNP in the first quarter and only .75% of real GNP by the fifth quarter. Taylor's results show remarkably large changes in German and Japanese real GNP for the sizes of the U.S. government spending changes. These changes are much larger than the changes for the Fair model, especially considering that there government spending fell by 1% of real GNP from the very beginning. Taylor's large changes are, of course, from the fact that future predicted values have an important effect on current predicted values in the model. This is another example in which the properties of a rational-expectations model can be quite different from those of nonrational-expectations models. The results in table 1 are likewise quite different for the exchange rates and the GNP deflators.

Are the large initial changes that Taylor gets to be trusted? I have my doubts. I doubt that very many people form expectations in the way that Taylor specifies that they do. The large differences between models like Taylor's and Fair's do show the importance of testing the rational-expectations assumption. Until more tests are made, Taylor's results must be interpreted with considerable caution.

Although I have used my space as a critic to be critical, I would like to end on a positive note. Taylor's modeling effort is an impressive piece of work. To be able to combine the rational-expectations assumption into an estimated multicountry model is a remarkable achievement. My critical comments are merely meant to needle John into giving the nonrational-expectations viewpoint more of a chance to emerge from the empirical estimates.

References

Fair, Ray C. 1987a. "Properties of a Multicountry Econometric Model." *Journal of Policy Modeling*, Spring, 83–123.

Fair, Ray C. 1987b. "The Use of Expected Future Variables in Macroeconometric Models." Mimeo.

3 THE IMPACT OF THE U.S. CURRENT ACCOUNT DEFICIT ON OTHER OECD COUNTRIES*

Jeffrey R. Shafer

3.1 Introduction

The emergence of an external current account deficit of the United States on the order of $150 billion is one of the most striking economic developments of the 1980s. When scaled by the size of the U.S. economy, the deficit is not uncommonly large. But given the weight of the United States in OECD output—more than 40%—it is no wonder that a wide range of developments have been ascribed to it. It has been seen as the transmitter of U.S. growth to the rest of the world. And it has been seen as the mechanism through which the savings of the rest of the world have been sucked into the United States. Now, the challenge of reducing it to

* The author is Counsellor for International Economic Policies in the Economics and Statistics Department of the Organisation for Economic Cooperation and Development. He wishes to acknowledge the important contribution of Byron Ballis, who gave advice on the design of the simulation around which the paper is built and implemented it. Derek Blades provided the data reported in the final section; Andrew Dean and Pete Richardson gave helpful comments. The views expressed are those of the author and do not necessarily reflect those of the Organization or the governments of its member countries.

sustainable levels without unhinging the world economy is a preoccupation of policymakers in the United States and in its partner countries. This challenge has taken on greater urgency as the large current account deficit of the United States, together with the large surpluses of Japan and Germany, have become identified as a source of instability in financial markets. Hence it seems important to sort out what effects this deficit has had—on other countries, as well as on the United States. Indeed, those who, like the author, are called upon to provide economic analysis to policymakers are often asked this question. It is not, however, an easy one for an economist to answer. Two aspects make it difficult.

First, the question does not take the form of a testable hypothesis. It calls for an analysis of a unique event—one that has not occurred before and is unlikely to occur again under the same circumstances in the same way. In this respect, it is of a different nature from questions that are clearly recognizable hypotheses—that the demand for money depends on the level of interest rates, for example, or that the imports of a country depend on a particular ratio of foreign prices to domestic prices. The question is more of an historian's question, calling for the counterfactual approach sometimes employed by that discipline. An historian who employs this approach attempts to build a convincing story of why things occurred as they did and not in some other way. The art in doing this involves developing a counterfactual view based on the identification of key events that could plausibly have turned out differently and tracing the implications through a convincing theory of the forces at work and their interrelationships. The goal is not to test or prove the theory, although the reasonableness of the analysis may enhance its standing. Rather it is to convey the meaning of the theory in concrete terms and to draw lessons.

The second difficulty with the question is that the emergence of the U.S. current account deficit, per se, is not acceptable as the key event on which to base the analysis. The current account of a country is the endogenous outcome of interactions within an international economic system. One must dig deeper to find other events which gave rise to it. There are, in principle, an infinity of combinations of more basic events that, had they occurred differently, would have left the U.S. current account in rough balance.

Most people who make statements about the effects of the U.S. deficit are aware of this. They have an implicit view of what exogenous forces lie behind it. These forces may be readily observable (as in the course of government spending and taxes in the United States or other countries), or they may not be (as a decline in the "export mindedness" of U.S. firms). The conclusions about the effects of the deficits depend on these views of driving forces—of what might have been different. It is important to be specific about these assumptions.

Some possibilities are more interesting than others and focusing the analysis on one or a few of them is a matter of judgement, or perhaps one should say, of taste. Plausibility must be the standard—one must be able to accept the possibility that something could reasonably have happened even though it did not, or not happen even though it did. This makes for an interesting analysis because it focuses on possibilities that could arise in a somewhat similar way in the future. Hence, it can provide insights to guide forecasts or policy decisions in the future. But there is no testable sense in which one set of causes can be called the true one and another set false.

The analysis in this chapter is presented in this spirit—no claim is made that it offers a scientific answer to the question of what were the effects of the U.S. current account deficit. It presents a counterfactual history, based on a model of the international economy and driven by plausible assumptions about how key variables might have been different so that the U.S. current account would have remained in rough balance.

Section 3.2 describes the model used in constructing a counterfactual history of the 1980s. Then, section 3.3 describes the key forces that are assumed to have been different and how policies in other countries are assumed to have responded. In section 3.4, the counterfactual history is presented, both in its own terms and as it compares with what acutally occurred. Section 3.5 provides a discussion of the points of tension in the counterfactual history and considers what alternative outcomes might have plausibly occurred. Finally, in Section 3.6, some lessons are suggested concerning likely policy challenges in unwinding the U.S, deficit and the costs and benefits of allowing such events to occur. This discussion draws on some observations concerning the evolution of trade and production patterns that accompanied the emerging U.S. deficit.

3.2 the Analytical Framework—INTERLINK

The model used is INTERLINK, a global model developed over a number of years by the Secretariat of the OECD. This is not the place to give a full description of the structure of this model or of its properties, but a few observations about its structure and historical tracking properties are essential. A number of papers describing the recent development of the model, giving details on its structure and simulation characteristics are listed in the references. Unfortunately, these do not provide a full description of INTERLINK as it stands now. However, papers in preparation and forthcoming in OECD *Economic Studies* and as OECD Department of Economics and Statistics Working Papers will fill this gap shortly.

The INTERLINK system comprises national macroeconomic models for each member country. The models for the major seven countries are more fully developed than those for smaller member countries. The country models incorporate both demand and supply blocks. The former include income-expenditure, monetary, and some wealth-expenditure mechanisms —that is, they are elaborations of the IS-LM approach. Supply blocks are built around production functions with optimizing behavior determining factor demands and, inter alia, price, wage, and output schedules. Behavior in labor markets is described by price-augmented Philips curves, which together with productivity trends generate nonaccelerating inflation rates of unemployment (NAIRUs). Country models are linked internationally by trade and investment income flows, together with determination of world prices for primary commodity groups and rudimentary relationships to determine trade with the rest of the world. INTERLINK also incorporates financial linkages through an exchange rate determination mechanism. These linkages, however, do not give a robust explanation of exchange rate determination—a deficiency that INTERLINK shares with its competitors—and they were suppressed for the purposes of conducting the analysis presented here. A particular important feature of INTERLINK for the present exercise is the care with whch identities, within countries and internationally, have been treated—not always perfectly, but published data do not observe identities perfectly either. These identities extend to relationships between stock changes and flows, as well as those for trade flows and income/expenditure accounts.

INTERLINK, if run hands off, has a mixed record in tracking history, but it seems to capture the broad interactions at work reasonably well. Of particular interest from the standpoint of the present exercise is how well it tracks the development of the U.S. current account deficit, given domestic conditions in the United States and its partner countries. This question has been explored by the author's colleague, Pete Richardson [1987a]. He found that while there are sizeable, persistent errors in components of export and import prices and volumes, these have tended to offset one another so that the predictions for the overall nominal current account are generally good, with essentially zero average errors over the period 1980–1985. The largest single-year error is $19 billion in 1984.

One development of that period which INTERLINK seems to have missed is the extent to which exporters in other countries kept up their dollar prices despite depreciations of their currencies, while expanding the volume of their shipments of nonmanufactures to the United States.

As a result, INTERLINK tends to overpredict U.S. import volume and underpredict import prices by as much as 10–15% during this period. The possibility ought not be excluded that this is at least partly due to an imperfect separation of import value changes into volume and price changes in the published data. The errors on export price and volumes were smaller, but an underprediction of export volumes reinforces the overprediction of import volumes in producing a predicted deterioration of U.S. real net exports even larger than the one that occurred—amounting to about 1/4 of one percent per year of U.S. GNP growth. While this is too large to be dismissed as trivial, it does not invalidate the use of INTERLINK to examine this period. The directions and rough magnitudes of the adjustments in the model coincide with those that occurred. And it should be noted that these are based on trade equations that have not been reestimated over the period under study.

Other models would tell stories that differed in detail from the one told by INTERLINK. But comparisons with other linked models indicate that INTERLINK is in the mainstream. (See Bryant and Holtham [1987].) The judgements made about what underlying forces might have been different, leading to the result of a roughly balanced U.S. current account, are more critical to the articular story that is presented here. These are described and motivated in the next section.

3.3 How a Different Course of the U.S. Economy Might Have Forestalled the Appearance of a Large U.S. Current Account Deficit

3.3.1 Macroeconomic Conditions in the United States and Dollar Exchange Rates

The nature of the question points toward a focus on events within the U.S. economy or those, such as the appreciation of the dollar, that are closely linked to it. One could identify other forces—policies and exogenous developments outside the United States, for example—but one would then be confusing causes and effects. Even focusing on forces emanating from the U.S. economy and from the behavior of dollar exchange rates, one can imagine a number of ways in which things could have evolved differently, so that a large current account deficit might not have emerged. Of course the outcome would still depend on interactions with the rest of the world and not on the United States alone. The approach taken in this paper is to identify four areas where developments in the 1980s diverged from the 1970s, and which have been linked in policy discussions to the emergence of the U.S. current account deficit. These are:

1. The U.S. household savings rate declined from over 7% in the late 1970s to 4% in 1986. In the counterfactual alternative, consumer behavior has been altered by introducing a trend add factor to the historical residuals in the consumption equation so that the household savings rate remains near the earlier level.
2. U.S. government expenditure rose as a share of GNP from less than 30% in the late 1970s to over 35% in 1986. In the counterfactual alternative, real non-wage government spending was lowered so that, if the same GNP had been achieved, the nonwage government spending share of it would not have increased. The endogenous response of other government spending (government wages and transfer payments) to price changes and to cyclical developments was allowed to operate, however.
3. Direct tax receipts fell as a share of household income from 14% in 1981 to 13.5% in 1986, a less dramatic development than often thought. Although it has a relatively small effect on the simulation, this ratio was held at its 1981 level in the counterfactual simulation.
4. The dollar appreciated sharply against foreign currencies—by 50% on an OECD weighted average calculation from 1980 to 1985. In the alternative, it is assumed that the dollar remained much more stable vis-à-vis other currencies over the decade to date. It seemed necessary to implement this assumption by making different assumptions about each currency to produce a realistic alternative pattern of cross rates:
   — The German mark/dollar rate was assumed to remain unchanged from its average 1980 level of 1.82 marks per dollar.
   — The currencies of the EMS partners of Germany were assumed to have followed paths on which their cross rates with the mark were those that occurred. Hence their levels against the dollar are much more stable in the alternative than in real history, but they decline against the dollar to the extent they decline against the mark.
   — The Japanese yen, which had begun declining against the dollar as early as 1979, but fell much less than the EMS currencies after 1980, was assumed in the alternative to have appreciated smoothly from 1980 to 1985 to reach the average level of 179 yen per dollar actually realized in that year. The further appreciation of the yen that took place in 1986 was assumed to have occurred.
   — The U.K. pound, which had a life of its own in this decade, is

assumed in the alternative to have followed an unchanged course against a simple average of the dollar and the EMS bloc.
— The Canadian dollar, which depreciated only moderately against the U.S. dollar over the first half of the decade, is assumed in the alternative to have followed the same path vis-à-vis the currency of its neighbour.
— Assumptions were made about the currencies of small OECD countries that are not members of the EMS according to judgments as to what key currency they are most influenced by. For example, the cross rate of the Swiss franc with the German mark was set according to its historical evolution, similarly for the Australian dollar/U.S. dollar rate.

The net effect of these assumptions is that the dollar appreciates slowly on a nominal effective basis to stand 13% above its 1980 level in 1985 and 14% above in 1986, as compared with the actual effective appreciation of almost 50%, measured from average rates in 1980 to average rates in 1985. The paths of exchange rate assumed for the counterfactual history are shown in table 3–1.

It should be stressed that the alternative produced by these assumed changes in the history of key variables is not an illustration of how the world would have been different if only U.S. policies had been different. Indeed, the assumed differences in U.S. fiscal policy are less important than those in private behavior—with respect to consumption and savings, and with respect to the pricing of currencies in markets.

It is not adequately understood what drove both of these off track in the 1980s. They are both undoubtedly at least partly an endogenous response to other macroeconomic developments—especially real interest rate developments in the case of exchange rates, and the rising valuation of net household assets in the case of saving. These possible effects are either absent or weak in the INTERLINK model and, in any event, would not seem to explain fully what happened. A range of other explanations could be offered for both of these developments—for example, perceptions of the United States as a safe haven for wealth in the first half of the decade and liberalization of capital outflows from Japan, leading to an ensuing adjustment of portfolios, very likely affected exchange rates.

It seems acceptable for the present purposes not to attempt to dig still deeper into fundamental causes—to leave unexplained why these developments occurred, and to refrain from tying the analysis to one explanation as to what might have caused these variables to behave as they

Table 3–1. Counterfactual Exchange Rates

	1978	*1979*	*1980*	*1981*	*1982*	*1983*	*1984*	*1985*	*1986*
United States	103	100	100	100	104	108	110	113	114
(effective, for. curr./dollar 1980 = 100)	(actual)			112	124	131	142	149	124
Japan	209	219	226	200	191	185	179	179	168
(yen/dollar)	(actual)			220	249	238	238	238	168
Germany	2.01	1.83	1.82	1.82	1.82	1.82	1.82	1.82	1.82
(marks/dollar)	(actual)			2.25	2.42	2.55	2.84	2.92	2.16
France	4.51	4.27	4.22	4.37	4.88	5.43	5.59	5.55	5.81
(francs/dollar)	(actual)			5.42	6.56	7.59	8.80	8.93	6.92
United Kingdom	1.92	2.12	2.33	2.26	2.04	1.82	1.71	1.68	1.61
(dollars/pound)	(actual)			2.02	1.75	1.52	1.34	1.29	1.47
Italy	847	833	855	909	1010	1087	1236	1190	1250
(lire/dollar)	(actual)			1130	1351	1515	1754	1923	1493
Canada	1.14	1.17	1.17	1.20	1.23	1.23	1.30	1.37	1.39
(Can. dollars/ U.S. dollar)	(actual)			1.20	1.23	1.23	1.30	1.37	1.39

did. The important point is that shifts in net savings, partly public and partly private, and the strong dollar stand at the center of most accounts as to how the U.S. current account deficit arose. And the spirit of the exercise is to focus on forces emanating from or closely linked to the United States rather than those that could be argued to have come from abroad.

One marked change in the U.S. economy, which occurred at the turn of the decade, was retained in the counterfactual alternative. This is the shift to a monetary policy much more strongly committed to reducing inflation. There are two reasons for retaining this event in the counterfactual history—one a matter of taste, the second a matter of analysis. As for the first, the shift in monetary orientation, although perhaps not its precise timing and intensity, had an aspect of necessity to it as a response that also occurred, albeit with varying degrees of intensity, in most OECD countries as inflation was seen to be running increasingly out of control. It would be unpleasant to contemplate an alternative history of easy monetary policy, with the inflation of the early part of the decade continuing to accelerate. As for the second reason, it would not be convincing to construct such an alternative in a model that was neither estimated nor tested over a period in which inflation in the United States was permitted to surge further upward from the rates of the early years of the decade. The behavioral changes that would have occurred, and indeed were beginning to appear then, very likely would have undermined the structural relationships in the model.

In designing the alternative, an unchanged commitment to an anti-inflationary monetary policy was taken to mean an unchanged path for M-2, given the actual pattern of residuals in the demand function for this aggregate. U.S. interest rates were thus the outcome of simulating the INTERLINK system. It turned out that this meant a slightly higher peak of interest rates in the early part of the decade, as inflation reduction came more slowly in the counterfactual history. By 1984, counterfactual U.S. interest rates are lower than the actual ones as the effects of slower real growth become dominant; and, in the absence of upward pressures on prices from a declining dollar, they are sharply lower by 1986.

The counterfactual assumptions were tested first in an unlinked simulation of the U.S. economy—that is, taking foreign aggregate demand and foreign export prices in domestic currency as given. The result was a current account that oscillated around zero. The swings would have been sizeable compared with earlier periods, but are insubstantial compared with actual experience in the 1980s. Counterfactual assumptions having been found that fall in the range necessary to achieve the required difference in the current account outcome, fine tuning of assumptions and add factors was eschewed and attention is turned to producing a linked counterfactual simulation.

3.3.2 Macroeconomic Policies in the Rest of the World

The model provides considerable flexibility in specifying government spending, tax and monetary conditions. How these might have been different outside the United States under conditions of much higher U.S. savings rates, private and public, and in the absence of upward pressure on the dollar, were among the most difficult questions that had to be addressed in constructing the counterfactual simulation. Choices were made based on the broad policy objectives that governments enunciated during the period—namely, a commitment to reduce inflation and to contain government spending and deficits, which had grown rapidly in the 1970s. These objectives reflected a broad shift in the orientation of economic policies away from short-run fine tuning and toward establishing conditions favorable for growth driven by private demand and more responsive supply.

For fiscal policies, these orientations seemed best reflected by assumptions of unchanged paths of real government spending and unchanged tax structures from those that were actually in place. The thinking behind this government spending assumption was that actual government spending in the first half of the 1980s was governed more by the politically feasible scope for expenditure restraint given by the interplay of interest groups than by short-run macroeconomic conditions. Most governments would have reduced spending from levels that were realized if they could have found palatable ways of doing so, even though economic activity was weak almost everywhere. Similarly for taxes, the motivation behind tax changes that were implemented was more long-run budgetary prospects and microeconomic efficiency than it was short-run macroeconomic.

These fiscal assumptions are not entirely satisfactory for two reasons. First, during the period, there were cases of fiscal action that were motivated by demand management considerations—France after the election of a Socialist government in 1981 is the most notable example. The expansionary course taken there led quickly to an unsustainable external position and to a reversal of course. As will be seen, the external macroeconomic conditions that initially forced the reversal of course in France appear even more compelling in the counterfactual simulation. Moreover, the eventual commitment to budgetary control by the Socialist government, and subsequently maintained by a government of the right, increasingly was founded on the medium-term objectives that were the focus of policy in many other countries.

The second not fully satisfactory feature of the assumption arises because the evolution of government deficits and debt is different in the counterfactual case—deficits are higher in some countries and in some periods, they are lower in others. These features of the counterfactual simulation reflect the effects of different inflation rates on unchanged real government spending and the dependence of tax receipts on both inflation and real income. In some cases, where deficits are higher, economic activity is weaker, and conversely where deficits are lower. It can be argued in these cases that the conflicting structural and macroeconomic considerations support the assumption that real spending and tax systems would not have been substantially different. There are other cases, however, where a weaker economy and a smaller deficit result because of the effects of lower inflation on nominal spending. While there is a stronger argument that the course of fiscal policy would have been different in these instances, the magnitude could not be very large without producing bigger deficits. And external constraints would have inhibited fiscal expansion in many of these cases. It seemed more transparent to identify them, as is done later on, rather than complicate the assumptions in the basic counterfactual alternative.

The objective of reducing inflation was pursued in most countries through the establishment of monetary targets, although other variables were given more-or-less weight in a number of countries as an intermediate target of monetary policy. In particular, various exchange rate objectives have played a role in the monetary policies of Germany's EMS partners, of the United Kingdom, and of Canada.

These general policy orientations were assumed to govern policies in the counterfactual environment. But it proved impossible to deal with monetary policy in a mechanical way. This is due partly to the properties of the INTERLINK model in its current form, and partly to the fact that monetary growth rates were clearly allowed by central banks to deviate from announced targets depending on macroeconomic conditions during the period, thus lending plausibility to the view that they would have been different in an alternative environment.

The first difficulty became apparent from a trial simulation in which the paths of monetary aggregates were kept unchanged. The model produced negative short-term interest rates for some countries, reflecting the fact that in the design of the monetary blocks in INTERLINK little attention has been given to money supply and demand processes at very low interest rates, since, at least until recently, these were remote from modern experience. Interest rates could, of course, not have been negative. Either interest elasticities of the demand for money would have proved much higher at low interest rates than they are in INTERLINK, or central banks would have found it difficult to maintain money growth at the rates achieved. The likely persistence of inflationary expectations, even with a more rapid unwinding of inflation, would have created market pressures tending to hold interest rates well above zero. Indeed, the record of Japan and Germany in late 1986 and early 1987, when inflation was negative and market short-term interest rates remained above 3%, supports the view that interest rates could have been forced below this level only very slowly, if at all.

These considerations governed the redesign of the counterfactual simulation, which was implemented by setting paths for short-term interest rates. This was done not because it was thought that interest rates were, or should have been, the central focus of monetary policymaking, rather this provided a way to deal expediently with an unrealistic feature of the model and to give some weight to the exchange rate considerations that were important in a number of countries. The short-term interest rate paths for Germany and Japan were set to follow roughly those from the unchanged monetary path simulation at the outset, but interest rate declines in these countries were moderated from those paths so that by 1987 they were only 100 basis points below the levels actually reached. The other EMS currencies and the U.K. pound were assigned interest rate paths that roughly maintained the historical pattern of interest differentials for Germany. Canada was assigned an interest rate path to roughly maintain historical differentials vis-à-vis the United States.

The resulting paths for short-term interest rates are shown in table 3–2. Given these and the other assumptions, money stocks in the counterfactual simulation (not shown in the tables) are below actual levels in Germany, France, and Italy; they are higher in Japan, the United Kingdom, and Canada. But they still have the look of money growth paths that are being managed by central banks—that is to say, they neither explode nor collapse.

The pattern of interest differentials imposed in the counterfactual simulation should be evaluated from the standpoint of its consistency with the assumed behavior of exchange rates and the resulting pattern of inflation rates. This issue will be taken up, together with other possible tensions in the counterfactual alternative, following a review of the main features of the alternative.

Table 3–2. Counterfactual short-term interest rates (percent)

	1978	*1979*	*1980*	*1981*	*1982*	*1983*	*1984*	*1985*	*1986*
United States	7.2	10.1	11.4	14.6	12.1	8.8	8.5	6.5	3.8
	(actual)			14.0	10.6	8.6	9.5	7.5	6.0
Japan	4.4	5.9	10.9	5.4	3.9	3.4	3.1	3.5	2.8
	(actual)			7.4	6.9	6.4	6.1	6.9	4.8
Germany	3.7	6.7	9.5	10.1	5.9	2.8	3.0	2.4	2.6
	(actual)			12.1	8.9	5.8	6.0	5.4	4.6
France	8.0	9.0	11.8	13.3	11.9	9.5	7.7	6.9	5.7
	(actual)			15.3	14.9	12.5	11.7	9.9	7.7
United Kingdom	8.6	13.1	15.0	11.0	8.4	6.6	5.3	8.6	8.3
	(actual)			13.0	11.4	9.6	9.3	11.6	10.3
Italy	11.5	11.9	17.1	17.3	16.9	15.3	13.3	12.3	11.4
	(actual)			19.3	19.9	18.3	17.3	15.3	13.4
Canada	8.8	12.1	13.2	17.8	12.7	9.5	10.2	8.6	7.2
	(actual)			18.3	14.2	9.5	11.2	9.6	9.2

3.4 The Counterfactual Alternative

Tables 3–3 to 3–6 present the counterfactual evolution of inflation, output, unemployment, and current account balances over the period 1978–1986 produced by INTERLINK, given the assumptions described in the previous section. The counterfactual diverges from the actual history beginning in 1981. It is interesting to get the flavor of how this counterfactual history might have been summarized in 1987 as if it had occurred, and without reference to history as we know it to have been. Since actual events are reflected in the counterfactual simulation where paths of exogenous variables and error terms have been left unchanged, they figure in the story. In broad terms, this counterfactual history might have been recounted as follows.

Following the second oil shock in 1979, governments of the OECD adopted a non-accommodating monetary stance, with greater commitment to monetary targets. Interest rates rose sharply, and substantially positive real interest rates became the norm after a protracted period of low or negative real rates. Inflation began to recede after peaking in 1980, but not without a slowing of the pace of output growth and outright recessions in a number of countries over the course of 1980–1983. The sharpest contractions occurred in the United Kingdom (1980–1981), the United States (1982–1983), and Canada (1982). Weak demand and the collapse of commodity prices that accompanied it, following several years of high nominal and real interest rates, precipitated a breakdown of private financial flows to developing countries in 1982 and a subsequent sharp import contraction by them. Although recovery in the OECD area got underway in 1983, it has remained weak throughout the 1980s to date. Unemployment has continued to rise in Europe and has fallen only marginally from peak levels in North America. Governments sought to contain government spending and budget deficits, which had ratcheted upwards over the 1970s, but made little or no headway given the weakness of economic activity. The tighter fiscal discipline, and the financial difficulties of developing countries, contributed to the continuing weakness in demand growth. But what has been striking is the failure of a stronger pace of recovery to appear, even in countries where inflation is low and where interest rates are at the lowest levels experienced in the postwar period.

Governments have recognized the need to improve the microeconomic functioning of their economies—to enhance the flexibility of labor markets and give greater play to market forces more generally. There was some progress made on this front, but in some countries subsidies to and protection of agriculture and declining industries have mounted. Reforms

Table 3–3. Counterfactual Inflation (Private consumption deflator, percent change)

	1978	1979	1980	1981	1982	1983	1984	1985	1986
United States	7.2	9.2	10.8	10.0	8.6	5.0	3.5	3.6	−0.8
Japan	4.5	3.6	7.1	4.4	1.3	0.5	2.1	1.2	0.7
Germany	2.8	3.9	5.8	4.0	2.0	0.4	−1.8	−3.3	−1.8
France	9.1	10.8	13.3	11.3	8.4	6.9	4.1	1.2	0.5
United Kingdom	9.2	13.5	16.3	11.1	8.2	5.6	5.2	3.9	3.7
Italy	12.9	15.0	20.3	14.1	11.1	10.3	6.3	5.2	8.7
Canada	7.6	8.5	10.0	12.0	12.5	8.8	6.9	6.5	3.3

Table 3–4. Counterfactual GNP/GDP growth rates (percent)

	1978	1979	1980	1981	1982	1983	1984	1985	1986
United States	5.3	2.5	−0.2	3.1	−3.1	−0.7	5.5	2.4	0.6
Japan	5.2	5.3	4.3	4.2	3.3	2.9	4.2	3.7	2.3
Germany	3.3	4.0	1.5	0.5	−0.3	0.7	1.3	1.5	1.4
France	3.4	3.2	1.6	1.4	2.6	0.3	0.9	0.8	1.6
United Kingdom	3.5	2.7	−2.4	−0.9	2.5	3.6	2.6	3.1	1.6
Italy	2.7	4.9	3.9	1.2	1.6	1.6	3.6	3.4	3.0
Canada	4.5	3.5	1.0	3.8	−2.5	2.7	5.0	3.6	1.3

Table 3–5. Counterfactual Unemployment Rates (percent)

	1978	*1979*	*1980*	*1981*	*1982*	*1983*	*1984*	*1985*	*1986*
United States	6.1	5.8	7.2	7.1	9.1	10.8	9.4	8.8	9.4
Japan	2.2	2.1	2.0	2.2	2.3	2.7	2.7	2.7	2.8
Germany	3.7	3.3	3.3	4.4	6.2	7.7	8.1	8.8	9.4
France	5.4	6.0	6.4	7.6	8.2	8.6	10.2	10.8	11.5
United Kingdom	5.1	4.8	6.4	9.5	10.7	10.8	10.8	11.4	12.0
Italy	6.8	7.2	7.1	7.9	8.4	9.0	9.0	8.8	9.5
Canada	8.3	7.4	7.5	7.3	10.1	10.2	11.0	10.4	10.9

Table 3–6. Counterfactual Current Account Balances (billions of dollars)

	1978	*1979*	*1980*	*1981*	*1982*	*1983*	*1984*	*1985*	*1986*
United States	−15	−1	2	−2	11	9	−37	−20	−12
Japan	16	−9	−11	9	8	5	19	29	46
Germany	9	−6	−16	3	7	1	7	8	8
France	8	7	−3	−4	−19	−15	−14	−17	−14
United Kingdom	2	−2	7	16	8	4	−1	−4	−10
Italy	6	5	−10	−9	−12	−7	−15	−22	−17
Canada	−4	−4	−1	2	−7	7	10	7	−4
Major Seven	22	−10	−32	15	−4	4	−31	−19	−3
Four Large European	25	4	−22	6	−16	−17	−23	−35	−33
Small OECD	−10	−19	−37	−30	−10	−15	−13	−21	−31
Total OECD	12	−29	−69	−15	−14	−11	−44	−40	−34
Excl. U.S.A.	27	−28	−71	−13	−25	−20	−7	−20	−22

could not be achieved on a broad enough scale to substantially alter macroeconomic structural relationships in the direction of strengthening the self-equilibrating mechanisms in economies.

Exchange rates were reasonably orderly over the period, with a stable mark/dollar rate and periodic adjustments within the EMS—but these adjustments of European cross rates, which roughly compensated for inflation differentials (falling somewhat short, however, in the case of Italy), were insufficient to avert persistent and ever-growing current account deficits in a number of Germany's EMS partners. Nevertheless, these deficits proved financeable, and the EMS held together despite rising concern in some quarters about its sustainability. The yen appreciated fairly steadily over the period against the dollar and other currencies as a sizeable surplus appeared in the Japanese current account. The Canadian dollar declined steadily as Canadian inflation persistently exceeded U.S. inflation.

In 1987, the major economic policy issues in international meetings would have been:

1. How can growth be induced to proceed at a more rapid pace across the OECD so as to reduce unemployment?
2. Is the European Monetary System sustainable in the face of the large current account imbalances in Europe?
3. Is there a way out of the LDC debt situation?

This counterfactual history shares many common features with history as it was—for example, successful disinflation and disappointing growth in Europe. The United States would have looked less different from Europe in these respects. And the behavior of exchange rates would not pose such great policy challenges or intellectual puzzles—purchasing power parity and current account economic equilibrium theories of exchange rate determination would have continued to hold sway as a rough guide to the medium-term. Tensions across the Atlantic would have been absent, those across the Pacific would have been more muted, and those within Europe would have been more acute. It cannot be described as a better outcome for any region of the world. Indeed, it would have been generally worse in terms of output and employment—most markedly so in the United States. But the buildup of a big external deficit in the largest country would not now be clouding prospects for the future.

The next section provides a closer look at the differences between the counterfactual and actual histories.

3.4.1 Comparing the Counterfactual and Actual Histories

The differences between counterfactual alternative and actual history for key macroeconomic variables are shown in tables 3–7 through 3–16 for the seven largest OECD countries and, where available, for groups including smaller OECD countries and the rest of the world. A brief discussion of the main differences for each variable follows. While the main purpose of this paper is to highlight what might have happened outside the United States, developments in that country are also of interest and are noted.

3.4.1.1 Inflation as Measured by the GNP/GDP Deflator. In the United States, disinflation proceeds more slowly in the counterfactual alternative, mainly because it is not accelerated by a strong dollar exchange rate in the first half of the decade. But with a weaker path for output and in the absence of dollar depreciation in 1985 and 1986, counterfactual inflation falls below actual inflation. By 1986 U.S. prices reach the same level. In Canada, higher inflation in the early part of the period is not offset by lower inflation later and the price level is nearly 10% higher by 1985/1986. The Canadian counterfactual inflation rate, however, is roughly the same as actually recorded by then. Elsewhere, inflation is generally lower—markedly so for EMS members and in some cases negative for a few years. Price levels in these countries are 15 to 20% below their actual level by

Table 3–7. Simtab Table: PGDP Deflator, GDP/GNP at Market Prices (difference in percent of actual)

	81	*82*	*83*	*84*	*85*	*86*
U.S.A.	0.49	2.24	2.72	2.25	1.94	−0.35
Japan	0.10	−0.61	−1.77	−2.01	−2.99	−3.45
Germany	−0.68	−3.30	−5.83	−9.58	−14.72	−17.40
France	−0.44	−2.73	−5.11	−7.71	−11.54	−14.53
U.K.	0.10	−0.38	0.34	1.28	0.03	−0.31
Italy	−1.18	−5.55	−9.53	−13.33	−16.82	−16.62
Canada	0.59	2.12	4.47	7.22	9.91	9.74
Major 7	0.11	0.14	−0.42	1.38	−2.78	−4.54
Small OECD	−0.39	−1.02	−1.61	−2.36	−3.49	−4.68
OECD Total	0.04	−0.03	−0.60	−1.54	−2.90	−4.56
Ex. U.S.A.	−0.27	−1.57	−2.81	−4.02	−6.00	−7.20
North America	0.50	2.23	2.87	2.69	2.65	0.54
OECD Europe	−0.50	−2.29	−3.84	−5.62	−8.16	−9.41
Pacific	0.06	−0.71	−1.98	−2.53	−3.96	−5.03

1986. Thus, the different exchange rate path redistributes inflation across countries and over time. But, on balance, average OECD inflation recedes a little more quickly owing to weaker output and employment.

4.1.2 Total Domestic Demand. In the United States, domestic demand grows substantially more slowly after 1981 and stands almost 10% below actual in 1986. Elsewhere, it generally grows more strongly earlier in the period, but then recedes to a slower pace leaving levels of domestic demand, on average, less than 1% above its historical level in 1986. Italy is notable in achieving a 6½% higher level of domestic demand in 1986. This is one of several aspects of the behavior of the Italian counterfactual history that are idiosyncratic. These will be reviewed together in the plausibility discussion below.

Real government consumption is, by assumption, unchanged except in the United States where it is 8% lower by 1986. But government budget balances as measured by the net lending of the public sector are affected by output, interest rates, and inflation. For the United States, these effects mean that there is not a consistently better budget outcome, despite the assumed fiscal policy change. Most other countries achieve somewhat smaller nominal deficits, but in Germany government deficits are larger in 1985 and 1986.

Consumption is, of course, weaker in the United States owing to

Table 3–8. Simtab Table: TDDV at Total Domestic Demand, Volume (difference in percent of actual)

	81	*82*	*83*	*84*	*85*	*86*
U.S.A.	0.76	−0.82	−5.90	−7.43	−8.36	−9.77
Japan	0.43	1.75	2.59	2.07	1.33	0.45
Germany	1.08	2.71	2.38	1.09	0.56	−0.89
France	0.83	1.74	1.82	1.99	1.57	−0.43
U.K.	0.39	1.90	2.45	2.46	2.82	1.88
Italy	0.79	3.08	4.58	5.33	6.66	6.46
Canada	0.06	0.78	0.65	0.33	0.48	−0.22
Major 7	0.69	0.67	−1.58	−2.61	−3.17	−4.40
Small OECD	−0.08	−0.33	−0.53	−0.77	−1.16	−1.14
OECD Total	0.57	0.52	−1.43	−2.35	−2.88	−3.93
Ex. U.S.A.	0.44	1.43	1.73	1.43	1.21	0.41
North America	0.70	−0.68	−5.35	−6.80	−7.64	−8.99
OECD Europe	0.53	1.52	1.73	1.55	1.50	0.67
Pacific	0.34	1.35	1.97	1.43	0.70	−0.05

Table 3–9. Government Net Lending (change from actual)

	1981	*1982*	*1983*	*1984*	*1985*	*1986*
United States (bill. dollars)	−6	25	10	−6	1	−14
Japan (trill. yen)	0	2	2	2	1	0
Germany (bill. marks)	3	12	13	4	−8	−23
France (bill. francs)	8	27	42	56	60	46
United Kingdom	1	2	5	6	7	6
Italy (trill. lire)	2	10	18	28	38	48
Canada	1	4	4	7	10	10

assumed higher saving and endogenously lower income. The endogenous response of investment to a weaker economy is strong enough to pull its growth down more than the other components of domestic final demand. In other countries several patterns of consumption and investment behavior can be observed. In Italy, both are strong; in Canada and the United Kingdom, investment is strong with consumption only a little stronger in the former and quite weak in the latter; in Japan, both are stronger in the early 1980s and then level off; in Germany and France, greater strength in both gives way to weakness, especially of investment, in the middle of the decade. Perhaps the most important general observation to make about these outcomes is that investment performance is not consistently higher outside the United States in the absence of net U.S. absorption of savings from the rest of the world.

Table 3–10. Business Investment Volume (percent difference from actual)

	1981	*1982*	*1983*	*1984*	*1985*	*1986*
United States	1.54	0.23	−8.03	−8.98	−9.36	−12.66
Japan	0.63	2.67	3.83	3.26	2.29	1.97
Germany	1.02	3.48	1.06	−2.78	−5.62	−8.44
France	2.44	3.64	2.57	1.02	−3.10	−10.61
United Kingdom	1.60	6.70	10.45	11.55	11.99	10.49
Italy	0.63	5.38	9.09	9.68	12.41	12.88
Canada	0.09	0.89	1.99	2.73	3.74	4.31

Table 3–11. Consumption Volume (percent difference from actual)

	1981	*1982*	*1983*	*1984*	*1985*	*1986*
United States	0.44	−0.80	−5.21	−6.97	−7.66	−8.69
Japan	0.30	1.36	2.12	1.54	0.96	0.17
Germany	1.38	2.96	3.16	3.36	3.96	2.48
France	0.61	1.59	2.09	2.52	3.09	2.45
United Kingdom	0.34	1.37	1.72	1.85	2.25	1.33
Italy	0.99	3.21	4.80	6.25	7.79	7.11
Canada	−0.10	−0.33	−0.94	−1.57	−1.98	−1.99

3.4.1.3 Exports of Goods and Services—Volume. U.S. export volume grows somewhat more strongly through 1985 as stronger U.S. price competitiveness in the alternative outweighs greater market weakness. (In several years, however, this means that export volume would merely have declined less than it did, not that it would have risen.) In 1986, without the boost in competitiveness from dollar depreciation and with slower growth abroad, export growth is weaker than in the actual history. However, the level of exports volume is still 6% higher. In Canada, competitive gains are

Table 3–12. SIMTAB Table: *XGSV* at Exports of Goods and Services, Volume, N.A. Basis (difference in percent of actual)

	81	*82*	*83*	*84*	*85*	*86*
U.S.A.	2.66	7.50	8.85	8.59	10.72	6.44
Japan	0.69	−3.40	−8.85	−10.86	−12.55	−12.49
Germany	−0.96	−2.33	−5.50	−7.59	−9.08	−8.99
France	−1.03	−2.96	−5.20	−7.79	−10.19	−9.35
U.K.	0.84	1.41	0.69	−0.74	−2.73	−4.72
Italy	−1.62	−2.54	−2.13	−4.34	−5.71	−4.49
Canada	1.52	1.66	−1.69	−3.18	−4.91	−8.50
Major 7	0.80	1.17	−0.52	−2.18	−3.09	−4.45
Small OECD	−0.08	−0.10	−1.33	−2.84	−4.03	−5.40
OECD Total	0.58	0.85	−0.74	−2.35	−3.34	−4.70
Ex. U.S.A.	−0.11	−1.15	−3.43	−5.30	−6.87	−7.55
North America	2.46	6.41	6.71	6.00	7.08	2.94
OECD Europe	−0.39	−0.92	−2.51	−4.34	−5.89	−6.53
Pacific	0.42	−3.17	−7.95	−9.84	−11.40	−11.23
Non OECD	0.07	0.38	−1.07	−3.32	−4.66	−6.17

Table 3–13. SIMTAB Table: *MGSV* at Imports of Goods and Services, Volume, N.A. Basis (difference in percent of actual)

	81	*82*	*83*	*84*	*85*	*86*
U.S.A.	−0.48	−4.99	−13.11	−17.91	−21.67	−21.73
Japan	0.17	2.77	4.64	2.78	2.32	−0.85
Germany	0.81	2.26	1.84	0.38	−0.27	−1.38
France	1.71	3.94	3.82	3.78	3.20	−0.79
U.K.	0.61	2.88	3.31	2.83	3.59	1.92
Italy	1.86	5.35	7.45	7.95	9.34	8.73
Canada	0.28	−0.18	−2.92	−3.94	−3.93	−4.13
Major 7	0.44	0.49	−2.09	−4.82	−6.19	−7.71
Small OECD	0.43	0.96	0.67	0.29	0.01	−0.99
OECD Total	0.43	0.61	−1.37	−3.54	−4.62	−6.02
Ex. U.S.A.	0.70	2.23	2.32	1.61	1.46	−0.13
North America	−0.33	−4.16	−11.58	−15.65	−18.71	−18.91
OECD Europe	0.81	2.22	2.20	1.69	1.55	0.23
Pacific	0.44	3.06	4.84	3.40	3.27	−0.07
Non OECD	−0.91	−1.01	−1.55	−4.23	−6.01	−5.87

more quickly swamped by weak market growth owing to weaker demand in the United States, its major trading partner. Hence, Canadian export volume falls increasingly below historical levels after 1982. Export volumes elsewhere in the OECD also generally follow lower paths, with Japan experiencing the largest difference owing to the assumed appreciation of the yen and the importance of the U.S. market for Japanese exports. Poorer export performance is not confined to the OECD area other than the United States: non-OECD export volumes are 6% below their historical level in 1986.

3.4.1.4 Imports of Goods and Services—Volume. U.S. and Canadian import volumes follow lower paths in the counterfactual simulation, substantially lower in the United States, as price competitiveness and domestic demand operate in the same direction. Indeed, about three quarters of the net difference in U.S. trade volumes in 1986 appears on the import side. Elsewhere in the OECD, imports are higher through 1984. By 1986 some countries, but not Italy and the United Kingdom (which both have higher levels of domestic demand), have lower imports in the counterfactual simulation. Financing constraints on import growth are even stronger for the non-OECD than in actual history owing to weaker exports. Hence import compression is more draconian in these countries.

3.4.1.5 Real Gross National Product/Domestic Product. GNP/GDP growth for the OECD area averages a little less over the period as a whole in the counterfactual history, standing about 3½% lower in 1986. As one would expect, given the assumptions, U.S. output is reduced the most—over 6% by 1986. For the rest of the OECD, output stands only a little more than 1½% lower in 1986. All of the G-7 countries, including the United States, experience slightly stronger growth in the early part of the period (when the exchange rate and interest rate paths are different, but U.S. total saving has not yet begun to diverge from its historical path). Countries stay ahead of actual history for varying lengths of time, with only Italy registering higher GNP (as well as a higher GNP growth rate) in 1986.

3.4.1.6 Employment. Employment is initially a little stronger and, in most countries, subsequently weaker in the counterfactual simulation, with the U.S. showing the largest employment loss relative to actual history. The United Kingdom and Italy, have higher employment throughout the period. The difference by 1986 is negligible in the former country, however. These employment developments correspond roughly to the evolution of GNPs, but employment is affected by wage and profitability developments, as well as by the path of output.

Table 3–14. SIMTAB Table: *GDPV* at Gross National/Domestic Product at Market Prices, *VO* (difference in percent of actual)

	81	*82*	*83*	*84*	*85*	*86*
U.S.A.	1.12	0.58	−3.53	−4.37	−4.69	−6.44
Japan	0.52	0.73	0.37	−0.48	−1.44	−1.64
Germany	0.53	1.22	0.07	−1.57	−2.52	−3.46
France	0.22	0.26	−0.13	−0.65	−1.50	−2.34
U.K.	0.46	1.51	1.74	1.42	0.99	−0.06
Italy	0.04	1.40	2.53	2.58	3.25	3.46
Canada	0.40	1.24	0.85	0.35	−0.04	−1.78
Major 7	0.75	0.79	−1.32	−2.13	−2.61	−3.78
Small OECD	−0.25	−0.70	−1.24	−1.90	−2.66	−2.79
OECD Total	0.60	0.57	−1.31	−2.10	−2.61	−3.64
Ex. U.S.A.	0.24	0.56	0.23	−0.49	−1.15	−1.66
Nth. America	1.05	0.64	−3.15	−3.97	−4.28	−6.03
OECD Europe	0.18	0.60	0.33	−0.34	−0.88	−1.47
Pacific	0.34	0.30	−0.16	−1.04	−2.03	−2.07

Table 3–15. SIMTAB Table: *ET* at Total Employment (difference in percent of actual)

	81	*82*	*83*	*84*	*85*	*86*
U.S.A.	0.56	0.79	−1.34	−2.14	−1.87	−2.77
Japan	0.10	0.06	0.01	−0.10	−0.30	−0.33
Germany	0.24	0.59	0.60	0.14	−0.57	−1.70
France	0.08	0.07	−0.04	−0.22	−0.55	−1.04
U.K.	0.09	0.39	0.93	0.93	0.53	0.05
Italy	0.05	0.05	0.18	0.32	0.43	0.55
Canada	0.39	1.40	1.12	0.57	0.31	−1.76
Major 7	0.30	0.47	−0.31	−0.73	−0.81	−1.44
Small OECD	−0.01	−0.04	−0.22	−0.48	−0.77	−1.11
OECD Total	0.23	0.37	−0.29	−0.68	−0.80	−1.38
Ex. U.S.A.	0.09	0.18	0.17	−0.02	−0.31	−0.72
North America	0.54	0.85	−1.11	−1.88	−1.67	−2.68
OECD Europe	0.08	0.20	0.25	0.09	−0.21	−0.66
Pacific	0.07	−0.05	−0.19	−0.36	−0.63	−0.70

3.4.1.7 Current Accounts. The U.S. current account is much stronger by design. The Japanese and German current account surpluses are substantially smaller, although a sizeable current account surplus emerges in Japan (about $25 billion in 1985 and $45 billion in 1986) despite the assumed appreciation of the yen. The much weaker current account positions that emerge for Italy (where the effects of weaker price competitiveness and weaker markets are reinforced by stronger domestic demand), France, and the aggregate of the smaller OECD countries, highlight one of the main tensions that appear in the counterfactual history. OECD Europe has a current account deficit in the neighbourhood of $40 billion in 1985 and 1986.

3.5 Could Things Have Worked Out This Way?

Several features of the counterfactual history warrant examination as to their plausibility. They involve questions about both the adequacy of the behavioral relationships embedded in INTERLINK and the policy assumptions imposed. It is fair to ask whether the broad features of the INTERLINK responses are plausible, given the assumptions. The main

Table 3–16. SIMTAB Table: *CBD* Current Balance Dollars (difference in dollars from actual)

	81	*82*	*83*	*84*	*85*	*86*
U.S.A.	−8.56	19.93	55.71	69.32	97.39	128.50
Japan	4.26	1.74	−16.25	−15.95	−19.36	−40.36
Germany	8.34	2.85	−2.75	0.17	−5.10	−27.70
France	0.88	−7.06	−9.79	−13.12	−17.21	−17.77
U.K.	3.26	0.97	−0.72	−3.03	−7.54	−8.87
Italy	−0.39	−6.32	−7.77	−11.87	−17.39	−20.69
Canada	2.74	5.00	5.40	7.78	7.83	1.95
Major 7	10.53	17.11	23.83	33.29	38.62	15.05
Small OECD	0.90	−2.29	−7.11	−11.62	−19.79	−29.05
OECD Total	11.43	14.32	16.72	21.67	18.83	−14.00
Ex. U.S.A.	20.00	−5.11	−38.99	−47.65	−78.56	−142.49
North America	−5.82	24.93	61.11	77.11	105.22	130.45
OECD Europe	13.99	−9.01	−24.27	−33.23	−59.28	−99.46
Pacific	3.26	−1.10	−20.11	−22.21	−27.12	−44.98
Non-OECD	6.13	−1.41	−2.60	6.73	11.87	12.38

focus of this section, however, is on the reasonableness of some of the assumptions when looked at in light of the resulting simulations. Two areas of tension are examined, then three kinds of alternative outcomes are discussed.

3.5.1 Exchange Rates

Given the puzzles thrown up by the actual behavior of dollar exchange rates in this decade, it is difficult to claim that any constellation of exchange rates is more or less plausible for a particular set of values of macroeconomic variables. In some respects, the counterfactual pattern of exchange rates would have been easier to explain; the rough stability of the dollar against the German mark would have been seen against conflicting pressures—much lower inflation in Germany and higher inflation in the United States, on the one hand, and nominal interest rate differentials much more in favor of the dollar on the other hand. If market psychology had somehow been different early in the decade and dollar appreciation had not taken hold, strengthening the disinflation process in the United

States as it did, and if the strong U.S. recovery from the 1982 recession had not occurred, one could perhaps accept the possibility that rather large nominal interest differentials in favor of the U.S. dollar would have been consistent with exchange rate stability.

Similarly, a continuing appreciation of the yen might have been sustainable in a different psychological climate as a Japanese current account surplus emerged. Expectations of such an appreciation would have been qualitatively consistent with the interest differential in favor of the U.S. dollar which appears. Nevertheless, the assumed alternative behavior of dollar exchange rates is not derived from a theory of exchange rate determination and must be taken for what it is—one of the key "what if" elements used to construct the alternative. If this element of the counterfactual simulation is not accepted, one would be forced to more extreme views about how other factors might have evolved, or to the conclusion that at least part of the U.S. current account deficit was inevitable.

The assumed behavior of exchange rates for Germany's largest EMS partners, Italy and France, given the mark/dollar rate, poses more intriguing questions. The interest rates and inflation performance of these countries relative to that of Germany is not markedly different in the alternative, and current account balances are reduced by slightly less in these countries than in Germany. These observations suggest that the historical EMS cross-rates might have been sustainable. But the absolute pattern of current accounts would have looked quite different. Germany would have still registered a surplus, while Italy and France would have developed very large, chronic deficits. The same would have been true for most of the smaller EMS members, for which individual country figures are not shown in the tables. Given the tendency for EMS pressures to emerge when sizeable deficits appear, policies might have had to have been quite different within Europe to have maintained the parities that actually prevailed.

While Italian policies could clearly have been more restrictive, given that Italy is the only country to have consistently higher GNP growth in the counterfactual simulation, France and the smaller EMS participants would have paid a higher price to uphold European currency stability. In an environment of greater stability of the dollar, intra-European stability may well not have been valued as highly as it was when the dollar was subject to wild swings. This consideration suggests also that Germany might not have modified its policy to any great extent in the interests of intra-European exchange rate stability. Might the EMS not have survived or survived only with much larger parity changes in such a world? This possibility needs to be assessed against the background of output and inflation performance.

3.5.2 Output, Inflation, and Macroeconomic Policies

The counterfactual simulation shows weaker output paths for Germany and Japan, while disinflation proceeds more quickly in these countries. Indeed, each country experiences earlier and larger periods of declining prices than actually occurred. Might private domestic demand have been substantially stronger autonomously with the given policies? Might policies in these countries have been much more stimulative?

The experience of 1985–1987 would suggest neither possibility should be considered very likely, although each is of course conceivable (as is the possibility of still weaker domestic demand). Both economies have grown more slowly in this decade than earlier, with Germany experiencing much higher unemployment. At first, this seemed the result of policies to control inflation—made more difficult by weak currencies—and of efforts to reduce budget deficits. But slow growth of domestic demand has persisted after these factors have receded. Both economies have failed to respond strongly to the elimination of inflation. Savings rates have edged up rather than down. In the face of weak growth of demand, investment has not responded strongly to high rates of profit—earlier on export activities, now on production for the domestic market. While there are some indications from very recent developments that this situation could be changing in Japan, the conclusion seems justified that domestic private demand in these countries, and especially in Germany, is not more strongly self-levitational, nor is it more strongly responsive to low money market interest rates and ample liquidity levels than INTERLINK allows for. (In this respect, it should be noted that the household savings rate is $1\frac{1}{2}$ percentage points lower in Japan and $3\frac{1}{2}$ percentage points lower in Germany by 1986 in the counterfactual simulation—there is considerable endogenous crowding-in of private consumption spending in INTERLINK.)

It is also not self-evident that policies would have been more expansionary than assumed, simply because of the different external environment. The real growth and employment developments in the counterfactual history are not so radically different from actual history as to call into question the basic orientations of monetary and fiscal policy assumed to be maintained in constructing the counterfactual history. As noted previously, interest rates are substantially lower through much of the period, reflecting lower inflation. And they fall somewhat below what the central banks and markets seem to view as floors in Germany and Japan. Moreover, they result in interest differentials vis-à-vis the dollar that cast some doubt on the assumed path of exchange rates. Much easier monetary policies in these countries, while the Federal Reserve was pursuing a tight anti-inflationery monetary policy, would very likely have triggered dollar appreciation, at least some shift toward deficit in the U.S. current account, and enough reason to be concerned about inflation in Germany and Japan to deflect the central banks of these countries from such a course. Indeed, this is akin to what actually happened.

As for other countries, the question arises whether the emergence of current account deficits would have forced tighter policies to maintain stable exchange rates. This is a possibility not only for Italy, where the response of private demand to lower inflation is strong and growth is higher, but also for other European countries where output falls below the levels actually achieved. It seems reasonable to believe that this tension in the counterfactual simulation, if it resulted in exchange rate pressures, would have been resolved partly through larger intra-European exchange rate changes and partly through more restrictive policies in countries with large current account deficits. The result would have been still weaker output, although perhaps not markedly so.

In Canada there is tension of a different sort. While the current account is somewhat stronger, the inflation differential with the United States is wider and the current account balance falls back to only $2 billion higher than in actual history by 1986. Under these conditions, greater monetary restraint than allowed for in the counterfactual history might well have been forthcoming. In its absence, the Canadian dollar might have slipped further against the U.S. dollar.

3.5.3 Plausible Alternatives

As noted in the Introduction, in principle, there are an infinite number of alternative sets of assumptions that would have produced a roughly constant U.S. current account. Many of them—such as different ways of distributing the reduction in U.S. absorption between government spending, investment, and private consumption—would matter little for an investigation focused on the rest of the world. This is all the more true because possible links among exchange rates, interest rates outside the United States, and U.S. interest rates were ignored in constructing the counterfactual history. But the mix between assumed different paths for exchange rates and the total size of ex ante U.S. absorption adjustments does affect the rest of the world. And, of course, starting from assumed changes in policies or behavior in the rest of the world would create a different-looking simulation.

The limits of possible outcomes must be imposed judgementally; they are not restricted by the model, except for possible failure of the solution algorithm for some extreme cases. The likelihood of fundamentally different macroeconomic policy responses and spending behavior outside the United States has already been discussed. Three other possibilities warrant reflection.

3.5.3.1 Different Behavior of U.S. Exchange Rate and the U.S. Economy. INTERLINK simulations prepared by colleagues of the author and presented elsewhere, indicate small short-run effects on the U.S. current account from policy changes of a plausible magnitude in other countries, although the simulated effects cumulate over time [Yoshitomi 1986; Dean and Koromzay 1987]. This suggests that it would be impossible to produce a realistic alternative case of a stable U.S. current account without imposing most of the ex ante absorption change in the United States. The reasons for this are the very large apparent elasticity of U.S. imports with respect to U.S. domestic demand, and the weight of the United States in OECD area demand. Moreover, it seems to require that all three key divergences from trend be corrected to eliminate the U.S. deficit. Hence, if more dollar appreciation were allowed, U.S. fiscal policy would have had to be tightened or the private savings rate would have had to increase in order to maintain an unchanged current account.

One possibility of particular interest, given the debate surrounding U.S. policy at the time, involves U.S. saving. Suppose the U.S. personal saving rate had risen over the early 1980s, as predicted at the time by a number of Reagan Administration advisors? U.S. interest rates might have been lower after 1982 than in either the actual or counterfactual history, and U.S. growth might not have been too far below the counterfactual historical path. This would depend on precisely how the Federal Reserve would have responded. The current account could have remained in balance with some appreciation of the dollar (say, owing to safe-haven flows) if growth were lower. As compared with the counterfactual simulation, the other OECD countries would have faced roughly the same net U.S. demand support for their output as in the counterfactual, but somewhat slower disinflation to the extent the dollar appreciated, and therefore monetary policies in these countries might well have been tighter. This would seem to suggest that even weaker growth abroad than in the counterfactual simulation would have resulted.

3.5.3.2 A Different Distribution of Effects Across OECD Countries. The precise pattern of output, inflation, and current account effects on countries other than the United States is the combined result of the specific assumptions made about the patterns of exchange rates and interest rates and of the properties of the individual country models. Neither of these can be assigned as much confidence as the broad behavior of this group of countries. Without an appreciation of the yen, for example, the Japanese current account surplus would have been larger and the deficit of Europe would have been even more disconcerting. The pattern within Europe could easily look quite different—especially the strong performance of Italy. But it seems unlikely that Germany would have failed to emerge in a relatively strong position within Europe—as judged by current account or inflation. Thus, the likelihood of greater tension within the EMS seems robust, although perhaps the countries under pressure will not be easily identified.

3.5.3.3 Structural Change—Endogenous Forces and Policies. A macroeconomic model such as INTERLINK assumes stability of the economic structure when subjected to changes in exogenous variables. The stability of the estimated macroeconomic relationships in such a model is a hotly debated issue in macroeconomics today. Rational-expectations theory predicts that INTERLINK's structure, which does not systematically embody this theory, might be unstable. The problems are especially likely to arise in determining financial prices such as exchange rates which are forward looking. This is one reason why exchange rates have been taken as exogenous in this analysis in the spirit of asking "what if?" When it comes to accounting for broad developments in the real economy, the potential instability of INTERLINK has seemed not to be an overwhelming problem in practice. Alternative models that are more satisfying in their treatment of expectations do not seem to have consistently better out-of-sample tracking or forecasting records. Thus one would seem to need to take on faith the stability of any model that is capable of providing an answer to the question posed. The degree of credence that one places in the counterfactual history is a matter of subjective judgement—history cannot be repeated in order to provide a test.

The possibility of structural change raises policy questions, as well as theoretical ones. It has become increasingly recognized that microeconomic interventions of governments—in labor markets, financial markets, and goods markets—shape the macroeconomic structure and hence have an important bearing on macroeconomic outcomes. It follows that the behavior observed in historical macroeconomic data—price sluggishness, weak responses to changing patterns of demand and relative price changes, and the persistence of high unemployment—should be seen as the macroeconomic reflection of microeconomic conditions. Thus policies to improve macroeconomic outcomes over the medium term extend to microeconomic reform and are not exclusively the domain of macroeconomic policies. Governments have acted in recognition of the possibilities to strengthen economic adjustment mechanisms by reducing regulation, reforming tax systems, and privatizing public corporations. But, at the same time, production subsidies for weak sectors have tended to increase in some countries, as have nontariff trade barriers to international trade. Thus, while there seems to be a trend toward increased flexibility of economies, progress has been uneven.

It has not proved possible to identify very large effects on macroeconomic structural relations of the microeconomic measures governments have taken, although there is some weak evidence of change. Perhaps one should not be surprised that the links between microeconomic policies and macroeconomic structural change are difficult to observe statistically. The effects of individual policy actions may be small and many of them have been quite recent. (See Chan-Lee, Coe, and Prywes [1987] for an examination of this issue in OECD labor markets.) To the extent that microeconomic structures have changed, the net macroeconomic effects are reflected in the error terms of a macroeconomic model. The question is, might these policies have been different and might they have affected coefficients or the error terms in the INTERLINK model if the U.S. current account deficit had not appeared?

The answer one gives to this question will depend on an evaluation of the balance of considerations in the debate over the politics of macroeconomic reform. Many policymakers and commentators have argued that the slow growth and high unemployment of the 1980s have created a poor environment in which to build political support for reform. In this view, the no-better situation in the counterfactual history would have made reform even more glacial and perhaps would have resulted in more recourse to subsidies and protection. As a result, inflation might have been higher and aggregate employment and output lower than in the counterfactual simulation, even if some groups might have managed to do better with greater protection.

Others argue that deep reform will occur only under intense distress. On this view, one might conclude that by the middle of the decade a stronger consensus for change might have emerged. But without the good growth and dazzling job-creating performance of the U.S. economy under a President committed to strengthening the role of markets, would this have been the direction of change that other countries would have moved toward? It seems more likely that the political economic dynamic would have corresponded more closely to that of the 1930s, with the crisis perceived to be one of the failure of capitalism rather than one of the failure of the interventionist state. What actually happened—a combination of moderately disappointing economic performance in Europe, combined with relative good performance in the United States (even though marred by a large current account deficit)—may have created conditions most favorable to addressing the rigidities and distortions that policies have introduced into national economies and the world trading and financial systems. Even with these developments, however, the longer-term outcome in this area is by no means certain. Perception that the current account imbalances and large swings in exchange rates reflect failures of markets, rather than safety valves in an economic system still in need of reform, lie behind mounting pressure to introduce new trade barriers and to reverse the trend toward less regulation of financial markets.

3.6 Some Lessons

The principal ways in which the assumed forces behind the growing U.S. current account deficit shaped world macroeconomic developments in the first half of the 1980s have been identified by comparing actual developments with a counterfactual history. The analysis certainly accords with the view that the emergence of the deficit was a major event in the world economy. It does not, however, lead to the conclusion that it was responsible for the generally poor economic performance over this period in Europe, or that by drawing savings to the United States that it resulted in lower business investment elsewhere. Most countries probably achieved higher levels of output and investment than they otherwise would have. Nor does it suggest that tensions in the international economic arena would have been less, although the lines of conflict might have been different —less focused on the United States, more focused within Europe, and perhaps within each country between those who saw the way to renewed prosperity through control of government spending, government deficits, and microeconomic reform on the one hand, and those who sought expansionary demand policies on the other hand.

The reasons the story comes out this way are important. There are two. First are the forces that shaped actual economic developments.

The major reason that output performance in the OECD area was so poor in the early 1980s would seem to be that policies were directed towards reversing the upward trend of inflation over the previous decade. Two other developments also contributed. (a) In Europe and Japan efforts were made to contain budget deficits that had built up over the previous decade. (b) the debt crisis constrained the import possibilities of the developing countries and compounded the global demand weakness. These features of the history of the 1980s were retained in the counterfactual history.

But the United States took a different budgetary course after 1982 and budget deficits ballooned even though the economy was expanding at a surprisingly strong pace. The appreciation of the dollar allowed this to occur while U.S. inflation continued to recede. Growth was driven, not only by fiscal stimulus, but also by strong consumption demand and an investment recovery sustained by both renewed confidence in future economic growth and a pro-business orientation in Washington. One consequence of this course of developments in the U.S. economy was considerable spillover of demand to other countries—the current account deficit.

The second reason the story comes out as it does is that INTERLINK predicts that stronger domestic demand growth outside the United States would not have fully compensated for the loss of U.S. demand, even though inflation would have receded more quickly, the terms-of-trade would have been more favorable, and interest rates might have been substantially lower. Does this reflect a model structure that is overly pessimistic about the response of consumption and investment to such developments? The author was inclined to this view 18 months ago. But the weak response of private spending outside the United States to the improving terms-of-trade, low inflation, lower interest rates that came in the wake of the decline of the dollar, and lower oil prices lends credence to the behavior embodied in the model. This is not to say that all countries failed to respond, either in the counterfactual simulation or in reality over the past year. But, on average, the pickup in investment and consumption spending has been weak. The weakness of German domestic demand is especially important in both the counterfactual history and in recent events because it has by far the largest current account surplus in Europe. If this is not shrunk through stronger domestic demand growth, a shrinking U.S. deficit in the future and a correspondingly shrinking European surplus is likely to impose external constraints on other European countries, at least some of which might otherwise be able to generate stronger domestic demand growth. The only other way out for these countries would seem to be a substantial revaluation of the German mark against other European countries.

The general conclusion would seem to be that there were deep problems in all of the OECD countries at the outset of the decade. Policies that were pursued exchanged some of those problems (inflation, large government debts in Europe and Japan), for others (high unemployment in Europe, large current account imbalance, and corresponding domestic imbalances between saving and investment). Fundamental solutions have not yet been put in place. The time for doing so may be short, as the October 1987 collapse of stock markets has signaled.

The story of the effects of the large U.S. current account deficit is not complete; how it will unwind is not yet known. This chapter's focus on macroeconomic developments in the first half of the decade has neglected some of the costs of the course that was followed. World patterns of trade and production have been distorted, and these distortions must now be reversed. The U.S. must reclaim lost markets. Others must accept this adjustment. Indeed, if this decade's shortfall in demand growth abroad is not made up, the market share developments of this period will have to be more than reversed.

While favorable changes may occur in commodities and services trade, manufacturing is likely to be where the forces of adjustment operate most strongly. The scale of the adjustment challenge in manufactured trade, which represents three-quarters of U.S. merchandise trade, is indicated by tables 3–17 and 3–18.

Table 3–17 shows the evolution of the G-7 countries' shares of exports in world trade of manufactures. These have declined on average, as nonmember countries have expanded their manufactured exports. They are likely to continue to do so. The United States, along with the United Kingdom, lost market shares most rapidly from 1979 to 1984. Since then both have gained, and the United States has returned to the middle of the standings. Japan continued to gain market share until 1984; its loss in 1986 is likely to have to be followed by many more if a better balance of current accounts is to be achieved. Germany, too, would seem to face market share loss.

A perspective on performance in each countries' own market for manufactures is given in table 3–18, which shows the evolution of ratios of domestic value-added to imports in manufacturing in index form. The

Table 3–17. Manufactured Export Market Shares (1979 = 100)

	1979	*1980*	*1981*	*1982*	*1983*	*1984*	*1985*	*1986*
United States	100	106	97	87	84	83	85	89
Japan	100	111	114	113	117	120	120	114
Germany	100	95	100	102	100	101	104	101
France	100	94	92	91	91	90	87	83
United Kingdom	100	95	85	85	83	83	87	86
Italy	100	91	89	88	92	92	93	92
Canada	100	99	96	93	89	86	85	81

Table 3–18. Index of Ratio of Manufacturing Value Added to Manufactured Imports (1979 = 100)

	1979	*1980*	*1981*	*1982*	*1983*	*1984*	*1985*
United States	100	95	90	84	75	63	60
Japan	100	111	104	110	116	107	115
Germany	100	97	98	98	89	86	86
France	100	90	91	86	89	88	n.a.
United Kingdom	100	92	89	82	75	71	68
Italy	100	92	101	100	102	87	82
Canada	100	103	103	109	100	96	90

general trend is downward, as one would expect so long as there is a trend toward increasing international integration of markets for manufactures. But Japan stands out against this general trend as having become more self-contained as a manufactured goods market. This cannot be ascribed to the emergence of the strong dollar and a large U.S. current account deficit: other countries have also clearly failed to penetrate the Japanese market. The establishment of a trend toward rising imports relative to domestic value-added will have to be a part of the process of reducing the Japanese current account surplus and the U.S. deficit. The United States stands out in this table as having lost domestic markets to imports more rapidly than other countries through 1985. Its producers must now take on the challenge of stemming this erosion and reclaiming a larger share of their domestic markets.

Table 3–19. Value-added Growth in Tradeables and Nontradeables (percent per year)

	1960–1984[a]		*1980–1985*[b]	
	Tradeables	*Nontradeables*	*Tradeables*	*Nontradeables*
United States	3.0	3.5	3.3	3.2
Japan	7.7	8.6	6.8	3.0
Germany	3.5	3.9	0.1	1.8
France	4.8	4.9	1.0	1.5
United Kingdom	1.3	2.4	1.7	3.3
Italy	4.9	4.4	−0.1	1.9
Canada	4.3	5.4	2.9	3.0

[a] 1961–1980 for Canada.
[b] 1980–1984 for Germany and France.

Japan does better than Germany in maintaining output growth in the counterfactual simulation, despite a greater loss of exports. Thus it might have got by better in a world of weak U.S. markets than is often supposed. But its current account surplus, although much reduced, would still have been large enough to be a point of some international tension. This underscores the magnitude of the challenge that lies ahead to achieve a better balance of competitiveness between Japan and others in world markets and in Japanese markets, even with the value of the yen having now risen to the path assumed in the counterfactual history. This surplus seems to have partly reflected trend developments in Japan's export prowess and the absence, at least until this year, of signs that the Japanese economy was becoming more receptive to imports. The developments assumed to have given rise to the U.S. deficit do not seem to have been more than half the story behind Japan's surplus.

If the view developed in this chapter is accepted as reasonable, it leads to a relatively pessimistic view about prospects for strengthening growth and reducing unemployment in Europe while the U.S. current account deficit is declining. There may be room for somewhat more expansionary demand policies if Germany were to take the lead. And it would seem to make sense to use all of the available means to correct unemployment problems that have deepened in Europe year by year. But when one looks at the contribution that larger budget deficits could make without building up future problems, it looks small in comparison with the need. So too does the contribution that could be expected from monetary policy, given the resistance levels that seem to appear in the market for mark bonds as money market conditions are eased.

One can hope that economies will begin to show more dynamic growth than INTERLINK would predict or than has been apparent thus far in this decade. But action is needed to improve the structural functioning of economies and brighten the prospects for such a development. Greater flexibility and better incentives in labor markets, more competitive and less insulated markets for goods and services, and more active capital markets could all strengthen the self-equilibrating mechanisms that seem weak when seen from a macroeconomic vantage point. Progress on all of these fronts could strengthen opportunities and incentives to work, impel firms to invest if they are to remain profitable, and put a richer and more enticing array of consumer goods and services in the marketplace. Governments have subscribed to the need for such action. But resistance of those in favored positions is great and progress has been halting. If the pace were accelerated, the structure of models such as INTERLINK, which point to chronic weak growth without unsustainable stimulus from exports or fiscal deficits, would become invalid. The future need not be as bleak as the past was, or might have been.

A third indicator of what structural changes might have accompanied the growth of the U.S. current account deficit reveals surprisingly little evidence of such changes. This is the relative growth of tradeable and nontradeable value-added in major countries, shown in table 3–19. Tradeables are defined here as goods less construction; nontradeables are market services plus construction. Nonmarket government services are excluded. The table shows no general skewing of relative growth rates in the 1980–1984 period as compared with the 20 previous years. Only for Japan, where nontradeable growth slowed down much more than tradeable growth, is there a strong correlation with current account developments. These observations are based on a disaggregation that is too crude to permit firm conclusions. But it seems possible that the shifts in market shares in international manufactures trade, while large in relationship to that trade, do not loom so large in the context of overall production patterns, especially as differential market growth has also accounted for much of what has happened to current accounts. Thus, for example, the United States has lost market share in its own market for manufactures, but it has had a relatively rapidly growing market since 1980.

Taken together, these indicators suggest that the main challenge of the future with respect to the evolution of trade and production patterns will be to reverse the relative market share developments in the early part of the decade. Productive capacity will need to evolve in line with these requirements. But adjustment may not require that past investments in productive capacity be abandoned in tradeables good sectors outside the United States if growth in the OECD area can be sustained.

References

Bryant, Ralph C., and Holtham, Gerald. 1987. "The U.S. External Deficit: Diagnosis, Prognosis, and Cure." *Brookings Discussion Papers in International Economics*, no. 55, March.

Chan-Lee, James H.; Coe; David T.; and Prywes, Menahem. 1987. "Microeconomic Changes and Macroeconomic Wage Disinflation in the 1980s." *OECD Economic Studies*, no. 8, Spring, pp. 121–157.

Dean, Andrew, and Koromzay, Val. 1987. "Current Account Imbalances and Adjustment Mechanisms." *OECD Economic Studies*, no. 8, Spring, pp. 7–34.

Richardson, Pete. 1987a. "Tracking the U.S. External Deficit 1980–1985: Experience with the OECD INTERLINK Model." OECD Economics and Statistics Department Working Paper, no. 38, February.

Richardson, Pete. 1987b. "Recent Developments in OECD's International Macroeconomic Model." OECD Economics and Statistics Department Working Paper, no. 46, June.

Richardson, Pete. 1987c. "A Review of the Simulation Properties of OECD's INTERLINK Model." OECD Economics and Statistics Department Working Paper, no. 47, July.

Richardson, Pete, 1988. "The Structure and Simulation Properties of OECD's INTERLINK Model." *OECD Economic Studies*, no. 10, Spring.

Yoshitomi, Masaru. 1986. "Growth Gaps, Exchange Rates and Asymmetry." Paper presented to a Conference on Exchange Rates, Macroeconomic Policies and Financial Market Innovations in New York, June 4–5, 1987.

COMMENTARY

by Richard D. Haas

I liked Shafer's chapter for several reasons, not the least of which is that it is, in my opinion, a good example of how to properly use a macroeconometric simulation model. All too often, models are forced to answer questions they are not well designed to answer, in particular forecasting questions. Counterfactual policy analysis should be the forte of structural econometric models. Often, by employing the full structure of a model, useful analytical results that are the outcome of the interplay within the model emerge; results that would be missed if the analysis were limited to a few variables.

I also agree with the strategy used. Specifically, the problem confronted is how to assess the effects of one endogenous variable, the U.S. current account deficit, on other endogenous variables, in particular the activity and price variables elsewhere in the OECD. As Shafer correctly points out, the combinations of exogenous variables that could be solved out are infinite in number; and, over time, all would produce the same U.S. current account path. This is a very important point. Each set of possible exogenous variables implies, however, altogether different outcomes for the other variables. This is to say that the answer the paper reaches concerning the effect of the U.S. current account on output and prices in the other OECD countries depends critically on the package of policy settings and values of other exogenous variables assumed at the outset of the exercise.

As the author points out, there is no right or wrong answer to the question of which set of assumptions to make for the exogenous variables. But some possibilities are more likely, or perhaps have more inherent interest, than others. Consequently, a defense of the assumptions made can only be by an appeal to the plausibility of how things might have been, were we to experience the recent past again. I, for one, find the counterfactual case plausible, certainly plausible enough to merit the exercise.

Whether or not the results are convincing depends not only on the plausibility of the assumptions, but also on the validity of the model used, in this case the OECD's INTERLINK model. INTERLINK is not a heretical model, most of its parameters and properties are broadly consistent with other similar models. It is, however, a fairly large model. This means that in its present state it cannot be run with forward-looking, model-consistent expectations. That is, values of such things as expected exchange rates, expected inflation rates, and expected interest rates are not generated by iteratively solving the model for their future values. Rather, they must be determined in some other fashion within the model, typically in an adaptive-expectations framework. Thus, changes in policy, even well-announced changes in completely credible policy, only affect such variables as interest rates and exchange rates with lags that are, in my opinion, unrealistically long. Consequently, I was not distressed, unlike many other readers, I suspect, to learn that exchange rates and interest rates had been exogenized. I have long been convinced of the futility of building empirical models of exchange rates and prefer either to impose open parity on the model or exogenize exchange rates. Similarly, I see no virtue in retaining on obviously flawed interest rate block. I am not sure if the exogenously imposed trajectory for interest rates and exchange rates is appropriate, but I am sure that I would not have found values of these variables generated by the model compelling. In fact, for this reason, I would have preferred to see not only short-term interest rates exogenized but also long-term rates. If this were done, there would doubtless have been a bigger difference in the actual and counterfactual simulations in the user cost of capital in the early years, and the path of output outside of the United States would have presumably been somewhat stronger.

There are, as I see it, two important lessons in Shafer's chapter. The first is that less of a fiscal deficit in the United States does not necessarily lead to more investment outside the United States, the second is that by eliminating one tension in the counterfactual scenario—the payments imbalance of the United States vis-à-vis the rest of the world—another one is created. In this case current account imbalances within the EMS become more pronounced, making EMS currency realignments likely in the counterfactual scenario. These are exactly the types of insights on which larger model simulations are capable of shedding light. That having been said, let's look at these two conclusions in a little more detail.

Taking the question of fiscal deficits and capital formation first, the INTERLINK results suggest that, at least over the range simulated, real interest rates do not fall enough either at home or abroad to increase the capital stock and, consequently, output. This is quite possible, but it is contrary to one of the advertised benefits of fiscal restraint and at odds with some theoretical models. Table 3—10 shows very pronounced multiplier/accelarator machanisms working to depress the capital stock in the United States, Japan, and Germany. At the same time, investment is greater in the counterfactual case in Italy, the United Kingdom, and Canada. This latter case is particularly paradoxical, given the strong financial and trade links between the United States and Canada.

Is it possible that this result might be due in part to a slow transmission link in the model between short and long rates, or to the absence of making the idea of the optimal capital stock operational in the model. The point is simply that one is unlikely to find results that depend on long-run properties in models designed to answer short-run questions. In MINIMOD, a small simulation model with forward-looking, model-consistent expectations—a model very much in the spirit of the model John Taylor uses in chapter 2—I don't find these results. In particular, a U.S. fiscal contraction will lower U.S. output on impact, but raise it after several years as the capital stock increases above what it otherwise would have been. Similarly, output abroad will increase as a direct result of lower real interest rates globally. These results are critically dependent on the assumption of forward-looking expectations and do not occur nearly so quickly when adaptive exceptional processes are used.

The second major conclusion—the emergence of EMS tensions in the counterfactual simulation—is particularly interesting because of its unexpected nature. The question here is to what extent this conclusion is dependent on the absence, as I read it, of an adding-up constraint in the model on global current account shifts? Table 3–16 suggests that the statistical discrepancy has not been kept constant throughout the simulation. It is doubtful that keeping it constant with a simulation rule would alter this result, but it might, so I raise the issue.

An examination of table 3–16 raises another point, the small role developing countries seem to play in the simulation. Large current account changes in the United States are accompanied by small changes in the same direction outside the OECD. While it is clearly outside the scope of the chapter, which is limited to the OECD countries, it would be interesting, and important, to subsequently expand the study to quantify the effects of the shock on developing countries—not only on their trade, but also on their capacity to service debt. I suspect that the conclusion of the paper—that the counterfactual simulation simply trades one set of unpalatable outcome for another—might well be amended if the developing countries were included in the analysis.

There are several additional questions about the results presented by Shafer. Some are somewhat more technical and might best be pursued bilaterally.

1. How was the savings ratio increased in the counterfactual simulation? Presumably, initially increased U.S. interest rates were not sufficient and the consumption function was shifted downward exogenously. I sympathize with Jeff's reluctance to dig too deep into the true exogenous shifts in the counterfactual simulation, but the rational for this is not as transparent to me as is the shift in government expenditures. It would be interesting to learn not only how the model was shocked, but also any explanation of why it was done that way.

2. Some of the weakness in U.S. growth in the counterfactual is due, if I understand INTERLINK properly, to the surprisingly strong negative effect that the higher inflation rate in that scenario has on U.S. consumption. In the absence of this effect, an effect that not all might subscribe to, the effect on U.S. output would be somewhat stronger in the counterfactual scenario.

3. It looks as if Canada has lost a lot of competitiveness vis-à-vis the United States (tables 3–1 and 3–7), but it shows a large current account increase (table 3–9). U.S. activity is much lower than Canadian activity in the counterfactual case, making this result even more surprising.

4. Is the Japanese current account so resilient because of differential import and export activity elasticities? Had simple trend terms been used in the trade volume equations, they would have canceled out in the two simulations. Are differential import and export elasticities in Japan behind the decision to let the yen rise in the counterfactual simulation, in contrast to the DM?

5. It would be interesting to know what is happening to the U.S. deficit or debt in the counterfactual simulation. Sustainability has a number of different meanings, but is the counterfactual simulation, in any sense of the word, sustainable?

6. Why were the counterfactual assumptions first run in an unlinked U.S. model? I would have thought the linked simulations would be the ones of interest.

But I don't want to end on specific, and somewhat technical points. Let me finish by saying that Shafer's contribution is a good example of how to intelligently use a large simulation model in order to extract useful information based on an interesting set of counterfactual assumptions.

SESSION III

4 TRADE DEFICITS IN THE LONG RUN*

Barry J. Eichengreen

4.1 Introduction

Among policymakers, the U.S. trade deficit is increasingly viewed as the problem that will not go away. In 1986 the deficit reached unprecedented levels in excess of $140 billion. The trade gap has widened in nominal terms in every calender year since 1980. While the deficit's growth over the early part of the decade could be straightforwardly attributed to the rise of the dollar and to the consequent decline in the relative price of U.S. imports and the rising cost to foreigners of U.S. exports, the persistence of deficits in the face of the dollar's subsequent decline has sent shudders through Washington, D.C. conference rooms and corporate boardrooms alike. Even those who anticipate that import and export quantities will eventually

* Prepared for the St. Louis Federal Reserve Bank Conference on the U.S. Trade Deficit. Much of the work on this paper was completed during a visit to the Department of Economics of Tel Aviv University, whose hospitality is acknowledged with thanks. Trevor Dick and Taka Ito provided valuable advice on Canadian and Japanese data. Anna Schwartz provided helpful comments in her role as conference discussant.

respond to the dollar's real depreciation entertain the possibility that the competitiveness of exporting and import-competing firms has been damaged permanently by the deficits experienced in the interim.

Unlike international trade theorists, who have recently freed themselves from the confines of two-sector, two-factor, two-country models, the thinking of economists and others about trade as a policy problem remains dominated by twos: two U.S. deficits (those on the trade and government budget balances), two countries (the U.S. and Japan), and two periods (the two terms of the Reagan administration). The confining nature of the framework makes it difficult to evaluate whether and in what respects the recent behavior of the U.S. trade deficit is unprecedented and to answer such questions as the following: Are there other modern periods when the trade deficits of the United States or of other countries have grown to comparable proportions? On prior occasions when the trade gap has grown exceptionally wide, how much time has been required to close it? In particular, what have been the roles of the two factors that have figured so prominently in recent discussions—relative prices and the government budget—in the creation and elimination of trade deficits?

My purpose here is to consider these questions from the perspective of comparative history. I examine the experience since 1870 of four countries: the United States, the United Kingdom, Canada, and Japan. Currently, popular accounts view Japan's trade surplus as the foreign counterpart to America's trade deficit. Hence it is of interest to ask whether Japanese trade has diverged so widely from balance in the past, for how long her trade surpluses and deficits have persisted, and with what factors they have been associated. Canada's and Britain's deficits have received less attention in the United States but are of equal interest. Late-nineteenth century Britain, like mid-twentieth century America, entered the period as the leading international creditor of her day. Like the United States after World War II, Britain at the turn of the century typically ran current account surpluses while exporting capital on a large scale. As the twentieth century progressed, her traded goods industries experienced growing competitive difficulties leading to trade deficits, the decline of Britain's net foreign asset position, and mounting protectionist pressures. Hence it is intriguing to explore parallels between early British experience and recent trends in the U.S. economy. Canadian experience between 1880 and 1913 provides a dramatic example of an economy running substantial trade deficits while importing capital on a huge scale. The capital imports that have figured so prominently in recent U.S. experience bear more than passing resemblance to this Canadian episode. If trade deficits behave differently in the long run when accompanied by capital imports (in contrast to deficits financed by reserve outflows or invisible earnings), then the differences should be evident in comparisons of Canada with these other countries.

While the focus here on the years since 1870 can be defended on the grounds that they comprise the period when these economies all had at least begun to undergo significant industrialization, that choice is dictated by the availability of historical statistics. Since imports pass through a small number of ports, making it easy for nascent governments to tax international transactions, trade accounts are among the first economic statistics gathered and published. But other information required to construct estimates of the economic variables upon which trade volumes and prices depend—notably national incomes—typically becomes available only in the nineteenth or twentieth centuries. Hence the focus on the post-1870 period.

The data employed derive from the painstaking work of economic historians of all four countries, who have backcast their national income accounts. These long time series are not without limitations, as their architects would be the first to admit. Readers can cultivate the appropriate sense of caution by referring to the data appendix at the end of the chapter.

This chapter does not offer formal structural models of U.S. import and export supplies and demands. Doing so would entail estimating separate models for different subperiods. The dramatic changes that have occurred in U.S. and international markets since the late nineteenth century warn against estimating a single set of structural equations over that period of time. The alternative, of estimating models for subperiods, even if possible would exceed the confines of one chapter. Rather than losing sight of the forest for the trees, this chapter will err in the opposite direction, focusing on the period since 1870 as a single economic era, and devoting most of its efforts to characterizing general features of that experience, to developing broad generalizations about the data, and to offering hypotheses about changes in the long-run behavior of the trade deficit.

The exclusive focus of this chapter is on the macroeconomics of the trade balance. Currently, import penetration and export competitiveness are of equal concern at a variety of other levels, including the sectoral, where the impact of foreign competition is felt unevenly and poses a threat to the continued survival of particular U.S. firms and industries, and the political, where import penetration is a source of political pressures threatening to transform the traditional free-trade stance of the post-WWII U.S.

economy. Both of these topics are the subject of a more extensive historical literature than the macroeconomics of trade deficits.[1] Neither receives more than passing attention here.

4.2 Recent U.S. Trade Performance

One of the most prominent features of the U.S. trade deficit in the 1980s has been its persistence. Table 4–1 shows for the post-WWII period (starting in 1948 taking account of lags) autocorrelations of two measures of the deficit in merchandise trade. The nominal deficit, in the first column, is highly persistent in the short run. On average, 95% of a deficit in one year has persisted into the next, more than 87% into the year subsequent to that. Even after four years less than a quarter of trade deficits are eliminated. Some but not much of the persistence in nominal deficits is due to persistence in the rate of growth of national income. But scaling the deficit by GNP does not do much to moderate the persistence; while autocorrelation is reduced at one-year lags, it is increased at lags two through four.[2]

Trade imbalances may persist not because disturbances take years to dissipate but because a country's trade balance can remain nonzero even in the long run. A country that specializes in producing and exporting services can offset a deficit in merchandise trade with a surplus on service account. Ignoring international interest payments, a country that persistently saves more than it invests and exports capital can remain in balance-of-trade surplus for substantial periods before corrective mechanisms equalize savings with investment and imports with exports. Once a country is a net foreign creditor, current account balance is entirely consistent with a trade deficit in equilibrium so long as the excess of imports over exports is offset by interest payments from abroad. To assess the speed of adjustment of the trade balance to its long-run (possibly nonzero) level, consider the following minimal model:

Table 4–1. Autocorrelations of Annual U.S. Trade Deficit, 1952–85

	Nominal Deficit	*Deficit/GNP*
Lagged 1 year	0.951	0.912
Lagged 2 years	0.875	0.825
Lagged 3 years	0.792	0.798
Lagged 4 years	0.774	0.789

Source: See text and data appendix.

$$D(t) - D(t-1) = \alpha\{D^*(t) - D(t-1)\} \quad (4.1)$$

where D is the observed deficit, D^* is its long-run value, and t indexes time. The deficit adjusts at speed α. Equivalently,

$$D(t) = (1-\alpha)D(t-1) + \alpha D^*(t) \quad (4.2)$$

In principle, D^* should be derived from a general equilibrium model of both domestic and foreign economies. Here, D^* is simply specified as a function of time, either linear ($D^* = B_0 + B_1 * t$) or quadratic ($D^* = B_0 + B_1 * t + B_2 * t^2$). Estimates of equation (4.2) under this assumption are shown in table 4–2. For the nominal deficit, estimates with a coefficient on the lagged dependent variable between zero and one are obtained only when the nonlinear term in time is included. The presistence of the nominal deficit, as reflected in the coefficient on the lagged dependent variable, is only slightly lower than that in table 4–1.[3] The nominal deficit moves only a tenth of the way toward its long-run equilibrium level in a year, less than 40% of the way in five years. When these equations are solved for the implied long-run value of the deficit, they imply a surplus from the mid-1950s through 1969 and a deficit thereafter. (The actual balance moves from surplus to deficit in 1971.)

Like the nominal deficit, the deficit share of GNP exhibits less persistence in table 4–2 than in table 4–1. Half of the deficit share of GNP is eliminated within a year whichever long-run specification is assumed.

Table 4–2. Speed of Convergence of the Annual U.S. Trade Deficit, 1952–1985

Coefficient	*Nominal Deficit*		*Deficit/GNP*	
Constant	−2.776	6.378	−0.010	−0.009
	(4.403)	(6.09)	(0.004)	(0.004)
Lagged deficit	1.121	0.903	0.557	0.311
	(0.097)	(0.140)	(0.163)	(0.180)
Time	0.299	−1.507	0.0006	−0.0001
	(0.248)	(0.903)	(0.0002)	(0.0003)
Time squared		0.059		−0.000003
		(0.029)		(0.000001)
R^2	0.91	0.92	0.87	0.89
DW	1.75	1.61	1.85	1.79

Notes: 1. Standard errors in parentheses.
2. The time trend runs from 1 in 1951 to 35 in 1985.

Source: See text.

The reduction in persistence when the possibility of a nonzero long-run deficit is introduced is considerably greater in the case of the deficit/GNP ratio than in that of the nominal deficit.

The different behavior of the deficit share than of the nominal deficit points to the behavior of the trade balance over the cycle. Figure 4–1 plots the deficit as a share of GNP together with a five-year moving average of the rate of growth of real GNP. It makes clear that GNP growth explains only part of the time-series behavior of the deficit. Another determinant is relative prices. Figure 4–2 shows the deficit as a share of GNP together with the real exchange rate (defined throughout as the price of traded goods, proxied by the average of import and export prices, relative to the GNP deflator). Figure 4–3 superimposes the terms of trade, defined throughout as the home country's export prices relative to its import prices. Over the third of a century since 1952, neither relative price series is highly correlated with the trade balance as a share of GNP. The strong association between the real exchange rate and trade deficit of which so much has been written in recent years appears to be limited largely to the final decade of the sample.

The other correlation of which much has been written is that between the government budget deficit and the trade deficit. Figure 4–4 displays these two variables scaled by GNP, with the appearance of a positive relationship throughout the post-WWII period.[4] Standard open-economy analysis like the Mundell-Fleming model suggests that the impact of the

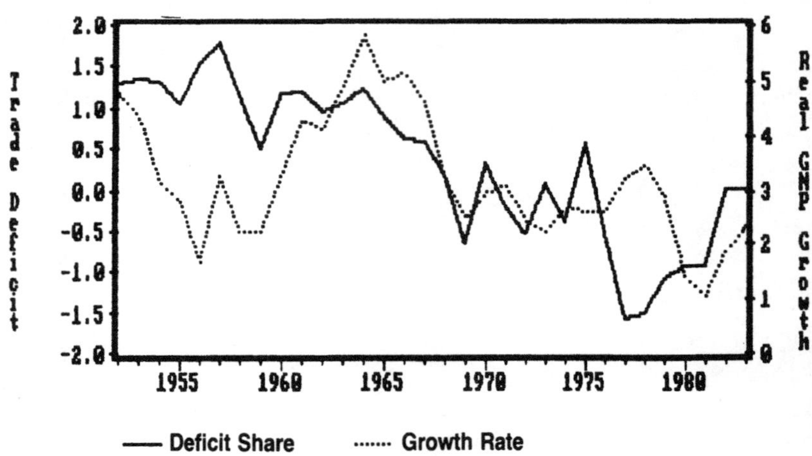

Figure 4–1. Deficit Share of GNP and Real GNP Growth

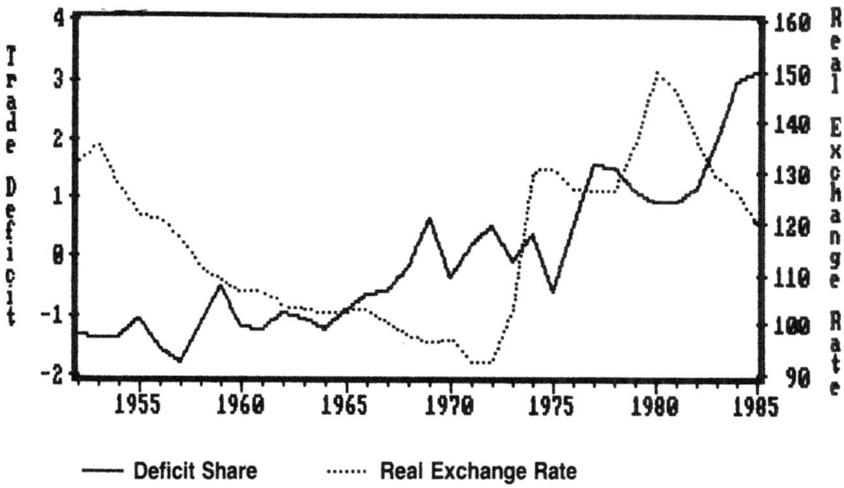

Figure 4–2. U.S. Deficit Share of GNP and Real Exchange Rate

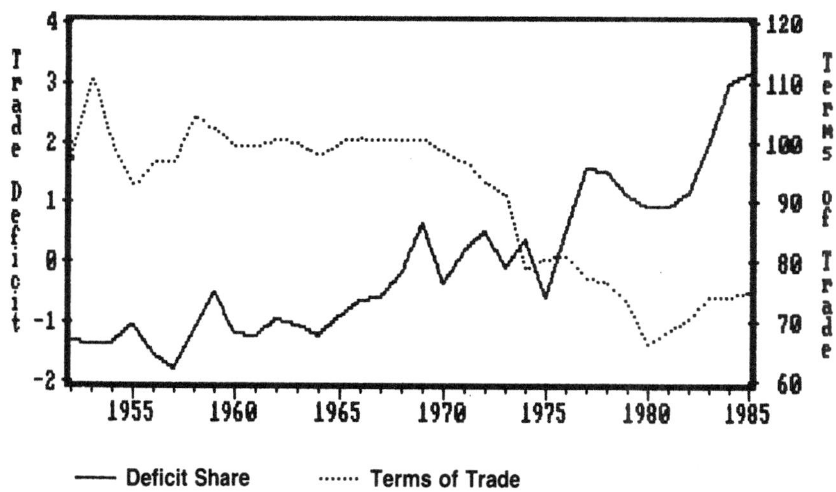

Figure 4–3. U.S. Deficit Share of GNP and Terms of Trade

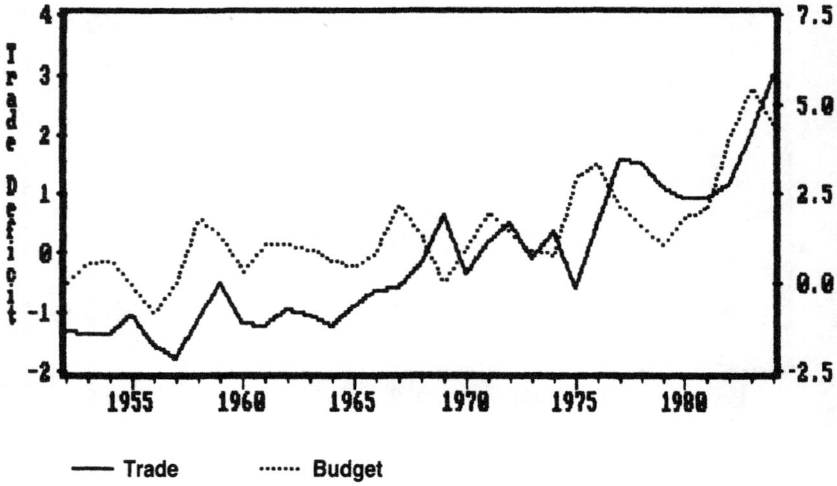

Figure 4–4. U.S. Trade and Budget Deficits as Shares of GNP

government budget on the trade balance should depend on the exchange rate regime. While there is evidence of a shift around the time of the collapse of Bretton Woods, it is not so much a change in the elasticity of the trade deficit with respect to the budget deficit as an upward shift in the level of the trade deficit given any level of budget deficit.[5]

4.3 The U.S. Trade Balance in Historical Perspective

A first question upon which an historical perspective can shed light is whether the magnitude of the recent U.S. trade deficit is unprecedented in any meaningful sense. Figure 4–5 shows the deficit share of GNP on an annual basis since 1890. It does suggest that the recent rise in the trade deficit represents a break with the past.[6] The deficit share seems to have risen in two stages, once in the second half of the 1960s, again in the 1980s.

From figure 4–5 it is clear that the U.S. trade balance has remained nonzero for substantial periods. Throughout the nineteenth century, the United States was a net foreign debtor, and there was relatively little change in her net external asset position from the turn of the century to the eve of World War I.[7] Trade surpluses were required to service the external debt, although these declined relative to GNP as the economy grew. During World War II, the United States emerged as a large-scale capital

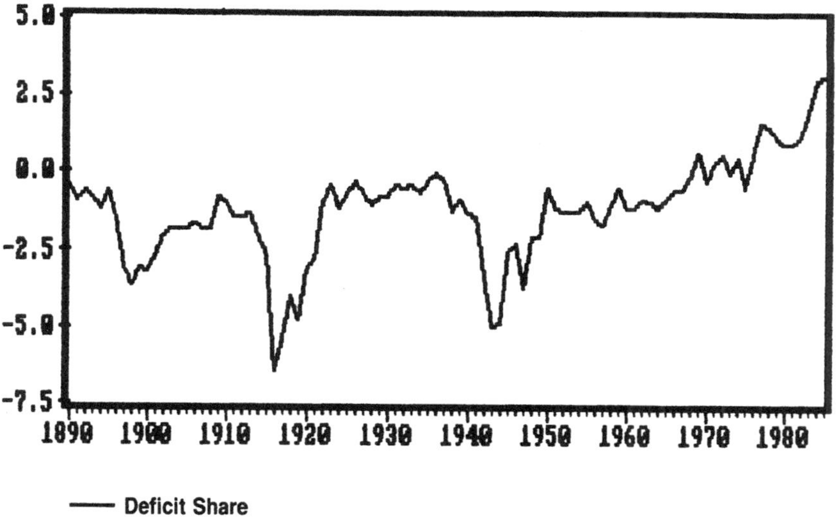

Figure 4–5. U.S. Deficit Share of GNP, 1890–1985

exporter and importer of reserves; for both reasons, persistent trade surpluses were implied. After World War II, the United States was the world's leading international creditor; trade surpluses no longer were required as a counterpart of external debt service but as a corollary of continued U.S. foreign investment.

If the recent behavior of the deficit/GNP ratio is unprecedented, must one turn for explanation to changes in the deficit relative to trade or in trade relative to national income? Figure 4–6 uses the identity $D/GNP = (D/T)(T/GNP)$ to decompose the deficit share, where D is the deficit and T is trade (measured as the sum of imports plus exports). Both components display considerable variability, and both have contributed to the recent rise in the deficit share of GNP. But the two components have moved differently over time. Relative to trade, the deficit falls sharply during World War I, recovers and remains steady over the 1920s, and then grows as the United States enters the Great Depression. D/T falls sharply during World War II, recovers and remains relatively stable over the 1950s, before rising after 1965 and again after 1980. Prior to World War II, movements in trade as a share of national income tended to offset movements in the deficit as a share of trade. T/GNP rises sharply during World War I, falls during the 1920s, and recovers gradually over the 1930s. It rises

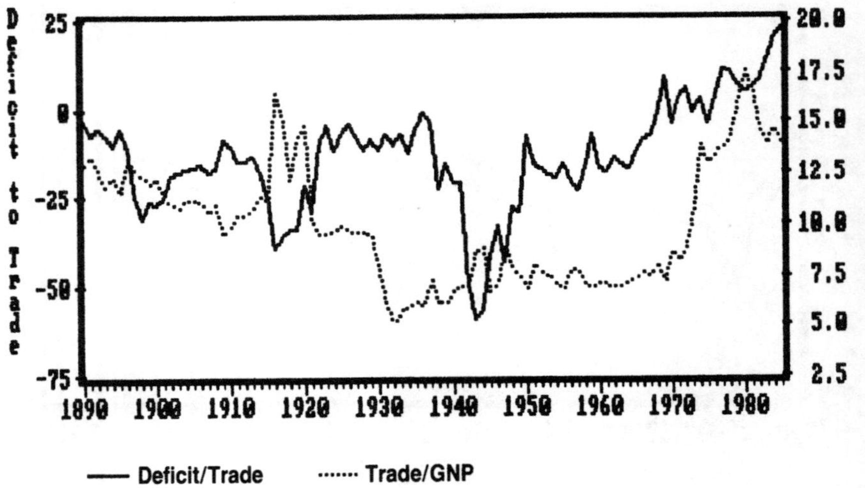

Figure 4–6. Proximate Determinants of U.S. Deficit/GNP Ratio

during World War II although, in contrast to fluctuations in *D/T*, *T/GNP* fluctuates less sharply during World War II than during World War I. It is steady through 1970 before rising dramatically to 1980 and falling back over the current decade. Overall, openness traces out a U-shaped pattern, recovering to pre-WWI levels after 1965. Thus, while openness has increased since the early 1960s, tending ceteris paribus to raise the deficit share of GNP, the recent behavior of *T/GNP*, unlike the recent behavior of *D/T*, is by no means historically unprecedented.

Table 4–3 compares the behavior of the trade deficit in periods of fixed and floating dollar exchange rates. It is not easy to partition the periods. Even under the gold standard, small but persistent variations occurred in the foreign currency value of the dollar. Even in periods when the dollar was tightly pegged to certain foreign currencies, its value was altered against others. Changes in a peg entail uncomfortable decisions about whether to assign the year in which the change occurs to the fixed or floating period. Hence the periodization underlying table 4–3 is very aporoximate. Neither is it easy to interpret the statistics, since differences in behavior under different regimes may reflect either the effects of the exchange rate regime or the effects of the underlying economic environment on both the regime and the variable of interest.[8] At this point, only overall patterns are noted. While there is relatively little difference in the

Table 4–3. Level and Variability of U.S. Trade Deficit as a Share of GNP, 1890–1985

Period	*Mean (% of GNP)*	*Standard Deviation*
1890–1985	1.220	1.634
1890–1913 1925–1931 1947–1972	1.279	0.921
1914–1924 1932–1946 1973–1985	1.135	2.326
1919–1924 1932–1939 1973–1985	0.091	1.750

Source: See text and data appendix.

average level of the deficit share of GNP under different exchange rate regimes, there are pronounced differences in variability. The standard deviation of the trade deficit relative to GNP is more than twice as large in periods of floating as in periods of fixed rates (lines 2 and 3 of table 4–3). While some of the difference in standard deviations is attributable to the war years (as shown in the fourth line of table 4–3), even after eliminating them from the floating period a difference in standard deviations of nearly 100% remains.

Table 4–4 presents autocorrelations of various deficit measures analogous to those in table 4–1 but since 1895. Remarkably, the autocorrelation in the nominal deficit has been almost precisely the same over the last 90 years as over the post-WWII era. There is no evidence here that trade imbalances have grown more persistent recently. But in contrast, the

Table 4–4. Autocorrelations of Annual U.S. Trade Deficit, 1895–1985

	Nominal Deficit	*Deficit/GNP*
Lagged 1 year	0.954	0.871
Lagged 2 years	0.881	0.730
Lagged 3 years	0.796	0.617
Lagged 4 years	0.769	0.513

Source: See text and data appendix.

Table 4–5. Speed of Convergence of U.S. Trade Deficit, 1895–1985 (dependent variable is deficit/GNP ratio)

Coefficient	*1895–1929*		*1930–1951*	
Constant	−0.010 (0.004)	−0.011 (0.005)	−0.003 (0.003)	−0.230 (0.035)
Lagged deficit	0.623 (0.110)	0.627 (0.114)	0.517 (0.190)	0.510 (0.193)
Time	0.0002 (0.0001)	0.0004 (0.0006)	−0.00001 (0.00002)	−0.00005 (0.00009)
Time squared × 1000,000		−0.353 (1.711)		−1.756 (2.316)
WWI	−0.014 (0.005)	−0.014 (0.005)		
WWII			−0.011 (0.005)	−0.009 (0.006)
R^2	0.70	0.70	0.67	0.68
DW	2.23	2.25	2.03	2.02

Note: *WWI* and *WWII* are dummy variables taking on values of unity in 1914–1918 and 1940–1945, respectively. For other definitions, see note to table 4–2.

Source: See text.

deficit share of GNP has somewhat lower autocorrelation coefficients over the longer period. Bearing in mind the problems with such comparisons due to the fact that retrospective GNP estimates may exaggerate the volatility and understate the persistence of income in earlier periods [Romer 1986], tables 4–1 and 4–4 suggest that the different time-series behavior of the trade balance after World War II reflects more than the different time-series behavior of GNP.

Table 4–5 follows table 4–2 in analyzing the speed of convergence of the trade balance to a nonzero long-run level. Table 4–5 concentrates on the deficit share of GNP. The long-run trade balance again is modeled as a function of time and time squared but in addition is permitted to shift during World Wars I and II. To minimize the problems of modeling the trade balance's equilibrium level over long time spans, the earlier period is divided into two segments: 1895–1929 and 1930–1951. Although there is little difference between tables 4–2 and 4–5 in the speed with which the trade balance converges to its long-run level, the coefficients on time and time squared are uniformly more important in the table 4–2 equations for the post-1952 period than in the table 4–5 equations for earlier eras. This suggests that insofar as the trade balance has exhibited greater persistence in recent years, this is due to more persistence in its long-run level rather than to a slower speed of adjustment.

One corollary of this very different long-run behavior of the trade balance has been a change in cyclical responsiveness. Recall from above that in recent years the deficit has tended to move procyclically. Figure 4–7, where the deficit share of GNP and a five-year moving average of the rate of growth of real income are plotted for the nine decades from 1895, suggests shifts in the relationship between these variables. Table 4–6 documents these shifts. In contrast to recent years, when the deficit has tended to worsen while GNP was growing rapidly, prior to 1952 the deficit tended to shrink during cyclical upswings.

The most appealing explanation is changes over the cycle in the composition of demand. For evidence the logical place to look is the behavior of relative prices. Figures 4–8 and 4–9, depicting the real exchange rate and the terms of trade, are long-term counterparts of figures 4–2 and 4–3. In contrast to recent years, over the longer period U.S. experience seems to be characterized by an inverse relationship between the terms of trade and the trade deficit. Prior to the 1950s, in periods when terms of trade tended to weaken (the mid-1890s and mid-1920s, for example), the deficit tended to grow. During the two world wars, when the

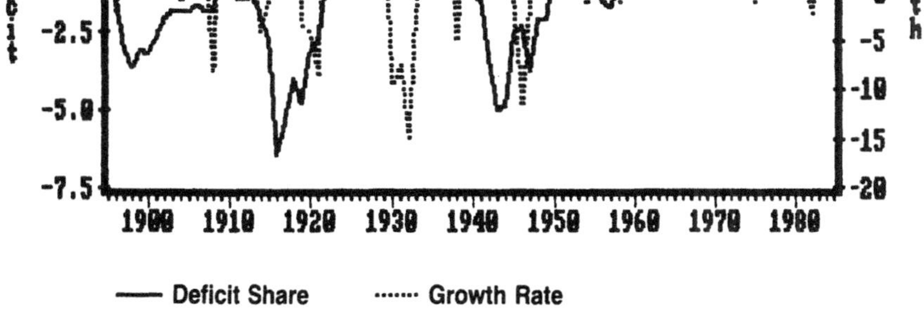

Figure 4–7. U.S. Deficit Share of GNP and Real GNP Growth Rate

Table 4–6. Long-Run Responsiveness of the Real Deficit to Real GNP, 1895–1980, Using Filtered Data

	1895–1925	*1930–1951*	*1895–1980*
Constant	−0.022	0.077	−0.058
	(0.010)	(0.022)	(0.008)
Real GNP	−0.00006	−0.00053	0.00009
	(0.00008)	(0.00008)	(0.00003)
Standard error of regression	0.013	0.019	0.027

Note: Filtered data use five-year moving averages of both the dependent and independent variables centered on the current year. The filter removes the influence of cyclical factors with a periodicity of less than five years.

Source: See text.

U.S. terms of trade strengthened dramatically, the trade deficit tended to fall. This suggests that prior to 1950 it was mainly fluctuations in foreign demands for U.S. exports that drove the trade balance over the cycle. An increase in the foreign demand for U.S. exports would drive up their price, improving the U.S. terms of trade, and move the trade balance into surplus (figure 4–9). Increased foreign demand would raise GNP, resulting in a negative relationship between the trade deficit and output (table 4–6).

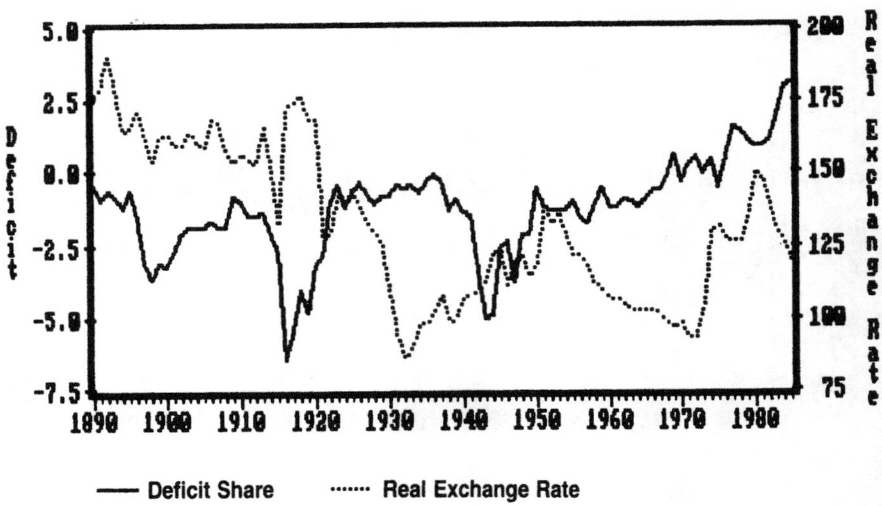

Figure 4–8. U.S. Deficit Share of GNP and Real Exchange Rate

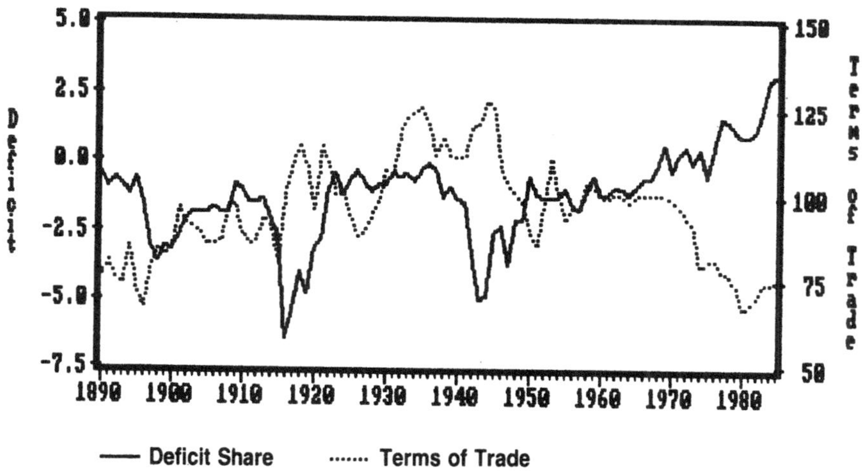

Figure 4–9. U.S. Deficit Share of GNP and Terms of Trade

After World War II, in contrast, there are as many instances of the terms of trade and the trade deficit moving together as of them moving in opposite directions. Between 1955 and 1965 and after 1980, as the terms of trade strengthened the deficit grew. The pattern suggests that in recent years it has increasingly been fluctuations in the domestic demand for imports (and in the residual supply of exports) that have driven the trade balance over the cycle. By increasing the demand for imports and curtailing the availability of exports, increased domestic demand has driven up U.S. export prices—improving the terms of trade—and moved the trade balance into deficit (figure 4–9). Increased domestic demand has stimulated GNP, resulting in a positive relationship between the trade deficit and output (table 4–6).[9]

The relationship of the real exchange rate to the trade balance (figure 4–8) is consistent with this interpretation. Overall, during periods when the real exchange rate (the price of tradeables relative to nontradeables) tended to rise, the deficit tended to fall, again as if it was mainly fluctuations in foreign demand that were driving the U.S. trade balance over the cycle. This relationship is attenuated after World War II, as if fluctuations in domestic demand began to play an increasingly important role.[10]

It is logical to turn to monetary and fiscal policies for shocks to domestic demand. The data on the government budget in figure 4–10 are dominated by the two world wars, when large budget deficits were associated—

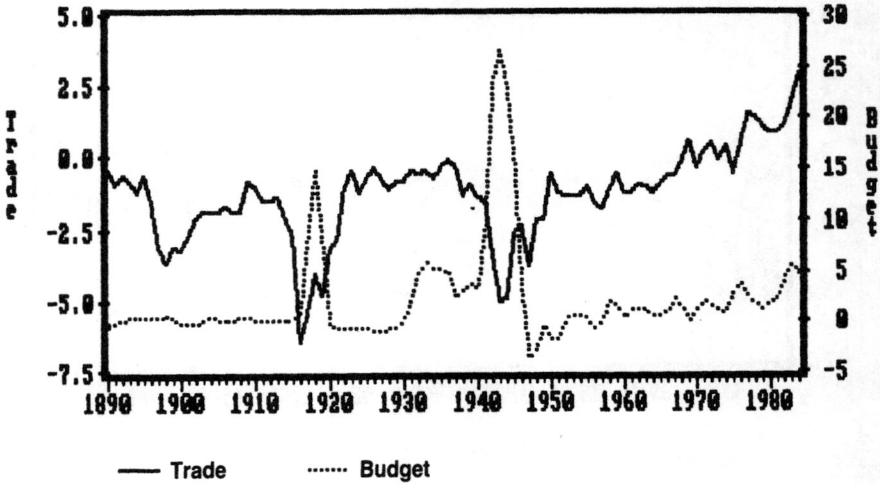

Figure 4–10. U.S. Trade and Budget Deficits as Shares of GNP

courtesy of controls on domestic prices and international transactions and even larger budget deficits abroad—with large trade-balance surpluses. But after eliminating the wartime periods, as in figure 4–11, the relationship is clearly positive. An OLS regression for 1896–1913, 1920–1938 and 1947–1984 yields

$$D/Y = -0.012 + 0.397 \; B/Y \qquad (4.3)$$
$$\quad (0.001) \quad (0.067) \qquad R^2 = 0.33$$

where B is the government budget deficit and other variables are defined as above. Thus, in peacetime the government budget and the trade balance have tended to move in the same direction, a common implication of models emphasizing the absorption effects of government spending.

A futher implication of those models is that the precise impact of government spending on the trade balance will depend on exchange rate and monetary policies. Under flexible exchange rates, perfect asset substitutability and high capital mobility, a fiscal expansion will put upward pressure on the exchange rate. As absorption rises, the increased demand for traded goods can be satisfied by increased imports and curtailed exports. The market for nontraded goods can only clear, however, if spending on them is restrained and resources are shifted into their production through a real appreciation. Under fixed exchange rates, in

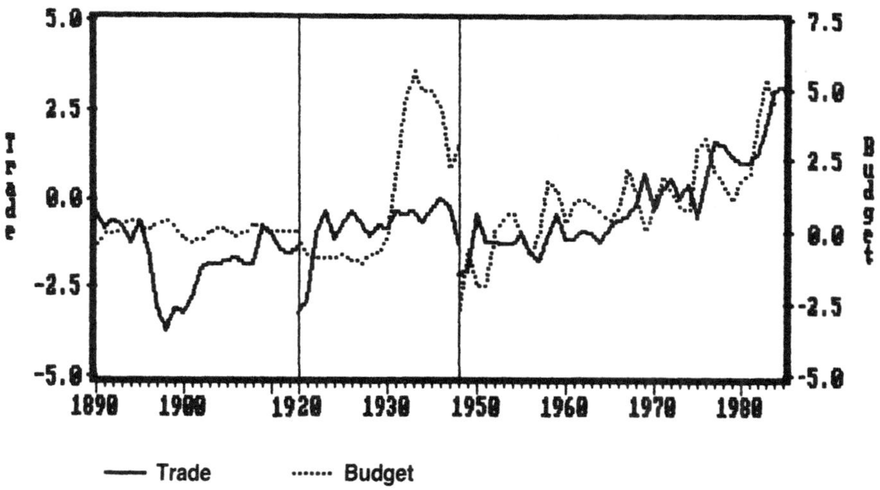

Figure 4–11. U.S. Trade and Budget Shares During Peacetime

contrast, monetary policy is used to prevent appreciation; and, due to the higher price of imports and increased competitiveness of exports, a smaller trade deficit results.[11] To probe for a difference in the trade-balance–budget-balance relationship between fixed- and flexible-exchange-rate periods. the budget balance has been interacted with a dummy variable equaling unity for years in which foreign currencies were floating against the dollar. Floating periods are defined as above. Conventional theories would suggest a positive coefficient. Using essentially the same sample as for equation (4.3):

$$D/Y = \underset{(0.001)}{-0.012} + \underset{(0.134)}{0.344}\ B/Y + \underset{(0.153)}{0.069}\ B/Y(FLOATING\ PERIODS) \qquad R^2 = 0.33 \qquad (4.4)$$

While consistent with the hypothesis, the data lend at best weak support to this interpretation.[12]

These differences in the behavior of the trade deficit during fixed- and floating-rate periods point to the role of monetary policy. Figure 4–12 shows the trade deficit share of GNP together with a five-year moving average of the rate of growth of real balances relative to real income (rate of growth of *M2* minus rate of growth of nominal *GNP*). On first glance, the relationship of real money growth to the trade deficit is not apparent.

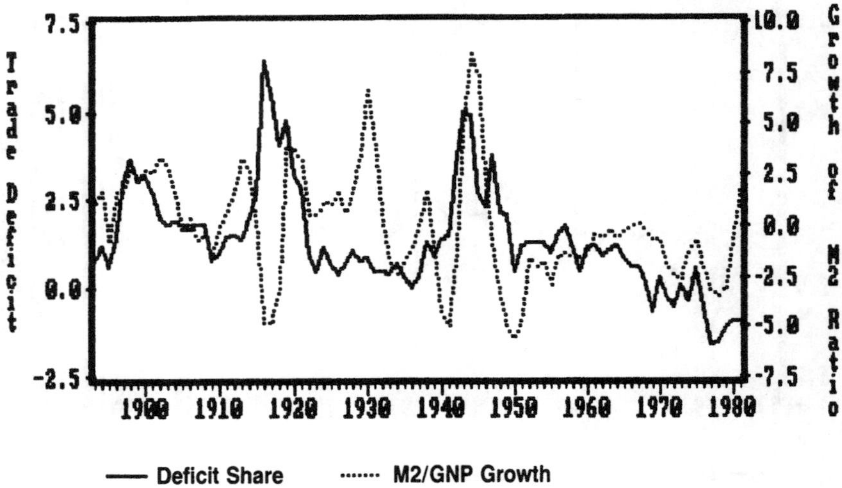

Figure 4–12. U.S. Trade Deficit and M2/GNP Growth Rate

But adding the percentage change in *M2* relative to *GNP* to equation (4.3) and estimating over peacetime periods yields

$$D/Y = \underset{(0.001)}{-0.011} + \underset{(0.055)}{0.193}\ B/Y - \underset{(0.023)}{0.074}\ \%\Delta(M2/Y) \quad R^2 = 0.19 \qquad (4.5)$$

Clearly, budget deficits have had different effects on the trade balance depending on the degree to which they have been monetized.[13] Fiscal deficits in conjunction with tight money tended to lead to trade deficits not just in recent years but over the preceding century. In contrast, in periods when fiscal deficits were accompanied by monetary expansion, the impact of domestic policy on the trade balance was attenuated.

This observation goes some way toward explaining the greater variability of trade deficits in periods of floating rates. In periods of fixed rates, the correlation of budget deficits and the growth of *M2/GNP* is positive (as if monetary policy was loosened in periods of fiscal expansion so as to prevent exchange rate appreciation, and tightened in periods of fiscal contraction to prevent depreciation). In periods of floating, the correlation of the two variables is negative. Thus, in floating-rate periods monetary and fiscal policies have tended to move deficits in the same direction, accentuating trade-balance swings; in fixed-rate periods they have tended to have offsetting effects.

In summary, a long-term perspective suggests conclusions with strong implications for understanding the recent behavior of the U.S. trade deficit. Relative to the size of the economy, the deficit has reached proportions never experienced previously in the modern history of the United States. The magnitude of that deficit is all the more noteworthy because movements in the trade balance have tended to grow more persistent over time. Yet there is little evidence that, once perturbed, the trade balance takes longer to return to its long-run underlying level. Rather, its persistence is a result of the persistence of policy affecting the long-run level of the balance of trade. Prior to World War II, fluctuations in the trade balance were dominated by foreign shocks with relatively little serial correlation; since World War II, fluctuations have been dominated by domestic shocks with considerably greater persistence. Rather than a result of changes in market structure in the United States and abroad, this suggests that the recent behavior of the U.S. trade deficit is predominantly a consequence of policy.

4.4 The U.S. Trade Balance in International Perspective

If at no time in the last century have U.S. trade deficits approached their current magnitude, have the deficits of other countries approached comparable proportions? Figures 4–13 through 4–15, where the U.S.

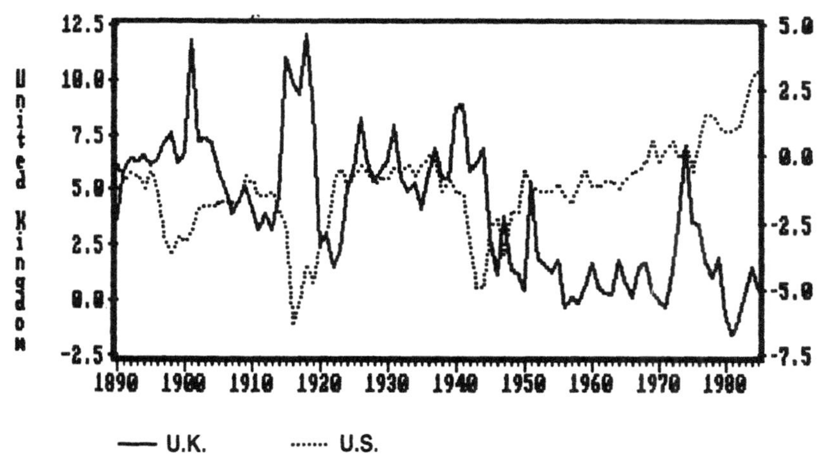

Figure 4–13. U.K. and U.S. Deficit Shares of GNP

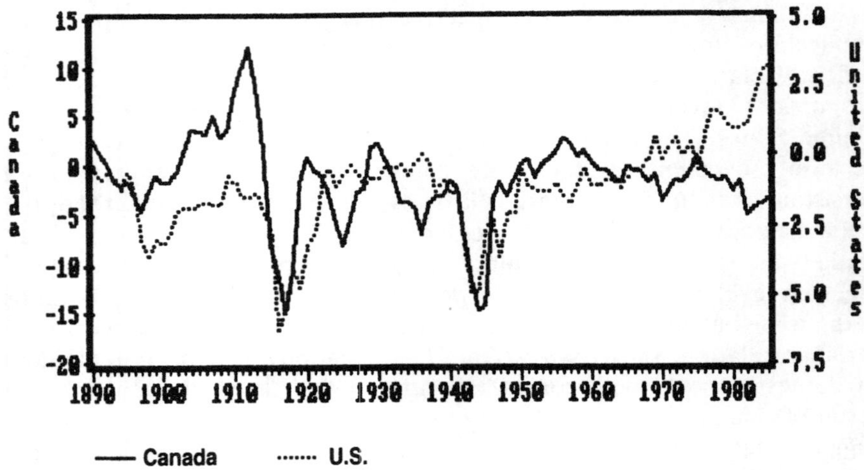

Figure 4–14. Canadian and U.S. Deficit Shares of GNP

deficit as a share of GNP is plotted along with comparable time series for the United Kingdom, Canada, and Japan, point to an answer of yes. Noteworthy are the large deficits run by the United Kingdom throughout the pre-WWII period, the large deficits run by Canada through much of the pre-WWI period and, by contrast, Japan's large surpluses during World

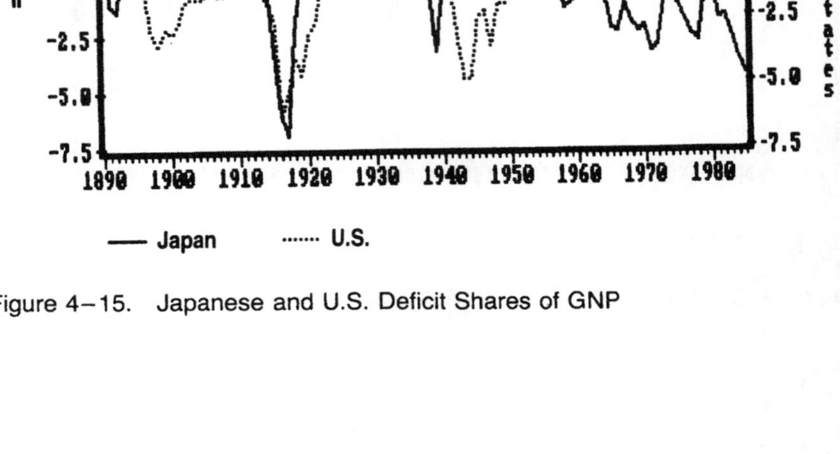

Figure 4–15. Japanese and U.S. Deficit Shares of GNP

War I, Yet the circumstances in which those deficits and surpluses were incurred were very different from those prevailing currently.

The magnitude of Britain's and Canada's pre-WWII deficits reflects more than their openness. Although compared to the United States, the share of imports and exports in GNP is higher in Britain, Canada, and Japan alike, the relationship of the import and export share of GNP in the United States and abroad has remained more or less constant over time and thus cannot account for the exceptional behavior of foreign deficits prior to the interwar years. Britain sustained her large deficits despite running capital account surpluses prior to World War I. She was able to export capital even while running merchandise trade deficits by virtue of invisible earnings derived from shipping, insurance and, most of all, the financial business in which the City of London specialized, and by virtue of interest earnings on British capital previously invested abroad. Although the precise magnitude of Edwardian Britain's foreign assets and liabilities is debated [Platt 1986; Kennedy 1987], historians agree that Britain's net foreign position continued to strengthen in the decades prior to the Great War. Thus, Britain's pre-WWI deficits offer no parallel to the increasing debt to foreigners currently being accumulated by the United States.

Like current U.S. deficits, pre-WWI Canadian deficits were accompanied by large-scale capital imports. Canada had neither invisible exports nor foreign investment earnings to defray merchandise trade deficits. Relative to the size of the economy, Canadian capital imports were exceptional, leading economists to study how her economy and her balance of payments accommodated such large capital inflows [Viner 1924]. Canada's ability to sustain her large pre-WWI trade deficits is readily explicable. Throughout this period the Canadian economy was undergoing rapid development of her resource-based and industrial sectors. Between the late 1890s and World War I, the wheat economy of the Canadian plains expanded with exceptional speed. Foreign capital was used to construct railways and navigable waterways and to purchase machinery and equipment. The uses to which foreign funds were put generated a stream of export revenues. Deficits which loomed large at the beginning of the period did not give rise to a heavy external debt burden relative to the size of the economy, given the latter's rapid rate of growth, while the development of Canada's capacity to export prevented serious transfer problems from arising along the way.

In contrast to Britain and Canada, there are no periods in recent economic history in which Japan has run large deficits relative to GNP. Moreover, Japan's current surplus has no peacetime precedent in that country's modern economic history. During World War I in Europe, however, Japanese merchandise trade surpluses reached 7% of GNP, a ratio in excess of current levels. Still, the parallels are limited, since these surpluses resulted from the sudden and substantial growth of Japanese exports arising from the disruption of intra-European and North Atlantic trade, of which Japanese exporters took full advantage [Eichengreen 1986], not from secular trends in competitiveness.

Thus, while comparisons with earlier British, Canadian, and Japanese experience permit one to dismiss alarmist accounts based exclusively on the magnitude of current U.S. deficits, they only underscore the relevance of the intertemporal budget constraint and the importance of putting capital imports to productive use.

The time-series behavior of U.S. trade deficits has differed from the behavior of deficits abroad, although more so in the post-WWII period than previously. Table 4–7 displays first- through fourth-order autocorrelations of the Canadian, British, and Japanese deficits. Movements in the U.S. trade balance are more persistent at both short lags (where only the autocorrelation of the Canadian balance approaches that of the American) and longer lags (where only the autocorrelation of the British balance approaches that of the American). The differences are most pronounced after World War II despite that, with the notable exception of the United Kingdom's foreign trade balances generally grow more persistent in the same way as the American.

In these other countries, as in the United States, increasing persistence seems to have resulted not from changes in the trade balance's speed of adjustment but from changes in the forcing variables driving the long-run balance toward which the current level adjusts. Table 4–8 reports convergence regressions like those in Tables 4–2 and 4–5 above. In every country the speed of convergence seems to have increased in recent years. The unusual persistence of U.S. trade deficits does not appear to be explicable in terms of exceptional sluggishness of U.S. market adjustment: coefficients on the lagged dependent variable in comparable regressions for the U.S. (0.77 for 1871–1951 and 0.31 for 1952–1985) suggest that, currently if not in earlier periods, speed of adjustment in the U.S. has matched or exceeded that in other countries.

Turing to the relationship of the trade deficit to the budget deficit, figure 4–16 displays these two variables for Canada in peacetime (1870–1913, 1920–1938, 1947–1984) in a manner comparable to figure 4–11 above. The trade deficits of Canada and the United States move together, reflecting the synchronization of the U.S. economy and its northern neighbor. As in the United States, the trade and budget balances of Canada move in sympathy over much of the period, the notable exception

Table 4–7. Autocorrelations for Canada, United Kingdom, and Japan of Trade Deficit as Share of GNP

	Canada		*United Kingdom*		*Japan*	
	1874–1985	*1952–1985*	*1874–1985*	*1952–1985*	*1904–1939 1946–1985*	*1952–1985*
Lagged 1 year	0.844	0.764	0.803	0.596	0.733	0.735
Lagged 2 years	0.582	0.668	0.650	0.250	0.460	0.411
Lagged 3 years	0.328	0.538	0.556	−0.012	0.308	0.416
Lagged 4 years	0.125	0.323	0.412	−0.011	0.199	0.522

Source: See text and data appendix.

Table 4–8. Speed of Convergence of Canadian, U.K., and Japanese Trade Deficits as Shares of GNP

	Canada		*United Kingdom*		*Japan*	
Variable	*1871–1951*	*1952–1985*	*1871–1951*	*1952–1985*	*1885–1939*	*1953–1985*
Constant	0.011	−0.023	0.016	−0.339	−0.004	0.261
	(0.010)	(0.217)	(0.007)	(0.256)	(0.021)	(0.283)
Lagged trade	0.804	0.488	0.618	0.553	0.574	0.446
deficit	(0.070)	(0.159)	(0.090)	(0.130)	(0.118)	(0.183)
Time	−0.0004	0.001	0.0004	0.007	0.0005	−0.005
	(0.0005)	(0.004)	(0.0004)	(0.005)	(0.001)	(0.006)
Time squared	0.311	−0.883	−0.549	−3.390	−0.683	2.040
× 100,000	(0.62)	(2.22)	(0.428)	(2.596)	(1.227)	(2.730)
R^2	0.74	0.66	0.46	0.39	0.32	0.61
DW	1.08	1.97	1.79	1.73	2.04	1.65

Notes: Standard errors in parentheses. Time trend starts at unity in 1870.

Source: See text and data appendix.

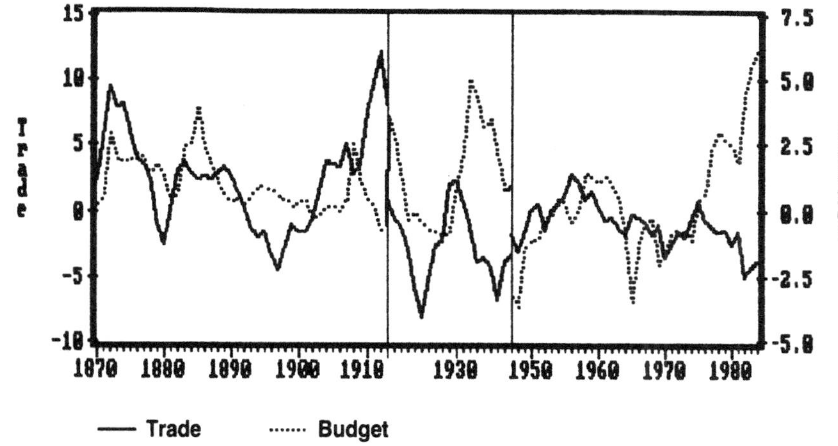

Figure 4–16. Canadian Trade and Budget Deficit Shares in Peacetime

before World War II being the experience of the Great Depression when, as in the United States, large budget deficits were paired with exchange depreciation and protectionism, preventing the emergence of significant trade deficits. More recently, the experiences of the two countries diverge. In contrast to the United States, the deterioration of the Canadian government's budget since 1975 does not have as a counterpart the emergence of a large trade deficit. It is tempting to explain this by the fact that Canada trades heavily with the United States and that if the United States runs a trade deficit its trading partners must run a surplus. But U.S. trade need not clear bilaterally with Canada. That Canadian exchange rate policies have followed a different course over the period is surely relevant: the Canadian dollar has sunk to some two-thirds the value of the U.S. dollar, and the real depreciation that resulted strengthened Canada's competitiveness and trade balance.[14] But the real exchange rate should be seen as a consequence of other policies affecting the trade deficit, not as an independent cause. The source of the divergence does not appear to be monetary policy, which, like fiscal policy, did not differ greatly between Canada and the United States. Rather, the difference lies in a higher level of household savings in Canada (which reduces the investment-savings imbalance that requires a capital inflow). This savings behavior is attributed by some to Canadian savings-promoting tax policies [Carroll and Summers 1987].

Figure 4–17 for Britain further undermines the simple view that budget deficits drive trade deficits. This is not to deny that Britain's budget balance and trade balance moved together, albeit at different levels, during the Edwardian period, the interwar years, and the quarter century following World War II. (While only peacetime periods are plotted, including the war years would reinforce the point.) The comovement of the two variables is particularly clear in their sawtooth pattern during the stop-go years of the 1960s. But after 1975, the two variables diverge. The explanation does not lie in monetary expansion, especially after 1979. And there is no significant depreciation of the real exchange rate to alter the trade balance-budget balance relationship. Clearly, the severe and protracted recession that has prevailed in Britain through much of this period has broken the trade-balance–budget-balance link, the fall in incomes at the same time reducing government revenues and depressing import demands. This underscores the point that government budget deficits can bear different relationships to the trade deficit depending on their source.

4.5 Eliminating Large Trade Imbalances

The historical experience of the countries considered here provides several examples of large trade deficits that have been eliminated rapidly. There is

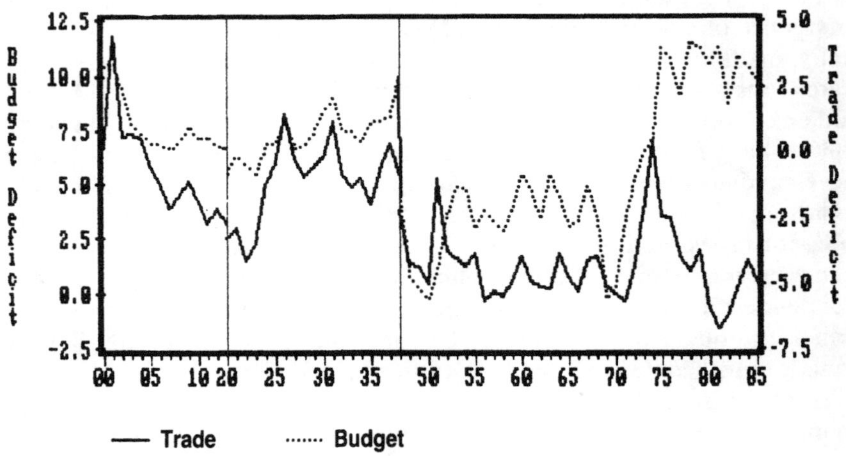

Figure 4–17. U.K. Trade and Budget Deficits as Shares of GNP

nothing mysterious about the mechanism: if domestic demand is radically curtailed, the volume of imports will fall with little delay. Unfortunately, so will output and employment. More interesting is whether historical experience provides instances where large trade deficits have been eliminated rapidly without incurring a sizeable and prolonged recession. If such instances exist, do their histories suggest some mix or sequencing of policies that might be recommended to U.S. authorities?

Identifying episodes to study is not as straightforward as one might suppose. Since at no time in the last 100 years has the United States run a deficit whose magnitude approaches the current U.S. deficit as a share of GNP, case studies of earlier American experience are not attractive. Many of the largest deficits experienced by Canada, Britain, and Japan resulted from those countries' entry into war or were eliminated by the economic effects of war abroad. Wartime experience is exceptional, although it may still contain implications of relevance for officials attempting to formulate policy in peacetime. The difficulty of identifying appropriate episodes reinforces the point that recent U.S. experience is highly unusual.

In fact, for those countries and periods depicted in figures 4–13 through 4–15, I have not been able to identify a large trade deficit that was eliminated without the intervention of a recession. But there are at least three episodes, one from each country and one from each period (prewar, interwar, postwar), where the recession was unusually short: Canada after 1912, Japan after 1924, and Britain after 1951. What was there about the sources of these deficits, the circumstances in which they were eliminated, or the policies pursued that rendered their reduction less painful than was typically the case?

Canada's trade deficits prior to World War I were associated with an exceptional surge of foreign capital inflows. Canada was by far the leading capital importer of the period—Viner [1924] estimated total foreign capital invested in Canada during the period 1900—1913 to have been in excess of $2.5 billion.[15] This was the period during which British capital exports reached their peak. According to Viner's review of contemporary estimates, more than two-thirds of Canadian capital imports were British in origin; $1.4 billion of the $2.5 billion total capital inflow was accounted for by British public investments in Canadian securities alone. After fluctuating unevenly around a mean of $290 million between 1907 and 1913, the gross capital inflow then fell abruptly with outbreak of World War I.[16]

Table 4–9 shows how the economy responded first to the inundation of foreign capital and then to the drought. The immediate effect of the capital inflow was to stimulate the economy. Economic growth proceeded at

Table 4–9. Canadian Economic Statistics, 1910–1916 (millions of Canadian dollars or 1910 = 100)

Year	*Deficit*	*Real GNP Growth (%)*	*Terms of Trade*	*Real Exchange Rate*	*Export Volume*	*Import Volume*
1910	140.0	8.3	100.0	100.0	100.0	100.0
1911	202.0	7.9	98.0	98.5	104.5	115.5
1912	274.3	4.3	98.6	90.3	127.2	149.5
1913	196.5	4.9	97.5	90.6	151.8	145.3
1914	37.3	−10.0	90.7	87.9	167.9	111.3
1915	−204.5	13.2	104.1	89.0	243.8	121.4
1916	−317.5	13.1	94.8	98.3	333.6	150.9

Source: See data appendix.

extremely rapid rates in 1910–1911, as gross domestic capital formation rose to more than a quarter of GNP.[17] Construction, most notably of Canada's second and third transcontinental railways and feeder lines, accounted for more than two-thirds of total investment between 1900 and 1914 and for a rising share as the period progressed. The rate at which the railways were expanded in the decade from 1906 has no precedent in either U.S. or Australian experience. Expansion of the Canadian railways stimulated other forms of investment, notably residential construction and infrastructure in the new urban centers of the plains. Investment in manufacturing and mining were also stimulated by the ready availability of foreign funds.

Although the volume of exports rose with the economy's expansion, import volumes rose more rapidly still, by 15% in 1911 and by 29% in 1912, pushing the trade balance deeply into deficit. The concurrent deterioration of Canada's terms of trade mainly reflected world market conditions, since Canada was a price taker in most markets. In contrast, the capital inflow and demand stimulus were directly responsible for driving up the price of home goods, as reflected in the 10% fall in the real exchange rate (price of traded relative to nontraded goods) between 1910 and 1912.

Although capital inflows terminated abruptly in 1913, economic expansion continued into the following year as new investments came on stream. Although imports fell only slightly as foreign capital dried up, the volume of exports continued to grow, considerably reducing the deficit. Thus, one lesson to which this Canadian experience points is the relative ease of eliminating large deficits when the excess of absorption over production is used to finance investment rather than consumption.

In 1914, as a result of the halt to capital inflows, Canada experienced a short but severe recession, output falling by 10%. Investment spending on construction fell by a fifth, on machinery and equipment by roughly a third.[18] The impact on Canadian incomes was reinforced by a deterioration of roughly 7% in the terms of trade, dominated again by conditions in the international wheat market. Yet the deficit was reduced to less than one seventh of its level two years before. There is nothing magical about the adjustment. Together, the recession and terms-of-trade shock reduced the volume of Canadian imports very dramatically, cutting the deficit at a stroke. The exceptional feature of this experience is that the volume of exports continued to grow despite the recession. While the decline in imports was mainly responsible for reducing the trade balance so dramatically, the continued rise in exports had a useful reinforcing effect. Continued export growth likely reflected both the final 1910–1913 investments coming on stream and strong demands for raw materials following the outbreak of the European war.

Neither is there anything mysterious about the short duration of the slump. Canada was pulled out of recession by buoyant wartime demands for her primary commodity exports. Export values and volumes rose dramatically in 1915, and volumes continued to expand the following year. That Canada was able to respond to foreign demands for her exports by increasing supplies again reflects the extent to which previous foreign borrowings had been devoted to investment.

Japanese experience in the 1920s offers an interesting contrast. As shown in table 4–10, Japanese deficits reached high levels in 1923–1924, before declining over the remainder of the decade. As in Canada after 1912, the reduction of deficits in Japan was accompanied by a relatively short recession, growth turning negative for only a year. But both the origins of Japan's deficit and the mechanisms through which it was reduced were entirely different from the Canadian case. The Japanese trade deficit rose in two stages, the first in 1919–1922 and the second in 1923–1924. The 1919–1920 upswing and 1920–1921 recession in Japan were synchronized with the postwar boom and slump abroad, although after the spring of 1920 Japanese prices fell less rapidly than prices abroad. The government adopted a silk valorization scheme and a Rice Control act to support the prices of these two commodities, and credit extended to finance these schemes prevented prices from falling as rapidly as they did abroad.[19] Meanwhile, the authorities expended foreign exchange reserves accumulated during the war to prevent the dollar exchange rate from

Table 4–10. Japanese Economic Statistics, 1922–1928 (millions of yen or 1922 = 100)

Year	*Deficit*	*Real GNP Growth (%)*	*Terms of Trade*	*Real Exchange Rate*	*Export Volume*	*Import Volume*
1922	331.2	−2.5	100.0	100.0	100.0	100.0
1923	694.8	−4.5	99.7	103.9	86.6	103.5
1924	851.4	12.1	90.0	115.3	108.9	116.8
1925	421.6	−2.9	81.1	115.5	133.5	106.5
1926	491.2	1.1	84.9	101.2	138.2	120.7
1927	314.5	2.9	82.9	90.9	156.0	124.4
1928	321.1	6.4	79.7	94.0	162.6	124.9

Source: See data appendix.

diverging from its prewar parity. The yen was rendered seriously overvalued: the real exchange rate (prices of imports and exports relative to GNP deflator) fell by more than 20% between 1919 and 1922, and a substantial deficit emerged.

The second stage in the growth of the deficit followed the 1923 Kanto earthquake and the recession for which it was responsible. The large quantities of raw materials and machinery required for reconstruction can be seen in the rise in the volume of imports in the midst of the 1923 recession. Meanwhile, export volumes declined precipitously. But if the 1923 recession was serious, the 1924 recovery was rapid. The Bank of Japan extended large amounts of credit to the private sector once the government guaranteed it against losses on discounts of bills for financial institutions whose solvency was threatened in the wake of the earthquake. As a result, not only did exports recover with reconstruction, but imports boomed. Japan's trade deficit reached its interwar peak in 1924. In contrast to Canada, where the deficit resulted from the shock to demand attendant on capital inflows, in Japan the deficit resulted from both supply and demand shocks.

Thereafter, Japan's trade deficit was progressively reduced. The economy experienced another brief downturn, as the government attempted to balance its budget by winding down reconstruction expenditures and increasing taxes. The main impulse tending to moderate the deficit was the steady growth of exports. Export volumes increased even in 1925 when the economy was in recession. The mechanism was depreciation of the yen. The 1924–1925 trade deficits had depleted the government's foreign balances, dictating the termination of support operations. The nominal exchange rate against the dollar was then allowed to fall by some 20%. The effects of depreciation are evident in table 4–10: the 1923–1925 decline in Japan's terms of trade is nearly 20%, while the prices of imports and exports rise relative to the GNP deflator by about half that amount.[20] Broadly speaking, Japan's deficits were reduced by a combination of domestic demand restraint resulting in stagnant economic growth and exchange-rate depreciation enhancing the competitiveness of Japanese exports and switching domestic expenditure away from traded goods.

British experience after 1951 was again very different (see table 4–11). The backdrop to the 1951 crisis was the 1949 devaluation of sterling.[21] 1949 was a year of neither serious trade imbalance nor obvious convertibility crisis, and a 30% devaluation in conjunction with wage and price restraints all but eliminated the existing deficit on merchandise trade account. But in 1951 the trade deficit suddenly rose to extremely high levels. Imports reached levels not to be matched until 1957. Here too a combination of factors was at work. Following U.S. entry into the Korean War in mid-1950 and purchases of raw materials by the American Munitions Board, the prices of primary products were bid up. This is evident in the deterioration of Britain's terms of trade in 1950–1951. There was no obvious problem on the export side: despite Korean-war-induced shortages of coal, steel, and other commodities, which hampered Britain's steel industry, export volumes rose by some 14% in the wake of the 1949 devaluation and remained steady in 1951.[22] The growth of the trade deficit

Table 4–11. U.K. Economic Statistics, 1949–1956 (millions of pounds or 1949 = 100)

Year	*Deficit*	*Real GNP Growth (%)*	*Terms of Trade*	*Real Exchange Rate*	*Export Volume*	*Import Volume*
1949	137	2.8	100.0	100.0	100.0	100.0
1950	51	4.0	92.8	109.1	114.4	101.1
1951	689	2.7	84.9	129.2	114.4	113.3
1952	279	−0.6	91.7	119.5	110.1	103.5
1953	244	4.5	100.8	108.0	108.9	111.5
1954	204	3.8	99.7	105.5	114.2	113.9
1955	313	3.0	99.3	104.7	123.2	125.5
1956	−53	1.8	101.7	100.3	130.8	122.0

Source: See data appendix.

resulted entirely, therefore, from terms-of-trade deterioration and import growth. While rapid import growth might seem curious in the wake of a substantial devaluation, in 1950–1951 it reflected the relaxation of wartime controls on imports and continued stimulus to aggregate demand. Under Hugh Gaitskell's 1951 budget, government expenditures (mostly on defense) were to increase by £973 million, but new taxation was projected at only one-seventh that amount.

The crisis was resolved through a general election and installation of a new Chancellor of the Exchequer.[23] Interest rates were raised, credit conditions were tightened, import restrictions were reimposed, and the rearmament program was scaled down. British firms had augmented their stocks in anticipation of continued increases in materials prices; as price increases first slowed and then reversed in mid-1951, inventory demands fell precipitously.[24] In 1952 the trade deficit was very considerably reduced by declining import volumes and recovering terms of trade, but at the cost of negative economic growth.

Britain's 1952 recession, like the Canadian and Japanese cases discussed above, is notable for its brevity; growth recommenced in 1953. Again, the key appears to lie in a fortuitous terms-of-trade improvement. In 1953 the government could afford to apply macroeconomic stimulus without violating the external constraint because of the very dramatic improvement in the terms of trade. Despite the fact that by 1953 import volumes had nearly returned to 1951 levels and export volumes still remained well below 1951, the trade deficit remained at manageable levels by virtue of the change in relative prices. In the words of Scott [in Worswick and Ady 1962, p. 217], the crisis, "was due very largely to . . . [a] gigantic fluctuation in [Britain's] terms of trade. As such, it largely cured itself."

4.6 Concluding Remarks

Judged by the country's historical experience, U.S. trade deficits have reached what are unprecedented levels. While other industrial countries have run comparable merchandise trade deficits at various points in their histories, this should be of little comfort to American observers. Those countries either financed their deficits out of interest earnings on prior foreign investments and through the large-scale export of services, or used the debt they incurred to finance investment in infrastructure and expand their capacity to export. Neither of these scenarios has a counterpart in current U.S. experience, the main legacy of which would appear to be a burden of debt service to foreigners.

That unprecedented trade deficit has its principal source, not in changes in market structure affecting the speed with which quantities respond to prices, but in the policy environment, namely the monetary-fiscal mix. While the positive relationship of the trade deficit to the budget deficit is predicted by every standard model of the balance of payments, a review of historical experience underscores a subtler point also conveyed by many of those models: that the precise impact on the balance of payments of fiscal deficits depends not only on the magnitude of those deficits but on their source, on accompanying policies, and on the structure of domestic and foreign economies. Recent U.S. fiscal deficits have had a sizeable impact on the balance of trade because they have occurred in an environment of high capital mobility and have not been accompanied by accommodating monetary policy.

How easily can the trade deficit be eliminated if historical experience is any guide? The answer, unfortunately, would appear to be "not easily." More often than not, the reduction of deficits has been achieved through the reduction of imports; typically this entails additional restraints on aggregate demand from which recession results. Trade deficits have been reduced most quickly and at lowest cost in terms of foregone output when at least one of two conditions prevails: a favorable shock to the terms of trade, and a reallocation of resources toward investment in export-oriented sectors. The first of these conditions is largely beyond the authorities' control; the second must be initiated well before other measures to reduce the deficit are adopted if it is to increase export revenues within the relevant period of time. Barring a fortuitous terms-of-trade shock, this does not give cause for optimism that the conditions are present for rapidly eliminating the U.S. trade deficit at low cost.

Notes

1. To cite but two examples, the relationship of trade to the political economy of trade policy is the subject of Kindleberger [1951], while the impact of trade at the sectoral and aggregate levels is the subject of Sayers [1965].

2. Throughout, the current value of exports and imports relative to nominal GNP is used to avoid the index number problems that arise when comparing import and export volumes to real GNP. These problems result from the significant changes in the commodity composition of imports, exports, and GNP that occur over long periods of time (see Lipsey [1963] or Matthews, Feinstein, and Odling-Smee [1982], p. 429). These same index number problems must be borne in mind when the price indexes of imports and exports are compared with the GNP deflator.

3. Throughout, it is impossible to reject that the coefficient on the lagged dependent variable is unity—in other words, that the trade deficit follows a random walk. However, the

Dickey-Fuller test used is likely to be of low power, and the random-walk hypothesis would seem to be difficult to interpret when applied to the trade deficit.

4. For 1952–1984 the correlation coefficient of the two variables is 0.72. Note that in this figure, separate scales are used for the trade and budget deficits, making the correlation look closer to the naked eye.

5. An OLS regression for 1952–1984 yields

$$\underset{(0.002)}{D/Y = -0.011} + \underset{(0.210)}{0.386}\ B/Y - \underset{(0.254)}{0.064}\ (B/Y)*F + \underset{(0.005)}{0.012}\ F$$

$$DW = 1.22 \qquad R^2 = 0.68$$

where D/Y is the trade deficit ratio, B/Y is the budget deficit ratio, and F is a dummy variable for the floating years from 1973. Standard errors are in parentheses here and throughout.

6. A t test of the hypothesis of no increase in D/Y after 1975 is rejected at the 99% level.

7. Eichengreen [1987], Table 1.

8. For further discussion, see Eichengreen [1988].

9. Many but not all of these conclusions for the period prior to 1952 are consistent with those of Mintz [1959].

10. A regression for the period 1895–1985 of the deficit relative to GNP (D/Y) on the real exchange rate (RER), with an additional slope coefficient for the post-1951 period, yields

$$D/Y = \underset{(0.008)}{0.003} - \underset{(0.006)}{0.017}\ RER + \underset{(0.003)}{0.015}\ RER(POST\ 1951)$$

$$P = 0.003 \qquad R^2 = 0.39$$

with a first-order autocorrelation correction and standard errors in parentheses. Thus, the tendency of the trade deficit to fall as the relative price of traded goods rose was weaker after World War II.

11. For a recent restatement of this literature, see Sachs and Wyplosz [1987].

12. One might object that the relationship between the trade balance and the budget balance simply reflects the influence on both budget and trade deficits of cyclical factors omitted from the equation. Adding the deviation of output from trend (computed as the residuals from a regression of real GNP on a constant, time and time squared) to the list of regressors had minimal impact on the results:

$$D/Y = \underset{(0.002)}{-0.022} + \underset{(0.102)}{0.173}\ B/Y + \underset{(0.113)}{0.095}\ B/Y(FLOATING)$$

$$+ \underset{(0.172)}{1.339}\ OUTPUT\ DEVIATION \qquad R^2 = 0.64$$

13. The sample period for this regression is 1896–1913, 1920–1938, 1945–1983. Other proxies for the stance of monetary policy yielded similar results. For example, when the level rather than the percentage change in the $M2/GNP$ ratio was used

$$D/Y = \underset{(0.709)}{0.218} + \underset{(0.065)}{0.362}\ B/Y - \underset{(1.622)}{2.334}\ M2/Y \qquad R^2 = 0.32$$

Entering both the percentage change in the $M2/GNP$ ratio and the budget deficit/GNP ratio interacted with a dummy variable for floating-rate periods supports the conclusion that it is monetary policy that accounts for the shift:

$$D/Y = \underset{(0.124)}{-1.220} + \underset{(0.130)}{0.440}\ B/Y - \underset{(2.143)}{5.719}\ \%\Delta(M2/Y) - \underset{(0.148)}{0.073}\ B/Y(FLOATING) \qquad R^2 = 0.35$$

14. In figure 4–16, the same tendencies are evident for the 1950s, when a floating Canadian dollar similarly loosened the link between budget deficits and trade deficits.
15. See Edelstein [1982, table 12.1] for international comparisons.
16. Viner [1924, p. 106].
17. Calculated from Firestone [1958]. Edelstein [1982, p. 272] suggests that the figure is inflated by an exceptional amount of inventory investment in 1910. Adjustments are likely to change the picture only slightly, however.
18. Buckley [1955, pp. 145–158].
19. Allen [1962, pp. 100–101].
20. Disaggregated relative price series are discussed by Shinohara [1962, pp. 68 et seq.].
21. For details, see Cairncross and Eichengreen [1983, ch. 4].
22. Flanders [1963, pp. 190–192]; M. Scott, in Worwsick and Ady [1962, p. 213].
23. See Mitchell [1963] for details.
24. The role of stockbuilding and adjustment in 1950–1951 is especially emphasized by Harrod [1963, pp. 134–135].

References

Allen, G. C. 1963. *A Short Economic History of Modern Japan*. New York: Praeger.

Buckley, K. A. H. 1955. *Capital Formation in Canada, 1896–1930*. Toronto: University of Toronto Press.

Cairncross, Alec, and Eichengreen, Barry, 1983. *Sterling in Decline*. Oxford: Blackwell.

Carroll, Chris, and Summers, Lawrence. 1987. "Why Have Private Savings Rates in the United States and Canada Diverged?" National Bureau of Economic Research Working Paper no. 2319.

Edelstein, Michael, 1982. *Overseas Investment in the Age of High Imperialism*. New York: Columbia University Press.

Eichengreen, Barry. 1986. "Understanding 1921–1927 (Inflation and Economic Recovery in the 1920s)." *Rivista di Storia Economica* 3:34–66.

Eichengreen, Barry. 1987. "The U.S. Capital Market and Foreign Lending, 1920–1955 in Jeffrey Sachs (ed.), *Developing Country Debt and Economic Performance: Special Topics*, Chicago: University of Chicago Press (forthcoming)."

Eichengreen, Barry. 1988. "Real Exchange Rate Behavior Under Alternative International Monetary Regimes: Interwar Evidence." *European Economic Review* 32, pp. 363–371.

Feinstein, Charles H. 1972. *National Expenditure, Output and Income of the United Kingdom, 1855–1965*. Cambridge: Cambridge University Press.

Firestone, O. J. 1958. *Canada's Economic Development, 1867–1953*, London: Bowes and Bowes.

Flanders, M. June. 1963. "The Effects of Devaluation on Exports." *Oxford Bulletin of Economics and Statistics* 25:165–198.

Harrod, Roy. 1963. *The British Economy*. New York: McGraw Hill.

International Monetary Fund (various years). *International Financial Statistics*.

Washington, D.C.: IMF.

Japanese Ministry of Finance. 1986. *Zaisei Tokei (Fiscal Statistics)* Tokyo: Ministry of Finance.

Kennedy, William. 1987. "Review of *Britain's Investment Overseas on the Eve of the First World War*." *Economic History Review* 2nd ser., 40:307–309.

Kindleberger, Charles. 1951. "Group Behavior and International Trade." Reprinted in Kindleberger, *Economic Response*, Cambridge: Harvard University Press, pp. 19–38.

Lipsey, Robert. 1963. *Price and Quantity Trends in the Foreign Trade of the United States*. Princeton: National Bureau of Economic Research.

Matthews, R. C. O.; Feinstein, C. H.; and Odling-Smee, J. C. 1982. *British Economic Growth*. Stanford: Stanford University Press.

Mintz, Ilse. 1959. "Trade Balances During Business Cycles: U.S. and Britain Since 1880." Occasional Paper 67, New York: National Bureau of Economic Research.

Mitchell, Joan, 1963. *Crisis in Britain 1951*. London: Secker & Warburg.

Ohkawa, Kazushi, and Rosovsky, Henry. 1973. *Japanese Economic Growth*, Stanford: Stanford University Press.

Ohkawa, Kazushi; Takamatsu, Nobukiyo; and Yamamoto, Yuzo. 1974. *Estimates of Long Term Economic Statistics for Japan Since 1868*. Vol. 1. Tokyo: Oriental Publishing Company.

Platt, D. C. M. 1986. *Britain's Investment Overseas on the Eve of the First World War*. London: Macmillan.

Romer, Christina. 1986. "New Estimates of Prewar Gross National Product and Unemployment." *Journal of Economic History* 46:341–352.

Sachs, Jeffrey, and Wyplosz, Charles. 1987. "Real Exchange Rate Effects of Fiscal Policy." *Journal of International Money and Finance* (forthcoming).

Sayers, Richard S. 1965. *The Vicissitudes of an Export Economy: Britain Since 1880*. Sydney: Sydney University Press.

Shinohara, Miyohei. 1962. *Growth and Cycles in the Japanese Economy*. Tokyo: Kinokuniya Bookstore Co.

United States Department of Commerce. 1976. *Historical Statistics of the United States*. Washington, D.C.: GPO.

Urquhart, M. C. 1986. "New Estimates of Gross National Product, Canada, 1870–1926: Some Implications for Canadian Development." In Lance Davis and Stanley Engerman, *The Development of the American Economy*, Chicago: University of Chicago Press.

Urquhart, M. C., and Buckley, K. A. H. 1965. *Historical Statistics of Canada*. Cambridge: Cambridge University Press.

Viner, Jacob. 1924. *Canada's Balance of International Indebtedness*. Cambridge, Mass.: Harvard University Press.

Weir, David. 1986. "The Reliability of Historical Macroeconomic Data for Comparing Cyclical Stability." *Journal of Economic History* 46:353–366.

Worswick, G. D. N., and Ady, P. H. (eds.). 1962. *The British Economy in the 1950s*. Oxford: Clarendon Press.

DATA APPENDIX

United States

The basic source for trade data for the United States is the Department of Commerce's *Historical Statistics of the United States* through 1970 and the International Monetary Fund's *International Financial Statistics* thereafter. Exports and imports of merchandise are at f.o.b. prices. Data through 1915 are for years ending June 30, entries thereafter for calender years. Since variables for items other than trade are conveniently available on a calender-year basis, the trade data has been realigned through 1915 to minimize problems of timing. On the assumption of a constant rate of flow over the fiscal year, the figures for pairs of successive years are averaged to generate calendar-year estimates.

It is tempting to use Lipsey's [1963] estimates of U.S. imports and exports, upon which many of Commerce's *Historical Statistics*...(*HS*) series are based. Lipsey presents calendar year estimates for years prior to 1915, based on monthly trade accounts. Thus, use of Lipsey's data would permit relaxation of the assumption of a constant rate of flow over the fiscal year. However, rather than total imports and exports, Lipsey studies (i) total imports and (ii) exports of U.S. merchandise only (excluding re-exports). While appropriate for his purposes, the exclusion of re-exports (which average about 1.5% of the total) is not desirable for this paper's exercise, the focus of which is the macroeconomics of trade deficits. Experimentation showed that differences due to the choice of series were consistently small, however. In the case of import and export price indexes, no fiscal-year–calendar-year adjustment is required, since these indexes prior to 1915 appear to be taken by *HS* directly from Lipsey (and apply only to domestic exports). The vast majority of the analysis in this chapter considers the nominal deficit as a share of nominal GNP; hence the fact that the export price index used covers only domestic exports is not a major problem. For regression analysis, all price indexes are benchmarked to 1967 = 100.

Total receipts and expenditures of the federal government are available in *HS* through 1970 for years ending June 30 and in the IMF's *International Financial Statistics* (*IFS*) thereafter for years ending September 30. Appropriately weighted averages of successive years were used to construct calender-year estimates. M2 is taken from *HS* through 1970 and *IFS* thereafter.

Through 1970 the *HS* series was used for GNP at current and constant 1958 prices, taking their ratio as the implicit price deflator. This series has been spliced to GNP for the post-1970 period as reported in *IFS*, and the IMF's series for GNP at constant 1980 prices has been rebenchmarked to 1958 prices. Romer [1986] has pointed to problems with the Kuznets and Commerce-Kendrick estimates upon which the *HS* series are based. The late nineteenth- and early twentieth-century estimates may exaggerate the cyclical volatility of national income, making comparisons over time of the income elasticities of imports and exports problematic. Others, such as Weir [1986], conclude that Romer's alternative estimates underestimate the cyclical volatility of national income prior to World War I. (See also section 4.3.)

United Kingdom

Data for the United Kingdom are drawn from Feinstein [1972] through 1965 and from *IFS* thereafter. All series are for calendar years. The export and import price indexes are again based on the unit value of exports of domestic products and of total imports. Through 1965 these are from Feinstein's Table 64. The volume of total exports and total imports is calculated from his Table 15. Through 1965, gross national product at market prices, in millions of pounds sterling and 1938 constant prices, is drawn from Feinstein's Tables 3 and 5. These are linked to *IFS* national income at market prices for subsequent years. Government receipts and expenditures (the current account of the central government, inclusive of National Health Insurance Funds) are from Feinstein's Table 12, linked to total government revenue and expenditure from *IFS*.

Japan

Most series for Japan are from *Long Term Economic Statistics* (*LTES*), as revised by Ohkawa and Rosovsky [1973] and supplemented by *IFS*. Gross national product at current market prices is from *LTES* through 1904 and from Ohkawa and Rosovksy thereafter. (The Ohkawa-Rosovsky series differs primarily by virtue of a revision of investment in agriculture.) GNP at constant prices is available for the pre-WWII and postwar periods separately, but no attempt has been made to link the two subsamples. Prewar GNP is at 1934–1946 prices, postwar GNP (from Okhawa and Rosovsky through 1965 and *IFS* thereafter) is in constant 1960 prices. The GNP deflators are normalized to 100 in 1937 for the prewar segment and in 1967 for the postwar segment. Current price GNP is linked to the counterpart series in *IFS*, and current price GNP is linked to GNP in 1980 prices from *IFS*, rebenchmarked to 1960 prices.

The value of imports and exports and the import and export price indexes are from *LTES*, Tables 5 and 15. As with GNP, no trade data exist for 1945, and no price indexes for imports and exports are available for 1940–1950. While Okhawa and Rosovsky provide import and export price indexes derived from the national income statistics for 1940–1944 and 1946–1950, these should be regarded as provisional. The 1940–1944 values have been rebenchmarked to link them to the 1939 *LTES* figure and the 1946–1950 values rebenchmarked to link them to the 1951 *LTES* figure. These series are then linked to *IFS* figures on import and export values (f.o.b.) and import and export prices (which are available in addition to unit values for the post-WWII period).

Finally, government revenues and expenditures, on a fiscal year basis, are taken from Japanese Ministry of Finance [1986].

Canada

The basic source for Canada is Urquhart and Buckley [1965], as supplemented and revised by Urquhart [1986] and extended by *IFS*. GNP at current market prices and constant 1913 prices is drawn from Urquhart for the period through 1925, to which the comparable series in Urquhart and Buckley are spliced through the period through 1960, followed by the comparable series from *IFS*. Real GNP is provided through 1925 at 1913 prices by Urquhart and from 1926 at 1949 prices by Urquhart and Buckley. The post-1926 component has been converted to 1913 prices by assuming no change in the GNP deflator between 1925 and 1926.

Export and import values (f.o.b.) are provided by Urquhart and Buckley. These are on a fiscal-year basis through 1918 (ending March 31 of the year given from 1908 through 1919 and June 30 from 1868 through 1906) and on a calendar-year basis thereafter. Fiscal-year figures are transformed to a calender-year basis by assuming a constant flow throughout the year and taking appropriately weighted averages. The import and export price indexes are drawn from Urquhart and Buckley, using their 1900 base series through 1915, their 1913 base series from 1916 through 1926, and their 1948 base series from 1927 through 1960. These were benchmarked to 1900 = 100, the unit values of imports and exports were appended for subsequent years, and the entire series was normalized to 1967 = 100.

Total government revenue and expenditure are from Urquhart and Buckley through 1960 and from *IFS* thereafter. Since Urquhart and Buckley's series are on a fiscal year basis for years ending June 30 before 1907 and for years ending March 31 thereafter, while the IMF's are for fiscal years beginning April 1, the revenue and expenditure series were adjusted to a calendar-year basis assuming a constant flow throughout the year and taking appropriately weighted averages.

COMMENTARY

by Anna J. Schwartz

Barry Eichengreen's contribution is admirable for the breadth of its coverage, given its compact size. Exploiting the evidence in 17 charts and 11 tables, Eichengreen touches on a number of macroeconomic themes related to the U.S. trade deficit. Annual data for the nominal trade deficit and GNP in nominal and real values are the empirical underpinning of his chapter.

Eichengreen has chosen to use U.S. trade numbers from *Historical Statistics*, where the data through 1915 are for years ending June 30, rather than the calendar-year series before 1915 back to 1879 in current and constant dollars of U.S. exports and imports in Robert Lipsey's *Price and Quantity Trends in the Foreign Trade of the United States* [Lipsey 1963, Table A–6, pp. 154–155]. Instead, he converted the *HS* numbers to calendar-year figures by averaging pairs of successive years. Eichengreen contends that Lipsey's exclusion of re-exports from total U.S. merchandise exports justifies his use of the *HS* numbers, though he concedes that re-exports averaged only 1.5% of total exports and that "differences due to the choice of series were consistently small." However, he uses the *HS* import and export price indexes before 1923 that are drawn from Lipsey's work. A consistent data base underlying the paper would have been preferable in my view.

Eichengreen expresses trade deficits mainly relative to GNP, rather than import and export volumes relative to real GNP, because of the index number problem resulting from changes in the composition of imports and exports and GNP that occur over long periods of time. It would nevertheless have been desirable to examine the breakdown of trade deficits into price and quantity components, especially since the breakdown is available in Lipsey's book in the form of price indexes for U.S. exports and imports of merchandise, and corresponding quantity indexes [Lipsey, Tables A-1 to A-4, pp. 142–150].

In addition to the U.S. time series, this chapter presents similar data for Canada, Japan, and the United Kingdom, plus tables of economic statistics for each of the foreign countries for a selected period of years. Those years, Eichengreen believes, exemplify the elimination of a trade deficit without marked recessionary effects. The econometric exercises that employ the data are limited to autocorrelations and OLS regressions.

A final observation in these preliminaries concerns the charts. Many of them require relabeling the scale for the trade deficit. Scales and labels have been altered to bring the level of the trade deficit closer to another series with which the chart compares it. The charts merely confuse when the deficit is labelled surplus and vice versa.

Now for the content of the chapter. The first half deals with the U.S. trade deficit initially from 1952 on and then extends the time period covered back to 1890. The second half of the chapter compares U.S. experience with that of the three foreign countries since 1870.

The author attempts to answer five questions, of which the first is whether the recent U.S. trade deficit as a percentage of GNP has been unprecedented.

An Unprecedented U.S. Trade Deficit?

Eichengreen finds that the U.S. trade deficit share of GNP since 1890 showed little trend until 1965, when it shifted to a moderately higher level which was maintained until the late 1970s, when once again it shifted upward to a more pronounced extent. On examining the role of the deficit relative to trade and trade relative to GNP, to see which explains more of the recent unprecedented deficit/GNP ratio, he reports more resemblance between the recent deficit relative to trade behavior than between trade/GNP behavior and the deficit. He also compares the average level of the deficit/GNP ratio under fixed and floating exchange rates since 1890, finding little difference in levels but a decidedly higher standard deviation and coefficient of variation in floating rate periods.

Compared to foreign country experience, the magnitude of the recent U.S. trade deficits is not unique. The United Kingdom had larger trade deficits before World War II, Canada likewise before World War I, and Japan had larger deficits during many periods from 1890 to 1950 but none since then. The current Japanese trade surplus is, however, without precedent, excepting only its huge World War I surplus.

A second question considered in this chapter is the time that has been required to close an exceptionally wide trade gap.

Time Required to Close a Trade Gap

The chapter examines persistence in autocorrelations lagged up to four years of the U.S. trade deficit, nominal or scaled by GNP. Whether examined from 1952 on or from 1895 on, Eichengreen finds a high degree of persistence, with no evidence of a rise in persistence in more recent years. Compared to foreign country autocorrelations, the U.S. trade balance tends to be more persistent both at short and longer lags, greater persistence after World War II characterizing also foreign country trade balances. It is not clear from the summary of the post-World War II autocorrelations whether here Eichengreen implies that persistence is currently greater than earlier for the U.S. deficit, that his earlier statement denied.

Since persistence may reflect long-run equilibrium of a nonzero trade balance, Eichengreen solves an equation for an equilibrium value for the deficit expressed as a function of a lagged dependent variable and an equilibrium value to which the deficit converges as a function of time, either linear or quadratic. For the more recent period, the implied U.S. long-run equilibrium value is a surplus from the mid-1950s through 1969 and a deficit thereafter. The actual balance moved from surplus to deficit in 1971. He does not comment on this result. If the current deficit is a long-run equilibrium value, is there any reason for concern about it?

For the earlier historical period, the coefficients on time are not significant, unlike the results for the later period, although the speed of convergence is similar both before and after 1952. This result is interpreted to mean greater persistence in the long-run equilibrium level in recent years.

He also finds increasing speed of convergence to a long-run balance in foreign countries. Speed of adjustment in the United States has been comparable to that in other countries.

Cyclical Behavior of the Trade Deficit

Although the focus of the paper is on the long run, Eichengreen also examines cyclical behavior of the trade deficit. The cyclical analysis is based in part on charts comparing the deficit share of GNP with a five-year moving average of the rate of growth of real GNP, first for 1952–1983, then for 1895–1985.

From the chart for the earlier historical period, he dates a break in cyclical behavior in 1952—earlier dates showing countercyclical behavior of the trade deficit, dates since then showing cyclical conformity. This pattern is not obvious to me in the post-Bretton Woods years. The trade deficit falls and then rises in both the contraction from 1973 to 1975 and the expansion from 1975 to 1980; thereafter, it rises during both contractions and expansions. Eichengreen also estimates a regression of the deficit as a function of real GNP growth, using a five-year moving average of both the dependent and independent variables. For two subperiods, 1895–1925 and 1930–1951, the sign of the coefficient on real GNP is negative. For the period 1895–1980, it is positive.

The explanation given for countercyclical behavior of the trade deficit before World War II is that foreign demands for U.S. exports were the driving force: an increase in foreign demand raised the price of exports, improved U.S. terms of trade, and moved the trade balance into surplus, while raising GNP and producing a negative relationship between the trade deficit and output. After World War II, the terms of trade and the trade deficit tended to move together rather than in opposite directions. The change in domestic demand for imports and the residual supply of exports is viewed as the driving force behind the trade deficit. Increased demand for imports and curtailed availability of exports increased export prices, improved the terms of trade, and moved the trade balance into deficit. Domestic demand raised GNP and led to a positive relation between the trade deficit and output.

Further, the fact that the real exchange rate tended to rise while the deficit tended to fall in the earlier period impresses Eichengreen as suggesting that it was mainly foreign demand that was driving the U.S. trade balance over the cycle. This relation with the real exchange rate is less obvious in recent years, which he attributes to an increasingly important role played by domestic demand. Before 1975, the real exchange rate shows little correlation with the trade deficit. In the decade 1975–1985, the relation between the real exchange rate and the deficit is inverse.

To explain domestic demand, he first regresses the deficit on the budget deficit in peacetime years and finds a positive relation. The deficit is then the consequence of "absorption effects of government spending." Here he introduces the exchange rate regime. Under flexible exchange rates, as absorption rises, increased demand for traded goods is satisfied by increased imports and curtailed exports. The market for nontraded goods can clear only if spending on them is restrained and resources are shifted into them through a real appreciation. He contrasts this outcome with fixed exchange rates, where monetary policy prevents appreciation—presumably it is expansionary—and a smaller trade deficit results due to the higher price of imports and increased competitiveness of exports. (How does expansionary monetary policy achieve these results?) He adds a dummy variable to floating-rate periods since 1895 in the regression of the trade deficit on the budget deficit and finds a positive relation as before, but the coefficient on the dummy is not significant.

This story could be correct, but would be more convincing if there were quantitative analysis of all the variables that are treated verbally. Countercyclical trade balance behavior is what Ilse Mintz [1959, "Trade Balances During Business Cycles: U.S. and Britain Since 1880," NBER Occasional Paper 67] found for the U.S. before 1954, when her study based on quarterly data ended. For the United Kingdom, however, she found high positive cyclical conformity before World War I. Thereafter the U.K. trade balance was countercyclical. There is obviously more to cyclicality than could be encompassed in one chapter.

Contribution of Relative Prices and the Government Budget to the Trade Deficit

Another question dealt with in this chapter is the contribution of relative prices and the government budget to the creation and elimination of trade deficits. A chart of the U.S. trade and government budget deficits both scaled by GNP has the appearance of a positive relationship throughout the post-WWII period, which Eichengreen notes should depend on the exchange rate regime. He sees such a change at the time of the Bretton Woods collapse, characterized not by a change in the elasticity of the trade deficit with respect to the budget deficit, but as an upward shift in the level of the trade deficit, given any level of the budget deficit.

To come back to the regression of the U.S. trade deficit on the budget deficit, Eichengreen adds the rate of change of the inverse of velocity, the sign of which is negative. In a footnote he also includes a variable interacting with the money variable for the floating rate periods, as he did for the budget deficit regression mentioned earlier. He tells a story about the difference between fixed- and floating-rate exchange rates. In fixed-exchange rate periods, budget deficits and monetary growth are positively correlated, attenuating the impact of domestic policy on trade policy. In floating-rate periods, budget deficits and monetary growth rates are negatively correlated. So it is the conventional view that he offers to explain the recent growth of the trade deficit: it is the result of both loose fiscal policy and tight monetary growth. Since the third quarter of 1982, monetary growth has alternated between very high and more moderate rates of increase. The pattern is not one I would describe as tight. Moreover, I interpret the inverse of velocity as the demand for money—the rate of change of the fraction of a year's income held as M2 money. What theory relates a change in the demand for money to the trade deficit? At a later point, referred to below, Eichengreen offers an explanation, alternative to the loose fiscal-tight monetary explanation, for trade deficits under floating exchange rates, but applicable to Canada. It is applicable also to the U.S.

Although Eichengreen contends that, in general, under floating exchange rates and high capital mobility, loose fiscal policy will drive up the real exchange rate, he notes that in Canada loose fiscal policy since 1975 has been paired with a depreciating Canadian dollar. At least one recent study by Paul Evans ["Is the Dollar High Because of Large Budget Deficits?" JME 18, Nov. 1986] has found a negative correlation between budget deficits and exchange rates. I believe Eichengreen correctly attributes the difference between the Canadian and the U.S. real exchange rate before 1985 to a higher level of household savings in Canada relative to the level in the U.S. He fails to observe, however, that the U.S. real exchange rate rose in 1981–1985 because of a low U.S. saving rate and the relative advantage of U.S. investment opportunities over opportunities in the rest of the world. These conditions stimulated a capital inflow, the counterpart of which was a large net inflow of goods. The real exchange rate has fallen since as investors worldwide reordered their portfolios to include assets in currencies other than the dollar. A market-determined dollar exchange rate might have fallen more since 1985, had other governments not intervened to support it—for the sake of their exports—thus maintaining the U.S. capital inflow and trade deficit.

Deficits Financed by Reserve Outlows or Invisible Earnings vs. Capital Imports

The final question examined in this chapter is what difference there is between deficits accompanied by capital imports and deficits financed by reserve outflows or invisible earnings. First, Eichengreen examines three episodes in Canada after 1912, Japan after 1924, and the United Kingdom after 1951, when the trade deficit was reduced without a prolonged recession. Chapter 4 tells a standard story about Canada—real shocks accounted for the capital inflows and raised the price of home goods; unlike Viner, Eichengreen mentions no monetary forces. Because Canada devoted foreign borrowings to finance investment rather than consumption, when capital inflows dried up, the volume of exports continued to grow, reducing the deficit in the course of a short but severe recession. In Japan, the trade deficit increased because of demand and supply shocks, but it fell rapidly thanks to export growth induced by exchange rate depreciation and stagnant economic growth, to which monetary restraint contributed. Likewise in the United Kingdom after World War II, regulatory restrictions on imports and monetary restraint reduced the trade deficit, thanks to improvement in the terms of trade.

This chapter contrasts the historical experience of the foreign countries with current U.S. trade deficits. Foreign countries financed their deficits out of interest earnings on prior foreign investments, export of services, or improvements in capacity to export. Eichengreen is pessimistic that the U.S. trade deficit can be reduced rapidly at low cost. The reason is that U.S. authorities cannot effect a favorable shock to the terms of trade and it is late in the day for a switch of U.S. resources to export-oriented sectors.

The response to that is that the pessimism is overdone. If at some future date, foreigners decide that they no longer want to invest in the United States, the trade deficit will undoubtedly decline. It is not obvious that in that event the burden of repaying the foreign debt will fall on the U.S. taxpayer. If foreigners have been misguided in acquiring U.S. equity, financial instruments, and direct investments, they will bear the cost of nonperforming assets. Predictions of how long it would take and at what horrendous cost to reduce the inflation rate in the early 1980s should remind us that predictions of how long it would take and at what horrendous cost to reduce the trade deficit are not to be credited.

5 AN EVALUATION OF POLICIES TO RESOLVE THE TRADE DEFICIT*

Sven W. Arndt

5.1 Introduction

In policy discussions of the "trade problem" three explanations of the U.S. experience in the 1980s have received particular attention. One is essentially macroeconomic in orientation and attributes the U.S. trade deficit to an excess of domestic aggregate demand over supply. The others stress the importance of trade-specific factors generally and of unfair trade practices and declining comparative advantage in particular.[1] The first sees restoration of macroeconomic balance at home as the principal means to trade balance improvement, while the other two focus on trade and industry specific policies.

Diagnosis clearly dictates remedy. If the problem is mainly macro-

---

* Prepared for a conference on "The U.S. Trade Deficit—Causes, Consequences and Cures," sponsored by the Federal Reserve Bank of St. Louis, October 1987.

This chapter draws on work sponsored by the Ford Foundation. I am indebted to Larry Bouton, Michael Hutchinson, Charles Pigott, William Poole, and Jack Tatom for valuable comments and to Cindy Beltz for able research assistance.

economic in nature, then industry and trade policies are impotent; if it is not, restrictive macroeconomic policies would reduce employment and output without solving the underlying problem. Section 5.2 evaluates the major explanations of the U.S trade problem in light of recent evidence. It is followed in section 5.3 by a detailed discussion of proposed solutions. A brief concluding section follows.

5.2 The Trade Deficit: Its Major Causes

The dollar appreciated sharply in the first half of the 1980s (as figure 5–1 shows) and the current account and trade balance deteriorated equally sharply. The decline in the trade balance was broadly based, affecting U.S. relations with a majority of its trading partners (as shown in figure 5–2) and across the spectrum of its commodity trade (as shown in table 5–1). The general nature and pervasive quality of these changes suggest that the

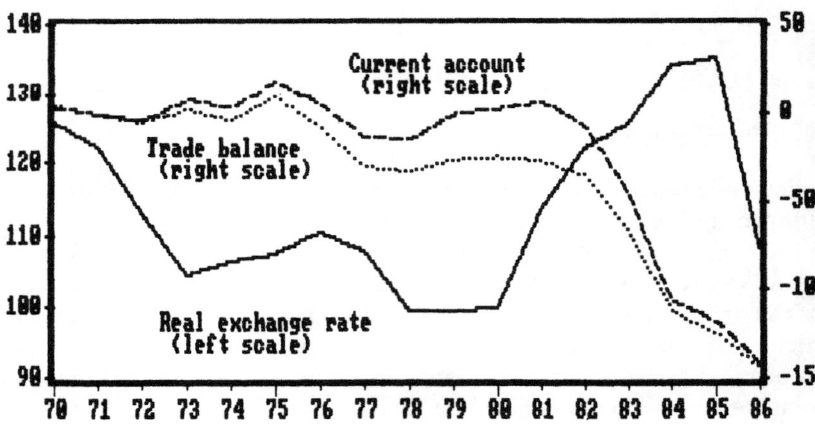

Notes:

[1] Right scale is in billions of dollars; left scale is indexed to base-year 1980.

[2] The real exchange rate is based on wholesale prices in the United States relative to a weighted average of wholesale prices in other industrial countries.

[3] The nominal exchange rate is the IMF MERM rate.

Source: International Monetary Fund, *International Financial Statistics* (various issues)

Figure 5–1. U.S. Merchandise Trade Balance, Current Account, and Real Exchange Rate, 1970–1986

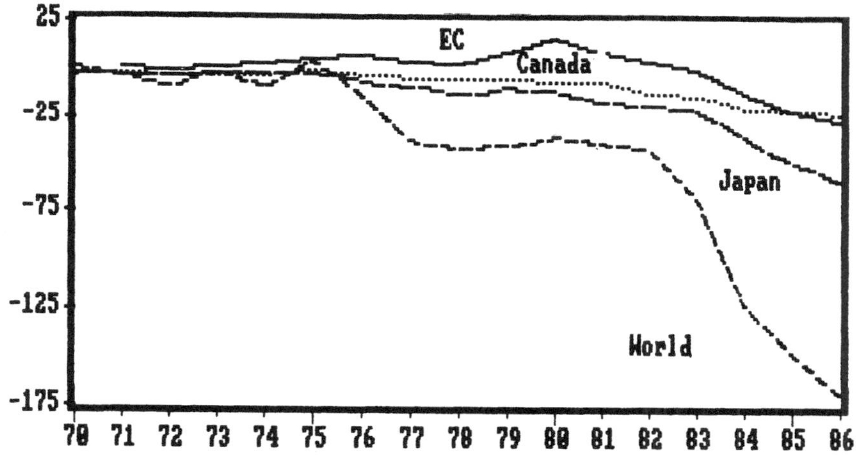

Source: International Monetary Fund, *Direction of Trade Statistics* (various issues) and U.S. Bureau of the Census, *Highlights of the U.S. Export and Import Trade*, FT 990 (March 1987)

Figure 5–2. U.S. Merchandise Trade Balance with Selected Countries, 1970–1986 (billions of dollars)

cause or causes were broad and economy-wide rather than microeconomic and trade specific.

Unfair foreign trade is one cause that cannot have made a major contribution because there is no evidence that America's trading partners suddenly and collectively escalated their discriminatory practices. Consequently, improvements in trade practices around the globe, however desirable in their own right, are not capable of bringing about a significant turnaround in America's trade balance.

The severity and pervasive nature of the trade balance deterioration also argue against shifts in global comparative advantage and in the global division of labor as a primary cause. Comparative advantage tends to shift slowly and selectively, rather than abruptly and in a wholesale manner. Although shifts in comparative advantage are no doubt taking place in relation to particular countries and products, a broad realignment in comparative advantage can be ruled out as a principal cause of the trade balance deficit.[2]

This leaves macroeconomic developments as the only comprehensive explanation of the trade deficit, but there exists substantial disagreement

Table 5–1. U.S. Trade Balance, Selected Industries, 1980–1986 (billions of dollars)

Industry	*1980*	*1981*	*1982*	*1983*	*1984*	*1985*	*1980–1985*	*1986*
Agriculture	19.6	21.2	16.5	15.2	15.3	7.3	−12.3	1.2
Mining	−62.4	−60.9	−45.1	−37.4	−37.1	−32.6	29.8	−22.4
Manufacturing	20.7	12.9	−2.0	−34.8	−84.3	−104.3	−125.0	−135.0
Food and kindred products	1.7	2.2	1.5	0.7	−0.9	−2.5	−4.2	−1.6
Tobacco manufactures	1.0	1.1	1.1	0.8	1.1	1.2	0.2	1.4
Textile mill products	0.5	−0.2	−0.5	−1.0	−1.9	−2.2	−2.7	−2.6
Apparel products	−4.9	−6.1	−7.2	−8.9	−12.9	−14.7	−9.8	−17.0
Lumber and wood products	0.1	−0.6	−0.2	−1.6	−2.1	−2.4	−2.5	−3.6
Furniture and fixtures	−0.6	−0.6	−0.8	−1.3	−1.9	−2.7	−2.1	
Paper and allied products	−0.8	−1.0	−1.3	−1.7	−3.1	−3.6	−2.8	−3.5
Printing and publishing	0.6	0.8	0.8	0.7	0.3	0.1	0.5	−0.2
Chemical products	14.1	13.8	12.4	10.4	10.3	9.0	−5.1	9.2
Petroleum and coal products	−10.6	−11.8	−9.3	−12.1	−16.1	−12.9	−2.3	−8.9
Rubber and plastic products	−0.1	−0.1	−0.3	−0.7	−1.4	−2.0	−1.9	−2.5
Leather products	−2.9	−3.4	−4.0	−4.8	−6.3	−7.2	−4.3	−8.2
Stone, clay, and glass	−0.3	−0.4	−0.5	−1.1	−1.9	−2.5	−2.2	−3.2
Primary metal products	−6.9	−12.4	−10.5	−11.0	−16.8	−15.7	−8.8	−17.9
Fabricated metal products	2.5	2.9	2.5	1.4	−0.3	−2.0	−4.5	−3.1
Machinery, except electrical	24.9	27.8	23.9	15.8	9.6	6.2	−18.7	−2.1
Electrical equipment	0.9	−0.4	−1.9	−6.4	−15.2	−19.0	−19.9	−23.2
Transportation equipment	−1.5	−0.9	−7.0	−11.7	−22.1	−27.9	−26.4	−40.4
Instruments	3.0	2.8	3.0	2.3	1.0	−0.2	−3.2	−1.5
Miscellaneous	−2.5	−3.7	−4.4	−4.5	−7.8	−9.4	−6.9	−6.6

Sources: Department of Commerce, Bureau of the Census, Foreign Trade Division, Report EA675, U.S. Exports, and Report IA275, U.S. Imports for Consumption and General Imports, various issues, Highlights of the U.S. Export and Import Trade, FT 990, December 1986.

on the channels through which the trade deficit is linked to domestic macroeconomic developments. The OECD calculates growth rates for the United States of real domestic demand of 5.0, 8.3, 3.4, and 3.5% in 1983, 1984, 1985, and 1986, respectively, compared with growth rates of real GNP of 3.4, 6.4, 2.7, and 2.5%, respectively.[3] In the public discourse such imbalances have been captured by the image of America "living beyond its means."

The relationship between the current account and the financial balances of private and public sectors is given in figure 5–3. The first several years of the 1980s resemble the recession/recovery of a typical business cycle, with the deficit of general government rising to fill the gap left by declining private demand. But when private investment and consumption rebound in 1983, the budget deficit retreats only partly and briefly and then expands again. It is at that point that the current account commences its long and sustained decline.

In late 1979, monetary policy became aggressively anti-inflationary in the United States, a new policy attitude that was soon emulated in other countries. The emergence of the debt crisis in 1982 was probably due at least in part to the worldwide shift toward anti-inflationary policies.

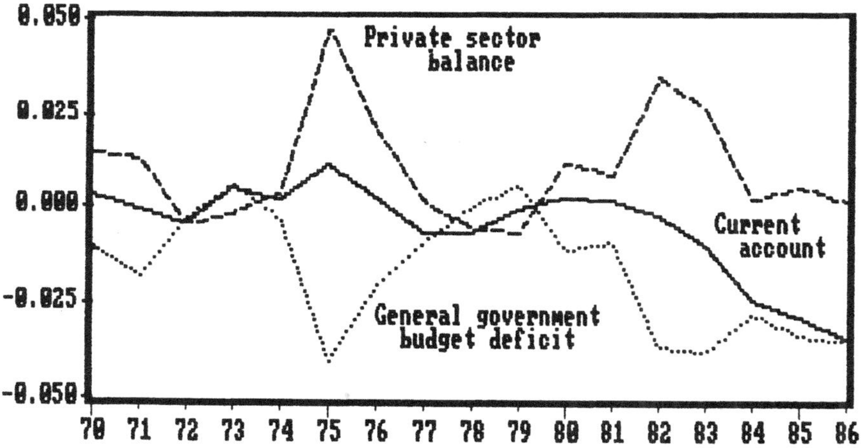

Source: U.S. Department of Commerce, *Survey of Current Business* (various issues) and *National Income and Product Accounts, Historical Data, 1929–1976*; and *Economic Report of the President, 1987*

Figure 5–3. U.S. Private Sector Balance, General Government Budget Deficit, and Current Account, 1970–1986 (percentage of GNP)

It introduced major adjustments in global asset preferences in favor of dollar-denominated assets.

Austerity policies in debtor nations helped weaken global demand and thereby contibuted to worldwide excess capacity. Prices in many world markets peaked in 1980, and the price pressures that had been so prominent in the preceding decade all but disappeared.

The global financial environment changed in important ways as financial deregulation and liberalization in Japan and other countries deepened financial interdependence and created new patterns of capital mobility.

Finally, the early years of the decade witnessed major changes in U.S. tax policy and in the fiscal stance of the federal government. The Economic Recovery and Tax Act (ERTA) provided tax incentives for private investment, especially in equipment, while significant reductions in taxes helped fuel the sustained growth of consumer demand and of the federal deficit.

In the first half of the 1980s, the price of tradables fell sharply relative to nontradables, as figure 5–4 shows. The decline shown there closely resembles the pattern followed by the real appreciation of the dollar in figure 5–1. Relative price changes of this magnitude should affect the share of resources devoted to production in the two sectors and, as figure 5–5

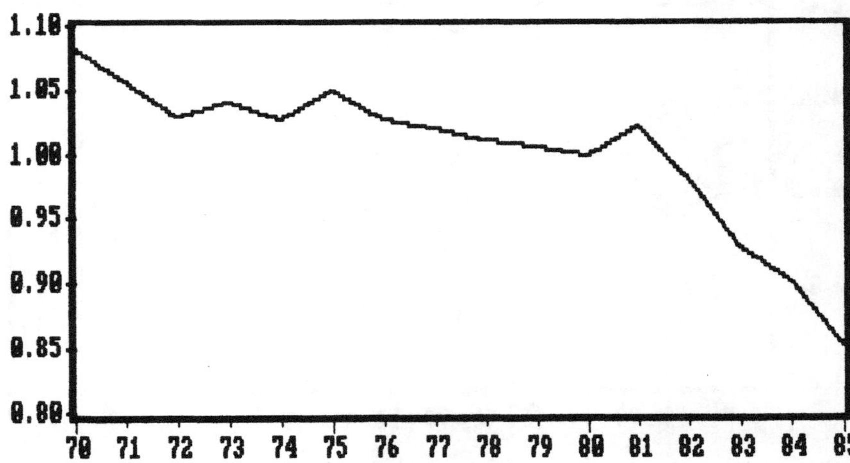

Source: U.S. Department of Commerce, *National Income and Product Accounts* (various issues)

Figure 5–4. U.S. Relative Prices, Tradables versus Nontradables, 1970–1985 (1980 = 100) illustrates, the share of tradables output in total private sector output declined significantly in the 1980s.

Private tradables consist of agriculture, mining, and manufactured goods, while nontradables are made up of construction; transportation and public utilities; wholesale and retail trade; and financial, insurance, and other services. The public sector produces mainly nontradables. Many industries do, of course, produce both types of products, but the intent here is to distinguish among different degrees of foreign competition faced by domestic producers. Tradables tend to be relatively exposed to foreign competition, which limits the price-making independence of their producers.

An important distinguishing feature of nontradables is that discrepancies between demand and supply in markets for nontradables cannot be bridged by exports or imports and must thus be corrected by price changes (after allowing for increases in order backlogs, delays in service, etc.). In the context of an integrated economy in which producers in the two sectors compete for consumer expenditure on the demand side and for resources on the supply side, the relative price of tradables to nontradables plays a key role.

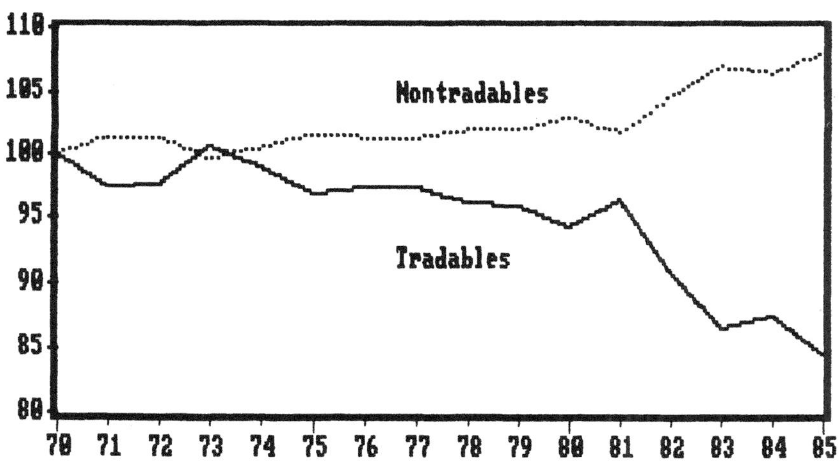

Source: U.S. Department of Commerce, *National Income and Product Accounts* (various issues)

Figure 5–5. Tradables and Nontradables in Total Private Sector Output (1970 = 100)

The relative price of tradables to nontradables moves in order to clear the market for nontradables, and in so doing plays an important part in the determination of the real exchange rate. Adjustments in real exchange rates and in the trade balance are thus closely linked to supply and demand conditions not only in the tradables sector, but in nontradables as well.

The role of intersectoral adjustment in the determination of real exchange rates and trade imbalances is sometimes ignored in the policy debate, where attention tends to focus on the interaction between the domestic tradables sector and the rest of the world. The connection between sectoral adjustment and external variables may be sketched with the aid of figure 5–6.[4] The figure shows the market for tradables in the right panel, with the relative price of tradables measured along the vertical axis. The left panel represents the market for nontradables, where the definition of relative price requires the positions of the demand and supply curves to be reversed.

Suppose that curves subscripted by 0 represent initial equilibrium, so that the relative price of tradables, P_0, clears both sectors. Consider next a rise in domestic expenditure that raises demand in both sectors (to demand curves subscripted by 1). In order to clear the market for nontradables, the relative price falls to P_1 and in the process the trade balance deteriorates. This deterioration comes in addition to the trade deficit created by the initial rise in expenditures on tradables.

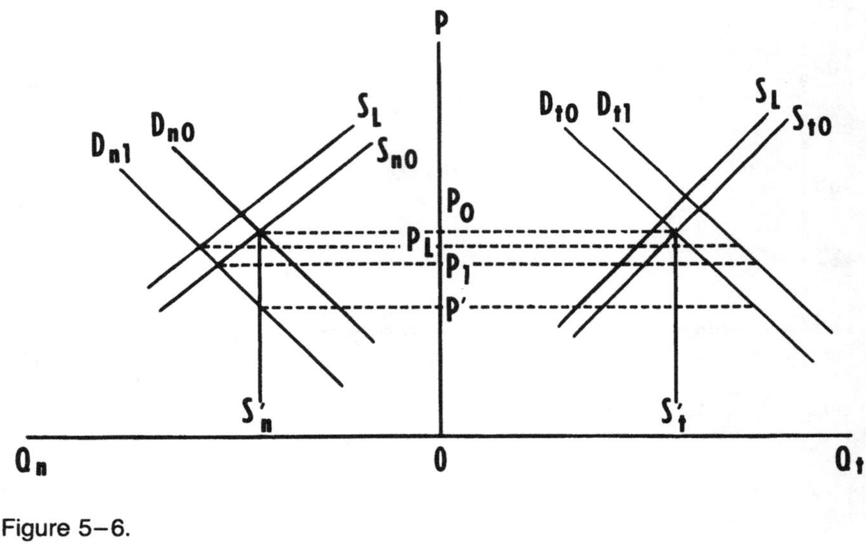

Figure 5–6.

The foregoing does not provide a complete picture of economy-wide adjustment, particularly in the financial sector, but it shows the important role played by the "domestic" side of the economy in determining movements in real exchange rates and in the trade balance.[5] The nontradables sector exerts its influence because the two sectors compete for productive resources on the supply side and for shares of national expenditure on the demand side. That competition is an important feature of the economy's overall adjustment to disturbances.

5.2.1 Budgetary Policy

Consider a debt-financed fiscal expansion that raises aggregate expenditure. In general, any large change in aggregate demand affects both sectors, but the particulars may vary from case to case. Its effect on the relative price of tradables depends on the share of nontradables in the expenditure increase. Its effect on the trade balance depends directly on the share of tradables in the expenditure increase and indirectly on the sensitivity of tradables supply and demand to the change in the relative price.

If the expenditure rise falls entirely on nontradables, there is no impact effect on the tradables demand curve. The curve shifts out eventually, however, as a result of the rise in income and private expenditure occasioned by the fiscal expansion. The impact effect of the fiscal expansion shifts the demand for nontradables to the left, reducing the relative price of tradables in order to preserve equilibrium in the market for nontradables. The price decline causes the trade balance to deteriorate. The trade balance deteriorates further as the effects of the fiscal-policy multiplier on private expenditure come into play.

If the fiscal stimulus falls entirely on tradables, then the demand for nontradables does not change initially. The relative price of tradables remains unchanged, but the trade balance deteriorates in response to the rise in domestic tradables demand. Eventually, as fiscal expansion stimulates private expenditure and the demand for nontradables rises, the relative price of tradables declines and the trade balance deteriorates further.

The ability of the home country to satisfy its increased demand for imports depends upon capacity constraints in world markets. If world output of tradables is perfectly elastic, the deterioration in the trade balance occurs without a run-up in the world price of tradables. If world supply is inelastic, then a rise in import demand or a decline in export supply forces up the world price of traded goods. The more inelastic is world supply, the more the outcome resembles the closed-economy case, for then a fiscal stimulus crowds out private expenditure. The outcome may still differ from the closed-economy case to the extent that the fiscal expansion crowds out foreign rather than domestic private expenditure.

5.2.2 Sector Specificity

Interdependence between the two sectors implies that shocks and disturbances in one have inevitable consequences for the other. At full employment, for example, a rise in resource utilization in one sector necessarily requires reduced utilization in the other. The sectoral supply curves are thus interrelated. Assuming that capital is sector specific in the short run, an upward movement along the tradables supply curve requires a rise in employment in that sector, which must be matched by a decline in employment in the nontradables sector. The accompanying upward movement along the nontradables supply curve releases labor for redeployment.

If labor is also immobile between sectors in the short run, then supplies are inelastic in both sectors (indicated by the vertical segments of the two supply curves—S_t' and S_n'). When factors are sector specific, factor markets are segmented and factor prices become unlinked. If factor prices are rigid downward in a market, a fall in the price of the relevant product creates unemployment or idle capacity in that sector without relief from intersectoral redeployment of the affected factor of production. Conditions of this type tend to produce a highly elastic sectoral supply curve.

When capital is sector specific, a decline in the relative price of tradables reduces capital rentals in the tradables sector while raising them in nontradables. This divergence between sectoral rentals creates incentives for long-run redeployment of capital away from tradables by means of capital accumulation in nontradables and decumulation in tradables. Although the evidence is still only fragmentary, it suggests that the share of total private nonresidential fixed capital (both equipment and structures) in tradables declined in the 1980s.[6]

Factor market conditions thus influence the economy's response to the fiscal disturbance. Compare, for example, the case of mobile labor and flexible wages (supply curves subscripted with 0) with immobile labor and flexible wages (supply curves vertical). The rise in nontradables demand produces a larger decline in the relative price of tradables in the second case and a larger real appreciation. Whether the trade balance deteriorates by more or less, depends upon the relevant elasticities.

Then, as time gradually restores labor mobility, the supply curves rotate in a clockwise manner from their vertical positions and the initial fall in the relative price of tradables, as well as the real appreciation, is to some extent reversed. The trade balance also changes, but its response is governed by two opposing forces and hence tends to be sluggish. As the relative price of tradables rises and the currency appreciates in real terms, the trade balance improves, but that improvement is diluted by the rotation of the tradables supply curve.

Under conditions of sector specificity, therefore, the relative price, and hence the real exchange rate, tends to overshoot its long-run value. Unlike overshooting in the Dornbusch [1976a] model, however, it is here the result of factor market conditions rather than rigid commodity prices.

It is thus possible to imagine a protracted process of adjustment governed by mobilities in the markets for capital and labor. If labor is more mobile than capital, adjustment is initially dominated by labor market flexibility. Then, as capital becomes mobile, further adjustment takes place. Redeployment of capital into a sector tends to increase output in that sector while reducing supply in the other. Redeployment of capital into nontradables, therefore, shifts supply curves left in both sectors, thereby tending to raise the relative price of tradables and causing the real value of the currency to fall.

Two forces operate on the trade balance during this process. The rise in the relative price of tradables tends to improve the trade balance, while the shift in the tradables supply curve tends to worsen it.

Once resources have been redeployed and the economy's industrial structure shifted toward nontradables, the extent of currency depreciation required to restore the trade balance to its original equilibrium is increased. It is clear from figure 5–6 that the relative price that clears the trade balance after intersectoral resource redeployment is higher than the original price (P_0).

The foregoing focuses on the constraints imposed by the need for the two sectors to share existing resource endowments. Under conditions of economic growth, however, supply curves can shift out in both sectors simultaneously, their relative movements depending upon the sectoral incidence of economic growth.

Economic growth raises not only productive capacity but income, and income growth boosts demand in both sectors. The net effect of economic growth in each market thus depends upon the relative magnitudes of demand and supply curve shifts. This insight is relevant to the popular argument that the rise in demand for tradables produced by U.S. economic growth was a major cause of the deterioration in the trade balance in the first half of the eighties. It is not absolute demand growth, however, but demand growth relative to supply expansion that matters.

The general framework developed above provides a useful tool for evaluating the effects of shocks like those of the early 1980s on the trade balance and the real exchange rate. The major shocks are monetary and fiscal policy in the United States and demand stagnation in the world economy.

5.2.2.1 Monetary Policy. In 1979, the Federal Reserve adopted new operating procedures as part of a determined and ultimately successful effort to control inflation. If wages and prices are flexible downward and resources mobile during such an exercise, a monetary "contraction" of this type tends to be neutral with respect to relative prices and real exchange rates.[7]

In the presence of market rigidities of one kind or another, however, a monetary contraction can alter relative prices, relative wages, and hence the real exchange rate. Inasmuch as nontradables include services of various types, whose prices tend to be less flexible than agricultural prices and those of many manufactured products, monetary contraction may drive down the relative prices of tradables, especially in the short run.

5.2.2.4 Fiscal Policy. The effects of a debt-financed fiscal expansion, whether it takes the form of an expenditure rise or tax cut, depend on the sectoral composition of the demand stimulus. A tax cut that raises household disposable income stimulates consumer demand for tradables and nontradables alike. In an advanced, high-income economy oriented toward services, a significant portion of any general demand rise is bound to fall on nontradables, with consequent downward pressures on the relative price of tradables and deterioration in the trade balance. This deterioration in the trade picture comes in addition to the direct trade balance effect of the rise in household demand for tradables.

If the fiscal expansion takes the form of a rise in expenditure, its effects again depend on the sectoral distribution of the expenditure rise. Government expenditure may be heavily biased toward military goods and services, thereby placing substantial pressure on the nontradables sector and hence on the relative price and the real exchange rate.

The mix of real-currency appreciation and trade-balance deterioration that follows a general expenditure increase depends not only on the sectoral distribution of the expenditure rise itself, but on the sectoral distribution of excess capacity in the economy. This is especially important in view of the fact that the fiscal expansion of the early 1980s began in the context of a relatively sluggish U.S. economy. By 1983–1984, however, aggregate expenditures were rising substantially faster than aggregate output, as we have already seen.

5.2.2.3 Global Economic Conditions. Monetary stringency and fiscal stimulus at home took place in the context of a relatively stagnant global economic environment. We have already noted that the open-economy response to aggregate disturbances approaches that of a closed economy when worldwide supply conditions are inelastic. A given policy package that produces real appreciation and trade balance deterioration when the world economy is relatively stagnant, generates outcomes that resemble the closed economy case under conditions of tight world capacity. Under such conditions, a rise in U.S. demand for tradables would simply raise tradables prices everywhere, forcing the demand rise back inside, raising the real rate of interest in order to crowd out domestic private demand, and inhibiting real exchange rate appreciation.

5.3 The Trade Balance Problem: Proposed Remedies

Hence, policies that aim to improve the trade deficit must reduce the excess demand for tradables, either directly through their effects on demand and supply conditions in that market or indirectly by lowering the equilibrium relative price of nontradables. Policies using the indirect approach produce real-currency depreciation followed by trade balance improvement. Policies using the direct approach generate improvements in the trade balance without necessarily doing much to real currency values.

As a practical matter, policy fine-tuning has its limits, so that both sectors are typically disturbed by intervention policy. Any comprehensive policy package must include reduction of the federal fiscal imbalance if significant realignments in sectoral equilibria are to be forthcoming.

To the extent that prices respond faster than the trade balance, the typical policy package is likely to move the relative price and hence the real exchange rate well before the trade balance. This is especially true, if trade balance improvement depends upon increasing tradables output by redeploying resources from nontradables to tradables.

It is to be expected, and the early anecdotal evidence confirms, that capacity limits in many tradables industries will slow the process of trade balance improvement. Indeed, the earlier discussion of overshooting suggests that it might be a problem in the reverse direction. Relatively large currency depreciation may be needed to produce even modest improvements in the trade deficit, especially one as large as ours. Then as labor, and eventually capital, resources flow back into the tradables sector and productive capacity expands, a partial reversal in the dollar's depreciation will occur. Overshooting, and hence exchange rate instability, will be larger, the greater the pressures for rapid adjustment. But in any event, the United States is in for exchange rate volatility during the transition period.

The transition period is also bound to be marked by rising prices generally, because the required increase in the relative price of tradables is likely to be achieved more through increases in the money prices of tradables than decreases in the money prices of nontradables. Price decreases are always difficult to achieve and especially in services sectors where they translate more or less directly into wage and salary cuts.

If increases in the relative price of tradables are achieved mainly by raising the money prices of tradables, the overall price level will rise. Federal Reserve policy will have to be accommodating, if monetary policy is not to inhibit and delay the needed intersectoral reallocation of the economy's productive resources. This places an additional burden on monetary policy, which must be lax enough to finance internal resource reallocation, yet tight enough to avoid monetary inflation.

A by-product of the budget deficits of the 1980s was a steady stream of Treasury securities into private domestic and foreign portfolios. As the share of debt in private holdings rose relative to equities, equity values were bid up as wealth owners strove to preserve portfolio diversification. This no doubt supported the long rise in stock market values around the globe. It also suggests that a partial reversal of these movements may be needed during the wind-down period.

5.3.1 Trade Policies

Various trade actions—from "Buy American" and local content promotions to selective and general trade restraints—have been proposed as means of reducing if not eliminating the U.S. trade deficit. If trade intervention is to improve the trade deficit it must reduce the domestic excess demand for tradables either directly at existing relative prices or indirectly by raising the relative price of tradables. Trade policy is not, in general, an efficient tool for this task.

Consider, for example, a "buy American" policy that encourages residents to use home rather than foreign goods. This could mean home produced tradables or nontradables or both. Given the size of the U.S. trade deficit, however, expenditure switching toward home tradables is unlikely to yield a great deal without a substantial rise in the relative price of tradables and a shift of productive resources into tradables.

A "buy American" policy may instead be aimed at switching resident expenditure from tradables to nontradables, so as to shift the tradables demand curve in and the nontradables demand curve out in figure 5–6. As is clear from inspection of the figure, however, a shift of the nontradables demand curve leads to a decline in relative price and thereby tends to dilute the beneficial effect on the trade deficit of the expenditure-switching trade policy. The main argument against a "buy American" policy in this instance is that it is not a very efficient means of changing the relative price between tradables and nontradables.

Trade sanctions against particular products or countries are also of limited value. Frequently, they do little more than alter the country or commodity composition of U.S. trade without much impact on the overall trade balance. They simply shift expenditures from sanctioned countries and commodities to others, without changing the overall equilibrium of the system.

A general trade action, such as a uniform surcharge on all dutiable imports, is a more complex measure whose effects depend upon the specifics of the situation. In order to improve the trade balance, imports must fall and/or exports rise. Under conditions of full employment, the only way to reduce the trade deficit at existing relative prices is to shift the tradables demand curve inward. As for the supply of tradables, it varies with the share of domestic resources dedicated to tradables production (technology and productivity changes aside). The share of productive resources available to the tradables sector can rise only if the relative price rises. Thus, the trade action must reduce demand in the nontradables sector, so that the relative price may rise and thereby support a redistribution of resources into the tradables sector.

Even when excess resources are available in the economy, only an absolutely flat and hence perfectly elastic tradables supply curve will enable tradables output to be increased without a rise in relative price. The anecdotal evidence for the United States in the mid-1980s is not reassuring, however, for it suggests that capacity is limited in many tradables industries, so that increasing tradables production requires large increases in relative price, that is, large real depreciation in the short run, and infusions of new resources into the tradables sector over time. Trade policy is a rather inefficient instrument for this task.

But is that not the purpose of protection, to raise the price of imports and therewith improve the trade balance? Economic theory after all suggests that a rise in the domestic money price of imports, brought about by protection, causes the quantity of imports demanded to decline, while raising the quantity demanded of domestically produced tradables and of nontradables. This traditional argument for trade policy rests heavily on demand considerations and the expenditure-switching effects of a rise in the money price of imports.

As the preceding discussion makes clear, however, supply considerations are crucial, especially as they pertain to the intersectoral movement of resources. A steeper price of imports, relative to other goods produced at home, provides incentives to supply more import-competing products by drawing resources from exportables and from nontradables. Inasmuch as resource redeployment between exportables and import-competing products does little to improve the trade balance, the main contribution must come from resource redeployments between tradables and nontradables. Since additional resources will be drawn into tradables production only if the relative price rises, the money prices of nontradables must rise less than those of tradables.

In the process, however, price pressures spread through the economy. As the price level rises, real cash balances and real wealth fall and aggregate expenditure drops. This drop causes the sectoral demand curves to shift inward, thereby creating the conditions for a rise in the relative price of tradables and an improvement in the trade balance. It is apparent that the effectiveness of trade policy in improving the trade balance depends on its ability to reduce overall expenditure by crowding out private demand.

The preceding result is, of course, built upon the assumption of full employment. It might be argued, therefore, that excess capacity and unemployment in the tradables sector could easily accommodate the demand shift toward import competing goods that a surcharge would generate. There can be little doubt that some tradables industries would benefit from the shift, but a major reduction in the large U.S. trade deficit cannot be achieved simply by making greater use of idle resources at existing prices.

In the first half of the 1980s, many tradables producers found that low world prices limited the extent to which existing capacity could be utilized profitably. Uneconomic operations were retired and capacity is now more limited than the official figures suggest. Hence, the speed and extent of trade-balance improvement are limited by a supply constraint, quite apart from the demand inelasticities that have received so much attention. In the short run, therefore, even large changes in the relative price of tradables and in the real value of the dollar are unlikely to make much of a dent in the large U.S. trade deficit. Ultimately, only restoration of productive capacity in the tradables sector can turn the trade balance around.

5.3.2 Foreign Expansion

U.S. officials have asked Germany and Japan to expand their economies in order to raise the demand for U.S. exports. The value of these measures for trade-balance improvement depends upon their effect on world tradables prices. If, as we have argued, existing world prices make additional production of tradables unprofitable in the United States, overseas expansion must raise world tradables prices.

In other words, foreign demand expansion must raise the relative price of tradables. For reasons discussed earlier, that rise is likely to raise prices generally in the United States, and hence a key to the success of the endeavor is the response of monetary authorities at home and abroad.

Tradables producers need a boost in relative prices, but it is precisely the fear of boosting prices that inhibits macroeconomic policy in Germany and Japan. This fear is misplaced to the extent that it mistakes a rise in overall prices due to a realignment of relative prices for a monetary inflation. Tradables prices have been depressed during this decade, and if a turnaround in relative prices cannot be achieved entirely by reduction in nontradables prices, then an improvement in tradables prices must inevitably lead to a rise in prices generally.

While pressing Germany and Japan, U.S. officials have all but ignored the effects on overall world demand of the debt crisis and of stagnation in debtor economies. Figure 5–7 shows the decline in U.S. exports to selected debtor countries in the 1980s. U.S. exports to Western Hemisphere developing nations declined from $42 billion to $31 billion between 1981 and 1985, far more than the drop from $10 to $9 billion of exports to Germany. During that period, exports to Japan actually rose slightly.

Together, the developing countries of the hemisphere accounted for 18% of U.S. exports in 1981 (declining to 13% in 1983 and recuperating to 15% in 1985), while Germany accounted for 4% in 1981 and 1985 and Japan for 9% in 1981 and 11% in 1985. The U.S. *share* of total imports into Western Hemisphere developing nations has actually increased from 33% in 1981 to 37% in 1985; but the sharp cuts in the total imports of those countries, made necessary by austerity, have led to equally sharp cuts in U.S. sales there.

Pressed to service their debt in an environment of capital scarcity,

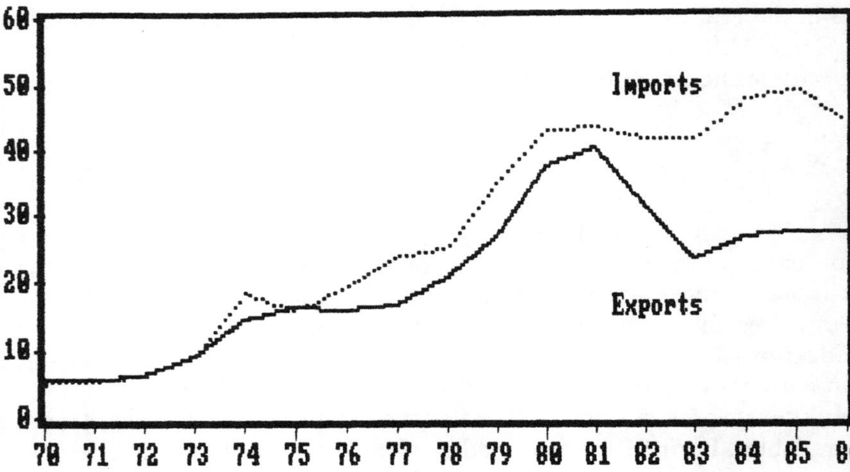

Note: Highly indebted countries include Argentina, Bolivia, Brazil, Chile, Colombia, Costa Rica, Cote d'Ivoire, Ecuador, Jamaica, Mexico, Morocco, Nigeria, Peru, Philippines, Uruguay, Venezuela, and Yugoslavia. See World Bank, *World Development Report, 1987* for definition.

Source: International Monetary Fund, *Direction of Trade Statistics* (various issues)

Figure 5–7. U.S. trade with Selected Highly Indebted Countries with debt servicing problems (in billions of U.S. dollars)

debtor countries have aggressively pushed exports while suppressing imports. This has affected the trade balances of the United States and other creditors directly, of course; but in addition, the slump in economic activity in those countries has contributed to the softness in world tradables prices.

From this perspective, therefore, improved economic performance in debtor countries would do more for the U.S. trade balance than even vigorous stimulation in Japan and Germany.

The debt crisis has affected the value of the dollar and the trade balance through an additional channel, as we have seen. By shifting asset preferences among U.S. and world investors toward dollar assets, the debt crisis contributed to the surge in capital inflows into the United States. This inflow facilitated Treasury debt sales and eased pressures on U.S. interest rates.

A major shift in portfolio preferences tends to push up the nominal and real value of the recipient country's currency. It tends to raise aggregate demand, through its effect on interest rates; and through its effect on the demand for nontradables, it raises their relative price, especially in the presence of ample worldwide productive capacity. Hence, improvement in the investment climate in debtor countries would lead to portfolio diversification away from the dollar and this would weaken the dollar and improve the trade balance.

5.2.3 Exchange Market Intervention

Coordinated intervention in exchange markets to push down the dollar has been advocated as a means to a better trade balance. The dollar has depreciated since early 1985, but the trade deficit response has been disappointing.

We have already seen how resource redeployment and sectoral restructuring reduces the trade balance response to exchange rate changes. The power of official intervention to force changes in real exchange rates has been vastly overrated in the debate. It is widely but erroneously believed that the Plaza accord among G-5 countries in September 1985 was the primary cause of the dollar's depreciation.

In fact, the dollar had already been depreciating for several months and its rate of depreciation after Plaza was very much like its rate before. The dollar began to depreciate when the growth of aggregate expenditure, which had been especially torrid in 1984, slowed significantly in relation to GNP growth. The "fundamentals" had changed and it is that change rather than official intervention which explains the depreciation since early 1985.

5.4 Conclusion

The pivotal role of U.S. budgetary policies in the trade balance developments of the 1980s stands out clearly. The preceding discussion has emphasized the role of domestic relative price adjustments and their effects on employment in industries producing tradables. Jobs and profits were not so much exported as redeployed within the economy from tradables to nontradables production.

Although the budgetary policies of the United States played a key role, monetary policy and the global environment of the time provided important support. Weakness in worldwide demand and softness in world prices facilitated an outcome that would not have been possible in a world of strong demand and scarce productive capacity. The debt crisis and austerity programs in debtor countries contributed to these conditions. For both, anti-inflationary monetary policies in the United States must take at least some blame.

Significant and pervasive changes in risk perceptions and asset preferences among the world's wealth owners, partly induced by the debt crisis and partly by widespread financial liberalization, provided timely changes in the pattern of world capital flows that helped finance the two U.S. deficits.

Reversal of any one of these factors would contribute to a turnaround of the U.S. trade deficit, but relying on a single policy change is unwise. The United States should be quite sensitive to a multipolicy approach and to the weight given each of several policies in a broad assault on the current global disequilibrium. For example, a combination of budget deficit reduction and debt crisis resolution is preferable to unilateral deficit reduction. Multipolicy approaches do, however, require policy coordination at home and collaboration with other countries. Domestic coordination has not been achieved, as policy makers continue to pursue the budget deficit, trade deficit, and debt problems along largely separate tracks. And collaboration with trading partners has produced few results thus far.

Trade action and exchange market intervention are of little use, because they are either incapable altogether of bringing about the internal changes needed for trade balance improvement or are rather clumsy and inefficient instruments for doing so. To the extent that trade and debt problems need coordinated approaches, moreover, trade policy only worsens the debt problem. Rather than encouraging collaboration, trade action runs the risk of inciting retaliation.

Notes

1. For a useful recent review of the issues, see Dean and Koromzay [1987]. See also Tatom [1986].

2. In a recent study, Arndt and Bouton [1987] examine the U.S. balance of trade in three product groups—product-cycle goods (p-c), Heckscher-Ohlin goods, and Ricardo goods. In all three cases, there is a sharp deterioration in the trade balance in the early 1980s. The long-run trend, however, is strongly positive for p-c goods, showing a rising trade surplus, while the trend for the other two groups is a moderately rising trade deficit.

3. OECD, *Economic Outlook*, various issues.

4. Two-sector modeling for tradables and nontradables may be found in Barry [1987], Mayer [1974], Dornbusch [1976], Minford [1981], Neary [1978], and Neary and Purvis [1983].

5. For a complete model, including a multiple-asset financial sector, see Arndt [1987b].

6. As reported in *Fixed Reproducible Tangible Wealth in the United States, 1925–85* [Washington, D.C.: U.S. Department of Commerce, Bureau of Economic Analysis, June 1987].

7. For a complete examination, see Arndt [1987a,b].

References

Arndt, S. W. 1987b. "Trade and Exchange Rates in a Diversified Economy." Discussion Paper no. 3, Commons Institute, August.

Arndt, S. W. 1987a. "Factor Markets in Open Economy Adjustment." Discussion Paper no. 4, Commons Institute, September.

Arndt, S. W., and Bouton L. 1987. *Competitiveness: The United States in World Trade*. Lanham, MD.: University Press of America.

Barry, F. G. 1987. "Fiscal Policy in a Small Open Economy." *Journal of International Economics* 22, February.

Dean, A., and Koromzay, V. 1987. "Current-Account Imbalances and Adjustment Mechanisms." *OECD Economic Studies*, no. 8, Spring.

Dornbusch, R. 1976b. "The Theory of Flexible Exchange Rate Regimes and Macroeconomic Policy." *Scandinavian Journal of Economics* 78, May.

Dornbusch, R. 1976a. "Expectations and Exchange Rate Dynamics." *Journal of Political Economy* 84, December.

Mayer, W. 1974. "Short-Run and Long-Run Equilibrium for a Small Open Economy." *Journal of Political Economy* 82, September-October.

Minford, P. 1981. "The Exchange Rate and Monetary Policy." In W. A. Eltis and P. J. N. Sinclair (eds.), *The Money Supply and the Exchange Rate*. Oxford: Clarendon Press.

Neary, J. P. 1978. "Short-Run Capital Specificity and the Pure Theory of International Trade," *Economic Journal* 88, September.

Neary, J. P., and Purvis, D. D. 1983. "Real Adjustment and Exchange Rate Dynamcs." In J. A. Frenkel (ed.) *Exchange Rates and International Macroeconomics*. Chicago: University of Chicago Press.

Tatom J.A. 1986. "Domestic vs. International Explanations of Recent U.S. Manufacturing Developments." *Review*. Federal Reserve Bank of St. Louis, April.

COMMENTARY

by William Poole

Sven Arndt provides a readable review of one approach to understanding the U.S. trade deficit, but I must be honest at the outset in saying that I have fundamental disagreements with this approach. However, many of Arndt's comments on policy are independent of his model. I support some of his policy analysis, but not all.

Arndt makes clear that the large change in the U.S. trade account is a macro phenomenon. That is an important and correct observation. What the paper is missing is an analysis of the economic conditions that determine both international capital flows and saving and investment in the United States and abroad. The only condition Arndt examines is the government budget deficit in the United States.

A focus on the U.S. budget deficit would be useful if the ceteris paribus proviso had real-world content. But changes in budget deficits in the United States and abroad in the 1980s did not occur through lump-sum changes in taxes and transfers. Fiscal policy and lower inflation have changed the marginal conditions facing households and firms, and it is essential that these changes be analyzed along with the changes in budget deficits. Concentration on the U.S. budget deficit alone is descriptively inaccurate and analytically misleading.

As a preliminary, note that Arndt—and, indeed, the conference program—take for granted that the U.S. trade deficit is a "problem." Without question, trade is a political problem but the trade deficit is not itself an economic problem. After all, most of the capital flow that is the counterpart of the current account deficit involves purchases and sales of assets by consenting adults. There is a problem, but it involves the low national saving rate in the United States and the declining investment and growth rates in Europe, Japan, and Latin America.

The "twin deficits," as they have come to be called, are not as closely connected as Arndt and many others would have us believe because fiscal policy adjustments affect private saving and investment as well as government saving. Before all this twin deficits talk started most economists would have predicted that a country facing an intractable budget deficit would suffer capital outflows, a weak currency, and slow economic growth. The reason is that investors fear that such a country would either inflate, raise taxes that depress investment returns, or both. Conversely, countries with strong fiscal situations generally have strong currencies. The twin deficits analysis predicts the opposite relation by neglecting all the economic conditions that give rise to the correlation actually observed in the real world.

Of course, any analysis must be consistent with the national income accounts identity that private saving plus government saving equals domestic investment plus investment abroad (or minus foreign investment flowing in). But the accounting identity does not reveal economic structure. Without an analysis of behavioral relations there is no justification for assuming that a change in economic conditions that increases or decreases one of these accounts will change a particular other account; what happens depends on supplies and demands in all the various markets and how they are affected by the change in economic conditions.

Arndt implicitly assumes, as do many other analysts, that a change in government saving occurs through a change in lump-sum taxes or transfers. This convenient assumption leaves other aspects of fiscal policy unaffected. That is, with the lump-sum assumption there is no change in marginal conditions from changes in government tax and spending rates. In fact, adjustments in U.S. fiscal policy in the 1980s have involved very large changes in marginal tax rates on labor and capital income. Real rates of return have also been importantly affected by changes in the inflation rate.

Bill Niskanen and I analyzed these issues in the 1985 *Economic Report of the President*. Our major point was that economic conditions in the early 1980s involved a large increase in the after-tax real rate of return on physical capital in the United States relative to the return abroad. This analysis also explains why the U.S. trade deficit per se is not an economic problem. If capital has indeed flowed across national boundaries in response to a higher relative rate of return on investment in the United States, then that capital flow is exactly what ought to occur for efficient international allocation of capital.

A careful documentation of this position would require a substantial monograph rather than a short discussion. But let me outline some of the principal considerations.

First, it seems clear that real rates of interest were high in the United States from 1981 through 1984. Moreover, these high real rates were not associated with a collapse of investment but rather with relatively strong investment once the 1981–1982 recession was out of the way. There is controversy about how to measure investment; in the 1985 *Economic Report* we focused on gross investment in real terms as a percentage of real GNP. Measured that way, investment growth looked very strong indeed in 1983–1984. Concentrating on net investment yields a substantially different picture, but net investment is difficult to interpret without a correction for the cyclical state of the economy.

Another investment measure is the ratio of nominal gross investment to nominal income, and that is the concept used in figure 1 below. The figure ends with 1985 because that is the last year of the available OECD data, which I want to use to have comparable data for the United States, Europe, and Japan.

On this nominal basis, U.S. domestic investment, which includes both fixed investment and inventory investment, has experienced a normal cyclical recovery to levels that are a little below average—but not much below—for the period from 1960 to 1980 as a whole. Investment has certainly not been severely depressed relative to GDP, as one might have anticipated from the very high real rate of interest.

With roughly normal investment performance in the United States it must be the case that the investment demand function shifted out sufficiently that the amount of investment realized at the high real rate was reasonably normal. An analysis that neglects the outward shift in the investment demand function is seriously misleading.

Of course, after late 1984 U.S. investment grew quite slowly and therefore we should consider that period differently from the early part of the decade. The Reagan tax reform proposal offered in late November 1984, and the eventual Tax Reform Act of 1986, were probably responsible in large part for the sharp decline in the growth of real investment. Both the proposal and the Act substantially reduced investment incentives. It is no accident that the real rate of interest in the United States declined, and

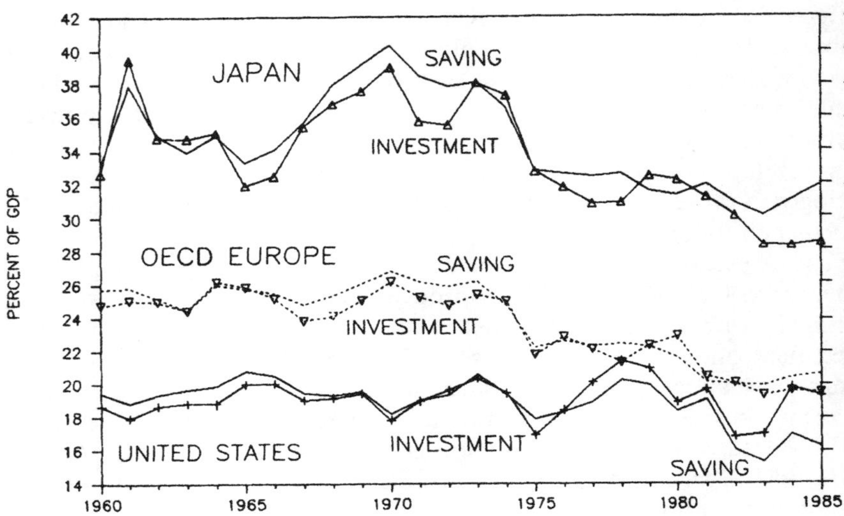

Source: OECD National Accounts Data Bank maintained by Data Resources, Inc

Figure 1. Saving and Domestic Investment in United States, Europe, and Japan

that the dollar declined as it became less attractive to move capital to the United States.

But U.S. international transactions depend as importantly on what happens abroad as on what happens in the United States. The figure includes relevant information for Japan and for OECD Europe (which consists of Austria, Belgium, Denmark, Finland, France, Germany, Greece, Iceland, Ireland, Italy, Luxembourg, The Netherlands, Norway, Portugal, Spain, Sweden, Switzerland, Turkey, and the United Kingdom). A striking characteristic of both of these cases is the marked decline in investment and saving as a percent of GDP. It appears that these economies are no longer providing as high a rate of return as earlier, and so domestic investment has declined as a percent of GDP. Saving rates in Europe and Japan have also declined but not by as much. Data on Latin America is missing, but we all know that these economies have even poorer investment climates than Europe and Japan.

Consistent with the observed behavior of domestic investment in Japan is the behavior of the real rate of return. There is only casual evidence to offer, but it appears that the return as measured by the price-earnings ratio in the Japanese stock market or the yield on government bonds is extremely low. Interest rates have also been quite low in Germany.

In the 1980s economic growth turned sharply lower and even negative in many countries of the world. European growth is low and unemployment rates have remained extremely high by earlier postwar standards. Growth in Latin America turned negative in most countries reversing the direction of capital flow. These developments cannot reasonably be attributed to events in the United States, and certainly not to the federal government budget deficit.

Turning to the model Arndt uses to analyze the U.S. trade deficit: the model is shown graphically in figure 5–5. Arndt assumes that the market for nontradable goods shown in the left-hand panel always clears. A fiscal expansion shifts both demands out, and the equilibrium is determined by the assumption that the market for nontradables clears at the intersection of the new demand function and the assumed stable supply function.

A key thing to note about this model is that Arndt works with the implicit assumption that international capital flows are totally passive—they finance whatever trade gap appears in the right-hand panel of figure 5–5. This assumption might be appropriate for a fixed-exchange-rate world, but it is surely inappropriate for the floating-rate world of the 1980s.

Suppose we drop the assumption of passive international capital flows and use instead the assumption that capital flow is exogenous to these markets. For convenience, assume that the capital flow is zero so that the tradables supply and demand must clear. How would we analyze a lump-sum fiscal expansion under that assumption?

Suppose both goods markets must clear, but nominal wages are fixed. There is a disequilibrium when the real demands in the two markets shift out as a result of the fiscal expansion. One possibility is that the fiscal expansion would simply bid up prices proportionately in both markets. With higher nominal prices the real demands would shift back, but not all the way, and the supply functions would shift out (because real wages would be lower). These shifts could occur in such a way as to leave the relative price of tradables unaffected.

Another possibility is that the fiscal expansion might have differential effects in the two markets. Suppose, for example, that the expansion had a larger effect on the demand for nontradable goods. Then, the nontradables demand might shift out and the tradable goods demand shift in. The markets might clear at a lower relative price of tradables, smaller quantities of both exports and imports, and a larger quantity of nontradables production. Conversely, the fiscal expansion might shift the demand function for tradables outward and for nontradables inward with the opposite effects.

If the labor markets also clear (the flexible-wages case) none of these disturbances will affect aggregate output, but fiscal expansion might alter the distribution of that output between nontradables and tradables. We could catalog the results from a number of different assumptions, but for understanding the trade account the key assumption will involve the nature of international capital flows.

As an aside, it is important to understand that this model is ill suited to analyze issues of inflation and unemployment. The vertical axis shows the price of tradables relative to nontradables. Because of the assumption that the goods markets clear—with the aid of passive capital flows in the case of tradables—there is no direct treatment in the model of employment issues. Arndt's discussion of the effects of nonclearing labor markets seems largely outside the model he offers.

Arndt argues that world supply conditions are crucial to the outcome. That is, he assumes that there is idle capacity in the tradable goods sector that permits substantial inflows of goods to the United States with little price impact. But why should we not adopt the same assumption for nontradables? If we did, then the supply of nontradables in figure 5–5 would be highly elastic. The outward shift of demand would then have little effect on the relative price and therefore would not be consistent with the observed substantial change in the relative price of tradables as the U.S. dollar appreciated between 1980 and 1985. Many observers would, of course, argue that the United States had substantial excess capacity in both sectors over these years.

Arndt takes up the issue of international capital flows. As noted earlier, the dynamic element in the 1980s was a substantial shift in capital flows due to a shift in relative rates of return. But Arndt argues that there was a shift in asset preferences. This argument seems to me to be inconsistent with the facts.

Consider the case of Japan. Financial liberalization should raise real interest rates in Japan as funds flow out of the country in response to higher returns abroad. At the same time, the flow into the United States should tend to lower real rates of interest. But that pattern of real rates is surely the reverse of what we actually observed between 1980 and 1985. Real rates were unambiguously high in the United States and low in Japan. The same observation holds for real rates of interest in Latin America and Europe relative to the U.S.

Turning now to Arndt's policy recommendations: it is important to underline his point that the trade deficit is a macroeconomic phenomenon.

Trade restriction not only is costly but also will not even have the advertised effects. The economic conditions that created the trade deficit have redistributed employment across industries and at the same time have increased total employment.

Arndt attributes some of the problems abroad to anti-inflationary policies in the United States. Even if that argument is correct, which is doubtful, it is not an argument for inflating here. Arndt also argues that the United States must be willing to foster a certain amount of inflation to obtain needed relative price changes. This argument is not acceptable. Changes in relative prices can and have occurred during periods of declining inflation. The United States needs stable prices for lasting economic stability at home, and stability at home is the greatest contribution the United States can make to world economic stability.

Finally, what about the budget deficit? What about the T-word? Many economists who support tax increases to reduce the budget deficit do so on political grounds—they believe that cutting spending is politically impossible. How many of these economists believe that the Defense Department is efficient, or that corporate welfare such as the Export-Import Bank promotes an important social function, or that agricultural programs provide justifiable income maintenance at minimal resource cost? If we give up on controlling federal spending we will eventually find ourselves in the same situation Europe and Latin America now face. The simple fact is that much government spending wastes resources while taxes and subsidies sap incentives for productive activity.

We as economists are feeding public hysteria about the deficit and promoting poor public policy. The budget deficit is poorly measured, and yet there is practically no serious work on the issue. (Robert Eisner is an exception.) Economists have contributed to irrational and dangerous public fears about the deficit. We are in a situation such that anything—bad that happens to the economy is the deficit's fault. Inflation, recession, stock market crashes, whatever—all the budget deficit's fault. The budget deficit is most of all a serious policy problem because of the harmful policies that may be adopted to reduce it.

Lest I be misread, I emphasize that I do not favor budget deficits. If we can not find ways to reduce federal spending we will in time raise taxes to reduce the deficit. If raising taxes were accompanied by policies to freeze federal expenditures as a percent of GNP to the current level of about 25% our fiscal problem would be largely solved. But I have no confidence that raising taxes now will do anything to control expenditures growth. If we give up on that matter now we will have to face the issue another day.

SPRINGER NATURE

GPSR Compliance

The European Union's (EU) General Product Safety Regulation (GPSR) is a set of rules that requires consumer products to be safe and our obligations to ensure this.

If you have any concerns about our products, you can contact us on ProductSafety@springernature.com

In case Publisher is established outside the EU, the EU authorized representative is:

Springer Nature Customer Service Center GmbH
Europaplatz 3
69115 Heidelberg, Germany

Kolibri 360 GmbH
Ferdinand-Jühlke-Straße 7
99095 Erfurt, Deutschland
produktsicherheit@kolibri360.de